Christopher Pickard

The

Insider's

Guide

To

Rio

de

Janeiro

1987

"Thomas Cook Travel & Guide Book Awards"
Finalist 1984

ISBN 85-85051-01-9

DISTRIBUTOR IN THE U.S.A.

> LUSO-BRAZILIAN BOOKS
> 33, NEVINS STREET
> BROOKLYN
> NY 11217
> TEL: (718) 624 4000

DISTRIBUTOR IN THE U.K.

> ROGER LASCELLES
> 47, YORK ROAD
> BRENTFORD
> MIDDLESEX TW8 OQP
> TEL: (01) 847 0935

DISTRIBUTOR FOR ALL OTHER TERRITORIES

> STREAMLINE
> Av. N.S. DE COPACABANA 605/1210
> RIO DE JANEIRO
> BRAZIL
> TEL: (021) 255 4433
> TELEX: 021 — 21791

Great care has been taken throughout this book to be as accurate as possible, but the publishers and author cannot accept responsibility for any errors which appear.

Changes in data, particularily in prices, may occur after going to press. Prices must be accepted as indications rather than firm quotes. All prices are given in U.S. dollars.

Impresso no Brasil/Printed in Brazil.

Published by Streamline Ltda. Av. N.S. de Copacabana 605/1210 — Copacabana — Rio de Janeiro — Brazil
Publicado por Streamline Ltda. Av. N.S. de Copacabana 605/1210 — Copacabana — Rio de Janeiro — Brasil

TEL: (021) 255-4433
TELEX: 21791 MANT BR

About the Insider's Guide

In the January of 1984 *The Insider's Guide to Rio de Janeiro* was launched quietly on to the Brazilian market by Streamline at a few select book stores in Rio de Janeiro.

One year later the launch of the second edition of *The Insider's Guide to Rio de Janeiro* was eagerly anticipated in not just Rio de Janeiro but also New York, London, Paris, Amsterdam and numerous other cities around the world, in fact anywhere where there was a reader with an interest in Rio de Janeiro or Brazil.

Since its launch, *The Insider's Guide to Rio de Janeiro* has become the largest selling guide book to Rio de Janeiro in the English language and the only one to be written, edited and published each year entirely from Rio de Janeiro itself.

Praise for the first editions of *The Insider's Guide to Rio de Janeiro* came not only from the Brazilian, American and European media but also from within the travel industry including the international airline companies, hoteliers, restaurant owners, travel agents and tour companies as well as Embratur (Brazilian Tourist Board) and Riotur (City of Rio de Janeiro Tourist Board).

The Insider's Guide to Rio de Janeiro's most important stamp of approval to date came in November 1984 when Thomas Cook, the world's most famous and prestigious travel agent and tour company, and a panel of travel experts chosen by them and the National Book League in London, judged the first edition to be one of the five best guide books produced around the world.

1987 sees the fourth English language edition of *The Insider's Guide to Rio de Janeiro* and because of demand Portuguese and Spanish language editions.

The author of *The Insider's Guide to Rio de Janeiro* is Christopher Pickard who was born in Guildford, close to London, in 1956. He was educated in Great Britain and lived in England, Scotland and Southern Ireland before moving permanently to Brazil in 1977.

As a journalist, Pickard was the arts and leisure editor of the *Latin America Daily Post* for more than two years and is the Brazilian correspondent for *Cash Box, down beat, Music Week, Prensario, Screen International* as well as Britain's *Independent Radio News*.

Contents

Prologue.

Acknowledgments.

About the *Insider's Guide.*

A

And Why Not Rio de Janeiro?
Important Facts to Know Before You Arrive in Rio.
Getting to Rio de Janeiro.
Travellers Please Note.
Arriving in Rio.
Rio At-A-Glance.
Getting Around.
Better To Be Safe Than Sorry: A Cautionary Tle.
Safety First: Dos and Dont's.

B

Hotels
Apart-Hotels.

C

Eating Out.
Entertainment and Night-Life.
Carnival.

D

Sugar Loaf.
Corcovado.
The Author's Tour.
The Beaches of Rio.
Things To See and Do.
The Art World of Rio.
Rainy Days and Cloudy Afternoons.
Tourist Timetable.

E

Sports and Recreation.

F

Shopping.

G

The History of Rio de Janeiro.
Historically Speaking: The Center of Rio.
Typically But Uniquely Brazilian.

'H

Day Trips and Longer.
Air Pass.
On From Rio To the Rest Of Brazil.
Brasília.
Foz do Iguaçu.
Manaus and the Amazon.
Minas Gerais.

I

Travel and Transport.
Leaving Rio de Janeiro.
Air Pass.

J

General Information.
Telephone Services.
Currency Exchange.
Business Rio.
Conferences, Congresses and Trade Fairs.
Health Matters.
Useful Words and Phrases.
Foreign Consulates.
Brazilian Contacts Abroad..
Annual Events and Holidays.
Emergency Services.

Maps.

Prologue

"The critic is the only independent source of information. The rest is advertising." — Pauline Kael (critic).

"Criticism may not be agreeable but it is necessary. It fulfils the same function as pain in the human body. It calls attention to an unhealthy state of things." — Sir Winston Churchill.

"A critic is a bundle of biases held losely together by a sense of taste." — Whitney Balliett (writer).

"I disapprove of much but I enjoy everything." — Harold Clurman (critic).

Rio de Janeiro is a unique city, of that there is no question, and a unique city deserves to have its own unique guide book, hence *The Insider's Guide to Rio de Janeiro,* which was first published in the January of 1984.

To arrive at the format used for the *Insider's Guide* in 1984 I studied other guides from the U.S., Europe, and the rest of South America. I looked at city guides, country guides, restaurant guides, shopping guides and entertainment guides, and while each had its own merits, none of them would have been suitable for Rio de Janeiro.

With the *Insider's Guide* I tried to produce a book that was as readable as it was informative. It was, and is designed to be of use to the traveller who is in Rio for a couple of days, but is equally at home with the foreign resident living in Rio. The *Insider's Guide* will help the tourist and the businessman, the student and the retired. It will help you get the most out of Rio de Janeiro, a city that has still to realize its full tourist potential, a city that is one of the world's most attractive destinations, a city that will turn Brazil into ''the long haul destination of the late 1980s and 1990s.

The *Insider's Guide* is now in its fourth edition and as I believed from the start any accurate guide to Rio must be updated yearly and from Rio de Janeiro itself. The city is too vibrant to stand still and allow a biennial update. Thus *The Insider's Guide to Rio de Janeiro 1987* is a complete revision which only closed to go to the press in January.

The experience with the first editions of the guide have allowed me to hone the edges and sharpen the information. I have also experimented with new layouts which are designed to help you find the information and facts you want more quickly.

To get the most out of the *Insider's Guide,* as opposed to Rio, you should take the time to read the contents thoroughly. The contents will give you a clearer and quicker understanding of what Rio has to offer, and will save you time later when you are looking for specific information.

The opinions aired in this book are mine and mine alone and can therefore be critized for being subjective. But while subjective they are based on living in Rio for ten years; of having travelled extensively, staying in many of the world's best hotels, and some of the worst; of having tasted some of the most delectable cuisines the kitchens of the world have to offer, as well as some of the most unpalatable.

My own opinions of Rio have, and continue to be sharpened, by my day to day activities which have me totally immersed in the workings of *Cidade Maravilhosa,* a city that has been constantly sold short by people who neither had the time not the inclination to help visitors to discover its hidden riches.

The *Insider's Guide* also reflects faithfully the opinions of the English speaking residents of Rio, the permanent "tourists" if you like, who over the years knowingly or not have supplied me with their thoughts and views on this fascinating city, and now, with several years under the guide's belt, I can also count on the hundreds of letters I have received from visitors who kindly took the time to jot down their own experiences. All of these opinions have been taken into account in this edition.

Finally I wish to stress that the *Insider's Guide* has no literary pretensions, and should the English at times appear to fall in the middle of the North Atlantic then I am to blame. The choice was deliberate, the aim to open the book up to as larger number of travellers as possible, many of whom do not use English as their first language.

And each and everyone of these travellers, like yourself, who comes to Rio becomes an "insider" and I want to hear from them and you. I want to know what you discovered; what you liked and what you didn't. I want to know about your problems and if and how they were solved.

If you can find the time please drop me a note, you will be helping all the visitors who come after you, who may be, who knows, your family and friends. The mailing address for the *Insider's Guide* is Av. N.S. de Copacabana, 605/1210 in Copacabana. Please write.

Welcome to the latest annual edition of *The Insider's Guide to Rio*, I hope that through it I can transmit to you just a fraction of the fun, enjoyment, and knowledge that I have experienced and continue to experience in this magnificent and marvelous city.

Christopher Pickard
Rio de Janeiro

Acknowledgments

I would like to express my gratitude to everyone who helped cajoled, encouraged and supported me during the preparation of this book and its continuous up-dates, and who turned a dream which resulted from a trans-Atlantic phone call into a success story. In particular I would like to thank the following people who gave me and Streamline their valuable advice, assistance, information, support and friendship when it mattered and continue to do so.

Claudio Sales, Igor and his staff at Editora Mory for putting up with me and my corrections with such professionalism and good humor; Francisco de Castro Azevedo for not only his masterful translation of the book to Portuguese but his help and advice over the years; Robin Brown and his team of ladies for unravelling and making sense of a mass of unrelated papers, the results of which we then ignore; Clem Kobrak for the use of his xerox, office equipment, and anything else we can take when he is not looking, his improvement at "palitos" has been noted however; Audrey, Madalena, Mary and Samantha for putting up with Chris "feio" and smiling at our requests however odd they may seem; Isabel for filling the gap; Curtis Dewees for taking on the challenge in the US and making it work through his own hard work and enthusiasm for the book and Brazil; Tuca, Bob, Brian and their crew for attempting the impossible of putting Rio on film with a Streamline budget and succeeding; Liz, Nigel and Steve who promise to put *life* back into Rio; Santiago and Tereza at Teatral; Embratur, without whose co-operation it would have been impossible to expand the book beyond Rio; Souza Cruz for their sponsorship and support which made *The Insider's Guide to Rio de Janeiro* possible; Fernando Amorim, Aureo Bonilha, John Buschman, Fernando Castro, Philip Carruthers, Mike Crawshaw and family, Jean-Louis Delquignies, Alvaro Diago, Ulrich Eckhardt, Ian Gillespie, Jacqueline Hoffmann, Roger Lascelles, Michael Parry, Luiz Raposo, Walder Saldanha, Frank Sanchez, Tony Sawyer, Hans Stern, John Stumpf, and John Vaughan who show in their support of me and the guide their faith and confidence in Brazilian tourism; and last but not least, the many press and information officers who assisted me. Without them a book of this type would be impossible to put together and keep up-to-date.

I would also like to express my appreciation for a second group of people without whom *The Insider's Guide of Rio de Janeiro* could not have been started or continue. My publisher and friend (except in matters of sport, bets or "Trivial Pursuit") Chris Wallace who having proved that the entrepreneurial publisher is alive and well, continues to serve excellent G & Ts even if he does insist on using diet tonic and his latest invention diet gin. Having completed his masterwork, *The Insider's Guide to the 9th and 18th at Teresopolis,* Mr. Wallace has been dedicating himself to a number of new publications including *My Best Round With My Favorite Caddy and No Witnesses, Video Editing and My Longest Putt On Film* and *Truck Driving Made Simple*. Mr. Wallace is 106; my PA and friend (except when losing whole chunks of the book or not believing that I am infallible), the world's "most efficient", Liane Raposo or Lia, who wears whichever hat we load her with good grace and a smile and who in less than a year has learnt to live with my warped British sense of humour and organize an office that is normally in total chaos thanks to a certain gentleman and his handwriting; Lulu and

Neiva for being there when I needed them, luckily I haven't with the guide so far; my close friends in Brazil, England and elsewhere, and especially the Castellanoses, Hubbards, Macdonalds, Smales, Miss Spalding, the "Copacabana (née Tijuca) Connection", Silvia and Marta, and the odd couple, Robin and Sonia, who were and are always game to try a new restaurant and pay; John and Jenny Byers and Edward, who did not have much say in the matter, for all the fun in getting the ball rolling in São Paulo and keeping it moving despite my slightly erratic timetable; Bruce and Mel for a bed in São Paulo, a record collection which I must partly be to blame for, and fun and true friendship which has now spread over more years than I care to remember; my family in England who can still cope with me after all this time and remain close if not closer despite the distance and the difficulties this entails; my advertisers who rarely see me, yet without whom none of this would be possible or viable; and the people of Brazil, especially Rio de Janeiro, to whom go my profound thanks and gratitude for allowing me to live and work in their wonderful country. I hope they will accept this book in the spirit it is meant and as a small token of my thanks and appreciation.

And finally, for my sister Thérèse, who gave me the push to start the book, brother-in-law Simon who has the misfortune to partner me in all the big money golf matches, and parents John and Jackie who help in every possible way but I hope get some enjoyment and fun from all the madness. This is for you. With love.

I have also over the years taken to dedicating each edition to one particular person or group of people and although it might sound rather odd I would like to dedicate the 1987 edition to Comlurb, Rio's refuse and garbage collectors, who against almost impossible odds and be it Carnival, New Year or an election, manage to keep Rio and its beaches so remarkably clean and tidy. We residents of Rio can take Comlurb somewhat for granted so I thought it might be nice to publicly say thank you.

Christopher Pickard
Rio de Janeiro
January 1987

A

Why Not Rio?
Important Facts
Getting to Rio
Travellers Note
Arriving
Rio At-A-Glance
Getting Around
Safety

And Why Not Rio de Janeiro?

Rio de Janeiro is quite probably the world's most ideal holiday destination. It gives the traveller the benefits of one of the world's largest cities, yet at the same time offers everything you could want from an idyllic tropical resort. About the only thing you would not want to come to Rio for is the winter sport scene, although even in tropical Rio you can find an ice-rink!

As a city Rio has all you would expect, and more. Excellent restaurants, sophisticated nightclubs, charming bars, musical extravaganzas, theatres, movie houses, museums, art galleries, fashionable shops and world class sport all abound, and for a fraction of the price you would expect to pay.

As a tropical resort Rio offers mile-after-mile of golden beaches, near perfect weather the year round, hotels to appeal to every taste and budget, folklore, typical foods and music, sightseeing and the feeling that you have really been abroad for your holiday.

And none of the above takes into account the overall beauty of Rio that has made the city famous and revered around the world.

Sadly though, most of the world is badly informed and frighteningly ignorant when it comes to South America. Most North Americans and Europeans cannot name the countries of South America — can you? — and when asked would be pushed to tell you if Rio de Janeiro is in Brazil or Argentina, or even what coast the city is on. And they would almost certainly guess that the language spoken in Brazil would be Spanish and not Portuguese.

Yet for all the ignorance Rio de Janeiro holds a special status; an exotic diamond twinkling somewhere to the south; a fashionable resort that is but a dream to most.

But a dream it no longer has to be. Since 1983 a number of tour operators in North America and Europe have been offering special deals well within the budget of the average traveller and in the coming years these deals promise to be even better.

Despite its reputation, Rio is relatively new to international tourism and still unspoilt.

According to the Brazilian Tourist Board's official figures only 1,7-million visitors came to Brazil in 1985 with an estimate of close to 2-million for 1986 and 2,1-million for 1987. Of the 1,7-million in 1985, 204,000 were from the U.S.A., 71,000 from Italy, 68,500 from West Germany, 51,000 from France, 34,500 from Great Britain, 32,000 from Spain, 30,000 from Switzerland and Canada, and 22,000 from Portugal and Japan. Of these, 620,000 entered Brazil via Rio, thus leaving Rio's unique atmosphere and character unchanged by the small influx of foreign visitors which at any one time make up less than 0,5% of the resident population

When you travel to Rio, be it to see the beautiful city or join in the Carnival, you will know that you have been abroad; to a place different from anything else that you have ever experienced, to a place that will leave you with the happiest and most lingering of memories, and at the end of the day memories are what travelling is all about.

Important Facts to Know Before You Arrive

When to Come: Before you plan to come to Rio de Janeiro you must decide what it is you want to see. Do you want to see Carnival or do you want to see Rio de Janeiro, the city?

Carnival, which in 1987 occupies the first week of March and in 1988 the third week of February, is mainly about night life, exotic parades and wonderful parties. Rio's carnival is for the young with money to spend. If this is what you want from your vacations then Carnival is the time to choose.

If on the other hand you want to see the "Cidade Maravilhosa" (Marvellous City) that has fascinated travellers for centuries for its warmth and outstanding beauty then you should think of coming to Rio at any other time of the year but Carnival. That is when you learn about the true Rio de Janeiro; Rio, the world's largest tropical city and its most beautiful.

Weather: Rio is blessed with a mild tropical climate where it is difficult to tell when spring becomes summer and summer, autumn.

Rio's average temperature is around 80°F which climbs in to the low hundreds during the summer months that stretch from December through March. In the middle of winter, July, the temperatures can drop as low as 65°F!

Language: The language in Brazil is Portuguese and not Spanish as you may have assumed. Spanish will help you get around though.

Visas: Many tourists need a visa to enter Brazil and this can easily be obtained from your local Brazilian Consulate. If you have any doubts consult the airline who will be flying you. Tourist visas normally allow the visitor to stay for three months and this can be extended for a further three months if necessary.

Size: With an area of 3.3 million square miles; a coast line of 4,500 miles of warm, white beaches; and a population of 141-million, Brazil is the world's fifth largest nation in terms of area and sixth in population.

Brazil has nine metropolitan areas with a population of over one million of which São Paulo is the largest with 15.3-million residents and Rio second with 10.2-million.

Dress: Cariocas, as the local residents are called, dress casually outside of the office. None of Rio's top restaurants insist on collar and tie although some business restaurants downtown do.

At the office the collar and tie still rules the day and most women wear dresses or skirts.

When you pack keep in mind that Rio is a big fashionable city and not a small tourist resort.

Ladies should remember to pack a jacket or shawl as some of the buildings can be a little over enthusiastic with their air-conditioning.

If you forget to bring some item of clothing with you don't worry, you will certainly be able to find it in Rio.

Drugs: If you can't get through your vacation without smoking a joint or snorting a line then stay away. Brazil, like most South American countries, takes a very dim view about drug offenses and your own consulate is likely to agree with them.

Money and Exchange Rates: The Brazilian currency since February 28, 1986 is the cruzado which is valued against the American dollar.

Previous to the cruzado Brazil's currency was the cruzeiro, a currency which, because of Brazil's high rate of inflation, was being devalued daily against the dollar. The cruzado, on the other hand, is, thanks to the dramatic fall in Brazil's inflation since February 1986, a fairly stable currency which at the time of going to press was valued weekly against the US dollar, the new rate being displayed in all the major newspapers.

In Brazil there is both an "official" rate for the dollar and a higher "parallel" rate. This situation is fully explained in the information section (I) of the book under "Currency Exchange". Brazilians understand dollars so if you are bringing traveler's checks bring them in US dollars, they are by far the most widely accepted.

It is advisable not to have any money wired to you in Brazil. The bank will have to pay the full amount over in cruzados and at the "official" — read "lower" — rate. When you leave Brazil you will only be able to turn 30% of the total money changed back in to dollars at the "official" rate.

All major credit cards are accepted throughout Brazil although *American Express, Diners* and *Visa* (*Credicard* in Brazil) are the market leaders.

Because the change from cruzeiro (Cr$) to cruzado (Cz$) is relatively recent the majority of notes in circulation are still in cruzeiros. The difference between a cruzeiro and a cruzado is a question of three noughts. A Cr$100,000 note is therefore today a Cz$100 note. The new notes are identical to the old but with the new values in cruzados.

It is worth getting hold of some low denomination notes — Cz$50 and below — on your arrival as nobody in Brazil ever seems to have any change. This is particularly true of cab drivers.

Getting to Rio de Janeiro

Travelling to Rio at the start of the century meant a lengthy sea voyage for both Americans and Europeans. From New York they came and went on the "Old Verdi" and "Voltaire" of the Lamport and Holt Line while from London the Europeans arrived on the "Alcântara", "Andes", and "Arlanza" of the Royal Mail Steam Packet Company. In 1914 it was a voyage for the rich, a round trip first class ticket from London costing 53 pounds!

Today's international travellers come ashore at Rio s modern airport from the fleets of 747s , DC-10s and Tristars which link Rio in a matter of hours with America, Europe, Africa, Asia and the rest of South America.

Nearly every visitor who arrives in Rio from abroad, be it for tourism, business or to live, comes by plane. Rio is the gateway to Brazil, and also the gateway to the Southern part of South America for North American, European and Asian travellers.

From the U.S.A.: Daily flights by Pan Am and the Brazilian flag carrier Varig link New York, Miami, Los Angeles and San Francisco to Rio, while Pan Am's internal American network joins more than 30 other American and Canadian cities with these services. Japan Air Lines also has twice weekly flights linking Los Angeles and Rio.

Flight time is eight-and-a-half hours from Miami, just over nine from New York, and thirteen from Los Angeles. Flights to-and-from Rio are normally overnight arriving in the early morning with a bonus for East coast travelers of the time difference between them and Rio being minimal. It is therefore feasible for a New York or Miami businessman to fly overnight to Rio, have a full day of meetings in Rio, fly back overnight to the U.S. and be back at his desk the next morning. In 1986 a number of daytime flights were introduced for those who prefer to fly in daylight.

Vacationers from the U.S. should note that the overnight flight allows them to maximise their holiday time and minimize the number of hotel nights. If, for example, you leave New York on a Friday night after work you arrive in Rio early Saturday morning with the whole day ahead of you. You might then stay through the following week returning to New York on the Sunday evening flight which arrives back in the Big Apple early Monday morning, still in time to go to work. In all you will have spent nine full days in Brazil, but only eight hotel nights, and missed just five days away from work.

Ticket prices to Rio vary greatly but thanks to an agreement between Pan Am, Varig, Embratur and the operators there are a large number of very attractive deals starting from as low as US$499 — which include hotel and flight — and that should put Rio in the reach of a large number of holiday makers who in the past only saw the trip to Rio as a distant dream.

Ask your local travel agent for the latest details on packages to Rio or look in the travel section of any of the major American newspapers.

From Canada: Both Aerolineas Argentinas and Varig operate direct flights between Toronto and Montreal and Rio while Air Canada flights link up other parts of Canada to New York, Miami, and Los Angeles where they connect with the daily direct flights of Pan Am and Varig.

From Europe: Flight time from Europe to Rio is just over eleven hours, depending on your starting point.

Because the time difference between Rio and Europe is two three, four of five hours most flights leave Europe in the evening arriving early morning in Rio, and on the return leg leave from Rio in the late afternoon or evening to get to Europe just after lunch on the following day.

Aerolineas Argentinas, Air France, Alitalia, British Airways, Iberia, KLM, Lufthansa, Royal Air Maroc, SAS, Swissair, Tap and Varig all run regular services between Europe and Rio which means that you have a daily choice of several different airlines linking the two continents.

Prices vary throughout Europe but there are some very attractive package deals to be picked up through travel agents, including for Carnival.

From South Africa and the African continent: Flight time between Cape Town and Rio is just over eight hours. Both South African Airways and Varig run weekly flights which also connect with Johannesburg. Other flights to the African continent connect Brazil to Abidjan, Lagos, Luanda and Maputo.

From Japan: Brazil has a large Japanese colony, of which São Paulo has the largest concentration of Japanese outside of Japan. At the end of 1984 Japan Air Lines inaugurated twice weekly flights between Rio and Tokyo via Los Angeles while Pan Am and Varig have daily flights to-and-from the U.S. and Rio which link with the flights of Japan Air Lines and Singapore Airlines in the U.S.

From Australia and Asia: There are no direct flights between Australasia and Brazil but the daily Pan Am and Varig flights, and the twice weekly Japan Air Lines flights, connect in Los Angeles and San Francisco with Air New Zealand, China Airlines, Korean Airlines, Philippine Airlines, Singapore Airlines and Qantas. Lan Chile also fly to-and-from Rio via Santiago, Papeete, Auckland and Sydney while the shortest and quickest flight linking Brazil to Australia and New Zealand is the weekly Aerolineas Argentinas Polar fight from Buenos Aires to Aukland.

From South America: Rio receives daily flights from virtually all the other South American capitals and is served by Aerolineas

Argentinas, Aero Peru. Avianca, Ladeco, Lan Chile, LAP, Lloyd Aereo Boliviano, Pluna, Viasa, and of course the Brazilian flag carrier Varig.

Because of its position as the gateway to the Southern part of South America, Rio is also linked to Buenos Aires, Montevideo, Santiago and Lima by other European and American carriers including Air France, British Airways, Iberia, KLM, Lufthansa, Pan Am, SAS and Swissair.

Charters: In recent years the number of charters both in and out of Brazil has grown and many of these do not use the regular airlines but instead reputable charter carries. From Brazil Vasp operate a number of charters to the U.S. and Europe at prices well below the normal standard fare.

By Ship: Since flying became so fast, cheap and popular no regular passenger service is left between Brazil and the rest of the world. The last regular service from the U.S. was run by Delta Line whose ships arrived fortnightly from San Francisco. The service closed in October 1984.

From Europe the only passenger services are aboard cargo ships, and so the service tends to be irregular, if at all.

Rio is however one of the prime ports of call for ships cruising the world, especially at Carnival time. Both the QE2 and Rotterdam are regular visitors as are many of the other famous liners. Your travel agent will be able to find out for you which ships are scheduled to call in Rio in the coming year and these will include the ships which come down from the U.S. and Europe to cruise in Brazilian waters during the Northern hemisphere's winter.

Travellers Please Note

— Before arriving in Brazil make sure you have the appropriate visa. Brazil has reciprocal visa agreements which result in strange situations such as American citizens requiring visas while British citizens don't.

Because the regulations are always changing ask the airline you are flying with about the rules currently in force, and ask, don't wait to be told.

— Don't make the mistake of thinking you will pick up a cheap ticket in Brazil for your return journey. There are no cheap flights out of Brazil.

— Bring your money with you. Current banking bureaucracy can delay the release of money that has been cabled to Brazil. If you have a choice bring American dollar traveller checks.

— If you are going to travel on within Brazil ask your travel agent about the Brazil Air Pass which gives almost unlimited air travel in Brazil for 21 days. The 21 days only start once you start travelling within Brazil so even if you are coming to live it is an excellent investment. At present the Air Pass costs $330 but must be bought before arriving in Brazil. There is also a $250 Air Pass which is valid for 14 days and allows you to visit four Brazilian cities.

— If you ask for any information from your local Brazilian Consulate get it in writing and bring it with you. Sometimes how

Brazilian Consulates interpret the law can be different from how the resident Brazilian authorities do. If you can prove what the Brazilian Consulate told you, by having it in writing, you can save yourself an awful lot of trouble at a later date, and this is especially true if you are coming to live or bringing special equipment.

— Finally, remember that Brazilians really do want you to come and visit their country. The authorities both in Brazil and abroad, in conjunction with Embratur, the national tourist board, and the airlines will do everything in their power to make your trip to Brazil as pleasant as possible. All they ask is that you ask.

Arriving in Rio de Janeiro

The traveller arriving in Rio by air is lucky enough to be landing at one of the world's most modern airports, the largest and most important in Latin America.

Rio's international airport has proven to be remarkably functional since opening in January 1977 and is praised by passengers for the short walking distances that link all parts of the airport.

On arrival you will disembark at one of the airport's 19 passenger bridges. Your first point of call is immigration who check your passport and visa and any other immigration formalities. Make sure your passport is stamped, sometimes visitors get through without and this causes chaos when they try to leave.

Past immigration you descend into the baggage claim area where you find a Duty Free shop. Rio is one of the few airports to offer duty free goods on arrival and you will be allowed on presentation of your passport to purchase $300 worth of duty free products. This can be $300 worth of Scotch whisky or champagne or even cigarettes. The choice is yours. The shop staff are bilingual and will help with any problems.

You will also find in the arrivals hall a desk run by ARSA, the airport authorities, who will help with any problems concerning the airport.

Customs formalities are strict in Brazil and they will inspect the baggage of 50% of incoming passengers. Customs, however, are not after tourists or foreign visitors so unless you are carrying something very strange you will have no problems. Customs are strictest about electronic equipment, especially if they think you are bringing it to sell. If you have any problems leave the item(s) with them and collect it when you leave. A genuine visitor has nothing to worry about.

Welcome to Rio then, you have arrived.

Having left the baggage hall and passed, through customs you are officially in Brazil. If you do not have a hotel reservation or need any information you will see desks in front of you. The state tourism board is called *Flumitur* and they have staff on hand to point you in the right direction.

Of the airport's three levels you are on the bottom. Above is the departure floor and on the top a restaurant, 24 hour post office, phone center and various shops. If you need to make a local phone call ask the information desk for the nearest sales point for the phone tokens called *fichas*. If you need to change money the airport bank, on the top floor, is open 24 hours a day.

Getting to Rio from the airport is remarkably simple. An executive airport bus links the international airport with Santos Dumont Airport in downtown Rio or you can take the bus that passes all the main hotels in Copacabana, Ipanema and São Conrado (See "Information Buses"). Taxis are plentiful at the airport and I would suggest that the best solution for a visitor is to take the official airport taxis run by Cootramo and Transcoopass. The joy of these taxis is you pay the fare before leaving the airport and this is posted on a board above the taxi company's desk. You do not therefore have to worry about being taken for a lengthy ride or any of the other tricks that normally greet foreign visitors at airports.

In dollar terms taxis are not expensive and will get you to your hotel in about 30 minutes depending or not if your arrival coincided with the rush hour.

Do not, by the way, be put off by the fairly unattractive drive in to the city from the airport, the only other time you will be in this area is on your way back to the airport.

If you are flying on to another location you should go to the departure desks on the second floor. National flights go from Sector A and international from Sector B and C, the airlines are split as follows.

Sector A: Cruzeiro — Transbrasil — Varig — Vasp — Ponte Aérea.

Sector B: Alitalia — British Airways — Japan Air Lines — KLM — Pluna — SAS — Swissair — Varig.

Sector C: Aeroperu — Aerolineas Argentinas — Air France — Avianca — Iberia — Iraqi Airlines — Ladeco — LAB — Lan Chile — Lufthansa — Pan Am — Royal Air Maroc — South African Airways — Tap — Viasa.

ARRIVING BY SHIP

You may be one of the few people who arrive in Rio by ship, if so, your ship will berth close to Praça Maua at the top end of Avenida Rio Branco. Because of the lack of passenger ships which come to Rio you will find the facilities adequate but basic. Your entry to the docks will be via the Touring Club do Brasil's building.

The docks themselves are not the most exciting area in town although quite safe in the day. If yours is a big ship you will find a waiting line of cabs and guides to take you around Rio, and even if they are not, Praca Maua is still an easy area to get away from.

If you decide to walk away from the docks make sure you take Av. Rio Branco. In less than six blocks you come to Av. Presidente Vargas, if you turn right you will find the metro station Uruguaiana three blocks up on the left, or by continuing up Rio Branco, after crossing President Vargas, you will come to the city's local bus terminal in the seventh road up on the left, called *Menezes Cortes*.

Should you take a cab from Praça Maua make sure you have an idea of where you want to go. It is a good idea to give the name of a hotel as it sounds as if you have been in Rio before. In Copacabana try the Copacabana Palace which is located about half way up the beach and in Ipanema you can do no better that asking for the Caesar Park. If you want to relax at a resort hotel then ask for the Inter-Continental in São Conrado or the Sheraton at Vidigal. If it is shopping you are after ask for Rio-Sul.

Rio At-A-Glance

It is the mountains and sea which surround tropical Rio de Janeiro that have given the city its unique beauty, and it is these same topographical and geographical features that have dictated how the city has spread since being discovered in the 16th century.

Lying on latitude 22° 54' 24'' S and longtitude 43° 10' 21'' W on the Tropic of Capricorn, Rio de Janeiro is home to over 9 million Cariocas, as the local residents are known.

Covering an area of 1,171 km2 Rio de Janeiro is, after São Paulo, Brazil's largest city, and after Santos, and Rio Grande the country's third busiest port.

Rio is broken by the mountains into two distinct zones, north and south. The north zone, *zona norte*, is where the bulk of Rio's industrial activity takes place around v hich the largest areas of poor housing are situated; the famous south zone, *zona sul*, houses the more expensive residential and cultural areas located along the sea shore.

The buffer between north and south is the city center, *Centro*, the commercial and banking heart of Rio.

As a visitor to Rio you need only be concerned with the *zona sul*, unless that is you are here to live and your factory is located in the *zona norte*. Starting back at Centro here is "at-a-glance" the main areas of Rio which you will want to get to know during your visit.

CENTRO

Centro is the business heart of Rio which buzzes with life during the week becoming a ghost town at the weekend. Rio grew out of Centro so this is where you find the historical sites that matter.

Eating Out — Good. Shopping — Good. Entertainment — Good. Hotel Accommodation — Poor.

FLAMENGO AND CATETE

Up until the 1940s Flamengo was Rio's most chic residential area and even as recently as 1954 home to the Brazilian President. As the city spread through to Copacabana so the wealthy moved on, but with the massive face lift that the area received in the late 1950s, resulting in Flamengo Park, and with the over crowding of Copacabana, many of Rio's older jet set found their way back to enjoy the luxury that the older, bigger, beach front apartments of Flamengo afford.

Commerce has also spread to Flamengo and the skyline is dominated by number 200 Praia do Flamengo, the office block which holds the distinction of receiving the most daily mail in the city.

Eating Out — Fair. Shopping — Poor. Entertainment — Poor. Hotel Accommodation — Poor.

BOTAFOGO

Botafogo is really an extension of Flamengo and today is a busy and important crossroads sifting the traffic pouring into town from Copacabana and the Lagoa. In recent years a number of palatial office blocks have been completed giving the area a more business like flavor than Flamengo, a flavor that has been enhanced further by a number of shops and movie houses.

Botafogo is more than just the beach front though, and stretches back to form the link between the bay and the Lagoa This part of Botafogo retains its residential air, once being the center of the magnificent mansions that housed the foreign Embassies, many of which still stand today.

Eating Out — Good. Shopping — Because of the Rio Sul Shopping Center, excellent. Entertainment — Good. Hotel Accommodation — Non-Existent.

COPACABANA

Copacabana is one of the most famous beaches in the world, yet ironically, like Flamengo, the beach you see is the result of a helping hand from man to widen both the beach and the road to cope with demand. Today Copacabana is Rio's most populous upper-middle class residential area and one of the most densely populated areas in the world. It is also Rio's tourist center, home to many of the city's best hotels.

Copacabana has everything you would expect of a major residential area including theaters, good restaurants, shops, movie houses, and nightclubs.

Eating Out — Excellent. Shopping — Excellent. Entertainment — Good. Hotel Accommodation — Excellent.

IPANEMA AND LEBLON

The brightest jewel in the Rio crown is the area known as Ipanema and Leblon. Highly residential with spectacular apartment blocks lining the beach front, Ipanema and Leblon boast the best and most sophisticated in nearly everything the city has to offer including restaurants, shops, nightclubs, the beach, and the world famous girls from Ipanema.

Eating Out   Excellent. Shopping - Excellent. Entertainment – Excellent. Hotel Accommodation — Very Good.

LAGOA AND JARDIM BOTANICO

Mainly residential, the Lagoa and Jardim Botanico offer as attractions the city's jockey club, the Botanical Gardens and on the shores of the Lagoa itself many of Rio's top restaurants.

Eating Out — Excellent. Shopping — Poor. Entertainment — Poor. Hotel Accommodation — Non-Existent.

SÃO CONRADO

São Conrado is home to the elegant and picturesque Gavea Golf Club and Rio's three major resort hotels (Inter-Continental, Nacional and Rio-Sheraton).

São Conrado is also a residential area of extremes. On the one hand you have the city's largest shantytown, *favela*, which sits picture postcard pretty clinging to the side of the mountain, then up the scale, and by a considerable amount, the new condominiums of high rise apartments that host many of Rio's foreign community, and then finally nestling in the trees above the golf course some of Rio's most spectacular houses.

Eating Out — Good. Shopping — Good thanks to the Fashion Mall. Entertaiment — Fair for live entertainment but getting better. Very good for movie houses thanks to the Fashion Mall. Hotel Accommodation — Excellent for the top resort hotels.

BARRA DA TIJUCA

Barra is the future of Rio. It already contains many of Rio's most pleasant residential districts. It has the sports clubs, the motor racing circuit, the city's much under used exhibition center (Riocentro), mile-after-mile of unspoilt beaches, and above all, the city's largest shopping center (Barra Shopping) and many of Rio's best stocked supermarkets including Carrefour and Makro whose names are known throughout the world. What Barra doesn't have yet are good restaurants or hotels, but it can only be a matter of time.

Eating Out – Fair. Shopping – Excellent. Entertainment – Fair but getting better, Hotel Accommodation – Poor.

Getting Around in Rio de Janeiro

Thanks to Corcovado it is impossible for a newcomer to get lost for any length of time in Rio; in fact Rio is probably the easiest of all the world's major cities for the visitor to find his or her way around.

Most of Rio's top residential and tourist areas can be found along the waterfront, so once you know what fits where, it is just a question of following the coast along. Starting in the city you have Flamengo then Botafogo, Leme, Copacabana, Ipanema, Leblon, Vidigal, São Conrado, Barra da Tijuca, Recreio dos Bandeirantes, Prainha and Grumari. Each and everyone a strip of golden sand backed by the mountains. So if you are staying at a hotel in São Conrado and want to go to Copacabana just follow the coast passing through Leblon and Ipanema. What could be simpler?

Once you have been in Rio for any length of time you will learn all about the short cuts, the most important of which is the Rebouças Tunnel that links Ipanema, Leblon and the Lagoa to the city. Depending on where your hotel is it is almost certain that your taxi or bus will come to the zona sul from the airport through this tunnel which runs under the Corcovado mountain.

Topped by the statue of Christ, the mountain of Corcovado dominates Rio's sky line and is a reference point the like of which no other city can claim. Just remember where your hotel is in relation to Christ and you will never get lost.

As he stands, Christ looks down directly on Botafogo. To his left is Gloria and Centro, to his right Copacabana and behind right Ipanema and Leblon.

The easiest way for a newcomer to understand Rio is a trip to the top of Corcovado from where the city lies below as a living map and everything slots nicely into place. It is only from Corcovado that a visitor believes for the first time that Ipanema and Copacabana sit at right angles to each other and don't run straight.

Public Transport

The best way to get around in Rio for both the resident and visitor is the city's taxi service. Clean. efficient and above all cheap, Rio's taxis are the answer to any commuters' prayer. In abundance in any part of the zona sul a taxi can normally get you to your destination in any other part of the zona sul in less than thirty minutes depending on the traffic conditions. With a cab you won't get lost and you won't waste valuable time.

With Rio's buses it is a case of "the good, the bad, and the ugly." The "good" is represented by the comfortable and regular air-conditioned executive service which links the zona sul with the city center and vice versa and the new *Jardineira* bus, routes; "the bad" by the normal bus services which although plentiful and cheap are best left to the residents, and "the ugly" by bus drivers in general (See: Information Buses.)

Rio's other major public transport system is the metro (subway) that links Botafogo with Centro. Unlike most city subway systems the Rio one is immaculately clean, comfortably air conditioned, and safe both as a transport system and for you personally.

Surviving in a Car

You may of course decide to take to the roads and drive yourself. Rio, being a tourist city, has a plentiful supply of car hire agencies which are listed in the information section of the book. To hire a car you should have an international licence although they may accept your normal national licence.

There is no secret to surviving on the roads of Rio except the will to survive and to remember that it is not what you do that matters, but what the other lunatics do.

Brazil has produced a number of motor racing champions including Nelson Piquet and Emerson Fittipaldi. After you have driven in Rio you will begin to understand why.

Any driver who is used to driving in a large city should have no major problems in Rio, but things to look out for are the way people pass on both sides, which comes as a bit of a shock at first; the total lack of any lane discipline and the habit of going through lights long after they have changed. In most parts of the city traffic signals are ignored after 10 p.m. so keep a look out even if your light is green.

To avoid accidents go with the flow of the traffic, it is never difficult to get back to where you were in Rio, and I am sure you value your life more than a ten minute detour.

If you have got the nerve, hire a car in Rio. It will be the only way you will get the chance of seeing some of the city's more unspoilt beaches and is a positive necessity if you want to go to Buzios, or the Green Coast. But don't forget, most car hire companies can also supply a driver who may help your peace of mind.

Parking in Rio is chaotic but not difficult. The locals have the attitude of: "If in doubt, park" and take full advantage of the fact that most restaurants take the responsibility of parking your car.

Rio, and Brazil in general, is well signposted so once you know where you are heading for it is just a question of getting in the car and going, but remember which areas you have to go through first, they will be the first to be posted.

Further information about car hire, taxis, buses, and even motor cycles can be found in the information section of the book.

Better to Be Safe Than Sorry:
A Cautionary Tale

A phrase you will see a lot in this book is "be sensible". Being sensible is the secret formula to having a trouble free and enjoyable stay in Rio.

Rio has in recent years suffered from an image of being a violent and crime ridden city. That is the image that sells newspapers, it is not the image that sells Rio. What most newspapers fail to mention in their reports is that the crime and violence taking place in Rio is happening in the zona norte, an area of the city which is unlikely to attract foreign visitors.

Like any major city with a booming tourist trade Rio does however suffer from a number of crimes which to work, play on tourists' gullibility.

I have never understood what comes over normal sane human beings but once they don the mantle of "tourist" they throw all intelligence to the wind and act in a manner they would never dream of in their own town. This is where the trouble starts.

Crime aimed at tourists in Rio is robbery. It would seem there are a lot of people out there who would prefer that tourists leave their money and belongings in Brazil when they return home.

The key to virtually all petty pilfering in Rio is your bag. The reasons are numerous, but basically a bag is easy for the thief to grab and run with. There is also the added factor that you are probably not used to carrying a bag. Back home you don't normally bother to lug around your guide book, sun hat, newspaper, towel, etc, etc. Not being used to a bag you will be amazed where you put it down. But before you do ask yourself: "Am I being sensible?" If you put a bag down somebody else is quite likely to pick it up, so keep your hand on it and don't leave it unattended.

To show you how bad things can get I have seen tourists getting on a bus hand their bags to local Brazilian children who were helping them on and then look surprised when the children don't get on the bus with the bag but run the other way. Now I ask you if you were a New Yorker would you give your brief case to some unknown kid while you get on the bus in Manhattan?

The simple answer of course is that you can't be robbed if you've got nothing with you to be stolen. Think about this before you leave your hotel room in the morning. Work out exactly what you want to take with you for the day and why? You certainly won't want all your traveller checks nor your passport or airticket. Items like these should be placed in the hotel safe deposit box where you won't have to worry about them for the rest of your holiday. For identification ask the hotel to photocopy your passport.

While we are in the hotel, and I know I speak for most of the hotel managers, please don't leave valuables lying around your room in the open. Rooms are too easy to break into, but somebody breaking in does not want to waste time looking for things so don't leave all your goodies sitting out in the open on the bed, lock them in a cupboard or out of the way in your suitcase.

Pickpockets in Rio

If somebody is not going to steal your bag they are going to have to pickpocket you and Brazil is no different from anywhere else in the world in that to do so the thief has to make bodily contact. Here Rio's tropical weather works against the thief. Because it is hot people don't group together but walk spaced out, it is rare that you are ever in a bodily crush, therefore take it as a warning if you are suddenly closed in on. Classic locations are the bus; going through doors; in markets, and that is true of Sunday's Hippie Fair; and in shops. Keep your wallet where you can feel it, and don't have it sticking out of your back pocket.

Jewelry is another item I have to warn you about. Here again the simple answer is if you don't wear any you can't lose it.

Despite all the jewelry sold in Brazil the women are not over dressy with their gems during the day, it is all too easy for somebody to grab a chain and run. In the evening Brazilians will dress up but only if they know they are going by car or cab. Don't for example go strolling along the streets at night laden down with your new jewelry. It would not be "sensible" would it?

Criminals in Rio are like criminals everywhere, they don't want to get caught. There are plenty of easy pickings for criminals in Rio it is sad to say but that does not mean that you must add yourself to the list, if you keep your wits about you you will not come to any harm. Behave how you would in your own home town and you will be alright. It's easy to avoid trouble if you want to.

Carnival Time

Carnival is no worse than any other time of year, I should add, except that you are likely to find yourself in more crushes where pickpockets can operate. The entry to club balls is one such location so hang on to your wallet until you get through the door.

Security at the big parade itself is first class although the same cannot be said for the carnival activities around Rio Branco.

You should also forget what you may have read about South American policemen. On the day, in Rio, they are on your side and will do their best to help. If you think you are being followed by a suspicious looking character during carnival go and stand next to a policeman. If he can't understand you he will call up one of the translators that are on hand at all the major carnival events.

It is advisable to let the police deal with the criminals in their own sweet way, don't get involved in heroics trying citizens arrests as you will get hurt. The vast majority of crime aimed at the foreign visitor is not violent. If the thief has a gun he will let you know from early on. If you see a fellow tourist in trouble try and help them but only help to scare away the potential thief, don't go chasing people up alleys, they may have friends waiting.

Finally a warning for the men.

If you go for a night time stroll along the front in Copacabana, which would be normal, be careful with overly friendly girls. You may think it is Christmas as they pounce and tell you how wonderful you are while in reality they are just getting in a little bodily contact so that they can remove your wallet while you are worrying about what the "lady" is doing with her other hand. The smile on your face won't last long when you realise you have been taken for a sucker. The same advice applies if you are going round Rio's raunchier bars, keep your money safe.

Welcome to Rio, now enjoy it by being sensible.

Safety First: Dos and Don'ts

DON'T...

.... leave bags unattended.

... put your wallet in your back pocket or the outside pocket of your bag.

... walk in unlit areas at night.

... wear lots of obvious jewelry in the streets.

... take more than you need to the beach.

... take the 553 bus from the Inter-Continental and Nacional under any circumstance. It passes close to one of Rio's worst shanty towns.

... walk from the Sheraton to Leblon and Ipanema and vice-versa, take a cab or a bus. More tourists have lost cameras and bags on this stretch or road than I care to remember.

... walk between Leblon and Ipanema at night or in the same Jardim de Alah area, especially the Leblon side of the canal, during the day. This is a Rio black spot for visitors and residents alike.

... ride on the Santa Teresa streetcar.

... take drugs or get involved with them while in Rio

... think it can't happen to you.

... be stupid.

DO

.... put your money, passport, airticket, and other valuables in the hotel safe deposit box.

... take cabs rather than buses.
... ask policemen for help.
... ask your hotel for any information you need, they know the answers.
... call on your consulate for help if you have any serious problems.
... avoid crushes.
... act more like a traveller than a tourist.
... have a good time.
... be sensible.

In recent years the Rio police department has been operating a special section, Poltur, whose specific job is to help tourists and other visitors in trouble. If you have any problems therefore visit Poltur at Av. Humberto de Campos, 315. Poltur is located next to the 14th District Police Station which sits on the corner of Av. Humberto de Campos and Av. Afranio de Melo Franco, almost opposite the Scala showhouse. The telephone number of Poltur is 259 7048. If you yourself run foul of the law and get taken to a police station ask them to contact Poltur for you.

If you are going to be travelling within Brazil make sure you purchase a Brazilian "Air Pass" when you buy your ticket to Brazil.

You can't buy the "Air Pass" in Brazil and internal air travel is not cheap.

B

Apart Hotels
Hotels

Rio's Hotel Scene

The Hotel section of *The Insider's Guide to Rio de Janeiro* is designed to be of help to the business traveller, the tourist, the travel agent, and even the local resident and from the letters and cards I receive I must assume that this section of the book is performing its task and well.

Today, more than ever, *The Insider's Guide to Rio de Janeiro* faithfully reflects the latest opinions of the paying customer, the person who, in my opinion, is always right.

As a city Rio offers hotels to fit every taste and budget. You can choose from small two-star hotels in the back streets of Copacabana and Ipanema for $15-a-night all the way up to the opulent luxury of the Presidential and Imperial suites of the top de-luxe hotels.

All the hotels listed in *The Insider's Guide to Rio de Janeiro* are chosen for their suitability for the foreign visitor. The hotels are to be found in safe, pleasant areas, they are comfortable and clean, have air-conditioning and private bathrooms, and each in its own way offers value for money.

Rio, it must be remembered, does not base itself around the European or North American visitor because the majority of visitors who come to stay in the city are from the other Latin American countries or from Brazil itself. Hotels operate on their local reputation and because of this you get what you pay for. Prices in Rio therefore become a fairly accurate guide to the degree of comfort you can expect and the facilities that go with it. They also reflect the hotel's position, so for the same money you can stay in a superior hotel two blocks from the beach to those in the same price bracket on the beachfront. It is for you to weigh up your own priorities.

As time waits for no man, or hotel, you should always check with the hotel about changes in its facilities or prices before making a firm reservation. If you have still to arrive in Rio write to the hotels which appeal to you and ask them to forward their latest brochure. It is still true that a picture can be worth a thousand words.

All prices quoted in this section of the guide are in American dollars at the "official" rate. In cruzados therefore your hotel room may become considerably cheaper by changing your dollars in Rio on the "parallel" market. This must, however, be balanced against the package deals offered in Europe and North America for most of Rio's top hotels. The advertised rate for your room, the rack rate, may be $80 while your tour operator will get it for you as part of a package for as little as $20. How else do you think they can offer seven days in Rio from New York, including air fare, for a little over $500? But remember if you want to pay in cruzados you will need hard currency or travellers checks to change, your plastic money, credit cards that is, will be charged at the "official" rate.

Hotels in the Past Year

1986 was an interesting year to say the least for hotels in Rio. On the one hand they had their busiest ever year, hotel rooms being at a premium for most of the time, yet on the other hand the boom in the Brazilian economy left the hotels of Rio with some embarrassing shortages like meat, eggs, etc.

In 1987 the only shortage in Rio looks like being the hotel rooms themselves so be warned you must book in advance, well in advance, if you want to stay in Rio during the high season.

A few mediocre four star hotels started operating at the end of 1986 but these are not the long term solution for Rio, that is on the drawing board of a number of companies in the shape of several deluxe resort hotels. When and where still remains a mystery though.

1986 saw the continued refurbishment of the top hotels the most dramatic of which was the completion of the Sheraton's lobby area, part of a $13-million facelift the hotel is undergoing which has helped lift the hotel in to the ranks of Rio's outstanding hotels.

The Inter-Continental continued making improvements which included the opening of a branch of Alfredo's of Rome; the Rio Palace transformed its Imperial Club in to a sophisticated executive floor for business travellers; while the Caesar Park and Meridien kept the high standards expected of them.

Outside of the group of outstanding hotels the Nacional finally started to spend money on itself, but a lot will need to be spent; the Copacabana Palace refurbished its main restaurant, but was still waiting for permission to start work on a new accommodation tower behind the main hotel; while the Gloria has done just about everything it can to satisfy the "package tour" traveller except move the hotel down to Copacabana.

The Best Area for Your Hotel

When choosing a hotel you must not be mistaken into thinking that Copacabana is the "be all and end all" of Rio. The distances between Copacabana, Ipanema and São Conrado are minimal and all are within easy reach of the city center.

This guide includes no hotels in the center itself because no visitor, including businessmen, should want to stay there. The city is a place which works by day and sleeps by night, you would find yourself constantly travelling at night to the zona sul in search of the better restaurants and night life.

The nearest hotel in the guide to the city center is the Hotel Gloria, just a short cab ride from any office in the center, and the furthest, discounting Barra, the resort hotels of the Inter-Continental, Sheraton and Nacional, which depending on traffic conditions are still only 30 minutes away by cab or executive coach.

Embratur's Star Rating

Embratur, the Brazilian tourist authority, visit every hotel in Brazil at least twice during the year and grades them against a strict series of guidelines which award stars, from one to five, to hotels for the facilities offered.

However, while the Embratur rating guarantees certain facilities, including private bathroom in all hotel rooms, it gives no guarantee of the overall quality of each individual hotel, and this is where you should look at the price.

Generally five star hotels are far superior to four star hotels while the difference between three and four star hotels is minimal. There is however a big difference between three and two star hotels, although even two star hotels, or certainly those included in this guide, offer comfortable and clean accommodation at low prices and with few additional frills. They are more than adequate for the traveller on a limited budget who wants a place to sleep and leave his bag in safety.

You will find the hotels are reviewed alphabetically and under their official Embratur rating, there are also preliminary listings by area, rating and alphabetically with phone number.

For 1987 I have chosen five hotels to be rated separately, the hotels that can be considered to be Rio's outstanding hotels. They are the Meridien and Rio Palace in Copacabana, the Caesar Park in.

Ipanema, the Sheraton in Vidigal, and the Inter-Continental in São Conrado.

Finally I return full circle and go back to where I started, the 1984 guide. I said then that the success of *The Insider's Guide to Rio de Janeiro* in the future and its aim to encourage the improvement of standards relies entirely on you, the paying customer. Then, as now, I ask you to take a little time and drop me a line and let me have your thoughts, praise and criticism, for the hotels that you were staying in, that way the *Insider's Guide* remains "the" insider's guide, only the insider will have been you.

Alphabetical Listing of Hotels

Acapulco	275-0022	Leme
Apa	255-8112	Copacabana
Arpoador Inn	247-6090	Ipanema
Astoria	257-8080	Copacabana
Atlântico Copacabana	235-7941	Copacabana
Atlantis Copacabana	521-1142	Ipanema
Bandeirantes Othon	255-6252	Copacabana
Biarritz	255-6552	Copacabana
California	257-1900	Copacabana
Caesar Park	287-3122	Ipanema
Canada	257-1864	Copacabana
Carlton	259-1932	Leblon
Castro Alves	257-1800	Copacabana
Copacabana Palace	255-7070	Copacabana
Copacabana Praia	521-2727	Copacabana
Copacabana Sol	257-1840	Copacabana
Debret	521-3332	Copacabana
Everest Rio	287-8282	Ipanema
Excelsior	257-1950	Copacabana
Gloria	245-8010	Flamengo
Inter-Continental Rio	322-2200	São Conrado
Ipanema Inn	287-6092	Ipanema
Lancaster	541-1887	Copacabana
Leme Palace	275-8080	Leme
Luxor Continental	275-5252	Leme
Luxor Copacabana	257-1940	Copacabana
Luxor Regente	287-4212	Copacabana
Marina Palace	259-5212	Leblon
Marina Rio	239-8844	Leblon
Martinique	521-4552	Copacabana
Meridien	275-9922	Leme
Mirimar	247-6070	Copacabana
Monza	342-3885	Barra da Tijuca
Nacional	322-1000	São Conrado
Novo Mundo	225-7366	Flamengo
Olinda	257-1890	Copacabana
Othon Palace	255-8812	Copacabana
Ouro Verde	542-1887	Copacabana
Plaza	275-7722	Copacabana
Praia Ipanema	239-9932	Ipanema
Real Palace	541-4387	Copacabana
Rio Copa	275-6644	Leme
Rio Palace	521-3232	Copacabana
Rishon	247-6044	Copacabana
Riviera	247-6060	Copacabana
Roalty Copacabana	255-7180	Copacabana

San Marco	239-5032	Ipanema
São Conrado Palace	322-0911	São Conrado
Savoy Othon	257-8052	Copacabana
Sheraton Rio	274-1122	Vidigal
Sol Ipanema	227-0060	Ipanema
Toledo	257-1990	Copacabana
Trocadero	257-1834	Copacabana
Tropical	399-0660	Barra da Tijuca
Vermont	247-6100	Ipanema

Hotels by Area

BARRA DA TIJUCA

Monza
Tropical

**COPACABANA
& LEME**

Acapulco
Apa
Astoria
Atlântico Copacabana
Bandeirantes Othon
Biarritz
California
Canada
Castro Alves
Copacabana Palace
Copacabana Praia
Copacabana Sol
Debret
Excelsior
Lancaster
Leme Palace
Luxor Continental
Luxor Copacabana
Luxor Regente
Martinique
Meridien
Mirimar
Olinda
Othon Palace
Ouro Verde
Plaza
Real Palace
Rio Copa

Rio Palace
Rishon
Riviera
Royalty Copacabana
Savoy Othon
Toledo
Trocadero

FLAMENGO

Gloria
Novo Mundo

**IPANEMA &
LEBLON**

Arpoador Inn
Atlantis Copacabana
Caesar Park
Carlton
Everest Inn
Ipanema Inn
Marina Palace
Marina Rio
Praia Ipanema
San Marco
Sol Ipanema
Vermont

SÃO CONRADO

Inter-Continental Rio
Nacional
São Conrado Palace

VIDIGAL
Sheraton Rio

Hotels by Category

OUTSTANDING

Caesar Park	Ipanema
Inter-Continental Rio	São Conrado
Meridien	Leme
Rio Palace	Copacabana
Sheraton Rio	Vidigal

FIVE STAR

Copacabana Palace	Copacabana
Everest Rio	Ipanema
Marina Palace	Leblon
Nacional	São Conrado
Othon Palace	Copacabana

FOUR STAR

Atlântico Copacabana	Copacabana
California	Copacabana
Copacabana Praia	Copacabana
Gloria	Flamengo
Lancaster	Copacabana
Leme Palace	Leme
Luxor Continental	Leme
Luxor Copacabana	Copacabana
Luxor Regente	Copacabana
Marina Rio	Leblon
Mirimar	Copacabana
Ouro Verde	Copacabana
Plaza	Copacabana
Praia Ipanema	Ipanema
Real Palace	Copacabana
Royalty Copacabana	Copacabana
São Conrado Palace	São Conrado
Savoy Othon	Copacabana
Sol Ipanema	Ipanema

THREE STAR

Acapulco	Leme
Apa	Copacabana
Arpoador Inn	Ipanema
Astoria	Copacabana

Atlantis Copacabana	Ipanema
Bandeirantes Othon	Copacabana
Castro Alves	Copacabana
Copacabana Sol	Copacabana
Debret	Copacabana
Excelsior	Copacabana
Novo Mundo	Flamengo
Olinda	Copacabana
Rio Copa	Leme
Rishon	Copacabana
Riviera	Copacabana
Trocadero	Copacabana
Tropical	Barra da Tijuca

TWO STAR

Biarritz	Copacabana
Canada	Copacabana
Carlton	Leblon
Ipanema Inn	Ipanema
Martinique	Copacabana
San Marco	Ipanema
Toledo	Copacabana
Vermont	Ipanema

ONE STAR

Monza	Barra da Tijuca

The Hotels of Rio

ACAPULCO ★ ★ ★
Rua Gustavo Sampaio, 854 — Leme.

Middle range unexceptional three star hotel located in a small, but busy, back road behind the Meridien Hotel, one block from the beach.

* 123 rooms.
* 6 suites.
* TV and mini-bar in every room.
* Restaurant and coffee shop.
* 24-hour room service.
* Parking

Rates: Single from $30. Double from $40 Suites from $46.
Telephone: 275-0022.
Telex: 021-32900.
Credit: All major cards.
Reservations: With the hotel.

APA ★ ★ ★
Rua República do Peru, 305 — Copacabana.

Bottom end of the three star market but with prices to match. The Hotel Apa offers comfortable if "dubiously" decorated accommodation three blocks from Copacabana Beach.

* 50 rooms.
* TV and mini-bar in every room.
* Coffee Shop.
* 24-hour room service.
* Parking.

Rates: Single from $30. Double from $36.
Telephone: 255-8112.
Telex: 021-30394.
Credit: All major cards.
Reservations: With the hotel.

ARPOADOR INN ★ ★ ★
Rua Francisco Otaviano, 177 — panema.

The Arpoador Inn is a tiny three star hostelry to be found facing Arpoador Beach, the most easterly extension of Ipanema Beach which since 1983 has been a quiet cul-de-sac.
The hotel itself stretches from the beach through to Rua Francisco Otaviano, the busy link road between Ipanema and Copacabana, and because of this you should insist on a beachfront room.

* 48 rooms.
* 2 suites
* Optional television in room.
* Mini-bar in every room.

MERIDIEN HOTELS.
"LE RAFFINEMENT."

MERIDIEN "LE RAFFINEMENT". THE EMBODIMENT OF THE FINEST FRENCH TRADITION IN HOTELS... "LE RAFFINEMENT". A SUBTLE ALLIANCE OF DECOR AND COMFORT, OF AMBIANCE AND SERVICE, OF THE ART OF ELEGANT DINING AND GASTRONOMY.

"LE RAFFINEMENT" IS A FINAL TOUCH, A SPECIAL CARE FOR DETAIL, A COURTEOUS ATTENTIVENESS TO EACH INDIVIDUAL GUEST, ALL COMBINING

TO CREATE A UNIQUE STYLE OF LIVING. WHEREVER YOU ARE IN THE WORLD, EXPERIENCE THE SOUL OF THE FRENCH ART OF FINE LIVING.

EXPERIENCE "LE RAFFINEMENT", ONLY AT MERIDIEN.

THE INTERNATIONAL HOTELS WITH A FRENCH TOUCH
GROUPE AIR FRANCE

HOTEL MERIDIEN COPACABANA
Av. Atlântica, 1020 - Tel.: (021) 275-9922 - Telex: 02123183

BRAZILIAN NAIVE ART

GALERIA DE ARTE JEAN-JACQUES

Brazilian Primitive Art
Open Tuesday through Saturday from 11 a.m. to 8 p.m.

Rua Ramon Franco, 49 — Urca — Rio de Janeiro
(5 minutes walk from the Sugar Loaf)
Tel: 021-542-1443

* Coffee shop / restaurant.
* Bar.
* Room service.
* On beachfront in Arpoador.

Rates: Single from $29. Double from $32.
Telephone: 247-6090.
Telex: 021-22833.
Credit: All major cards (except Diners).
Reservations: With the hotel.

ASTORIA ★ ★ ★
Rua República do Peru, 345 — Copacabana.

The opening of an extension, or annex, in 1984 lifted this hotel from the "ordinary" to the "exceptional" within its price range. The new extension includes a sun-deck with small pool and bar area, while below is located the sauna, games and TV rooms.

The Astoria is situated three blocks from Copacabana Beach in a relatively quiet side street.

* 120 rooms.
* 3 suites with own dip pool.
* TV and mini-bar in every room.
* Coffee shop and bar.
* Swimming pool and sauna.
* Parking.

Rates: Single from $25. Double from $40.
Suites from $65.
Telephone: 257-8080.
Credit: All major cards.
Reservations: With the hotel.

ATLÂNTICO COPACABANA ★ ★ ★ ★
Rua Siqueira Campos, 90 — Copacabana.

A new purpose built four star hotel which opened as the guide was going to press.

* 130 rooms.
* 13 suites.
* TV and mini-bar in every room.
* 24-hour room service.
* Restaurant.
* Coffee shop.
* Sundeck with pool.
* Sauna

Rates:
Telephone: 235-7941.
Telex:
Credit: Most major cards.
Reservations: With the hotel.

ATLANTIS COPACABANA ★ ★ ★
Rua Bulhões de Carvalho, 61 — Copacabana.

Despite its name and postal address, this smart purpose built three star hotel is closer to Ipanema Beach — one block away — than it is to Copacabana Beach — three blocks away.

Inaugurated in 1984, the Atlantis Copacabana is still to make its mark but is certain to become a popular choice with agents for tour groups.

* 87 rooms.
* TV and mini-bar in every room.
* 24-hour room service.
* Coffee shop.
* Lobby bar.
* Sundeck with pool.
* Gaivota Bar.
* Sauna.

Rates: Single from $40. Double from $45.
Telephone: 521-1142.
Telex: 021-35392.
Credit: All major cards.
Reservations: With the hotel.

BANDEIRANTES OTHON ★ ★ ★
Rua Barata Ribeiro, 548 — Copacabana.

A smart modern hotel built with the business traveller on a restricted budget in mind.

Three blocks from the beach, the Bandeirantes Othon was constructed in 1978 for the Othon group.

* 90 rooms.
* TV and mini-bar in every room.
* 24-hour room service.
* Coffee shop and bar.
* Limited parking.

Rates: Single from $28. Double from $32.
Telephone: 255-6252.
Credit: All major cards.
Reservations: With Othon Hotels — Av. Atlântica, 3264 — Copacabana. Tel.: 235-7292 or 255-8812. Telex: 021-22655. Worldwide with LRI.

BIARRITZ ★ ★
Rua Aires Saldanha, 54 — Copacabana.

Small hotel located in a quiet Copacabana back street half-a-block from the beach behind the five star Othon Palace.

* 29 rooms.
* Room service.
* TV Room.

Rates: Single from $15. Double from $30.
Telephone: 255-6552.
Credit: All major cards.
Reservations: With the hotel.

CALIFORNIA ★ ★ ★ ★
Av. Atlântica, 3264 — Copacabana.

Not quite the *Hotel California* the Eagles had in mind when they wrote their song Rio's Hotel California is still one of Copacabana's most traditional beachfront hotels and lies mid way along its sweeping curve.

Some of the California's rooms have pleasant balconies which overlook the beach and overall the hotel is comfortable if a little dated.

* 117 rooms and suites.
* TV and mini-bar in every room.
* 24-hour room service.
* Le Colonial Restaurant.
* Bar
* Beauty parlor and barber shop.
* Sidewalk bar.
* Meeting rooms.
* On beachfront.

Rates: Singles from $40. Double from $46. Suite from $65.
Telephone: 257-1900.
Credit: All major cards.
Reservations: With Othon Hotels — Av. Atlântica, 3264 — Copacabana. Tel.: 235-7292 or 255-8812. Telex: 021-22655. Worldwide with LRI.

CAESAR PARK (OUTSTANDING) — ★ ★ ★ ★ ★
Av. Vieira Souto, 460 — Ipanema.

The Caesar Park is the first, and until now, only hotel to do justice to the charm and sophistication of Ipanema.

Cooly elegant, the Caesar Park puts comfort and impeccable service above everything else, keeping the gimmicks to the bare minimum. It is hardly surprising to learn therefore, that this towering but graceful hotel has established itself as a firm favorite with many Latin American, European and North American business travellers since its inauguration in 1978.

Located in the heart of Ipanema, close to Rio's best shops and restaurants, the Caesar Park offers rooms that are stylishly furnished with views across Ipanema Beach to the ocean. All the rooms and suites were fully redecorated in 1986 as the lobby will be during the coming year.

The hotel's main restaurant is the highly regarded Petronius, one of Rio's most elegant, a restaurant where the dinner is as much at home dining alone or in a group.

The Caesar Park also offers its guests the Mariko sushi-bar and the roof top Tiberius, a restaurant which is popular in its own right with the residents of Ipanema for light lunches and its highly rated teas.

The hotel serves each Saturday one of Brazil's best and most famous feijoadas, the country's national dish.

The views from the Tiberius, and the sundeck and pool it leads on to, should not be missed by any visitor to Rio, even if you just pass by for an early evening drink or nightcap.

The Caesar Park is a top choice for travelling business executives, as is its sister hotel in São Paulo, and offers every support facility to these guests including an ample choice of conference, banqueting and meeting rooms.

The hotel's Imperial Suite offers the ultimate in luxury and comfort, covering an entire floor of the hotel. In recent years the suite has been the temporary Rio residence of the royal families of Spain and Sweden as well as countless Presidents and celebrities.

* 226 rooms and suites.
* TV and mini-bar in every room.
* 24-hour room service.
* Petronius restaurant.
* Tiberius restaurant.
* Mariko sushi-bar.
* Three bars.
* Sundeck and pool.
* Sauna.
* Beauty parlor and barber shop.
* Safe deposit boxes.
* Parking.
* Banquet and convention facilities.
* On beachfront in Ipanema.

Rates: Single from $130 to $150. Double from $150 to $170. Suites from $250.
Telephone: 287-3122.
Telex: 021-21204.
Credit: All major cards.
Reservations: With the hotel in Rio or worldwide with HRI, the Leading Hotels of the World.

CANADA ★ ★
Av. N. S. de Copacabana, 687 — Copacabana.

Located in the heart of Copacabana on the extremely busy and noisy crossroads of N. S. de Copacabana and Santa Clara.

The Canada completed a major restoration programme at the end of 1985 which enlarged and up-dated many of the rooms.

Two blocks from Copacabana Beach.

* 72 rooms.
* TV room.
* Room service.
* American Bar.

Rates: Single from $17. Double from $20.
Telephone: 257-1864.
Credit: All major cards.
Reservations: With the hotel.

CARLTON ★ ★
Rua João Lire. 68 — Leblon.

A hidden gem for anybody looking for cheap, clean, comfortable accommodation at the bottom end of the market for their holiday in Rio.

Tucked away in a quiet back street in Leblon, one block from the beach and close to the Marina Palace, the Carlton has a homely atmosphere which is helped by the hotel's friendly management who keep the standards high but without pretention.

A hotel for families who can't afford the large resort hotels.

- 45 rooms.
- TV and mini-bar in every room.
- Room service.
- Restaurant / Coffee Shop.
- Bar.

Rates: Single from $32. Double from $35. Suites from $40.
Telephone: 259-1932.
Credit: All major cards.
Reservations: With the hotel.

CASTRO ALVES ★ ★ ★
Av. N.S. de Copacabana. 552 — Copacabana.

A founder member of the Othon group, now South America's largest hotel operator, the Castro Alves today looks badly dated in comparison to some of the chain's newer hotels in Rio.

The Castro Alves is located in Praça Serzedelo Correia, a busy Copacabana square two blocks from the beach. Alongside the hotel is a branch of La Mole, Rio's best value Italian restaurant chain.

- 76 rooms.
- TV and mini-bar in every room.
- Room service.

Rates: Single from $28. Double from $32.
Telephone: 257-1800.
Credit: All major cards.
Reservations: With Othon Hotels — Av. Atlântica, 3264 — Copacabana. Tel. 235-7292 or 255-8812. Telex: 021-22655. Worldwide with LRI.

COPACABANA PALACE ★ ★ ★ ★ ★
Av. Atlântica, 1702 — Copacabana.

A grand hotel, in the traditional sense of the word, the Copacabana Palace in the past has hosted kings, queens, presidents, politicians and top Hollywood stars and even today boasts no less than three presidential and 78 other smaller suites.

Rio's most famous hotel was once one of the world's "great" hotels and it is not unconceivable to imagine that some day soon, if the owners are allowed to implement their planned improvements, that it may once again obtain that exalted position.

In 1986 the newly refurbished "Bife de Ouro" re-opened, inspired by the Negresco in Nice, and quckly re-established itself as one of the city's "in" eating places and better restaurants. The hotel's "Pergula" restaurant also benefitted from the face lift and is a pleasant location for a light lunch.

Even without the planned changes the Copacabana Palace's bedrooms can be considered comfortably plush, many already having been redecorated. The suites are outstanding.

The hotel's swimming pool is one of Rio's largest and most attractive.

For many travellers Rio would not be Rio without the Copacabana Palace. Let us hope, therefore, that the improvements continue in the coming years.

- 222 rooms and suites.
- TV and mini-bar in every room.
- 24-hour room service.
- Bife de Ouro restaurant.
- Pergula restaurant.
- Two bars.
- Swimming pool.
- Sauna.
- Beauty parlor.
- Safe deposit boxes in the room.
- Conference and convention facilities.
- Golden Room nightclub and banqueting hall.
- Theatre.
- On beachfront in Copacabana.

Rates: Single from $125. Double from $140. Suites from $225.
Telephone: 255-7070.
Telex: 021-21482
Credit: Most major cards.
Reservations: With the hotel or worldwide with Loew's Reservations or Utell International.

COPACABANA PRAIA ★ ★ ★ ★
Rua Francisco Otaviano. 30 — Copacabana.

Located behind the Rio Palace and not on Copacabana Beach as the name might suggest, the Copacabana Praia is still a short stroll to both Copacabana and Ipanema beaches.

The hotel itself has a rooftop sundeck and small pool. All rooms face forward and have balconies.

* 55 rooms.
* TV and mini-bar in every room.
* Room service.
* Picollo restaurant.
* Bar.
* Small swimming pool and sundeck.
* Sauna.

Rates: Single from $64. Double from $76.
Telephone: 521-2727.
Telex: 021-31734.
Credit: All major cards.
Reservations: With the hotel.

COPACABANA SOL ★ ★ ★
Rua Santa Clara, 141 – Copacabana.

Recently built hotel located three blocks from Copacabana Beach in Rua Santa Clara a busy cut-through.

* 70 rooms.
* 10 suites.
* TV and mini-bar in every room.
* Restaurant and bar.
* 24-hour room service.
* Parking.

Rates: Single from $50. Double from $57.
Telephone: 257-1840.
Telex: 021-33907.
Credit: All major cards.
Reservations: With the hotel.

DEBRET ★ ★ ★
Rua Almirante Gonçalves, 5 (Corner of Av. Atlàntica) – Copacabana.

This ex-apartment block on Copacabana beachfront was transformed in to a hotel back in 1972 and has since established itself as one of Rio's more traditional hotels.

Comfortably furnished, with a touch of the Brazilian colonial, the Debret offers good value for money.

* 96 rooms and suites.
* TV and mini-bar in every room.
* 24-hour room service.
* Bar / coffee shop / tea room.
* On beachfront.

Rates: Single from $43. Double from $50.
Telephone: 521-3332.
Telex: 021-30483.
Credit: All major cards.
Reservations: With the hotel.

EVEREST RIO ★ ★ ★ ★ ★
Rua Prudente de Morais, 1117
Ipanema.

Offering almost everything the business traveller could want, the Everest has become particularly popular for businessmen out on short contracts or families looking for their first apartment in Rio. At any time a good number of the hotel's guests will have been in residence for a month or more.

The bedrooms, which come as "standard", "deluxe", and "grand suite", are tastefully decorated with modern and functional fittings which include television, mini-bar and radio.

The hotel is located one block back from Ipanema Beach behind the Caesar Park hotel in the heart of the area's best shopping and restaurant district.

For those who want a break from the beach the Everest has a large sundeck and dip pool with panoramic views across Ipanema and the Lagoa to Corcovado.

* 169 rooms and suites.
* TV and mini-bar in every room.
* 24-hour room service.
* Restaurant.
* Coffee shop.
* Three bars.
* Sundeck with swimming pool.
* Sauna.
* Beauty parlor.
* Executive meeting rooms.
* Parking.

Rates: Single from $112. Double from $125.
Telephone: 287-8282.
Telex: 021-22254.
Credit: All major cards.
Reservations: With the hotel.

EXCELSIOR ★ ★ ★
Av. Atlàntica, 1800 – Copacabana.

One of Copacabana's most traditional beachfront hotels, the Excelsior, like the Horsa group's other Rio hotel, the five star Nacional, needs money spending on it to bring it up to date and the standard it is obviously capable of attaining.

Located in the same block as the Copacabana Palace, the Excelsior is one of the city's most spacious three star hotels and therefore a good choice for large tour groups of budget travellers.

* 183 rooms.
* 13 suites.
* TV and mini-bar in every room.
* 24-hour room service.

* Restaurant.
* Bar.
* Beauty parlor and barber shop.
* Meeting rooms.
* Parking.
* On beachfront.

Rates: Single from $35. Double from $39.
Telephone: 257-1800.
Telex: 021-21076.
Credit: All major cards.
Reservations: With Horsa Hotels on (011) 287-7522. Toll Free (011) 800-8011 and (011) 800-8210.

GLORIA ★ ★ ★ ★
Praia do Russel, 632 – Gloria.

The days when the Gloria stood alongside the Copacabana Palace as one of the great hotels of South America are long past. Time has moved the tourist activity of Rio on to Copacabana and Ipanema while the landscapers, to rub salt in the wound, even managed to steal the hotel's beach right from under its very nose.

Today what was beach is a park, leaving the hotel's guests a brisk stroll across Flamengo Park to find the sands of Flamengo Beach.

But markets change and so do hotels. Gone are the princes and princesses, the millionaire playboys and the Hollywood stars, gone to the plusher "de-luxe" hotels of Copacabana, Ipanema and São Conrado.

Today Brazil's largest hotel fills its 700 rooms with tourists visiting Rio on cheap package deals from the U.S. Happily a $7.5-million refurbishment programme has kept the Gloria good enough to satisfy these visitors despite its location which requires constant cab rides to find Rio's night life and the better beaches.

In spite of the constant movement of tour groups in the lobby, the business traveller who is in Rio to work, and work downtown, would do well to remember that the Gloria is less than a five minute cab ride from the city's main business center in Centro and certainly the best hotel in the area.

It must say something for the Gloria that the hotel's presidential suite is the choice of the Brazilian President when he visits Rio from Brasilia.

* 700 rooms and suites.
* TV and mini-bar in every room.
* 24-hour room service.
* Three restaurants.
* Three bars.
* Piano Bar.

* Two swimming pools.
* Sauna.
* Beauty parlor and barber shop..
* Conference and convention facilities.
* Theatre.
* Parking.
* Close to the marina.

Rates: Single from $75. Double from $90.
Telephone: 245-8010 and 205-7272.
Telex: 021-23623.
Credit: All major cards.
Reservations : With the hotel or through the reservation hot-line, 265-3436.

INTER-CONTINENTAL (OUTSTANDING) ★ ★ ★ ★ ★
Av. Prefeito Mendes de Morais, 222 São Conrado.

The Inter-Continental is Rio's premier resort hotel, each year offering an even wider number of services especially designed to help the holiday maker and the business traveller.

Set in its own grounds, facing on to the beach at São Conrado and backing on to the beautiful Gávea Golf Club, the Inter-Continental has recently been renovated to bring the hotel up to the highest international standards, standards which should satisfy the most discerning traveller and has in the process become one of the flagship hotels of Inter-Continental Hotels Corporation.

As a major resort hotel, the Inter-Continental offers plenty of options including for the visiting gourmet the "Monseigneur", one of Rio's outstanding restaurants, and a branch of Rome's famous "Alfredo di Lello" which opened its doors at the end of 1986.

The hotel also has the poolside "Varanda", which serves a daily buffet of the highest quality, as well as the pool snack bar and a 24-hour coffee shop. During the year the hotel has a full programme of food festivals which in the past have taken us to Paris, San Francisco, New Orleans, Rome, Lisbon and Holland.

For a thrist quenching drink the guest can choose between the Lobby Bar, a popular choice with Americans in Rio for its live satellite coverage of American football and sport; the "Jakui", which offers live music and dancing; and the swim-up pool bar which is reached from the swimming-pool itself.

In the evening the guests can retire to the "Jakui" or the "Papillon discotheque" which has been one of

Rio's most popular night spots with the young since opening.

For the sports fan the Inter-Continental offers the choice of three swimming-pools, tennis courts, sauna, gymnasium, and the chance to play golf at one of the city's championship courses. The hotel is also the base hotel for the Brazilian Formula 1 Grand Prix.

For the business traveller the hotel boasts the support facilities expected of a top "de-luxe" hotel including an extensive choice of rooms for banquets, conventions and smaller meetings.

The Inter-Continental is well located for congresses and trade shows taking place at Riocentro and the Convention Center of the Nacional Hotel and that means for the city's film and jazz festivals.

* 483 rooms and suites.
* TV and mini-bar in every room.
* 24-hour room service.
* Monseigneur restaurant.
* Alfredo di Lello restaurant.
* Varanda restaurant.
* 24-hour coffee shop.
* Pool snack bar.
* Lobby bar.
* Jakui bar and nightclub.
* Papillon discotheque.
* Three swimming pools.
* Tennis courts.
* Sauna.
* Gymnasium.
* Beauty parlor and barber shop.
* Safe deposit boxes.
* Parking.
* Banquet and convention facilities.
* Close to the São Conrado Fashion Mall.
* On beachfront in São Conrado.

Rates: Single from $105 to $145. Double from $115 to $155.
Telephone: 322-220.
Telex: 021-21790.
Credit: All major cards.
Reservations: With the hotel in Rio or worldwide with any member of the Inter-Continental group.

IPANEMA INN ★ ★
Rua Maria Quitéria, 27 — Ipanema.

Tucked in behind the outstanding Caesar Park Hotel, just half-a-block from Ipanema Beach, the Ipanema Inn offers similar simple accommodation to that offered by the Arpoador Inn but in the heart of Ipanema and with fewer frills.

* 56 rooms.
* Optional television in room.
* Mini-bar in every room.
* Bar.
* Room service.

Rates: Single from $35. Double from $38.
Telephone: 287-6092.
Telex: 021-22833.
Credit: All major cards (except Diners).
Reservations: With the hotel.

LANCASTER ★ ★ ★ ★
Av. Atlântica, 1470 — Copacabana.

Comfortable, rather than luxurious, the Lancaster is another of the Othon group's Copacabana beachfront hotels.

Located next to the superior Ouro Verde, close to the Copacabana Palace, the Lancaster underwent a facelift at the end of 1984 to keep her up to the Othon's standards and those of a Brazilian four star hotel.

* 70 rooms.
* TV and mini-bar in every room.
* 24-hour room service.
* Lancaster bar and restaurant.
* Sidewalk bar.
* Parking.
* On beachfront.

Rates: Single from $39. Double from $47. Suites from $75.
Telephone: 541-1887.
Credit: All major cards.
Reservations: With Othon Hotels
Av. Atlântica, 3264 – Copacabana.
Tel: 235-7292 or 255-8812. Telex: 021-22655. Worldwide with LRI.

LEME PALACE ★ ★ ★ ★
Av. Atlântica, 656 — Leme.

After the Ouro Verde and Hotel Gloria, the Leme Palace Hotel is Rio's most well known and respected four star hotel.

Located on Leme Beach, the Leme Palace is quieter than the other Copacabana hotels and appeals to both the business traveller and tourist.

The rooms are spacious with modern furnishings.

The best Rio hotel in the Othon group after the Othon Palace.

* 193 rooms and suites.
* TV and mini-bar in every room.
* 24-hour room service.
* La Fourchette Restaurant.
* Le Café coffee shop.
* Leme Pub with live music.
* Beauty parlor.
* Swimming pool.
* Reception and meeting rooms.
* Parking.
* On beachfront.

Rates: Single from $60. Double from $75.
Telephone: 275-8080.

Telex: 021-23265.
Credit: All major cards.
Reservations: With Othon Hotels —
Av. Atlântica, 3264 — Copacabana.
Tel: 235-7292 or 255-8812. Telex:
021-22655. Worldwide with LRI.

LUXOR CONTINENTAL ★ ★ ★ ★
Rua Gustavo Sampaio, 320 —
Leme.

One of three similar four star
hotels run by the Brazilian chain of
Luxor in Copacabana and Leme.
Well managed, comfortable and
clean, the Luxor Continental is
located one block back from Leme
beach behind the Leme Palace
Hotel.

* 250 rooms.
* TV and mini-bar in every room.
* 24-hour room service.
* "320" restaurant.
* Poty Bar.
* Caramelo coffee shop.

Rates: Single from $65. Double from
$73.
Telephone: 275-5252.
Telex: 021-21469.
Credit: All major cards.
Reservations: With the hotel or
Luxor Hotels — Av. N. S. de
Copacabana, 828, Tel: 256-2680.
Telex: 021-22410. In the U.S. with
Luxor Hotels — Biscayne Boulevard,
3000 — Miami. Tel: 800-327-3201 or
305-357-5221.

LUXOR COPACABANA ★ ★ ★ ★
Av. Atlântica, 2554 — Copacabana.

This pencil thin modern four star
hotel offers comfortable beachfront
accommodation backed by the
Luxor chain's know-how.
Located in the central part of the
beach, the streets behind the Luxor
Copacabana contains the area's best
stores.

* 123 rooms.
* TV and mini-bar in every room.
* 24-hour room service.
* Fogareiro bar and restaurant.
* On beachfront.

Rates: Single from $74. Double from
$82.
Telephone: 257-1940.
Telex: 021-23971.
Credit: All major cards.
Reservations: With the hotel or
Luxor Hotels — Av. N. S. de
Copacabana, 828. Tel: 256-2680.
Telex: 021-22410. In the U.S. with
Luxor Hotels — Biscayne Boulevard,
3000 — Miami, Tel: 256-2680.
305-357-5221.

LUXOR REGENTE ★ ★ ★ ★
Av. Atlântica, 3716 — Copacabana.

The best of the three Luxor hotels
is, in my opinion, to be found at the
Ipanema end of Copacabana where
the comfortable, spacious and more
modern Luxor Regente is located.
The hotel's *Forno e Fogão* restaurant underwent a facelift in 1985
and offers above average fare in
comparison with the restaurants of
most of the other four star hotels.

* 258 rooms and suites.
* TV and mini-bar in every room.
* 24-hour room service.
* Forno e Fogão restaurant.
* Cochicho bar.
* Presidential suite with private dip
pool.
* On beachfront.

Rates: Single from $80. Double from
$105.
Telephone: 287-4212.
Telex: 021-23887.
Credit: All major cards.
Reservations: With the hotel or
Luxor Hotels — Av. N. S. de
Copacabana, 828. Telex: 256-2680.
Telex: 021-22410. In the U.S. with
Luxor Hotels — Biscayne Bulevard,
3000 — Miami, Tel.: 800-327-3201 or
305-357-5221.

MARINA PALACE ★ ★ ★ ★ ★
Av. Delfim Moreira, 630 — Leblon

The Marina Palace should be one
of Rio's best four star hotels but as
it was built to conform with
Embratur's "star" rating it carries
the burden of five stars and therefore must suffer comparison with
the Caesar Park, Inter-Continental,
Meridien, Rio Palace, Sheraton, and
the other more sophisticated hotels
which fall in to this category.
The bedrooms are comfortable
and adequately equipped but fall
short of what a seasoned traveller
would expect from a "de-luxe" or
five star hotel.
The Marina Palace has become a
popular choice with a number of
overseas tour companies whose
clients will in no way feel disappointed if they are told in advance that
they will be staying in one of Rio's
better "four star" hotels.

* 160 rooms and suites.
* TV and mini-bar in every room.
* 24-hour room service.
* Restaurant.
* Coffee Shop.
* Two Bars.
* Sundeck with pool and bar.
* Sauna.

* Beauty parlor.
* Parking.
* Executive meeting rooms.
* On beachfront in Leblon.

Rates: Single from $115. Double from $130.
Telephone: 259-5212
Telex: 021-30224.
Credit: All major cards.
Reservations: With the hotel.

MARINA RIO ★ ★ ★ ★
Av. Delfim Moreira, 696 — Leblon.

The Marina Rio is to "four star" hotels as the Marina Palace" is to "five"

Modern and functional, the Marina Rio was the forerunner to the larger and better equipped Marina Palace, offering similar but cheaper accommodation just one block up Leblon Beach.

Residents of the Marina Rio are allowed to use the facilities, including the roof top pool, of the Marina Palace.

* 60 rooms and suites.
* TV and mini-bar in every room.
* 24-hour room service.
* Restaurant.
* Bar
* Parking.
* On beachfront in Leblon.

Rates: Single from $70. Double from $75. Suites from $110.
Telephone: 239-8844.
Telex: 021-30224.
Credit: All major cards.
Reservations: With the hotel or the Marina Palace. Tel: 259-5212.

MARTINIQUE ★ ★
Rua Sá Ferreira, 30 — Copacabana.

One block back from Copacabana Beach in a quiet side road close to the Miramar.

* 52 rooms.
* TV and mini-bar in every room.
* Room service.
* Bar

Rates: Single from $15. Double from $30.
Telephone: 521-4552.
Telex: 021-30366.
Credit: Most major cards.
Reservations: With the hotel on 521-4393.

MERIDIEN COPACABANA — (OUTSTANDING) ★ ★ ★ ★ ★
Av. Atlântica, 1020 — Copacabana.

The Meridien brings all the class, style and *je ne sais quoi* of the French together to produce one of Rio's outstanding hotels.

Typically French, but at the same time undeniably Brazilian, the Meridien offers the travelling business executives and demanding tourist everything they could want.

Towering 37 floors above Copacabana Beach, the Meridien is a Rio landmark and no more so than on New Year's eve when the hotel transforms itself in to a giant Roman Candle to mark the turning of the year, a spectacle watched by millions each year.

The hotel is a gourmet's paradise offering the finest food of any Rio hotel be it from the roof-top "Saint Honoré" restaurant which is under the guidance of Paul Bocuse, one of France's greatest chefs, or in the ground floor "Café de la Paix, a Parisian brasserie in the heart of Copacabana which has a reputation for serving one of the city's best breakfasts.

Located on the beach where Copacabana becomes Leme, the Meridien has a large terrace on the fourth floor which houses the ample swimming-pool, a snack bar and sauna. For the night owl the hotel offers nothing less than a branch of Regine's itself and the popular Rond Point jazz bar.

The rooms are of the high standard you would expect from the prestigious Meridien chain with modern furnishings and views across Copacabana and the beach.

The hotel has 17 de luxe suites, 34 junior suites, and two presidential suites which in 1985 appropriately hosted the President of France, François Mitterrand.

For the business traveller the Meridien has a business center which includes meeting rooms, secretarial services, telex and translators which are complimented by the support facilities to be expected of a top international hotel.

* 497 rooms.
* 53 suites.
* TV and mini-bar in every room.
* 24-hour room service.
* Saint Honoré restaurant.
* Café de la Paix restaurant.
* Saint Trop pool side snack bar.
* Rond Point jazz bar.
* Regine's nightclub.
* Large sundeck.
* Swimming pool.
* Sauna.
* Beauty parlor and barber shop.,
* Safe deposit boxes.
* Parking.
* Banquet and convention facilities
* Business center.
* Cinema screening room.
* On beachfront in Copacabana.

Rates: Single from $145. Double from $155. Suites from $250.
Telephone: 275-9922.
Telex: 021-23183.
Credit: All major cards.
Reservations: With the hotel in Rio or worldwide with any member of the Meridien chain or Air France office.
Note: The Meridien group also operate a hotel in Bahia.

MIRAMAR ★ ★ ★ ★
Av. Atlântica, 3668 — Copacabana

The Miramar is one of Rio's most comfortable and cozy hotels which within its category offers value for money.

Tastefully and elegantly decorated, many of the public areas having recently been refurbished, the Miramar has become increasingly popular with both business travellers and tourists in the know.

* 133 rooms and suites.
* TV and mini-bar in every room.
* 24-hour room service.
* Ancoradouro restaurant.
* Passadiço coffee-shop.
* Convés tea room.
* Sidewalk bar.
* Rooftop bar with live music.
* Reading room.
* Meeting rooms.
* On beachfront.

Rates: Single from $56. Double from $63. Suite from $120.
Telephone: 287-6348.
Telex: 021-21508.
Credit: All major cards.
Reservations: With the hotel. Toll Free: 021-800-0783.

MONZA ★
Av. Embaixador Adelardo Bueno, 1000 — Barra da Tijuca.

I only mention the one star Monza, in reality a motel, because it sits opposite the entrance to the motor racing circuit where the Brazilian Formula 1 Grand Prix takes place each year, and therefore if you are a journalist or a mechanic you could find yourself staying here.

All the rooms at the Monza have television and telephone and the suites have individual suanas!

* 72 rooms.
* TV in every room.
* 24-hour room service.
* Opposite the motor racing circuit.
Telephone: 342-3885.
Reservations: With the hotel.

NACIONAL ★ ★ ★ ★ ★
Av. Niemeyer, 769 — São Conrado.

Rio's Nacional hotel has all the facilities to be a first class resort hotel. Sadly though, the hotel let itself slip over the years to become second class and at times third but help, or even salvation, may be just around the corner.

Since the start of 1986 the Nacional has slowly started to refurbish the rooms and physical plant, which have taken such a sorry beating over the years, with the hope of fully up-grading the hotel by the end of 1987. Personally I hope that the priority list includes the elevator system and the telephone switchboard both of which are prone to interminably long delays.

In spite of itself, the hotel has the best conference facilities of any Rio hotel, the largest in Latin America they claim, and an excellent modern auditorium with a capacity for 1600 which has hosted in the past Liza Minnelli, Shirley Bassey, Julio Iglesias, Roberta Flack, Ray Conniff, Burt Bacharach and Mikail Baryshnikov. The threatre is also home to Rio's excellent film (Fest Rio) and jazz (Free Jazz) festivals.

There is no reason not to believe that in the coming years with a bit of thought, a lot of money and new staff that the Nacional will take its place amongst the best hotels in Rio and justify its position as one of Latin America's most important convention hotels.

Despite my rather harsh words, I am certain that no tour group will be disappointed with the Nacional, especially when they compare the price they are paying against Rio's other five star hotels. Indeed I have visited several worse "five" star hotels in the holiday areas of Spain but please don't expect to find an American style "deluxe" hotel. For that you have to pay.

* 520 rooms and suites.
* TV and mini-bar in every room.
* 24-hour room service.
* Céu restaurant.
* Barbecue restaurant.
* Breakfast room.
* Three bars.
* Apocalypse nightclub.
* Swimming pool.
* Tennis courts.
* Sauna.
* Beauty parlor.
* Safe deposit boxes in the room.
* Large conference and convention center.
* Theatre.
* Parking.
* On beachfront in São Conrado.

Rates: Single from $80. Double from $90.

Telephone: 322-1000.
Telex: 021-23615.
Credit: All major cards.
Reservations: With the hotel or any of the Horsa Hotel group.

NOVO MUNDO ★ ★ ★
Praia do Flamengo, 20 — Flamengo.

Like its neighboring Hotel Gloria, the Novo Mundo has seen better days. Today it seems to appeal to the up-market "back-packers" who arrive in Rio and to their dismay learn that you can't just pitch your tent in the middle of Copacabana Beach or sleep rough in Ipanema. Looking for good value, but comfortable surroundings where they won't waste too much of Daddy's "lovely money", these adventurers find their way to the Novo Mundo.

* 217 rooms.
* TV and mini-bar in every room.
* 24-hour room service.
* Restaurant and breakfast room.
* American bar.
* Reading room.
* Parking.
* Beauty parlor and barber shop.

Rates: Single from $12. Double from $15.
Telephone: 225-7366.
Telex: 021-33282.
Credit: All major cards.
Reservations: With the hotel.

OLINDA ★ ★ ★
Av. Atlântica, 2230 — Copacabana.

Another of the Othon group's hotels which dominate the beachfront in Copacabana.

The Olinda offers comfortable but dated accommodation in the heart of Copacabana.

* 100 rooms.
* TV and mini-bar in every room.
* Room service.
* Olinda restaurant and bar.
* Sidewalk bar.
* Beauty parlor.
* On beachfront.

Rates: Single from $35. Double from $43.
Telephone: 257-1890.
Credit: All major cards.
Reservations: With Othon Hotels — Av. Atlântica, 3264 — Copacabana, Tel.: 235-7292 or 255-8812.
Telex: 021-22655. Worldwide with LRI.

OTHON PALACE ★ ★ ★ ★ ★
Av. Atlântica, 3264 — Copacabana.

Since its inauguration in 1976 the Othon Palace has been the flag ship of Othon Hotels, South America's largest hotel chain, and a landmark on Copacabana Beach.

Towering 30 floors skyward the Othon Palace dominates the center of Copacabana Beach and quickly becomes a reference point for any newcomer to Rio.

A complete hotel, the Othon Palace appeals to travellers who like their hotel to be modern and functional.

The rooms are large and well equipped and are pleasing to both tourist and business travellers.

The rooftop Skylab Bar should not be missed by any visitor to Rio with its spectacular view of the whole sweep of Copacabana and its world famous mosaic pavements.

The bar opens on to the hotel's sundeck and pool while 27 floors below the "Estância" restaurant serves above average hotel food which is complimented by the stunning views of Copacabana beach. Behind the "Estância" is the "Samambaia" coffee shop and "Tropical Patio".

In the basement of the Othon Palace is the "Studio C", one of the city's better private nightclubs which is open to guests of the hotel.

* 584 rooms and suites.
* TV and mini-bar in every room.
* 24-hour room service.
* Estância restaurant and bar.
* Semambaia coffee shop.
* Tropical breakfast patio.
* Skylab rooftop bar.
* Lobby bar.
* Studio C nightclub.
* Sundeck with swimming pool.
* Sauna.
* Beauty parlor and barber shop.
* Safe deposit boxes.
* Conference and convention facilities
* Parking.
* On beachfront in Copacabana.

Rates: Single from $100. Double from $115.
Telephone: 255-8812.
Telex: 021-22655.
Credit: All major cards.
Reservation: With the hotel or worldwide with LRI.

OURO VERDE ★ ★ ★ ★
.Av. Atlântica, 1456 — Copacabana.

If quality was taken in to consideration by Embratur then there is no question that the Ouro Verde would be a "five", rather than "four" star hotel, yet however you choose to grade the Ouro Verde it is.

unquestionably one of Rio's finest hotels.

Justifiably famous, the Ouro Verde offers the business traveller no gimmicks, just extremely comfortable, traditional rooms backed by outstanding and correct service. As the hotel says about itself, "We are a contribution to the art of elegant and gracious living." Anyone who has stayed in the Ouro Verde will not argue with those sentiments.

The hotel's restaurant is famous in it's own right and considered, including by myself, to be one of Rio's top eating spots with a firm tradition which dates back to the 1950s.

The Ouro Verde is a hotel to be remembered by all discerning business travellers, yet because of its popularity you would be well advised to remember the Ouro Verde well in advance and make the necessary reservations.

* 64 rooms.
* 5 suites
* TV and mini-bar in every room.
* 24-hour room service.
* Ouro Verde restaurant
* Bar.
* Sidewalk bar.
* Reading room.
* On beachfront.

Rates: Single from $80. Double from $85, Suites from $175.
Telephone: 542-1887.
Telex: 021-23848.
Credit: Most major cards.
Reservations: With the hotel.

PLAZA ★ ★ ★ ★
Av. Princesa Isabel, 263 Copacabana.

At totally the other end of the four star scale to the Ouro Verde (see above) the Plaza is a typically modern hotel which lacks a lot in atmosphere and imagination but which offers value for money as the cheapest of the four star hotels.

As it is located two blocks from the beach in the middle of the red light district it should be avoided by ladies travelling un-escorted.

* 165 rooms.
* TV and mini-bar in every room.
* 24-hour room service.
* Restaurant and coffee shop.
* Meeting rooms.

Rates: Single from $40. Double from $45.
Telephone: 275-7722.
Telex: 021-31198
Credit: All major cards.
Reservations: With the hotel.

PRAIA IPANEMA ★ ★ ★ ★
Av. Vieira Souto, 706 — Ipanema.

A hotel built with the tourist and beach and sun worshipper in mind.

Smart modern hotel on Ipanema beachfront with own dip pool on rooftop sundeck.

Tastefully decorated bedrooms, most with own balcony.

* 105 rooms.
* TV and mini-bar in every room.
* 24-hour room service.
* La Mouette restaurant.
* Bar.
* Dip pool and bar on sundeck.
* Beauty parlor.
* On beachfront.

Rates: Single from $68. Double from $86.
Telephone: 239-9932.
Telex: 021-31280.
Credit: All major cards.
Reservation: With the hotel.

REAL PALACE ★ ★ ★ ★
Rua Duvivier, 70 — Copacabana.

Purpose built four star hotel in the back streets of Copacabana, two blocks from the beach.

Inaugurated in 1984, the rooms, as in many modern hotels, are on the small side, like don't bring a cat to swing, but functional.

The roof houses a small sundeck and dip pool.

Do not mix up the *Real Palace* with the *Rio Palace* as some tour companies would like to. The Real Palace does not deserve to be mentioned in the same breath as the outstanding *Rio Palace* (see below).

* 59 rooms.
* 5 suites
* TV and mini-bar in every room.
* 24-hour room service.
* Restaurant and bar.
* Dip pool and sundeck.
* Sauna.
* Beauty parlor and barber shop.
* Meeting rooms.

Rates: Single from $70. Double from $80.
Telephone: 541-4387.
Telex: 021-34218.
Credit: All major cards.
Reservations: With the hotel.

RIO COPA ★ ★ ★
Av. Princesa Isabel, 370 — Leme.

A favorite with the budget minded business traveller, the Rio Copa offers value for money in a hotel which in certain aspects is unlucky not to be "four" rather than "three" star.

Not a beachfront hotel, Rio Copa being setback three long blocks from Copacabana Beach on the very busy Av. Princesa Isabel, the main link-road between Copacabana and Botafogo.

The rooms offer standard modern US motel style furnishings and double glazing to cut the noise from the passing trafic.

* 110 rooms and suites
* TV and mini-bar in every room.
* Room service.
* Le Baron restaurant.
* Coffee Shop.
* Bar.
* Meeting rooms.

Rates: Single from $32. Double from $35.
Telephone: 275-6644.
Telex: 021-23988.
Credit: All major cards.
Reservations: With the hotel.

RIO PALACE — (OUTSTANDING) — ★ ★ ★ ★ ★
Av. Atlântica, 4240 — Copacabana.

Rarely, if ever, out of the headlines since its opening in 1979, the sheer richness of the Rio Palace and the agressive marketing of its owners made the hotel Rio's "in" location and as a result helped improve hotel standards in the city with the Caesar Park, Inter-Continental, Meridien and Sheraton all rising to meet the challenge set by the Rio-Palace.

Luxuriant, but at the same time discreetly tasteful, the Rio Palace has over 400 rooms and suites each with private balcony and views across Copacabana and Ipanema.

The hotel revolves around its large terrace which houses the hotel's two swimming-pools and boasts one of the most beautiful views of Copacabana and the coastline to the east. Above the pools are the rooms, below the outstanding public areas.

The conference and banqueting facilities have in the past hosted shows by Franck Sinatra, Julio Iglesias, Barry White and Bobby Short, while the "Le Pré Catelan" restaurant offers the highest standard of French cuisine supervised by Gaston Lenotre.

The Atlantis restaurant on the terrace level is popular with local residents for lunch at the weekend, including its feijoada, and dinner during the week. Other choices are the "Horses Neck Bar", where

Brazilian music and jazz is presented in a distinctly British atmosphere, the enchanting "Cha & Simpatia" tea room, while for the late night reveller there is the hotel's own private nightclub, one of the city's most exclusive, the Palace Club.

For the executive traveller the Rio Palace offers the Imperial Club, a self-contained floor with the full support services demanded by top travellers including full butler and valet service, private breakfast and meeting rooms.

During 1987 the Rio Palace will further pamper its guests with the opening of a fitness center.

Below the hotel is the 150 store Cassino Atlântico shopping center where a number of fine art galleries and souvenirs stores are housed.

The Rio Palace is the base hotel for the foreign journalists coming to the city to cover Carnival and in 1985 was the headquarters for "Rock in Rio", hosting most of the top international acts.

* 418 rooms and suiites.
* TV and mini-bar in every room.
* 24-hour room service.
* Le Pré Catelan restaurant.
* Atlântis restaurant
* Cha & Simpatia.
* Horse's Neck Bar.
* Lobby Bar.
* Palace Club.
* Two swimming pools.
* Sauna.
* Fitness Center.
* Beauty parlor and barber shop.
* Safe deposit boxes.
* Parking.
* Conference and convention facilities.
* On beachfront in Copacabana.

Rates: Single from $120 to $170. Double from $140 to $190. Suites from $340 to $1400.
Telephone: 521-3232.
Telex: 021-21803.
Credit: All major cards.
Reservations: With the hotel in Rio or worldwide with HRI,the Leading Hotels of the World.

RISHON ★ ★ ★
Rua Francisco Sá, 17 — Copacabana.

Located in one of Copacabana's quieter side streets, one block from the beach, the Rishon is little known even among the local residents.

Its' rooms are large and comfortable with color television and mini-bar.

On the roof the Rishon has a small pool and large sundeck.

The Rishon offers many of the

facilities of Rio's better four star hotels but at the price of a three star hotel making it a good choice for both the tourist and business traveller.

* 65 rooms.
* TV and mini-bar in every room.
* Room service.
* Swimming pool and sundeck.
* Coffee shop.

Rates: Single from $47, Double from $54.
Telephone: 247-6044.
Telex: 021-32486.
Credit: All major cards.
Reservations: With the hotel.

RIVIERA ★ ★ ★
Av. Atlântica, 4122 — Copacabana.

Small Copacabana beachfront hotel one block from the Rio Palace which can be considered to be at the lowest end of the three star market with prices and service to match.

Furnishings are basic to say the least.

* 108 rooms.
* TV and mini-bar in every room.
* 24-hour room service.
* Restaurant and bar.
* On beachfront.

Rates: Single and double from $37.
Telephone: 247-6060.
Telex: 021-23851.
Credit: All major cards.
Reservations: With the hotel.

ROYALTY COPACABANA
★ ★ ★ ★
Rua Tonelero, 154- Copacabana.

A new purpose built four star hotel in the busy, and noisy Rua Tonelero which opened as the guide went to press.

* 143 rooms.
* TV and mini-bar in every room.
* 24-hour room service.
* Restaurant and breakfast room.
* Bar.
* Swimming pool.
* Sauna.

Rates:
Telephone: 255-7180.
Telex:
Credit: Most major cards.
Reservations: With the hotel.

SAN MARCO ★ ★
Rua Visconde de Pirajá, 524 — Ipanema.

An excellent choice for the student traveller or anyone else looking to save money but who wants a comfortable safe place to sleep.

The San Marco is located in the heart of Ipanema, in the main shopping street, just two blocks from Ipanema Beach.

* 56 rooms.
* TV and mini-bar in every room.
* Room service.
* Bar.

Rates: Single from $22. Double from $24.
Telephone: 239-5032.
Credit: All major cards.
Reservations: With the hotel.

SÃO CONRADO PALACE ★ ★ ★ ★
Av. Niemeyer, 776 — São Conrado.

Opening as the guide went to press, I have to have reservations about the São Conrado Palace due to its location in front of one of Rio's largest shanty towns. 1987 will show if these concerns are justified.

* 160 rooms.
* TV and mini-bar in every room.
* 24-hour room service.
* Restaurant.
* Bar.
* Parking.

Rates:
Telephone: 322-0911.
Telex:
Credit: Most major cards.
Reservations: With the hotel.

SAVOY OTHON ★ ★ ★ ★
Av. N. S. de Copacabana, 995 — Copacabana.

A popular choice with the business traveller on a limited budget who wants to stay in the heart of Copacabana.

Two blocks from Copacabana Beach, the Savoy Othon offers value for money to the traveller who puts comfort before a sea view.

One of the Othon group's better hotels.

* 154 rooms and suites.
* TV and mini-bar in every room.
* 24-hour room service.
* Savoy Grill.
* Savoy pub bar and coffee shop.
* Meeting rooms.

Rates: Single from $36. Double from $51.
Telephone: 257-8052.
Credit: All major cards.
Reservations: With Othon Hotels — Av. Atlântica, 3264 — Copacabana.

Tel.. 235-7292 or 255-8812. Telex: 021-22655. Worldwide with LRI.

SHERATON RIO (OUTSTANDING) — ★ ★ ★ ★ ★
Av. Niemeyer, 121 — Vidigal.

A $13-million facelift, which is due for completion in the first half of 1987, has transformed a very good hotel into an outstanding hotel and made the Rio-Sheraton one of the most respected and admired members of the Sheraton Hotel and Inn chain.

Set on Vidigal Beach, between Leblon and São Conrado, the Rio Sheraton has all the facilities expected of a top class international resort hotel, facilities which should help any visitor to have a memorable trip to Rio be they in town for business or tourism. The hotel also brings to Rio all the experience and know how of the Sheraton chain.

The rooms and suites, all with private balconies and sea views, are pleasantly decorated and all will have been refurbished in a new restful color scheme by the end of 1987.

In 1984, the Rio-Sheraton inaugurated "Valentino", one of city's most attractive restaurants which serves gourmet, and I do mean gourmet, Italian cuisine. Other options at the hotel include "O Casarão", a self-service barbacue housed in the extensive grounds, the poolside Trampolin snack bar, and the "Mirador" coffee shop.

For drinks the hotel offers the picturesque "Casa da Cachaça", a small house serving typical Brazilian drinks to the accompaniment of live music and the sounds of the ever present South Atlantic, and the One-Twenty-One bar in the hotel's magnificent new lobby which at night swings to the sound of live music.

For the fitness fan the Rio-Sheraton has three fresh water swimming-pools, flood lit tennis courts, a well equipped gymnasium and its own beach.

The business traveller can make use of the Sheraton's *Distinguished Customer Service* or the *Sheraton Executive Traveller programme* which boast their own lounge and other special amenities. The hotel can also accommodate banquets, meetings and conferences of every size with the infrastructure to support it.

* 617 rooms and suites.
* TV and mini-bar in every room.
* 24-hour room service.
* Valentino's restaurant.
* O Casarão barbecue.
* Trampolin restaurant and snack bar.
* Mirador coffee shop.
* One-Twenty-One bar.
* Three swimming pools.
* Tennis courts.
* Sauna.
* Gymnasium.
* Beauty parlor.
* Safe deposit boxes.
* Parking.
* Banquet and convention facilities.
* Located directly on the beach.

Rates: Single from $105 to $140. Double from $115 to $140.
Telephone: 274-1122.
Telex: 021-23485.
Credit: All major cards.
Reservation: With the hotel in Rio or worldwide with any member of the Sheraton group.

SOL IPANEMA ★ ★ ★ ★
Av. Vieira Souto, 320 — Ipanema.

Under the same management as the Praia Ipanema, the Sol Ipanema appeals more to the business traveller than the tourist yet is still situated on the beachfront in Ipanema close to the city's best stores and restaurants.

Rooms are comfortable but not as modern as those of Praia Ipanema.

The roof of the hotel has a sundeck and small dip pool.

* 78 rooms and suites.
* TV and mini-bar in every room.
* 24-hour room service.
* Restaurant.
* Bar.
* Beauty parlor.
* Sundeck and dip pool.
  On beachfront.

Rates: Single from $68. Double from $75.
Telephone: 227-0060.
Telex: 021-21979.
Credit: All major cards.
Reservations: With the hotel.

TOLEDO ★ ★
Rua Domingos Ferreira, 71 — Copacabana.

This pleasant little hotel located in a quiet back street mid-way down Copacabana, one block from the beach, is possibly the best two star hotel on offer in Rio, giving excellent value for money.

* 54 double rooms.
* 48 single rooms.
* Room service.
* Coffee shop and bar.

* TV Room.
* TV in some rooms.

Rates: Single from $27. Double from $30.
Telephone: 257-1990.
Telex: 021-30366.
Credit: Most major cards.
Reservations: With the hotel via telex or call 521-4443.

TROCADERO ★ ★ ★
Av. Atlântica, 2064 — Copacabana.

One of the better three star hotels to be found on the beachfront in Copacabana.
The Trocadero, part of the Othon group, is a fine choice for both the business and tourist traveller.
The hotel's restaurant is considered to be one of Rio's better Brazilian restaurants serving typical dishes as well as offering a full international menu.
The hotel's prices reflect its higher standards.

* 120 rooms and suites.
* TV and mini-bar in every room.
* 24-hour room service.
* Moenda Brazilian restaurant.
* Bar.
* Sidewalk bar.
* On beachfront.

Rates: Single from $40. Double from $46.
Telephone: 257-1834
Credit: All major cards
Reservations: With Othon Hotels — Av. Atlântica, 3264 — Copacabana. Tel: 235-7292 or 255-8812. Telex: 021-22655. Worldwide with LRI.

TROPICAL BARRA ★ ★ ★
Av. Sernambetiba, 500 — Barra da Tijuca.

The Tropical Hotel, which has pioneered the hotel industry in Barra, is often used by charter groups from the U.S. who opt for the cheapest accommodation package.
Other than its location, some distance from the action in Copacabana and Ipanema, patrons should have few complaints about this modern, functional three star hotel which overlooks the beach at Barra.

* 86 rooms.
* 1 suite.
* TV and mini-bar in every room.
* 24-hour room service.
* Restaurant.
* Bar.
* Coffee shop.
* On beachfront.
* Parking.

Rates: Single from $26. Double from $29.
Telephone: 399-0660.
Telex: 021-30366.
Credit: Most major cards.
Reservations: With the hotel or telephone 521-4443.

VERMONT ★ ★
Rua Visconde de Pirajá, 254 — Ipanema.

Offering similar comfortable and clean budget accommodation as the San Marco.
Located in the heart of Ipanema and just two blocks from the beach.

* 54 rooms.
* TV and mini-bar in every room.
* Room service.
* Bar.

Rates: Single from $17. Double from $19.
Telephone: 247-6100.
Credit: No credit cards.
Reservations: With the hotel.

Rio's Apart Hotels

Over recent years the sector of the hotel trade which has shown the most growth has been the apart-hotel sector with new establishments springing up along Barra da Tijuca.
Most of the apart-hotel complexes offer small well equipped apartments backed by the facilities you would expect at one of the top four star hotels.

Apart hotels have been a popular choice with business travellers who are staying in Rio for a couple of months and don't wish to be confined to a small hotel room.
Discounts of up to 30% or more are offered for long let periods.

Alfabarra
Av. Sernambetiba, 6600
Barra da Tijuca — 385-4350

Telex: 021-21244
Reservations: 233-3636
Rates: Single from $35. Double from $36.

Apart Hotel
Rua Barata Ribeiro, 370
Copacabana — 256-2633
Rates: Single from $35. Double from $55.

Atlântico Flat Service
Rua Santa Clara, 15
Copacabana — 257-8090
Telex: 021-32914
Reservations: 274-9546
Rates:; Single from $58. Double from $62.

Barra Beach Rio
Av. Sernambetiba, 1120
Barra da Tijuca — 389-6333
Rates: Single from $50. Double from $75.

Barra Palace
Av. Sernambetiba, 2916
Barra da Tijuca — 399-3366
Rates: Single from $35. Double from $54.

Barrabela Hotel
Av. Sernambetiba, 4700
Barra da Tijuca — 385-2000
Reservations: 385-2222
Rates: Single from $54. Double from $76.

Barraleme Hotel
Av. Sernambetiba, 600
Barra da Tijuca.

Barramares Flat
Av. Sernambetiba, 3300
Barra da Tijuca — 399-5656
Telex: 021-21244
Reservations: 233-3636
Rates: Single from $36. Double from $43.

Copacabana Hotel Residência
Rua Barata Ribeiro, 222
Copacabana — 256-2610
Telex: 021-34162
Reservations: 235-1828
Rates: Single from $50. Double from $57.

Golden Coast
Av. Sernambetiba, 6000
Barra da Tijuca — 385-3300.

Ipanema Sweet
Rua Visconde de Pirajá, 161
Ipanema — 267-7015
Telex: 021-21244
Reservations: 233-3636
Rates: Single from $60. Double from $72.

Leblon Flat Service
Rua Prof. Antonio Maria Teixeira, 33
Leblon — 259-4332
Telex: 021-32914
Reservations: 274-9546
Rates: Single from $58. Double from $75.

Rio Flat Service
Rua Almirante Guilhen, 332
Leblon — 274-7222
Telex: 021-32914
Rates: Single from $57. Double from $65.

Rio Hotel Residência
Av. Sernambetiba, 6250
Barra da Tijuca — 385-5000
Telex: 021-21803
Reservations: 385-5000
Rates: Single from $62. Double from $90.

Rio Ipanema
Rua Visconde de Pirajá, 66
Ipanema — 267-4015
Telex: 021-21244
Reservations: 233-3636
Rates: Single from $60. Double from $78.

Saint Paul
Rua Barão de Ipanema, 95
Copacabana — 257-8110
Telex: 021-21244
Reservations: 233-3636
Rates: Single from $42. Double from $47.

Santa Clara Flat
Rua Santa Clara, 212
Copacabana — 256-2690
Rates: Single from $50. Double from $57.

C

Eating Out
Entertainment
Night Life
Shows
Carnival

Eating Out in Rio

FOOD FOR THOUGHT — AN EXPLANATION OR AN APOLOGY

It will come as no surprise to hear that the "Eating Out" section of *The Insider's Guide to Rio de Janeiro* has been the most controversial and talked about section of the guide.

People, and I include myself, never tire of lists. We all like to see what other people think and if our own opinions tie in with those of the "experts"

So you know where we stand from the start I hasten to add that I am no expert nor do I have any pretensions as a gourmet, in fact I would class myself as an extremely fussy and conservative eater. I am, if you like, Mr. Joe Public.

I do believe however that I know a good restaurant when I see one and can certainly judge good cooking, correct service and anything else the most discerning of gourmands demands. You may also like to know that I am an extremely critical person — you can ask anyone who knows me to confirm that — so if anything my reviews are harsher than they need to be.

While the choice of restaurants reviewed in the *Insider's Guide* is essentially personal, it is also based on the opinions of the hundreds of people that I have spoken to over the years who have been kind enough, knowingly or not, to give me their thoughts on eating out. These are the people who eat out in Rio because they want to, be it for pleasure or for business. They are the customers, the paying public, and for me their opinions easily out-weigh the thoughts and opinions of the experts. If you are one of those people I am indebted to you. I am also indebted to the hundreds of visitors to Brazil who have taken the time to jot down their thoughts about Rio's restaurants and send them to me. All these thoughts and opinions are reflected in this year's edition.

Finding Your Way Around

The main body of restaurant reviews runs alphabetically. You should note, however, that restaurants with a *le* or *la* drop the pronoun. Thus you will find Le Prê Catelan under P and Le Saint Honoré under S. Spanish restaurants, on the other hand, have been left with their pronoun of *el*. El Cordobes and El Pescador are therefore to be found under E. If this should all sound a little unusual I can assure you that the decision is based on the opinion of a number of resident readers of the guide who confirmed that they think of the *"Prê Catelan"* and *"Saint Honore"* but *"El Cordobés"* and *"El Pescador"*.

Before the main body of reviews you will find a listing of restaurants in alphabetical order by area and by type of cuisine. As I have emphasized in the past, the "type" of restaurant is to be treated lightly. Any restaurant in Rio can be classed as "international" because all are basically willing to try and cook any dish you want as long as they have the ingredients. In Brazil a menu should be regarded as a list of suggestions. No top restaurant, for example, is going to list "Steak and French Fries" because they presume that if you want it you will ask for it. And don't be afraid to ask, even if it is for changes to a given dish. If something which takes your fancy would be spoilt because of cooked cheese ask them to prepare it without. They won't mind.

The Ratings Game

In the first edition of the *Insider's Guide* I wanted to try and avoid the star system which I considered to have become a bit stereotyped. Restaurants in the first edition were classified instead as "Outstanding", "Posh Nosh and Fine Fodder", "Worth Remembering" and. "For a Change", and while today I still stand by those categories I had to bend to the prevailing wind which continuously asked, "But how many stars?"

In 1985 the star system was introduced. Five stars for Rio's "Outstanding" restaurants, four stars for those which were very close to outstanding but just missed, three for "Posh Nosh and Fine Fodder", and one star for "Worth Remembering" and "For a Change".

In 1986 a two star category was introduced for those restaurants "Worth Remembering" and "For a Change" that served the better food, yet this, it turned out, was still not enough so for 1987 the stars, one to five, reflect the food and overall ambience equally. This allows a restaurant like Saborear-te to be rated at three stars where in the past it would have been two, the three star rating being kept for restaurants suitable for business lunches and dinners, hence the previous title of "Posh Nosh & Fine Fodder".

The ultimate rating, and the success of this section, however, remains very firmly in your hands. I want to hear from you about the restaurants and bars you visit. Were they up to standard? Was I too kind or too harsh? Did I give them too many stars or too few? Have you found a restaurant I don't even know about?

Read on then for a fuller explanation of the 1987 ratings and how the listings themselves work.

RIO'S OUTSTANDING RESTAURANTS

Nine restaurants have been chosen this year as outstanding — five stars - restaurants that can hold their own against the best in the world, restaurants which Rio can justifiably be proud of.

Everybody deserves to eat "outstandingly" but so few do, a question of the right mental attitude I believe.

To eat outstandingly you should be willing to devote a considerable amount of time to eating and nothing else, good food should never be rushed.

Take your time at the restaurant, and above all use the *maitre's* experience and knowledge to the full. A good *maitre*, and all the outstanding restaurants have them, will help marry your choice of dishes to achieve a subtle blend of flavors that can produce such remarkable results, especially with French *nouvelle cuisine*.

The outstanding restaurants are classified in the listings as expensive because it is assumed that you will work your way through at least three courses and accompany the meal with good wines, the better wines of South America. Only Mr. and Mrs. Nouvéau-Rich would consider drinking European wines in Brazil because they do not travel well. Wine, I was told by one of France's top chefs, only travels well from south to north an old wife's tale perhaps, but worth considering. A selection of South American wines is listed a little later on.

As a year, 1986 was even more difficult for the top restaurants than 1985 had been, but for very different reasons.

Thanks to the country's new "economic miracle" and the price freeze, Brazilians started to eat out again and at the better and more expensive restaurants. The problem was that the demand the "miracle" brought in its wake for *all* products led to shortages which ranged from meat and eggs and even sugar and salt all the way to freezers and other electrical goods. It was not uncommon at times in 1986 to find that a restaurant could only offer a choice of one or two dishes, normally chicken and fish, and this has made it peculiarly difficult to judge the restaurants of Rio fairly since March 1986.

Because of the problems they faced in 1986 I decided to allow all of Rio's outstanding restaurants the benefit of the-doubt in regard to their rating in 1987 especially as the few complaints I did receive about them from readers were nearly all related to the problem of shortages.

The vast majority of correspondence and comments received about the *Insider's Guide's* ratings were in agreement with the listings and a further vote of confidence in the nine outstanding restaurants.

During 1986, Rio lost one of its outstanding restaurants, Le Flambard, which transformed itself in to The Cattleman a restaurant which while pleasant is far from outstanding. Another sad loss was Serendipity (four stars) which having established itself as one of Rio's best restaurants promptly changed hands and its name.

To balance the closures 1986 saw the opening of Laurent, owned and run by chef Laurent Suaudeau, the man responsible for establishing Le Saint Honoré as one of Latin America's top restaurants, and Le Sirenuse, the sister restaurant to Stefano Monti's outstanding Le Streghe. Both restaurants are unlucky not to get a fifth star but I prefer to wait a year to see what standard these two excellent restaurants maintain on a day to day basis.

Antiquarius and Valentino's were also unlucky not to get fifth stars while it was nice to see a marked improvement in Sal & Pimenta and Petronius who join Antiquarius, Valentino's, Café de la Paix and Rodeio as well as Laurent and Le Sirenuse on four stars.

★ ★ ★ ★ ★

Le Bec Fin	**Monseigneur**	**Le Saint Honoré**
Clube Gourmet	**Ouro Verde**	**Le Streghe**
Equinox	**Le Pré Catelan**	**Troigros**

★ ★ ★ ★

Antiquarius	**Petronius**	**Sal & Pimenta**
Café de la Paix	**Rodeio**	**Le Sirenuse**
Laurent		**Valentino's**

RESTAURANTS FOR EVERY TASTE

All the starred restaurants in the *Insider's Guide* offer an acceptable level of cuisine, some obviously more acceptable than others. Experiment with these restaurants and go to them often, you are unlikely to come across such a wide selection at such accessible prices again, unless, of course, you go to São Paulo.

To add a bit of spice to the ratings I would like to give special mentions to some of the restaurants in the three and two star categories.

Of the three star restaurants Baroni Fasoli, after Le Streghe, is the Italian restaurant most talked about by Rio's Italian community; the English Bar is the best restaurant in downtown Rio, and by a large margin, Mr. Zee is the city's best and most elegant Chinese restaurant, while Saboreante at times served dishes worthy of the outstanding restaurants and became one of my personal favorites.

Alt Munchen, of the two star restaurants, had a new lease of life in 1986 serving an interesting men Of German and Swiss dishes, Buffalo Grill served some magnificent meals in 1986 despite the crisis and with T-Bone is one of the best barbecue houses in Rio; the Lord Jim is an institution with the English speaking community; Neal's has great ribs and a really fun atmosphere; while Raajmahal is the city's Indian Restaurant.

★ ★ ★

Alfredo di Roma
Antonino
Atlantis
Baroni Fasoli
Barracuda
Bife de Ouro
Candido's
Casa da Suiça
Castelo da Lagoa
English Bar
Enotria
Florentino
Grottammare

Hippopotamus
Mariu's
Monte Carlo
Mr. Zee
Le Petit Paris
Quatro Sete Meia
Rio's
Rive Gauche
Sabor & Arte
Satiricon
Sol e Mar
Via Farme

★ ★

Alt Munchen
Buffalo Grill
Cattleman
Le Champs Elysées
Club 1
El Pescador
Helsingor
Lord Jim
Neal's
Negresco

Nino
Porcão
Quadrifoglio
Raajmahal
Shirley
T-Bone
Tia Palmira
Tiberius
Varanda

★

Albamar
Antonio's
Café Pacifico
Café do Teatro
Cota 200

Del Mare
El Cordobés
A Esquina
Jardim
Jockey Club

Majorica
Mediterraneo
Nobili
Plataforma
Pomme d'Or

COMING SOON AND OBITUARIES

I have to close the book sometime even knowing that many restaurants are set to open and others to close or change management.

In 1986 we lost for good Carpaccio, Bistro da Praia, the Gold Steak Bar, Maxim's, and Stones. Chez Phillipe became Allisca, Le

Flambard became The Cattleman, Four Seasons became Double Dose, Grand Finale became Del Mare, Michel became the Old Bistro Club, The Orchid became Raajmarhal; Serendipity became Quadriofoglio and VIP Club became Escriptório.

Mistura Fina Studio and Michelangelo also closed in 1986 and at the time of going to press it was impossible to tell what was planned for their locations in 1987. Also at the time of going to press T-Bone, Le Relais, and The Fox were all being redecorated but were set to open early in the new year.

Sadly there are no exciting projects to report on in the immediate future, except the opening of a new Neal's in Barra, but it is Rio's ever changing restaurant scene that makes eating in Rio such fun. Experiment because if "familiarity breeds contempt" so "absence makes the heart grow fonder".

CHURRASCARIAS

You cannot come to Brazil without going to a churrascaria where you will try the magnificent Brazilian barbecued meats.

In Rio there are two types of churrascaria. One is a standard barbecue house where you yourself choose the type and cut of meat you wish and the accompaniments that go with it, while the other, called a *rodízio*, brings you a little, or rather a lot, of everything.

If you go to a *rodízio*, as you should, don't panic. You don't have to order, they bring everything to you, and keep bringing it until you beg them to stop. This is all served for one set price.

At any *rodízio* you can expect to be served filet mignon, rib of beef, brisket of beef, rib of pork, pork filet, ham, turkey, chicken, and a few Brazilian delicacies for good measure. All this will be served with salads, french fries, and many other accompaniments.

I don't suggest that you go to a *rodízio* until you are hungry, you just won't survive. And one tip to survival. Don't rush. Take it gently, refuse meat if your plate is full with a wag of the finger, they will return to offer it again, and again, and again, and.......

For me personally the best standard churrascaria, and by a long way, is Rodeio in Barra da Tijuca while for a *rodízio* try Mariu's in Leme or Porcão in Ipanema and Barra.

COPACABANA BEACH FRONT (AV ATLÁNTICA)

From my listings you could be forgiven for thinking that Ipanema and Leblon have many more restaurants than Copacabana while the opposite is in fact true. The reason for this discrepancy is related to the eating habits of the resident Copacabana population.

The residents of Copacabana are less mobile than their neighbors in Ipanema and because of parking problems tend to walk everywhere; when it is hot you don't want to walk far, hence in Copacabana you find shops and restaurants on every corner.

The beachfront bars you see in Copacabana have become the Brazilian equivalent of the local British pub. All offer the same menu, and all present food of a reasonable standard. Prices are almost identical so throughout the year they survive on their local regulars and the clients they pick up from the nearby hotels.

In the length of Copacabana and Leme there were no less than 35 bars at the last count, and this does not include the ones that go with the 17 hotels. Wherever your hotel is in Copacabana you will never be more than a block away from a beachfront bar-restaurant, a few of which deserve a special mention.

In Leme look out for *La Fiorentina* which used to be the hang out for the art set. At any time of day or night you would have found a large group of artists, actors and such like. Today it is still popular.

but most of the bohemian crowd has moved on.

Further down the beach, just past the Copacabana Palace Hotel, you will come across *Bolero* which has operated in the same location since 1945, and is always open for a quick beer. Bolero is the most traditional and famous of all the beachfront bars and one of the largest.

Becoming a dominant feature in Copacabana, if not a land mark, is the massive *Terraço Atlântico* complex which boasts an indoor and outdoor restaurant, a nightclub restaurant (*Sobre as Ondas*) and Rio's biggest discotheque, *Help*. Terraço Atlantico is located smack in the middle of Copacabana at Av. Atlântica, 3432 (Tel.: 521-1296).

The final traditional Copacabana eatery is *Lucas* on the corner of Souza Lima. Now in its 46th year, Lucas serves a good honest menu of German cuisine and other international dishes.

EATING IN DOWNTOWN RIO

Restaurants in downtown Rio (Centro) generally cater for people working in the area. The cooking is of a reasonably high standard but, the service rushed, and the decor of most of the restaurants uninspiring.

The restaurants that I have reviewed in the downtown area are those which serve the better food in more interesting surroundings. It should not be forgotten, however, that many of the "English speaking" community use the luncheon clubs of the American Club (Av. Rio Branco, 123 — .21st Floor. Tel.: 242-6105) and Halfway House (Av. Franklin Roosevelt, 39 — 15th floor. Tel.: 220-6528).

Because of the expressway that links the center of Rio quickly with Copacabana, many businessmen choose to schedule their business lunches in the calmer atmosphere of the zona sul, especially in restaurants like Rio's, Saint Honoré and Ouro Verde.

The best of the "downtown" restaurants reviewed in this guide are The English Bar, Le Champs Elysées, and Café do Teatro as well as Barracuda in the Marina and Casa da Suíça in Rua Cândido Mendes.

TIPS ON EATING OUT

Eating out in Rio is cheap by world standards and Cariocas take full advantage of this by using it as one of their main forms of relaxation.

Cariocas eat late in the evening; if you go out much before 9 p.m. you can expect to eat alone unless you meet a Brazilian who is finishing lunch.

In Rio you can eat or drink at any time of the day or night, unlike many countries there are no legal restrictions. Most restaurants listed in this guide will take last orders well past midnight and in many cases until 3 a.m. or later.

If you are very particular about your food you should avoid eating out at the weekend or in large groups. In any restaurant in the world standards drop when the kitchen is working under pressure.

And please I beg of you, go out and experiment, don't get stuck in a rut and continuously return again and again to the same old haunts. There is no point telling you that Rio has nine outstanding restaurants if you are only going to visit one and be satisfied with that. If you are here for a week, why not go to all of them. And to the resident reader, how many of the establishments listed here have you been to during your time in Rio? Don't you think it is time to experiment?

WINES

The general standard of Brazilian wines is quite high although even Brazilians will admit that they cannot compare with the excellent wines produced in Chile and Argentina.

Brazilian wines are not expensive so you should have fun experimenting until you find the one that suits your palate. As a rule Brazilian white wines are far superior to the reds while with Chilean and Argentinian wines it is the other way round.

All of Rio's restaurants offer a fairly complete choice of wines but chances are only the waiters at the better restaurants will know anything about them. Supermarkets carry a wide range of Brazilian and imported wines while if you are downtown you can check out Lidador at Rua da Assembléia or Casa do Vinho (House of Wines) at Rua Sacadura Cabral, 228 (corner of Rua Sousa e Silva), a ten minute walk from Praça Mauá.

The two most consistent vintners in Brazil are Almaden and Forestier while the other names to look out for are:

Brazilian White: Almaden, Baron de Lantier, Chateau Chandon, Chateau Duvalier, Chateau Lacave, Clos de Nobles, Cotes de Blancs, Dijon, Dom Eudes, Edelweine, Forestier, Gran Blanc Fasano, Johannisberg, Jolimont, Katzweine, Kiedrich Riesling, Lejon, Liebfraumilch, Maison Rosselot, Marjolet, Marquês de Borba, Schwarze Katz, Weinzeller, Wunderwein, and Zahringer.

Brazilian Reds: Almaden, Baron de Lantier, Castel Chatelet, Chateau Chandon, Chateau Duvalier, Clos de Nobles, Conde de Foucaud, Cru de la Terre, Dijon, Dom Eudes, Erben Kabenett, Forestier, Grand Cru Fasano, Jolimont, Maison Rosselot, Marjolet, Marquês de Borba.

Argentine Red or White: Dom Valentin, Pinot, Rincon Famoso, Roccas Viejas, and Rodas.

Chilean Red or White: Concha y Toro, Cousino Macul, Santa Carolina, Santa Emiliana, Santa Helena, Santiago, and Undurraga.

The best Brazilian champagne is M. Chandon. Other good names are de Greville, Dijon, and Georges Aubert.

HOW THE LISTINGS WORK

The listings are designed to push and not to pull. The idea is to offer you the options that you might like to try and an explanation of what to expect.

Below each explanation you will find the hard information:

Hours: Times of opening vary widely in Rio, but it is true that most restaurants which open for lunch at the weekend stay open through until dinner. This is also true of many of the medium priced restaurants during the week.

Cuisine: As I have already stated, the type of "cuisine" a restaurant serves is to be taken lightly because at the end of the day we are in Brazil so even if the cooking is billed as French, it is still French/Brazilian

Telephone: Correct at going to press but if you don't have any luck call the operator and give them the name and address of the restaurant.

Numbers have been known to change in Rio!

Reservations: *'No'* can but does not always mean that the restaurant does not take reservations, more that it is not normal to bother for that particular establishment. If in doubt it is always safer to make a reservation, especially in the better restaurants or if you want a table by the window.

Price: The price indications are exactly that, indications and not firm quotes. As a rough guide use the following: Inexpensive — Below $6; Medium — $6 to $15; High — $15 to $25; Expensive — Over $25.

It is very unlikely that you will ever run up a bill of over $50-a-head unless you go berserk on expensive imported liquor. The prices listed are for one person including drinks and at the "official" dollar rate.

Credit: All major credit cards are accepted in Brazil yet despite what I list you should always call the restaurant in advance if your credit card is going to be a matter of life and death as far as the payment goes.

The most widely accepted international credit cards are American Express and Visa with Diners close behind. Only a few restaurants accept Master Charge. American Express, Visa (Credicard) and Diners all issue cards locally as do Elo and Nacional.

Restaurants By Type of Food

Please note that some of the restaurants appear under more than one category.

INTERNATIONAL

Allisca
Antiquarius ★ ★ ★ ★
Antonino ★ ★ ★
Antonio's ★
Atlantis ★ ★ ★
Barril 1800
Le Bistro
Botequim 184
Cabeça Feita
Café Lamas
Café do Teatro ★
Caneco 70
Carinhoso
Casa da Suiça ★ ★ ★
Castelo da Lagoa ★ ★ ★
Cattleman ★ ★
Cochrane
Colombo
Cota 200 ★
English Bar ★ ★ ★
Escriptorio
Os Esquilos
A Esquina ★
Estancia
Florentino ★ ★ ★
A Floresta
The Fox
Harry's Bar
Hippopotamus ★ ★ ★

Jockey Club ★
M.A.M.
Mare Nostrum
Monseigneur ★ ★ ★ ★ ★
Monte Carlo ★ ★ ★
O Navegador
Negresco ★ ★
Nino ★ ★
Nobili ★
Old Bistro Club
Ouro Verde ★ ★ ★ ★
Performance
Pomme d'Or ★
Queen's Legs
Le Relais
Rio's ★ ★ ★
Rive Gauche ★ ★ ★
Sal & Pimenta ★ ★ ★
Tarot
Tiberius ★ ★
La Tour
Un, Deux, Trois
Valentino's ★ ★ ★ ★
Varanda ★ ★
Vice-Rey
14 Bis

AMERICAN

Neal's ★ ★

AUSTRIAN

Hansl

BARBECUE (CHURRASCARIAS)

Bife de Ouro ★ ★
Bragado's
Buffalo Grill ★ ★
Carreta
Casarão
Copacabana
Jardim ★
Majorica ★
Plataforma ★
Rodeio ★ ★ ★ ★
T-Bone ★ ★

BARBECUE (RODIZIO)

Bragado's
Carretão
Estrela do Sul
Gaucha
Mariu's ★ ★ ★
Oasis
Palace
Pampa
Porção ★ ★

BRAZILIAN

Arataca
Chale Brasileiro
Maria Tereza Weiss
Moenda

BRITISH

Lord Jim ★ ★

CHINESE

Mr. Zee ★ ★ ★

CUBAN

La Bodeguita

FRENCH

Le Bec Fin ★ ★ ★ ★ ★
Café de la Paix ★ ★ ★ ★
Le Champs Elysées ★ ★
Club Gourmet ★ ★ ★ ★
Equinox ★ ★ ★ ★ ★
Laurent ★ ★ ★ ★
Monseigneur ★ ★ ★ ★
Ouro Verde ★ ★ ★ ★ ★
Performance
Le Petit Paris ★ ★ ★
Piccadilly Bar
Le Pre Catelan ★ ★ ★ ★ ★

Saborear-te ★ ★ ★
Le Saint Honore ★ ★ ★ ★ ★
Troisgros ★ ★ ★ ★ ★

GERMAN

Alt Munchen ★ ★
Suppentopf

HEALTH FOOD

Natural

INDIAN

Cantinho de Goa
Raajmahal ★ ★

ITALIAN

Alfredo di Roma ★ ★ ★
Angolo Blu
Baroni Fasoli ★ ★ ★
Club 1 ★ ★
Enotria ★ ★ ★
Ettore
Giancarlo
La Mole
Quadrifoglio ★ ★
Satiricon ★ ★ ★
Le Streghe ★ ★ ★ ★ ★
Tarantella
Trattoria Torna
Valentino's ★ ★ ★ ★
Via Farme ★ ★ ★

MEXICAN

Cafe Pacifico ★
Lagoa Charlie

POLISH

A Polonesa

SALADS

Molho Inglês
Steak & Salads
Super Salads

SCANDINAVIAN

Helsingor ★ ★

SEAFOOD

Albamar ★
Barracuda ★ ★ ★
Cabaça Grande
Candido's ★ ★ ★
Del Mare
El Pescador ★ ★

Grottammare ★ ★ ★
Marimbas
A Marisqueira
Mediterraneo ★
Petronius ★ ★ ★ ★
Por do Sol
Principe
Quatro Sete Meia ★ ★ ★
Real
Satiricon ★ ★ ★
Shirley ★ ★
Le Sirenuse ★ ★ ★ ★
Sol e Mar ★ ★ ★
Tia Palmira ★ ★
Via Farme ★ ★ ★
Le Vieux Port
Vice-Rey

SPANISH

El Cordobés ★

El Pescador ★ ★
Shirley ★ ★

STEAK HOUSE

Alberico
Buffalo Grill ★ ★
The Cattleman ★ ★
El Cid
Entrecote
Steak House
T-Bone ★ ★

SWISS

Alt Munchen ★ ★
Casa da Suiça ★ ★ ★
Le Mazot

Restaurants By Area

CENTRO

Albamar ★
Barracuda ★ ★ ★
Cabaça Grande
Café do Teatro ★
Casa da Suiça ★ ★ ★
Le Champs Elysées ★ ★
Colombo
English Bar ★ ★ ★
Entrecote
A Esquina ★
M.A.M.
Molho Inglês
O Navegador
Nino ★ ★
Oasis
Steak House
La Tour
14 Bis

FLAMENGO & LARANJEIRAS

Barracuda ★ ★ ★
La Bodeguita
Café Lamas
Gaucha
Majorica ★
Rio's ★ ★ ★

BOTAFOGO

Allisca
Botequim 184

Cafe Pacifico ★
Chalé Brasileiro
Club Gourmet ★ ★ ★ ★ ★
Cochrane
Cota 200 ★
Estrela do Sul
Laurent ★ ★ ★ ★
Maria Tereza Weiss
La Mole
Neal's ★ ★
Nino ★ ★
Raajmahal ★ ★
Sol e Mar ★ ★ ★
T-Bone ★ ★

LAGOA — JARDIM BOTANICO

El Cordobés ★
Jockey Club ★
Quadrifoglio ★ ★
Queen's Legs
Troigros ★ ★ ★ ★ ★

COPACABANA & LEME

Atlantis ★ ★ ★
Arataca
Le Bec Fin ★ ★ ★ ★ ★
Bife de Ouro ★ ★ ★
Café de La Paix ★ ★ ★ ★
Carretão
Copacabana
El Cid
Enotria ★ ★ ★

Estancia
Jardim ★
Marimbas
A Marisqueira
Mariu's ★ ★ ★
Le Mazot
Moenda
La Mole
Monte Carlo ★ ★ ★
Nino ★ ★
Old Bistro Club
Ouro Verde ★ ★ ★ ★ ★
Palace
Pomme d'Or★
A Polonesa
Le Pre Catelan ★ ★ ★ ★ ★
Principe
Real
Le Saint Honore ★ ★ ★ ★ ★
Shirley ★ ★
Suppentopf
Le Vieux Port

IPANEMA

Alberico
Angolo Blu
Baroni Fasoli ★ ★ ★
Barril 1800
Le Bistro
Cabeça Feita
Carinhoso
Club 1 ★ ★
Del Mare ★
Equinox ★ ★ ★ ★ ★
The Fox
Grottammare★ ★ ★
Hippopotamus ★ ★ ★
Lord Jim ★ ★
A Marisqueira
Mediterraneo ★
Natural
Negresco ★ ★
Performance
Petronius ★ ★ ★ ★
Porcão ★ ★
Sal & Pimenta ★ ★ ★ ★
Satiricon ★ ★ ★
Le Sirenuse ★ ★ ★ ★
Le Streghe ★ ★ ★ ★ ★
Tiberius ★ ★
Trattoria Torna
Via Farme ★ ★ ★

LEBLON

Alt Munchen ★ ★
Antiquarius ★ ★ ★ ★
Antonio's ★
Arataca

Buffalo Grill ★ ★
Caneco 70
Cantinho de Goa
Entrecote
Escriptorio
Florentino ★ ★ ★
Harry's Bar
Helsingor ★ ★
La Mole
Mr. Zee ★ ★ ★
Nobili ★
Piccadilly Bar
Plataforma ★
Le Relais
Saborear-te ★ ★ ★
Tarot
Un, Deux, Trois

LAGOA — IPENAMA

Antonino ★ ★ ★
Castelo da Lagoa ★ ★ ★
Cattleman ★ ★
Lagoa Charlie
Rive Gauche ★ ★ ★

SÃO CONRADO & VIDIGAL

Alfredo di Roma ★ ★ ★
Casarão
El Pescador ★ ★
Monseigneur ★ ★ ★ ★ ★
Oasis
Valentino's ★ ★ ★ ★
Varanda ★ ★

BARRA DA TIJUCA & JOÁ

Barra Shopping
Bragado's
Carreta
Ettore
Giancarlo
Hansl
Mare Nostrum
La Mole
Nino ★ ★
Pampa
Le Petit Paris ★ ★ ★
Porcão ★ ★
Rodeio ★ ★ ★ ★
Steak & Salads
Super Salads
Tarantella
Vice-Rey

FLORESTA DA TIJUCA

Os Esquilos
A Floresta

PEDRA & BARRA DE GUARATIBA

Candido's ★ ★ ★

Quatro Sete Meia ★ ★ ★
Por do Sol
Tia Palmira ★ ★

Business Lunches & Dinners

The following are recommended for more formal business lunches and dinner. L = Lunch. D = Dinner.

★ ★ ★ ★ ★

Le Bec Fin — D
Club Gourmet — D
Equinox — D
Monseigneur — D
Ouro Verde — L & D
Le Pre Catelan — D
Le Saint Honoré — L & D
Le Streghe — D
Troisgros — D

★ ★ ★ ★

Antiquarius — L & D
Cafe de La Paix — L & D
Laurent — D
Rodeio — L & D
Petronius — D
Sal & Pimenta — L & D
Le Sirenuse — D
Valentino's — D

★ ★ ★

Alfredo di Roma — L & D
Antonio — L & D
Atlantis — L & D

Barracuda — L & D
Bife de Ouro — L & D
Casa da Suiça — L & D
Castelo da Lagoa — L & D
English Bar — L
Enotria — D
Florentino — L & D
Hippopotamus — D
Monte Carlo — L & D
Mr. Zee — D
Le Petit Paris — D
Rio's — L & D
Rive Gauche — D
Satiricon — L & D
Sol e Mar — L & D

★ ★

Le Champs Elysées — L
Negresco — D
Nino's — L & D
Quadrifoglio — D

★

Cafe do Teatro — L
Del Mare — D
A Esquina — L
Pomme d'Or — D

Late Night Eating

Most restaurants in Rio serve until 2 a.m. If you want to eat later you might like to try.

Botafogo & Flamengo
La Bodeguita (Till 3:30 a.m.)
Cafe Lamas (Till 4 a.m.)
Neal's (Till 3 a.m.)
Sol e Mar (Till 3 a.m.)

Copacabana
Bella Blu (Till 4 a.m.)

Bella Roma (Till 4 a.m.)
El Cid (Till 4 a.m.)
La Fiorentina (Till 6 a.m.)
Suppentopf (Till 3 a.m.)

Ipanema
Alberico (Till 4 a.m.)
Castelo da Lagoa (Till 4 a.m.)

Hippopotamus (Till 3 a.m.)	Antonio's (Till 3 a.m.)
Pizza Palace (Till 6 a.m.)	Caneco 70 (Till 4:30 a.m.)
Rive Gauche (Till 3 a.m.)	Buffalo Grill (Till 3 a.m.)
	Harry's Bar (Till 3 a.m.)
Leblon	Pizza Guanabara (Till 5 a.m.)
	Tarot (24-hours)
Alt Munchen (Till 3 a.m.)	Un, Deux, Trois (Till 3 a.m.)

The Restaurants of Rio de Janeiro

ALBAMAR ★
Praça Marechal Áncora, 184 — Centro

A tourist attraction, an historic monument, and fish restaurant is the best way to describe Albamar which sits close to the waters edge a short walk from Praça XV.

Founded in 1933, Albamar is located in the last remaining tower of the old municipal market. Simple and unpretentious, Albamar lets the historic tower give the restaurant its atmosphere, the tower plus a little help from the glorious view across the bay and the water born traffic that buzzes in and out of the docks at Praça XV.

The cooking, like the restaurant, is simple and to the point but sadly was far from consistent in 1986, disappointing many. Stick with the seafood and the simpler the better.

Hours: 11:30 a.m. to 10 p.m. (Closed Sunday). **Cuisine:** Seafood. **Telephone:** 240-8378. **Reservations:** For large groups. **Prices:** Medium to high. **Credit:** American Express.

ALBERICO
Av. Vieira Souto, 236 — Ipanema

Alberico is somewhat of a disappointment and certainly does not live up to its expectations as only the second restaurant on the beachfront in Ipanema.

Offering a mixture of "steak house", "pizzaria" and "snack bar" Alberico misses on all counts and although packed-out most days thanks to its location it does tend to attract a young crowd who don't know any better.

A restaurant which could and should do better.

Hours: 11 a.m. to 4 a.m. **Cuisine:** Grills, pizzas and snacks. **Telephone:** 267-3793. **Reservations:** No. **Prices:** Low to medium. **Credit:** Most major cards.

ALFREDO DI ROMA ★ ★ ★
Hotel Inter-Continental — São Conrado

After years of speculation and rumor Alfredo di Roma finally opened the doors of its Rio branch on November 27 and became an instant hit.

A classically attractive restaurant with large windows that overlook the Inter-Continental's Varanda restaurant, pool area and the mountainous backdrop of São Conrado, Alfredo's presents, as you would expect, a menu of Italian specialities, with the emphasis firmly on the pastas, many of them made famous over the years by the original Alfredo's in Rome, dishes like *Fettuccine all' Alfredo*.

Alfredo's, I am sure, is going to be a success with not only the guests of the Inter-Continental, where the restaurant is located, but also with the residents of Rio who will enjoy its attractive and restful ambience.

Hours: 12 a.m. to 3:00 p.m. and 7:30 p.m. to 11:30 p.m. **Cuisine:** Italian. **Telephone:** 322-2200. **Reservations:** No. **Prices:** High. **Credit:** All major cards.

ALLISCA
Rua Paula Barreto — Botafogo

As predicted in last year's guide Chez Phillipe did lose direction and slip away in the night and its location has now been taken by Allisca a new "international" restaurant with a touch of the Brazilian which is a little bit bland for my liking.

Nothing too wrong with Allisca in either its location or cooking but I think it will have to do something more exciting if it is to survive the rough waters of the Rio restaurant trade.

Hours: Noon to 4 p.m. and 7 p.m. to 2 a.m. (No lunch Saturday). **Cuisine:** International/Brazilian. **Telephone:** 295-5494. **Reservations:** No. **Prices:** Medium to high. **Credit:** Most major cards.

ALT MUNCHEN ★ ★
Rua Dias Ferreira, 410 — Leblon

Alt Munchen was one of Rio's most improved restaurants in 1986 as the level of food offered rose from the "honest" to "very good".

Now serving a varied menu of German and Swiss dishes, including a very acceptable fondue, Alt Munchen gives the diner the choice of the cozy inside restaurant, which due to demand has spilled down in to the basement, or the more airy veranda. Demand has also led to the owners opening for lunch.

Hours: 11 a.m. to 3 p.m. and 6 p.m. to 3 a.m. (Closed Monday) **Cuisine:** German/Swiss. **Telephone:** 294-4197. **Reservations:** Yes. **Prices:** Medium to high. **Credit:** Most major cards.

ANGLO BLU
Rua Barão da Torre. 673 — Ipanema

On opening Anglo Blu splashed ads liberally through the Brazilian press but without much luck judging by the number of people frequenting it on my visits.

Smarter than many of the other Italian restaurants in town the food, despite the dressing, is of much the same standard as the simpler eateries to be found in the neighborhood and certainly nothing to get over excited about.

If you are looking for a change, if you live in Rio, you could do worse but I have a hunch the Anglo Blu won't be around this time next year.

Hours: 6 p.m. to 2 a.m. Lunch on Sunday. (Closed on Monday). **Cuisine:** Italian. **Telephone:** 274-0431. **Reservations:** No. **Prices:** Medium to high. **Credit:** Most major cards.

ANTIQUARIUS ★ ★ ★
Rua Aristides Espínola, 19 — Leblon.

Antiquarius has rightly figured amongst Rio's finest and most fashionable restaurants for a number of years and indeed on some occasions the food has been known to suffer when the fashionable has been given priority over the fine food.

One of Rio's most attractive restaurants, Antiquarius is both relaxed and elegant, the interior highlighted by beautiful antiques.

Undoubtedly brilliant at times, especially for its Bacalhau dishes, both the quality of food and service appear to drop if you are not known. However, if you can fight your way through the parked Mercedes pay this smart restaurant a visit, you may just get one of the "brilliant" meals that I sometimes hear about. Certainly though your chances of a better meal will be improved as an unknown foreigner if you go for lunch rather than dinner when it is always packed.

Hours: Noon to 2 a.m. **Cuisine:** International/ Portuguese. **Telephone:** 294-1049. **Reservations:** At night. **Prices:** High. **Credit:** All major cards.

ANTONINO ★ ★ ★
Av. Epitacio Pessoa, 1244 — Ipanema.

Fashions come and go, seasons change but Antonino remains one of Rio's best and most consistent restaurants.

Nothing spectacular or special, just standard international dishes of a high quality served by courteous waiters in surroundings that are conventional, elegant and formal but with a magnificent view across the Lagoa from the window seats.

Nothing you can put your finger on makes Antonino stand out except that it is what you would call in simple old fashioned terms "a good restaurant". The only criticism that could be levelled is that at times the dishes can be a bit bland.

Below the restaurant is a pleasant piano-bar which is a good location to either meet friends before dinner, whether or not you are going upstairs to the restaurant, or to appreciate the fine pianist.

Hours: Noon to 2 a.m. **Cuisine:** International/ French. **Telephone:** 267-6791. **Reservations:** Yes at night. **Prices:** High to expensive. **Credit:** All major cards.

ANTONIO'S ★
Av. Bartolomeu Mitre. 297 — Leblon

In the 1970s Antonio's was considered to be one of Rio's best restaurants, a restaurant heavily frequented by the art set who have stayed faithful over the years.

The cooking hit the heights again during 1984 but has since slipped, overpowered, perhaps, by its neighbor, the excellent Saborear-te. Despite this it is almost impossible to find a space at one of Antonio's few tables during the weekend.

Small and intimate internally, Antonio's has a brighter, lighter terrace which is a good option for a quiet lunch with friends despite the busy road outside.

Hours: Noon to 3 a.m. **Cuisine:** International/Italian. **Telephone:** 294-2699. **Reservations:** Yes. **Prices:** Medium to high. **Credit:** All major cards.

ATLANTIS ★ ★ ★
Av. Atlântica, 4240 — Copacabana

Although the decoration of the Rio Palace's Atlantis restaurant could be accused of being a little too typical of a hotel, the food, and that is after all what matters, is well above average and offers an interesting menu of full meals and snacks which is highlighted by the traditional *feijoada* on Saturday lunch time and the New York brunch on Sunday.

The outside tables have a magnificent view of Copacabana and the coast line, making it one of my personal favorites for lunch on any sunny day.

At night live music helps add to the atmosphere while at all times the standard of service is up to what we have come to expect from the Rio Palace, one of Rio's outstanding hotels.

Atlantis is a good place to recover from the night before or prepare for the night to come, and no more so than at Carnival when a true party spirit takes over the restaurant and terrace area.

Hours: 6 a.m. to 1 a.m. **Cuisine:** International. **Telephone:** 521-3232. **Reservations:** No. **Prices:** High. **Credit:** All major cards.

ARATACA
Rua Dias Ferreira, 135 — Leblon
Rua Figueiredo Magalhães, 28 — Copacabana

Arataca, with branches in Leblon and Copacabana, is for the more adventurous gourmet offering dishes from Pará including fish such as *pirarucu, surubim* and *tucunare* that are to be found in the rivers of the Amazon region.

Arataca also offers a good selection of exotic fruit juices and batidas.

Simple and to the point, Arataca certainly offers a change of taste and style.

Hours: 11:30 a.m. to 1 a.m. **Cuisine:** Para (Brazilian). **Telephone:** 274-1444 (Leblon), 255-7448 (Copacabana). **Reservations:** No. **Prices:** Medium. **Credit:** All major cards.

BARONI FASOLI ★ ★ ★
Rua Jangadeiros, 14 (Praça General Osorio) — Ipanema

Baroni Fasoli offers what a select few, including a good number of the Italian community, consider to be the best pasta dishes in town, dishes that are complimented on the extensive menu by a number of well prepared and interesting non-pasta based selections.

Offering a relaxed and typically "Italian restaurant" atmosphere, Baroni Fasoli is a restaurant that residents can return to time and time again. Its location in the Hippie Fair also means that close by is Le Streghe, Le Sirenuse, The Fox, and a number of other interesting restaurants, while the parking at night is relatively painless.

If pushed to say what is wrong with Baroni Fasoli — after all I can't be nice all the time — I would choose the inconsistency of the kitchen which can lead to the occasional disappointing meal.

Hours: Noon to 1 a.m. (Dinner only Monday). **Cuisine:** Italian. **Telephone:** 287-9592. **Reservations:** No. **Prices:** Medium to high. **Credit:** Most major cards.

BARRACUDA ★ ★ ★
Marina da Glória — Glória

Behind the dark glass facade of the marina shops lurks a truly individual restaurant which since 1984 has established itself as a firm favorite with downtown businessmen and women.

Rustic, yet at the same time discreetly elegant, Barracuda offers a small but imaginative menu of which the center piece are the giant shrimp, barbecued and served on the skewer.

The cooking is correct and the service attentive but expect to have to wait in the small bar area if you don't make a lunchtime reservation.

When the hustle and bustle of lunch dies down Barracuda takes on a more romantic air which helps make it a pleasant and different location for both lunch and dinner.

Note: Barracuda has a 70 ft motor launch built in 1980 which acts as a restaurant for up to 50 people. Information about the boat is available from the restaurant.

Hours: Noon to midnight. **Cuisine:** Seafood/International. **Telephone:** 265-3997 and 265-4641. **Reservations:** Essential for lunch. **Prices:** High. **Credit:** All major cards.

BARRA SHOPPING
Barra Shopping — Barra da Tijuca.

At the end of 1985 Barra Shopping moved its playground and ice-rink on the lower floor to a new location at the back of the center and used the free space for restaurants and snack bars to make Barra Shopping a complete entertainment and leisure center.

Sadly none of the restaurants deserve a special mention and all are poor copies of the original, the copies being Churrascaria Copacabana (barbecue), Bar Luiz (international), Edo Port (Japanese), Grande Muralha (Chinese), and La Truite Cocagne (seafood).

In their favor is the fact that Barra Shopping offers ample parking, other entertainment possibilities including three movie houses and a bowling alley to come, and between them offer most types of cuisine.

Hours: Noon to midnight. **Cuisine:** All types. **Telephone:** 325-8555 (La Truite Cocagne), 325-7600 (Copacabana). **Reservations:** No. **Prices:** Medium to high. **Credit:** Most major cards.
Telephone: 541-6748. **Reservations:** No. **Prices:** Medium. **Credit:**

BARRIL 1800
Av. Vieira Souto, 110 — Ipanema.

Barril 1800 is an Ipanema land mark, one of only two bars to operate on Ipanema beach.

Today Barril 1800 is unrecognizable from the simple beachfront bar that used to serve local residents, but while the face-lift has given us the more sophisticated facade of Jazzmania, Barril 1800, the bar, retains its festive atmosphere.

Open from early to late, Barril 1800 offers a typical beach front menu which basically means that if they have the ingredients they will try and make the dish for you, but please don't hold any gastronomic expectations.

You should during your times in Rio, even if only here for one week, stop at Barril 1800 for at the very least one cold beer or a caipirinha.

Hour: 10 a.m. to 3 a.m. **Cuisine:** International. **Telephone:** 227-2447. **Reservations:** No. **Prices:** Inexpensive to medium. **Credits:** All major cards.

LE BEC FIN ★ ★ ★ ★
Av. N.S. de Copacabana, 178 — Copacabana

It is interesting to note that of the four outstanding restaurants to be found in Copacabana only one, Le Bec Fin, is not in a hotel and of the four, two offer French *nouvelle cuisine* created by two of France's top chefs, while the others, Le Bec Fin and Ouro Verde, offer the more traditional French dishes which have been capturing the hearts of residents and visitors for decades.

Founded in 1948, Le Bec Fin is one of Rio's most traditional of eateries and was under the same direction for over 30 years before passing to the present owners some years back.

Rejuvenated and completely renovated, Le Bec Fin is again one of Rio's best restaurants and looks set for many more years of success.

Offering a menu of classical French dishes, the menu also holds enough surprises to tempt back the city's gourmands.

Le Bec Fin's service, under the watchful eyes of owner José Fernandes Costa, is nothing short of impeccable and the decor unostentatious luxury, a degree of comfort that you cannot imagine from the simple street side facade that announces the restaurant.

Hours: 8 p.m. to 2 a.m. **Cuisine:** French. **Telephone:** 542-4097. **Reservations:** Yes. **Prices:** High to expensive. **Credit:** All major cards.

BIFE DE OURO ★ ★ ★
Copacabana Palace Hotel — Copacabana

1986 saw Bife de Ouro receive the facelift it had been waiting for, a facelift which will remind its patrons of the Copacabana Palace's glorious past when the Bife de Ouro was Rio's premier restaurant.

Serving a small but interesting menu where barbecued meats from one of Brazil's top butchers, Weissel of São Paulo, dominate, the simple but well prepared dishes are supported by service which is also a reminder of the hotel's stately past.

Bife de Ouro offers elegant and expensive dining and is a very welcome addition to the list of Copacabana's better restaurants.

The media attention which followed its re-inauguration quickly made the new Bife de Ouro one of Rio's "in" locations, a burden it has happily survived.

Hours: Noon to 3:30 p.m. and 7:30 p.m. to 1 a.m. **Cuisine:** International/Barbecue. **Telephone:** 255-7070. **Reservations:** Yes. **Prices:** Expensive. **Credit:** All major cards.

LE BISTRO
Rua dos Jangadeiros. 10 — Ipanema

Of the new restaurants to open in 1986 Le Bistro was for me one of the most disappointing.

This ordinary restaurant, located next to the Fox in the Hippie Square, serves the standard Brazilian "international" menu which shows little or no imagination.

Le Bistro's atmosphere and decor can be classed as cosy, which is a bit like describing a girl as nice.

A restaurant I hope will do a lot better during 1987 and do justice to its location.

Hours: Noon to 2 a.m. **Cuisine:** International. **Telephone:** 287-0555. **Reservations:** No. **Prices:** Medium to high. **Credit:** Most major cards.

LA BODEGUITA
Rua Ipiranga. 78 — Laranjeiras

La Bodeguita's claim to fame in Rio's culinary circles is that it is the city's, if not Brazil's, only Cuban restaurant. That said, I have to admit that I would not know good authentic Cuban cooking if I fell over it, I will therefore reserve my judgement of La Bodeguita until I have dined there with Cuban friends who live in Rio.

For the record, La Bodeguita is based on Havana's La Bodeguita del Medio which I am told has other La Bodeguita's in Mexico, Spain, Japan, and not surprisingly Miami, while the owner, Marilia Guimarães, spent the 1970s in Cuba which must be some guarantee of authenticity.

La Bodeguita also offers some interesting drinks as well as live music.

Hours: 7:30 a.m. to 3 a.m. (Closed Monday). **Cuisine:** Cuban. **Telephone:** 205-0645. **Reservations:** No. **Prices:** Low to medium. **Credit:** Elo.

BOTEQUIM 184
Rua Visconde de Caravelas, 184 — Botafogo.

Botequim 184 is typical of the type of restaurant to be found in the heart of Botafogo between the beach and Lagoa.

Small, simple, but with lots of atmosphere Botequim offers cooking that is cheap but never less than honest.

The crowds that fill these cute restaurants are usually students with an eye on the bottom line yet their atmosphere and unpretentious cooking attracts a clientele that also frequents Rio's more expensive eating houses.

If you are in Rio for any time make sure you use some of it to track down these simple back street restaurants, many of which are within a short walk of Botequim.

Hours: 11:00 a.m. to 2 a.m. **Cuisine:** International/Brazilian. **Telephone:** 266-0437. **Reservations:** No. **Prices:** Inexpensive. **Credit:** Most major cards.

BRAGADO'S
Av. das Americas, 16331 (Km. 17,5) — Barra da Tijuca

When Bragado's opened its doors in 1986 it had already been the talk of the social columns for a number of years and probably because of this it has never lived up to the expectations the city created for it.

A purpose built churrascaria Bragado's is more attractive than many of the larger barbecue houses but falls down in the quality of the meat served and the sloppy service when working under pressure.

Its location makes it an unlikely choice for visitors, Bragado having to survive in the week on the clients attracted from Jacarepagua, when it offers an *à la carte* menu, and at the weekends, when it serves the *rodizio* system, by families returning from the beach at Recreio and Grumari.

Hours: Noon to midnight. **Cuisine:** Barbecue. **Telephone:** 327-6177. **Reservations:** No. **Prices:** Medium to high. **Credit:** Most major cards.

BUFFALO GRILL ★ ★
Rua Rita Ludolf, 47 — Leblon

I was quite hard on the Buffalo Grill in the 1986 guide, for which I now apologise, as during a difficult year it constantly served some of the best meat in town and in the process put to shame many of its larger and more famous competitors.

Visually the Buffalo Grill is still a bit of a mess. Smart and business like from the outside but confused internally, the piano bar doubling as the restaurant when the small upstairs area is packed, which is often.

More a steak house than a traditional churrasco, serious carnivores should not miss the Buffalo Grill, or the similar T-Bone, while in Rio.

Hours: Noon to 3 a.m. **Cuisine:** Steak House/Barbecue. **Telephone:** 274-4848. **Reservations:** Yes. **Prices:** Medium to high. **Credit:** Most major cards.

CABAÇA GRANDE
Rua do Ouvidor, 12 — Centro.

Despite its appearance as a simple sidewalk café, Cabaça Grande serves some of the best fish and seafood dishes in Rio and the fish soup should not be missed by anyone (one portion will easily serve two or three).

Cabaça Grande is definitely worth a visit if you are working in town.

Note: Two doors down from Cabaça Grande is Rio Minho (231-2338) which also serves a high standard of fish and sea food dishes. Both Cabaça Grande and Rio Minho are located in Rua Ouvidor between Av. 1° de Março and Av. Pres. Kubitschek, behind Praça XV.

Hours: 11 a.m. to 4 p.m. (Closed at weekends). **Cuisine:** Seafood. Telephone: 231-2301. **Reservations:** Only accepted up to 12:30 p.m. **Prices:** Medium to high. **Credit:** Visa and Diners.

CABEÇA FEITA
Rua Barão da Torre, 665 — Ipanema.

Simple, friendly, and typical of young Ipanema, Cabeça Feita is popular at any time over the weekend for a cold beer, snack or full meal.

The food is always good value and can be excellent or ordinary depending on the chef's mood.

A lot more character than many of its opposition, Cabeça Feita appeals to a predominantly young crowd and is a good call for a late lunch at the weekend after a morning on the beach at Ipanema. Cabeça Feita lies three blocks back behind the Country Club.

Hours: 5 p.m. to 2 a.m. (Mon. — Fri.) and Noon to 2 a.m. (Sat. & Sun.). **Cuisine:** International. **Telephone:** 239-3045. **Reservations:** No. **Prices:** Low to medium. **Credit:** No.

CAFÉ LAMAS
'Rua Marquês de Abrantes, 18 — Flamengo.

Although no longer at its original location, Café Lamas with 113 years of tradition is one of Rio's oldest restaurants, if not the oldest.

Nothing more than a streetside café in a Flamengo back street, Café Lamas serves food that has been cooked with care and competence be it meat, fish or anything else on the extensive menu.

Everybody receives the same warm welcome at Lamas and you will soon feel at home be it that you dropped in for a snack, a full meal, or an ice cold *chopp* (beer). The atmosphere is striking, many of its regular patrons being famous in the art world.

Not particularly a restaurant for the casual tourist who many not appreciate its bohemian atmosphere, it should not be forgotten by anybody who is in Rio for any length of time or who is looking for a late, late night meal.

Hours: 7 a.m. to 4 a.m. **Cuisine:** International. **Telephone:** 205-0799. **Reservations:** No. **Prices:** Low to medium. **Credit:** No.

CAFÉ PACIFICO ★
Rua Visconde Silva. 14 — Botafogo

Café Pacifico is typical of many of the restaurants to be found in Botafogo (see Botequim 184) except for the details that it is only Rio's second Mexican restaurant, and according to the readers, the city's best.

Tacos, Enchiladas, Tortillas etc., and all the appropriate accompanying drinks, have made Café Pacifico a popular haunt with many of the resident foreign readers a proportion of whom have written, called me, or cornered me at cocktail parties to demand that at "the very least" their favorite restaurant is given one star. Their wish is my command!

Hours: Noon to 3 p.m. (Monday through Friday) and 6:30 p.m. to 2 a.m. **Cuisine:** Mexican. **Telephone:** 246-5637. **Reservations:** No. **Prices:** Low to medium. **Credit:** No.

CAFÉ DE LA PAIX ★ ★ ★ ★
Av. Atlântica, 1020 (Hotel Meridien) — Copacabana.

Café de la Paix is one of Rio's outstanding restaurants, and it is only my natural British reserve which would hate to see one outstanding French hotel boast two outstanding, five star, restaurants that keeps it from a fifth star.

It is the Café de la Paix which sets the standard for all the other four star restaurants, and it is because of this that so many other restaurants fall short at three stars. If you don't believe me just test any restaurant that you think is worth a fourth star against the food served at the Café de la Paix, but be warned it won't be cheap.

The Café de la Paix, for those who like the more intimate details, has the charm of a Parisian brasserie, yet despite its informal atmosphere serves an extremely high quality of French cuisine from a menu that always holds some delightful surprises. From 3 p.m. to 6 p.m. the restaurant serves one of Rio's better teas.

In my opinion, you cannot do much better in Rio for a light business or holiday lunch, unless of course you choose the Meridien's Saint Honoré restaurant located thirty-seven floors above.

The service, as you would expect from the Meridien, is impeccable.

Hours: Noon to 1 a.m. (without a break). **Cuisine:** French. **Telephone:** 275-9922. **Reservations:** No. **Prices:** Expensive. **Credit:** All major cards.

CAFÉ DO TEATRO (ASSYRIUS) ★
Av. Rio Branco (Teatro Municípal) — Centro.

One of the superior Nino-Antonino group, the Café do Teatro has to be seen to be believed, being so over the top that it deserves a scene in an old Hollywood B-Epic set in Egypt.

Elegantly cool, despite the rest of the decor, the Café do Teatro should be high on your list of places to eat in Rio, especially downtown.

Only open for lunch, when it offers a acceptable level of international cuisine, it comes into its element when hosting the big cast parties held on the opening nights of the ballet and opera. Sadly these are "invitation only" affairs so you will just have to appreciate the setting and beauty and elegance of the occasion when you stop by for a drink in the interval.

Hours: 11:30 p.m. to 3:30 p.m. (Closed at the weekend). **Cuisine:** International. **Telephone:** 262-4164. **Reservations:** Yes for large parties. **Prices:** High. **Credit:** All major cards.

CANDIDO'S ★ ★ ★
Rua Barros de Alarção, 352 — Pedra de Guaratiba.

I bowed to the demands of my resident readers who insisted that Candido's, 476, and Tia Palmira, were all included in the restaurant section despite being an hours drive from Rio (see Trips — Costa Verde).

Candido's is the largest and possibly most famous, of these three outstanding fish and seafood restaurants, and should be visited by anybody with a car who has time to spare for a long leisurely lunch.

Rustic, but at the same time sophisticated, Candido's appeals to the most demanding of gourmands and has in the past hosted both Paul Bocuse and Gaston Lenotre among other famous chefs.

A lunch at Candido's is not something that will easily be forgotten. I myself have had many memorable lengthy lunches there and would not be fair if I did not dedicate this review to Nick and Sue Hillyard, now resident in Canada, who discovered this restaurant for me many years ago.

Hours: 11:30 a.m. to 7 p.m. (Mon. — Fri.), 11:30 a.m. to 11 p.m. (Sat. & Sun.). **Cuisine:** Seafood. **Telephone:** 395-2007 and 395-1630. **Reservations:** Essential at the weekend. **Prices:** High to expensive. **Credit:** Diners.

CANECO 70
Av. Delfim Moreira, 1026 — Leblon.

Caneco 70 is Leblon's beachfront bar, and while a recent face lift did nothing for the atmosphere of the place, unlike that of Barril 1800, it does have a pleasant upper restaurant terrace which allows you not only to watch the world go by but also the comings and goings on Leblon beach in front.

Caneco 70 offers straightforward, honest cooking and like many of the beachfront bars is open from early until late.

Hours: 10 a.m. to 4:30 a.m. **Cuisine:** International. **Telephone:** 294-1180. **Reservations:** No. **Prices:** Inexpensive to medium. **Credit:** Most major cards.

CANTINHO DE GOA
Rua Alm. Pereira Guimarães, 65 — Leblon

Discovered by the readers of this guide back in 1984, Cantinho de Goa was Rio's first, and for a long time only, curry house.

As the Cantinho de Goa is nothing more than a small store in a Leblon side road the best suggestion I can make is to think in terms of a take away. Go down, try the various curries, explain to the owner just how hot and spicy you like your curry, and then you will be set to order it at any time for any occasion, except please don't invite me as the one food I cannot abide is curry.

For curries in a more elegant setting you should think in terms of the Raajmahal, Rio's top Indian restaurant.

Hours: 11:30 a.m. to 9 p.m. Cuisine: Indian. Telephone: 259-0945. Reservations: No. Prices: Medium to high. Credit: No.

CARINHOSO
Rua Visconde de Pirajá, 22 — Ipanema.

Carinhoso used to be the old New York Disco, but fashions change and so must bars and restaurants. Today Carinhoso is not so much a restaurant, although serving an adequate level of international cuisine, but rather designed for people who wish to drink and enjoy a little romantic late-night dancing.

Hours: 8 p.m. to 4 a.m. Cuisine: International. Telephone: 287-3579. Reservations: No. Prices: High. Credit: All major cards.

CARRETA
Praça São Perpétuo, 116 — Barra da Tijuca.

Until Rodeio arrived, Carreta was the best barbecue house in Barra and one of the area's most consistent restaurants.
Carreta is a traditional Rio churrascaria and used to be located in a beautiful house in the heart of Ipanema. The move to Barra was a major set back but they have worked hard to re-establish the same atmosphere as the old house and can still count on a large number of faithful regulars who enjoy the friendly and helpful service which has become the restaurant's trademark.

Hours: 11 a.m. to 1 a.m. Cuisine: Barbecue: Telephone: 399-4055. Reservations: No. Prices: Medium to high. Credit: Most major cards.

CARRETÃO
Rua Siqueira Campos, 23 — Copacabana

As Carretão is only a short stroll from my office in Copacabana its opening in 1986 was more than welcome as it is an excellent churrascaria *rodizio*.
From its first day it was clear that Carretão held a few hidden secrets. The meats were first class and the chef certainly knew all about the deceptively difficult task of barbecuing. It was no surprise to learn therefore that Carretão had family ties to Mariu's, Rio's top churrascaria *rodizio* along with the Porcão chain.
While missing the theatrical flair of its larger competitors, meat fans should not miss this simple but homely churrascaria if they are in the area. You can even play "Spot the Author"!

Hours: Noon to 12:30 a.m. (Closed on Monday). Cuisine: Barbecue. Telephone: 236-3435. Reservations: No. Prices: Medium to high. Credit: All major cards.

O CASARÃO
Rio Sheraton Hotel — Vidigal.

The attractive O Casarão Churrascaria, set in the grounds of the Sheraton Hotel, offers for a set price a complete self-service barbecue with appetizers and desserts to support it.
A pleasant holiday atmosphere helps the overall ambience and can help even the local foreign residents to believe that they are in Rio on holiday again.
A visit to O Casarão can be combined with a stop at the Casa da Cachaça, also to be found in the hotel grounds, where Brazilian batidas are served.

Hours: Noon to 4 p.m. and 7 p.m. to midnight. **Cuisine:** Barbecue. **Telephone:** 274-1122. **Reservations:** No. **Prices:** High. **Credit:** All major cards.

CASTELO DA LAGOA ★ ★ ★
Av. Epitácio Pessoa, 1560 — Lagoa (Ipanema side)

The flag ship of Chico Recarey's group, which includes such diverse houses as El Pescador, Un Deux Trois, Carinhoso, Mediterrâneo, Bella Blu, Bella Roma and the showhouses of Asa Branca and Scala, is the Castelo da Lagoa which is one of the restaurants that helped establish the Lagoa as one of Rio's best eatings spots.

The restaurant is more informal than it looks from the road, and the prices on the large international menu more accessible than you would imagine.

The most attractive part of the restaurant is at the back so go right the way through otherwise you may think that the restaurant is empty when you arrive.

Castelo da Lagoa is a reliable choice for business lunches, when the restaurant is not as full as the nights when it fills with people going on to shows, many of them at Mr. Recarey's other houses.

In the same location as Castelo da Lagoa, facing on to the lake, is Chiko's Bar, Rio's most traditional night spot. You can't really say you have done Rio without dropping by Chiko's for a nightcap and to listen to the excellent jazz and Brazilian music that is presented nightly.

Hours: 12 a.m. to 3 a.m. **Cuisine:** International. **Telephone:** 287-3514. **Reservations:** At weekends. **Prices:** Medium to high. **Credit:** All major cards.

CASA DA SUIÇA ★ ★ ★
Rua Candido Mendes, 157 — Gloria

Casa da Suiça is one of Rio's most traditional restaurants and is in demand with the foreign business community for its proximity to the city center and the Rio Squash Club.

Located in the same building as the Swiss Consulate, Casa da Suiça offers traditional Swiss cuisine of the very highest quality and is popular at both lunch and dinner for its fondues.

The service is always correct, if a little stiff, a complaint that could also be levelled at the decor. The overall ambience however, is helped by the lush greenery viewed through the large windows.

Casa da Suiça is without question one of Rio's better restaurants and would rate in most residents' list of their ten favorite restaurants.

Hours: Noon to 3 p.m. and 7 p.m. to midnight. (Dinner only at the weekend). **Cuisine:** Swiss. **Telephone:** 252-5182. **Reservations:** Yes. **Prices:** Medium to high. **Credit:** No.

THE CATTLEMAN ★ ★
Av. Epitacio Pessoa. 864 — Lagoa (Ipanema)

Half way through 1986 one of Rio's outstanding restaurants, Le Flambard, closed its doors to be refurbished, sadly when it re-opened the attractive Le Flambard was no more and in its place was The Cattleman.

Following the trends of Rio's night-life Le Falmbard was transformed by its owners into a piano bar while up-stairs, in what used to be the private dining rooms, was installed The Cattleman restaurant, an up-market grill house offering good quality grills and other more interesting dishes.

By itself, The Cattleman would, and is, a worthwhile edition to Rio's restaurant scene. It is just a pity that it had to be at the expense of Le Flambard.

1987 will see The Cattleman establish its own identity and it is going to be interesting to see what catches the imagination of the Carioca public, the downstairs piano bar or the restaurant.

A restaurant worth trying in 1987 if you want a better steak.

Hours: 10 a.m. to 1 a.m. **Cuisine:** Grills. **Telephone:** 259-1041. **Reservations:** Yes. **Prices:** Medium to high. **Credit:** All major cards.

CHALÉ BRASILEIRO
Rua da Matriz, 54 — Botafogo.

A small narrow house in a Botafogo side street is the home to one of Rio's oldest Brazilian restaurants.

Chale presents a Brazilian menu in colonial surroundings, with local knick-knacks spread throughout.

Service is by waiters or girls dressed in typical Bahian dress.

The restaurant offers a selection of international dishes for those who can't take the spicy dishes of Bahia.

Hours: Noon to 4 p.m. and 7 p.m. to 1 a.m. **Cuisine:** Brazilian. **Telephone:** 286-0897. **Reservations:** At the weekend. **Prices:** Medium to high. **Credit:** All major cards.

LES CHAMPS ELYSEES ★ ★
Av. Antonio Carlos, 58 (Maison de France) — Centro

As a restaurant Les Champs Elysees promises so much but sadly always seems to fall short which is a great pity because in Dominique Raymond they have one of the city's most creative chefs.

An extremely attractive restaurant, probably the best dressed in the city center, with magnificent views across the roof tops to Sugar Loaf, Les Champs Elysees serves cuisine which is nouvelle French, which while adequate falls well short of the level maintained by the Saint Honoré. Pré Catelan, Café de la Paix, Troisgros, Laurent, and a host of others.

Hours: Noon to 5 p.m. (closed at the weekend). **Cuisine:** French. **Telephone:** 220-4129. **Reservations:** Yes. **Prices:** High to expensive. **Credit:** All major cards.

CLUB 1 (TAVERNETTA MACHIAVELLI) ★ ★
Rua Paul Redfern. 40 — Ipanema

Club 1 is a critic's nightmare because it simply won't leave itself alone. It started as a steak house then became a fairly non-descript Italian restaurant before finally, in the last year, metamorphosing in to something called the *Tavernetta Machiavelli* which is still in truth Club 1.

The change in name did however herald the arrival of a more interesting selection of dishes which, with a more informal atmosphere including the addition of paper table clothes and crayons, helped Club 1 stand apart from the "also rans"

Worth trying but please don't hold me responsible if you get there and you find that they have decided to make it a Chinese restaurant.

Hours: 6 p.m. to 2 a.m. **Cuisine:** Italian. **Telephone:** 259-3148. **Reservations:** Yes. **Prices:** Medium to high. **Credit:** All major cards.

CLUB GOURMET ★ ★ ★ ★
Rua General Polidoro, 186 — Botafogo.

Recent years have proved beyond all doubt that Club Gourmet is one of Rio's truly outstanding restaurants, the standard only slipping when the owner, and head chef, José Hugo Celidônio, travels.

Located in a most unlikely road in Botafogo, opposite a large graveyard, Club Gourmet offers a near perfect eating environment with few pretentions.

Club Gourmet has an air of elegance yet at the same time a more relaxed atmosphere than any of Rio's other outstanding restaurants.

Offering a complete dining experience you should go for dinner, the menu being a touch limited at lunch for my liking, and choose the full gourmet menu which allows you to pick one item from each course. All the dishes have been chosen for their flavors to subtly combine and produce the heavenly results that are a trademark of this fine restaurant.

The service is unassuming and at times unprofessional, but this helps add to the charm of a restaurant which is about good food and not being pompous with it.

The success of Club Gourmet is based around the master stroke of Mr. Celidônio in taking the sacred cow of French cooking and tampering with it, using the best Brazilian ingredients until we arrive at a cuisine which is a credit to both countries.

Hours: Noon to 3 p.m. (Closed for lunch on Saturday) and 8:30 p.m. to 1 a.m. (Closed for dinner on Sunday). **Cuisine:** Its own (French/Brazilian). **Telephone:** 295-3494. **Reservations:** Yes. **Prices:** High to expensive. **Credit:** No.

COCHRANE
Rua das Palmeiras, 66 — Botafogo.

Run by an English couple, Cochrane first opened serving traditional English fare then reverted to hamburgers, sandwiches and other snacks before returning to a stronger and more varied menu.

In surroundings that while simple are elegant, Cochrane is a fun place and whatever course it takes I am sure it will be unique in its conceptions.

Hours: 11 a.m. to 2 a.m. **Cuisine:** International. **Telephone:** 226-8844. **Reservations:** No. **Prices:** Medium to high. **Credit:** No.

COLOMBO
Rua Gonçalves Dias, 32 — Centro

If you want to eat in the past then Colombo is the place, a restaurant which should be visited by any traveller who finds himself downtown at lunchtime.

This magnificent continental café has hardly changed since opening on September 17, 1894 and retains in its upstairs restaurant an air of restfull elegance. The cooking is competent and the prices reasonable.

In Rio, Colombo is considered a tourist attraction in its own right.

Hours: 8:30 a.m. to 6:30 p.m. (Closed at weekends). **Cuisine:** International. **Telephone:** 232-2300. **Reservations:** No. **Prices:** Medium. **Credit:** No.

COPACABANA
Av. N.S. de Copacabana, 1444 — Copacabana
Barra Shopping — Barra da Tijuca

The original Churrascaria Copacabana is located in the center of Copacabana, closer to the Ipanema end, and has over the years become a firm favorite with the residents of the *zona sul* while establishing a reputation for serving good quality meats in pleasant modern surroundings backed by attentive service.

In 1986, Copacabana inaugurated a branch in the new restaurant area of Barra Shopping.

Churrascaria Copacabana is a suitable choice for couples or large groups and offers a full menu for those who don't like barbecued meats.

Hours: 11:30 a.m. to 2 a.m. (Copacabana) and 11:30 a.m. to midnight (Barra). **Cuisine:** Barbecue. **Telephone:** 247-8257 (Copacabana). 325-7600 (Barra). **Reservations:** No. **Prices:** Medium to high. **Credit:** All major cards.

COTA 200 ★
Morro da Urca (Sugar Loaf) — Botrafogo

It may seem a bit gauche to predict that by the end of 1987 Cota 200 will be the city's most improved restaurant but that is exactly what I am going to do.

Cota 200 would get a one star rating just for its spectacular location on top of Morro da Urca, and in the past that seemed to be the limit of its owners ambitions. That has now changed and plans are a foot for Cota 200.

During 1987 the restaurant will be refurbished and the honest food and service up-graded. The aim is to put Cota 200 on the map as a restaurant for the residents as well as foreign visitors.

Cable-cars are to be scheduled to allow business executives to lunch in this spectacular location while the restaurant will also operate at night before the shows of Beija-Flor and the other musical attractions planned for the weekends.

Hours: Noon to 7 p.m. (until 11 p.m. on the days of shows). **Cuisine:** International. **Telephone:** 541-3737 or 295-2397. **Reservations:** No. **Prices:** Medium. **Credit:** All major cards.

DEL MARE ★
Rua Paul Redfern, 37 — Ipanema

Purpose built seafood restaurant which emerged from the shell of the Grand Finale.

Attractive and popular, but not up to the standards of Grottammare, Del Mare is a comfortable choice for unpretentious dining or lengthy, relaxed lunches.

Italian dishes support the seafood selection.

Del Mare's position in Rio's gourmet circles is greatly enhanced for me by the fact that along with Club 1 and Mediterraneo it is within safe staggering distance of the Lord Jim.

Hours: Noon to 2 a.m. **Cuisine:** Seafood. **Telephone:** 239-1842. **Reservations:** No. **Prices:** Medium to high. **Credit:** All major cards.

EL CORDOBÉS ★
Av. Borges de Medeiros, 3207 — Lagoa (Botafogo end).

El Cordobés established itself in less than a year as one of Rio's most popular restaurants offering umpteen different environments in an attractive house on the shores of the Botafogo end of the Lagoa.

El Cordobes professes to specialize in seafood and Spanish cuisine, which includes a traditional paella, although like many similar restaurants it also serves a large number of standard international dishes.

El Cordobés is worth remembering if you are a large group. They seem to able to cope without flinching.

Hours: 6 p.m. to 2 a.m. (Mon.-Sat.). Noon to. 2 a.m. (Sun.). **Cuisine:** Spanish. **Telephone:** 246-7431. **Reservations:** For large groups. **Prices:** Medium to high **Credit:** All major cards.

EL CID
Rua Min. Viveiros de Castro, 15 — Copacabana.

When assessing a restaurant you must always deal with intangibles, that certain *je ne sais quoi*, and that is the case with El Cid.

El Cid is a small pavement café in one of Copacabana's busiest backstreets. From the street it looks a mess, the last place anyone would want to eat, yet time and time again I had residents asking me why El Cid was not rated. For all of them El Cid simply produced the best steak in Rio. Now I don't want to spoil the party but I did, as a confirmed steak and chips man, try the delights of El Cid and sadly I must report, I was not impressed. But don't take my word for it, please try El Cid's because this does come as an inside tip and at the very worst you may get caught by an attack of the *je ne sais quois*.

Hours: Noon to 4 a.m. **Cuisine:** Steak house. **Telephone:** 275-4597. **Reservations:** No. **Prices:** Medium. **Credit:** No.

EL PESCADOR ★ ★
Praça São Conrado, 20 — São Conrado.

On opening in 1985 El Pescador immediately became one of Rio's most popular and talked about restaurants and is the type of restaurant that residents find themselves returning to time and time again to eat with friends.

By Rio standards El Pescador is a large restaurant but remains attractive, the architect making good use of large wooden beams and nautical effects.

The menu holds no mysteries, offering a large choice of seafood and Spanish dishes, including probably Rio's best paella and, surprisingly, an excellent mixed grill. Suffice to say, the menu has something for every taste, which depending on the chefs mood can vary from excellent to good.

The portions served at El Pescador are some of the largest in Rio, which means enough to feed an army, and offers remarkable value for money if they get your bill right. The one smack on the hand I have to give them.

The seafood cover is enough to satisfy most people so think about sharing your main dish.

El Pescador is a short cab ride from both the Inter-Continental and Nacional hotels.

Hours: Noon to 2 a.m. **Cuisine:** Spanish/Seafood. **Telephone:** 322-0851. **Reservations:** No **Prices:** Medium to high. **Credit:** All major cards.

ENGLISH BAR ★ ★ ★
Rua do Comércio, 11 — Centro.

The best food served in the center of town has been found for a number of years at the English Bar and I expect it to continue this way.

Set in the historic Rua do Comércio, under the Arco do Telles off Praça XV, the English Bar offers a comfortable British atmosphere with a small pub bar and restaurant area downtairs and a large, although less attractive, eating area upstairs.

The cooking, from the imaginative menu, offers European dishes that spread from Portugal, through Spain and France and on up to Britain for roast beef. A truly international restaurant.

For the resident businessman the English Bar offers a break from the hustle and bustle of work in the city, and being set in a pedestrian precinct only helps the atmosphere of this tranquil haven.

The service is impeccable, as it should be in a top "business" restaurant.

Hours: Noon to 4 p.m. (Closed at the weekend). Drinks until 8 p.m. **Cuisine:** International. **Telephone:** 224-2539. **Reservations:** Yes. **Prices:** High. **Credit:** Most major cards.

ENOTRIA ★ ★ ★
Rua Constante Ramos, 115 — Copacabana.

Enotria is the exception that proves the rule, or if you prefer highlights why the *Insider's Guide's* ratings will always be different to any other guide

According to people in the catering business, many of them linked with Rio's outstanding restaurants. Enotria is one of Rio's best restaurants, especially as far as Italian cuisine goes. On the other hand I have yet to hear any customer get overly excited about Enotria. All agree that the food is good, even very good, but nothing that special, and this has been reconfirmed by the opinion of readers in 1986. In this case, as in every case, I must side with the paying customer.

Enotria, which in no way should you dismiss from your list of restaurants to try while in Rio, seats just 40 (reservations a must), is simply but tastefully decorated, serving dishes from a small inventive, and ever changing, menu which for the most part originate in Northern Italy.

Perhaps like Valentino's, Enotria suffers from being too good for its own good, especially as far as the "gourmet in the street" is concerned, and that would appear to be the majority of this guide's readers.

Hours: 8 p.m. to 2 a.m. (Closed on Sunday). **Cuisine:** Italian. **Telephone:** 237-6705. **Reservations:** Yes. **Prices:** High to expensive. **Credit:** Most major cards.

ENTRECOTE
Rua Rainha Guilhermina, 48 — Leblon
Rua Gonçalves Dias, 82 — Centro

Entrecote is the answer to eating cheaply without having to think. Basically a steak house. Entrecote offers four cuts of meat, eight types of potato and many different sauces to slosh over the top, and all for one very accessible price.

Popular with the *zona sul* crowd of every age, Entrecote is a good choice for large groups as ordering is simple and the standard guaranteed.

Service is quick and friendly, but never hurried.

Hours: Noon to 1 a.m. (Leblon); 11:00 a.m. to 4 p.m. Mon.-Fri. (Centro). **Cuisine:** Steak House. **Telephone,** 294-2915 (Leblon), 222-2603 (Centro). **Reservations:** No. **Prices:** Inexpensive. **Credit:** Visa and Diners.

EQUINOX ★ ★ ★ ★ ★
Rua Prudente de Morais, 729 — Ipanema.

Delightfully attractive, there is no one theme of elegance that can be pinned down at Equinox either in the restaurant on the first floor or the popular piano/jazz bar below. It reflects the taste of its owners, men who have travelled the world and sampled the best.

A touch of French, a smattering of Italian, a suggestion of the Orient, and holding it all together an atmosphere that can only be Brazilian, and to be more specific Rio.

The creative menu, which changes on the Equinox — around March 21 and September 23 — offers a well balanced selection of interesting dishes which allow the dinner to stick to the classical or experiment with the adventurous. All the dishes are lovingly and expertly prepared.

During 1986, a year when Equinox, like so many of the small independent restaurants, suffered badly from the shortages, the owners started to place more emphasis on the piano/jazz bar which has now built its own following quite separate from the regulars of what is one of Rio's outstanding restaurants and one of my own personal favorites.

Hours: 7:30 p.m. to 2 a.m. **Cuisine:** French. **Telephone:** 247-0580. **Reservations:** Yes. **Prices:** High to expensive. **Credit:** Most major cards.

ESCRIPTORIO
Rua Conde Bernadote, 26 — Leblon.

Located on the corner opposite the large Sendas supermarket in Leblon, Escriptorio took its location from VIP Club, a restaurant which had lasted less than a year in the torrid waters of the Rio restaurant trade.

Simple and with few pretentions, Escriptorio is really a bar with a menu added as a second thought, a menu which although small should satisfy the hungry.

Its location, and food, helps Escriptorio compliment one of the city's most popular bars, the Academia da Cachaça, and discos, Mikonos, both of which are close by.

Hours: 5 p.m. to 3 a.m. (Lunch on Saturday and Sunday. Closed on Monday). **Cuisine:** International/Brazilian. **Telephone:** No. **Reservations:** No. **Prices:** Medium. **Credit:** Most major cards.

OS ESQUILOS
Estr. Escragnolle, Km. 2 — Floresta da Tijuca.

Os Esquilos is one of two restaurants, the other being A Floresta, that is hidden away in the depths of the Tijuca Forest.

The smarter of the two, Os Esquilos, serves a traditional international menu which has few epicurean pretentions, the cooking never less than honest though.

What Os Esquilos does have in its favor, is the flavor of the forest which surrounds it and which makes it the ideal location for a long lazy lunch especially on a hot day when the height of the forest and its lush canopy keeps the temperatures several degrees lower than in the city.

Os Esquilos is a 40 minute drive from anywhere in the *zona sul* or Centro and should not be forgotten by residents.

You will certainly need a car to get to both Os Esquilos and A Floresta.

Note: Os Esquilos also has a full tea service.

Hours: 11 a.m. to 7 p.m. (Closed on Monday). **Cuisine:** International. **Prices:** Medium. **Credit:** Diners and Nacional.

A ESQUINA ★
Rua do Ouvidor, 14 — Centro.

A very welcome addition to the downtown restaurant scene in 1986 was A Esquina which is located at the bottom, 1° de Março, end of Rua do Ouvidor.

A touch bland and still a little "new", A Esquina has a good pedigree with links to the English Bar, which should help it fully establish itself in 1987 as one of the top choices for business executives in the city center.

A Esquina offers a standard menu of international dishes

Hours: 11 a.m. to 4 p.m. (Closed at the weekend). **Cuisine:** International. **Telephone:** 231-2362. **Reservations:** Yes. **Prices:** High. **Credit:** Most major cards.

ESTÂNCIA
Av. Atlântica, 3264 — Copacabana.

The Estância restaurant of the Othon Palace Hotel is unlikely to win any awards for its cooking at present which is a pity because the restaurant itself has spectacular views over Copacabana Beach and its location alone could make it one of Rio's better restaurants.

The menu offers a traditional balance of international dishes to be found in any hotel restaurant, while in its defense it serves a popular *feijoada* on Saturday.

Hours: Noon to 3 p.m. and 7 p.m. to midnight. **Cuisine:** International. **Telephone:** 255-8812. **Reservations:** No. **Prices:** High. **Credit:** All major cards.

ESTRELA DO SUL
Av. Repórter Nestor Moreira — Botafogo

One of the original churrascaria *rodízios*, Estrela do Sul still holds a soft spot for many despite getting left behind by the newer, better competition in Ipanema and Copacabana.

But a *rodízio* is a *rodízio* and Estrela do Sul will more than fit the bill if that is the sort of meal you are looking for.

Like all *rodízios*, remarkable value for money.

Note: In 1986 Estrela do Sul opened a new branch in the car park area of the large Free Way supermarket in Barra da Tijuca and also have a branch at Av. Maracanã, 649 (Tel. 254-0630) within walking distance of the Maracanã stadium.

Hours: 11 a.m. to midnight. **Cuisine:** Barbecue. **Telephone:** 295-0970 (Botafogo), 254-0630 (Maracanã). **Reservations:** No. **Prices:** Medium. **Credit:** Most major cards.

ETTORE
Av. Armando Lombardi, 800 — Barra da Tijuca.

El Show de Folclore Mas Famoso Del Mundo
The Most Famous Folklore Show In The World

Assista no primeiro andar do Plataforma 1 ao melhor musical já feito no Brasil, nos últimos vinte anos. Todas as noites às 23 horas.

Mr. Lenotre turns up at regular intervals throughout the year to re-orchestrate the menu and check that everything is up to his exacting standards, standards which Le Pré Catelan and the Rio Palace Hotel continue to reafirm beyond all doubt.

If anything is certain in Rio in 1987 it is that Le Pré Catelan will continue to present Rio with some of its most interesting and tasteful dishes.

Hours: 7 p.m. to midnight. **Cuisine:** French *nouvelle* cuisine. **Telephone:** 521-3232. **Reservations:** Yes. **Prices:** Expensive. **Credit:** All major cards.

PRÍNCIPE AND REAL
Av. Atlântica, 514 & 974 — Leme.

I rate these two restaurants together because they are almost identical in every manner including ambience which can hardly be considered one of their strong points.

Famous for seafood dishes, Principe and Real have become a traditional haunt for tourists and residents alike who take their eating seriously and don't worry about the uninteresting surroundings.

Accustomed to dealing with foreigners the waiters at both restaurants will take the time to describe the various dishes and types of fish which can make for an interesting and educational meal.

Both restaurants are within walking distance of the Meridien, Leme Palace and Luxor Continental.

Hours: Noon to 2 a.m. **Cuisine:** Seafood. **Telephone:** 275-3996 (Principe), 275-9048 (Real). **Reservations:** No. **Prices:** Medium to high. **Credit:** Most major cards.

QUADRIFOGLIO★ ★
Rua Maria Angelica, 43 — Jardim Botanico/Lagoa.

Quadrifoglio took the place of Serendipity, one of my own personal favorites, and therefore never really stood a chance with me.

Serving better than average Italian cuisine the best part of Quadrifoglio is still its attractive ambience, a direct result of the taste of the previous owners.

Despite my own opinion, Quadrifoglio managed to become one of the "in" locations in 1986 and should in 1987 re-inforce its own following so that Serendipity will soon be a distant memory.

Worth trying in 1987 as a change from the more sober and standard Italian eateries.

Hours: 8 p.m. to 2 a.m. (Closed on Sunday). **Cuisine:** Italian. **Telephone:** 226-1799. **Reservations:** Yes. **Prices:** High. **Credit:** Most major cards.

QUATRO SETE MEIA ★ ★ ★
Rua Barros de Alarcão, 476 — Pedra de Guaratiba.

This tiny seafood restaurant in Pedra de Guaratiba, about an hours drive from Rio, has had its praises sung by just about everyone including in the pages of the hallowed *New York Times*.

Owned by a Canadian and a Brazilian, Quatro Sete Meia only operates at the weekend. Serving a maximum of 24 guests in each sitting it is not a question that you *should* make a reservations but you *must*.

The menu at this rustic, but at the same time elegant restaurant, is always innovative and reflects the moods of its owners. The menu though be warned is limited and heavily features *muquecas* (a type of Brazilian stew) and so should be avoided by anyone who prefers simpler food. They would be more at home in the larger Candido's just a few doors down the road.

Quatro Sete Meia is a very special restaurant. If you live in Rio don't miss it.

Hours: 1 p.m. to 11 p.m. (Fri.-Sun.). **Cuisine:** Seafood. **Telephone:** 395-2716. **Reservations:** Essential. **Prices:** High to expensive. **Credit:** No.

QUEEN'S LEGS
Av. Epitacio Pessoa, 5030 — Lagoa (Botafogo end).

Decorated as an attractive Victorian pub, the Queen's Legs is a hospitable place to drop by for a drink and a game of darts, especially during the week when you can get on the dart board without too much trouble.

On the first floor the Queen's Legs has one of Rio's prettier restaurants although sadly the cooking is not up to much and was virtually ignored in 1986. Personally I recommend that you stick to drinks and a snack in the ground floor bar.

Hours: 6 p.m. to 2 a.m. **Cuisine:** International. **Telephone:** 226-3648. **Reservations:** No. **Prices:** Medium to high. **Credit:** American Express.

RAAJMAHAL★ ★
Rua General Polidoro, 29 — Botafogo.

If anyone was to open a proper Indian restaurant in Rio the odds must have been heavily on those people being British, and that is exactly what has happened.

The owners started out in the same Botafogo location with Habeas Corpus which bloomed in to The Orchid before transforming, in early 1986, to the Raajmahal after they had noted the heavy demand for the curries on their menu.

The next step was to engage a fully trained Indian chef and then adapt the ambience of the restaurant to something suitably Indian while still retaining its Carioca charm, all of which had been accomplished by the end of 1986.

Raajmahal's menu extends the delights of Indian cuisine beyond the simple curry and on into the realm of India's more interesting and lesser known dishes. It is worth noting, however, that the local taste is for mild curries so ask for it hot if you want the real McCoy, but please don't ask me, I detest curries.

Hours: Noon to 3 p.m. and 7 p.m. to 1 a.m. **Cuisine:** Indian. **Telephone:** 541-6999. **Reservations:** Yes. **Prices:** Medium to high. **Credit:** No.

LE RELAIS
Rua General Venancio, 365 — Leblon.

As the guide went to press Le Relais, once one of Rio's better and more charming restaurants, was being totally refurbished.

How Le Relais will return is anyone's guess but it will certainly be worth checking out once it is back in business.

The following information was correct when Le Relais closed.

Hours: 7 p.m. to 1 a.m. **Cuisine:** French. **Telephone:** 294-2897. **Reservations:** Yes. **Prices:** Medium to high. **Credit:** All major cards.

RIO'S ★ ★ ★
Parque do Flamengo — Flamengo.

This large purpose built restaurant complex is the perfect location for prestigious business lunches or smart dinners. The international dishes are cooked with care and competence and supported by service befitting a top restaurant.

Comfortable and smartly appointed, Rio's has magnificent views across the bay to Sugar Loaf and Niterói.

The international menu is extensive but imaginative and offers something to please every palate.

Its' large car park makes Rio's a popular location for lunch with businessmen and women, lying half way between Centro and the residential areas of Copacabana and Ipanema.

While a jacket and tie is not the rule at Rio's, it does predominate at lunch.

Note: Rio's also has a large outdoor beer terrace which serves excellent snacks and sandwiches and boasts the same magnificent views as the restaurant.

Hours: Noon to 2 a.m. **Cuisine:** International. **Telephone:** 551-1131. **Reservations:** Yes. **Prices:** High to expensive. **Credit:** All major cards.

RIVE GAUCHE ★ ★ ★
Av. Epitacio Pessoa, 1484 — Lagoa.

In the last couple of years Rive Gauche has managed to re-establish itself as one of Rio's more elegant restaurants with spectacular views across the Lagoa to Corcovado.

While the cuisine is billed as French it is in truth more international in flavor and of a quite acceptable quality.

Rive Gauche features live music which ranges from jazz to bossa nova and if the urge takes you there is a small space to dance in. Below, at street level, is Biblos Bar, one of Rio's most popular singles/nightclub.

Service is attentive and polite and in 1986 I did not even have any problems with the staff who organize the parking of the cars who in 1985 had brought a new meaning to the phrase "petty minded".

Rive Gauche today remains one of the best kept secrets in Rio's restaurant world.

Hours: 8 p.m. to 3 a.m. **Cuisine:** International. **Telephone:** 521-2645. **Reservations:** No. **Prices:** Medium to high. **Credit:** All major cards.

RODÉIO ★ ★ ★ ★
Casa Shopoping — Av. Alvorada, 2150 — Barra da Tijuca.

By a large margin Rodeio is not only the best restaurant in Barra da Tijuca but also the best churrascaria in Rio, just falling short of the exalted heights reached by the original Rodeio at Rua Haddock Lobo, 1498 in São Paulo.

I myself am not ashamed to admit that Rodeio is the only restaurant in the Barra area that I currently travel out to eat in, but sadly this same distance makes it very difficult for the average visitor to discover this outstanding barbecue house. Rodeio, as in São Paulo, is a residents' watering hole.

Not much can be said about the cooking at Rodeio except that the menu features some of the finest barbecued meats you will discover anywhere. Rodeio is not a *rodízio* — a category of churrascaria where Mariu's reigns supreme — and is considerably more elegant than the normal barbecue houses you find throughout Brazil.

It is worth remembering that Rodeio is very close to the Barra Shopping Center and Carrefour and across the road from the three Art Casa Shopping movie houses.

I must add, however, that Rodeio became dangerously close to losing a star this year for its irritating habit of allowing the staff to start clearing the restaurant on slow nights while there are still customers eating. I know these reports are true because it happened to me. By the time they had finished I could hardly get out the restaurant for the stacked tables and chairs.

Hours: Noon to 3 p.m. and 7 p.m. to 1:30 a.m. (At weekends the restaurants works straight through from noon to 1:30 a.m.). **Cuisine:** Barbecue. **Telephone:** 325-6163. **Reservations:** Yes, if they accept them. **Prices:** High to expensive. **Credit:** Most major cards.

SABOREAR-TE ★ ★ ★
Av. Bartolomeu Mitre, 297 — Leblon.

Simple sophistication best described Saborear-te in the 1986 edition of the guide and I see no reason to change that.

This small, simple bistro was one of the finds of 1985 serving a small, interesting and changeable menu which lent heavily towards the French thanks to a chef who had learned his trade under José Hugo Celidônio at Club Gourmet.

Not for a business dinner, Saborear-te is a restaurant that no Rio resident should miss if they are out with a small group of friends.

Try and get a table on the upper deck if you can.

Hours: 8 p.m. to 1,30 a.m. Lunch on Sunday. **Cuisine:** French. **Telephone:** 511-6999. **Reservations:** Yes. **Prices:** Medium to high. **Credit:** Most major cards.

LE SAINT HONORE ★ ★ ★ ★ ★
Av. Atlantica, 1020 (Hotel Meridien) — Copacabana.

Since opening the Saint Honoré has figured predominantly on every list of Rio's, Brazil's and South America's top restaurants.

Under the direction of the world famous French chef, Paul Bocuse, the Saint Honoré offers an imaginative menu of Bocuse's own creations which reflect the high standards set by the chef himself and the host hotel.

In 1986 the Saint Honoré lost its brilliant resident chef Laurent Suaudeau, who left to open Laurent, and while this would have shaken the best of restaurants the Saint Honoré took it in its stride, Bocuse appointing the equally brilliant Bernard Troulier who in a short time has already made a name for himself in Rio.

Situated 37 floors up, on top of the Meridien Hotel, the Saint Honoré has the most exquisite views over the whole sweep of, Copacabana Beach which is equally dramatic by day or by night.

The restaurant itself is one of Rio's most elegantly appointed and the service faultless.

At lunch the Saint Honoré offers a special menu set to appeal to the most demanding of business executives and because of this is enticing an ever growing number of diners through the tunnel from the city. Because the lunchtime menu is offered for a set price, excluding drink, it is a perfect introduction for anyone experimenting for the first time. It is also remarkable value for money.

A visit to the top of the Meridien would have been a must even if they had installed a McDonald's up-top, but with Bocuse in residen-

'ce you really cannot afford to miss the opportunity of dining at one of the world's, never mind Rio's, best restaurants, and with a view that is simply unforgettable.

Hours: Noon to 3 p.m. and 8 p.m. to midnight (Dinner only on Saturday. Closed on Sunday). **Cuisine:** French *nouvelle cuisine*. **Telephone:** 275-9922. **Reservations:** Yes. **Prices:** Expensive. **Credit:** All major cards.

SAL & PIMENTA ★ ★ ★
Rua Barão da Torre, 368 — Ipanema.

As soon as Sal & Pimenta dropped the pretence of trying to be Rio's most important restaurant the food and service improved dramatically so that today it is a restaurant that you can go and enjoy rather than simply pose in.

The menu has much improved since its opening and is now more international than Italian-Brazilian. Service is still a little stiff but efficient.

The restaurant itself is light, airy and very attractive and reflects the taste of the owner Ricardo Amaral who is also responsible for Hippopotamus and Club A in New York. If you can try and get one of the window tables that overlook the square below.

Prices at Sal & Pimenta are high by Rio Standards and the 15% service charge on top is almost unforgivable but fashion, it would seem, does have a price.

Below Sal & Pimenta is the "Alo-Alo" piano bar which opens from 5 p.m. to 5 a.m. and at night offers a nice selection of jazz and Brazilian music and is without question one of Rio's smartest night spots where you go to see and be seen.

Hours: Noon to 2 a.m. **Cuisine:** International. Telephone: 521-1460. **Reservations:** Yes. **Prices:** Expensive. **Credit:** All major cards.

SATIRICON ★ ★ ★
Rua Barão da Torre, 192 — Ipanema.

The Rio branch of the popular Buzios eatery is unlike VIP Club, which came and went in 1986, infinitely superior to the original making full use of the fresh seafood catch which comes daily from Buzios.

Large and smart, pink predominates, Satiricon is one of Rio's better dressed. medium priced restaurants where happily the food compliments and is not a disappointment.

The restaurant is as happy with large groups as it is with couples, each managing to blend with the surroundings.

If you live in Rio and have not tried Satiricon yet, which is located next to Porcão in Ipanema, do. You won't be disappointed and it is a restaurant you can return to often.

Hours: 8 p.m. to 2 a.m. Lunch on Sunday. **Cuisine:** Italian/Seafood. **Telephone:** 521-0627. **Reservations:** No. **Prices:** Medium to high. **Credit:** No.

SHIRLEY ★ ★
Rua Gustavo Sampaio, 610 — Leme.

When you first see Shirley's you will be certain that I have made a big mistake but fight your way to one of the few tables at the back of this street side bar behind the Meridien and you won't be disappointed in either your stomach or your wallet.

A favorite with those in the know, Shirley offers some of the best Spanish and seafood dishes in Rio. The service is modest but friendly.

Because of its high reputation you will have to wait for a table at nearly any time of day and as you can't make reservations expect to stand in line.

Not a restaurant to take the boss to unless you know him well but one which gives you the full flavor of Rio and its residents, many of them cabinet ministers and famous socialities.

Hours: Noon to 1 a.m. **Cuisine:** Seafood/Spanish. Telephone: 275-1398. **Reservations:** No. **Prices:** Inexpensive to medium. **Credit:** No.

LE SIRENUSE ★ ★ ★ ★
Rua Jangadeiros, 28 (Praça General Osório) — Ipanema.

Le Sirenuse was one of the best new restaurants to open in 1986 which came as no surprise as the man in charge is Stephano Monti, the owner of the outstanding Le Streghe located close by in the same square.

To create Le Sirenuse Monti took over the Novo Prive nightclub, which had opened and sunk without trace in less than 18 months, and adapted its surroundings, including the balcony area which overlooked the dance floor, to make one of Rio's smartest seafood restaurants which like Le Streghe still manages to "breath summer informality".

Le Sirenuse offers a small compact menu of seafoods all of which are expertly cooked and these are complimented by a few Italian dishes in the tradition of Le Streghe.

Le Sirenuse is a quality restaurant which deserves to do well. The food is excellent, the service good and the atmosphere relaxing and enjoyable. It also boasts one of Rio's most comfortable bars.

Hours: 8 p.m. to 2 a.m. **Cuisine:** Seafood. **Telephone:** 267-3588. **Reservations:** Yes, **Prices:** Expensive. **Credit:** Most major cards.

SOL E MAR ★ ★ ★
Av. Reporter Nestor Moreira, 11 — Botafogo.

Sol e Mar is strangely enough one of Rio's very few water side restaurants with views across the bay and to Sugar Loaf and Corcovado.

As a complex, Sol e Mar has been one of the most improved restaurants in recent year. The most attractive part is the *Terraço Polinesio* with its ample cane furniture, glass topped tables and hanging plants, but demand has pushed the "terrace" on out in to the bay where normal wooden tables offer still elegant dining.

The menu is small but includes an intriguing selection of seafood and Spanish dishes, many of which will satisfy the most demanding gourmet.

Behind the restaurant is the Bateau Mouche Bar which presents shows and/or music to dance to after you have finished dinner.

Lunch or dinner, you can't go far wrong with Sol e Mar, and remember it is the starting point of the Bateau Mouche itself.

Because Sol e Mar is so popular with visitors I feel I must pass on a word of warning that has come to my own attention through local Cariocas. The warning is watch your wallet, and I mean watch your wallet on the table. I have heard several alarming stories of wallets going walkabout by themselves only to be recovered at the restaurant next day with the documents intact but the money missing. You have been warned, and so now have the owners, so let's hope things improve in 1987 and that this is not a habit that is going to spread to other restaurants.

Despite the problems, Sol e Mar is still a must for visitors and residents alike.

Hours: 11 a.m. to 3 a.m. **Cuisine:** Seafood/Spanish. **Telephone:** 295-1947. **Reservations:** Yes, **Prices** High to expensive. **Credit:** All major cards.

STEAK HOUSE
Rua Buenos Aires, 20 — Centro.

Steak House 1 in Centro is the original Rio steak house that helped start the craze which exploded at the end of 1983.

Smart but simple, Steak House 1 caters to Rio's better heeled young executives who want a good grill in rather better surroundings.

Hours: Noon to 4 a.m. (Closed at tne weekend). **Cuisine:** Steak House. **Telephone:** 263-5565. **Reservations:** No. **Prices:** Medium to high. **Credit:** No.

LE STREGHE ★ ★ ★ ★ ★
Prudente de Morais, 129 (Praça General Osório) — Ipanema.

Informal elegance is the style of this comfortable restaurant, Rio's best Italian restaurant by a large margin, and if you don't believe me ask the Italian community.

Located on the top floor of its own attractive house in the Hippie Square, Le Streghe breathes summer informality, an atmosphere that is sadly lacking in so many of Rio's darker, more somber restaurants. Le Streghe it would seem is one of the few restaurants in Rio which recognize that we live in a tropical city.

The light cuisine borders on the *nuova cucina* of Italy, and many of the ingredients are brought by the owner from Italy to keep the standards consistently high. But please don't expect a menu full of pizzas and spaghetti, that is not the style of Le Streghe.

Service at Le Streghe is courteous and punctual and helps the overall air of elegant restfullness which they also maintain at their outstanding branch in Búzios.

Below Le Streghe is Caligola one of Rio's most popular night-clubs and discotheques which will probably become a private club during the year unless, I hope, you are dining at Le Streghe. Caligola also has a comfortable and attractive piano bar.

Le Streghe, the restaurant, is a must for hot summer nights.

Hours: 7:30 p.m. to 2 a.m. **Cuisine:** Italian. **Telephone:** 287-1369. **Reservations:** Yes, **Prices:** High to expensive. **Credit:** All major cards.

SUPER SALADS/STEAK & SALADS
Av. Armando Lombardi, 601 — Barra da Tijuca.

I don't have much to say about these two restaurants located at the start of Barra, or the Italian eatery Siciliano which is wedged between them, other than to comment on their existence which shows that there is life in Barra.

Personally I would not travel out to either of these restaurants for a meal but it you live in the area or have just finished a game of squash at the near by KS Academy I am sure you could do a lot worse and if you actually want a salad I can't imagine you have much choice.

I am, however, a firm believer that if God had wanted me to eat salad I would have been a rabbit and will make no comment on the fact that these two salad bars are to be found close to the motel area of Rio but perhaps at the end of the day you would do better with a plate of oysters at one of Barra's sea food eateries!

And in case you want to know the answer to the question "Where's the beef?" it is in Steak & Salads who serve sliced file, picanha to be exact, which accompanies the other hot dishes and salads.

Hours: Noon to 4 p.m. and 7 p.m. to 1 a.m. (Closed on Monday). **Cuisine:** Salads and accompaniments. **Telephone:** 399-1026 (Super Salads), 299-2185 (Steak & Salads). **Reservations:** No. **Prices:** Medium. **Credit:** No.

SUPPENTOPF
Av. Princesa Isabel, 350 — Copacabana.

Tucked at the back of a small gallery off Princesa Isabel Suppentopf is to the German community what the Lord Jim is to the British.

A cozy cave like atmosphere, Suppentopf serves a reasonable level of South German cuisine with few pretentions, standards that the restaurant has maintained over the years.

Suppentopf can be visited for a quick beer or full meal.

Hours: Noon to 3 a.m. **Cuisine:** German. **Telephone:** 275-1896. **Reservations:** At the weekend. **Prices:** Medium. **Credit:** No.

TARANTELLA
Av. Sernambetiba, 850 — Barra da Tijuca.

Pleasant Italian restaurant, at the lower end of the scale, which has been popular with Barra residents for a number of years.

Tarantella is Barra's answer to Ipanema's Trattoria Torna.

Hours: Noon to midnight. **Cuisine:** Italian. **Telephone:** 399-0995. **Reservations:** No. **Prices:** Medium. **Credit:** Most major cards.

TAROT
Rua General Urquiza, 104 Leblon.

Colorful and super trendy thanks to an incredible amount of hype in the media, Tarot, despite everything, is a welcome addition to the cheap and cheerfull end of the restaurant market although the bill is not always that cheap.

Tarot's biggest claim to fame is the fact that it never closes, operating 24-hours a day. As I am sure this was an early publicity stunt it is going to be interesting to see how long they can maintain the costs of never closing.

The menu can best be described as international with a little bit of everything for every taste and the cooking honest considering the turnover of clients and pressure of being open continuously.

A restautant to remember if you are young and trendy in 1987, even if it is only in your own mind.

Hours: 24-hours-a-day. **Cuisine:** International. **Telephone:** 294-2994.
Reservations: No. **Prices:** Medium to high. **Credit:** No.

T-BONE★ ★
Rio-Sul Shopping Center — Botafogo.

T-Bone is a cross between a churrascaria and a steak house and compliments both categories.

The first, and with the demise of Maxim's, only "better" restaurant to open in the busy Rio-Sul shopping center, T-Bone, like Leblon's Buffalo Grill, is run by one of Brazil's most famous maitres, Garrincha, who has been a well known figure in Rio night life, especially good churrascarias, for a number of years.

T-Bone can from its outside appearance and shopping center location be underestimated which is a pity because it serves some of the best barbecued meats in Rio which are always supported with friendly and personal service which makes for an enjoyable meal be it lunch or dinner.

Despite its location, T-Bone allows the last diners to arrive as late as 11 p.m. and you can stay through till 3 a.m.

A must for carnivores.

Hours: 11 a.m. to 11 p.m. (Closed on Sunday). **Cuisine:** Barbecue.
Telephone: 275-7895. **Reservations:** No. **Prices:** Medium to high.
Credit: Most major cards.

TIA PALMIRA ★ ★
Caminho do Souza, 18 — Barra de Guaratiba.

The Costa Verde, which spreads west from Rio through the Angra dos Reis region, boasts three excellent fish restaurants, 476, Candido's, and the newest member of the triumvirate, Tia Palmira.

Unlike Candido's and 476, Tia Palmira is located in Barra de Guaratiba, and not Pedra de Guaratiba, and takes some finding in a back street of the village up a steep hill. The easiest way to find Tia Palmira, short of me drawing a map, is to ask when you reach Barra de Guaratiba. In Barra de Guaratiba everyone knows Tia Palmira.

The success of Tia Palmira is based on home cooking. No menu is offered, just a set meal which covers a full range of traditional Brazilian seafood delicacies, from *camarão* to *muquecas*. You certainly won't leave Tia Palmira hungry, and the cost won't hurt your wallet too badly either.

Hours: 11:30 a.m. to 6 p.m. (Closed on Monday). **Cuisine:** Seafood.
Telephone: 310-1169. **Reservations:** Not accepted. **Prices:** Medium
Credit: No.

TIBERIUS ★ ★
Av. Vieira Souto, 460 (Caesar Park Hotel) — Ipanema.

The Caesar Park does itself a disservice by billing the roof-top Tiberius as a coffee shop because it is so much more, and is in fact one of my favorite locations for lunch in the week when I have visitors in town.

Open from breakfast right throughout the day until dinner. Tiberius serves an interesting international menu which offers everything from a quick snack to a full meal.

The view from the top of the Caesar Park is spectacular and shows Ipanema and Leblon beaches and the mountains beyond at their best. Tiberius is definitely a name to remember for breakfast, lunch, tea or dinner, or even a drink around the pool from where you can still enjoy the magnificent views.

Hours: 7 a.m. to 12:30 p.m. **Cuisine:** International. **Telephone:** 287-3122. **Reservations:** No. **Prices:** Medium to high. **Credit:** All major cards.

LA TOUR
Rua Santa Luzia, 651 — Centro.

Like many tourist attractions around the world the food at La Tour is not what it should be and over priced for what it is.

La Tour's main claim to fame is that it is Rio's only revolving restaurant, completing a full circle once every 50 minutes.

The restaurant itself is comfortable but uninteresting, a criticism that can also be levelled at the cooking.

La Tourist would perhaps be a more appropriate name for this restaurant, which as a visitor you will find difficult to avoid.

Hours: Noon to midnight. **Cuisine:** International. **Telephone:** 240-5795. **Prices:** High **Credit:** All major cards. **Reservations:** Yes.

TRATTORIA TORNA
Rua Maria Quitéria, 46 — Ipanema.

Trattoria Torna is one of Rio's more attractive and hospitable restaurants at the lower end of the market (see Cheap and Cheerful), bringing a touch of Italy to the center of Ipanema highlighted by the hanging cheeses and chianti bottles and our old friend the checkered tablecloth.

Serving fairly indifferent Italian cuisine at accessable prices the overall quality of your meal will depend directly on how overworked the kitchen is, which can be "very" as it is located close to the Caesar Park, Everest and Ipanema Inn.

The ambience covers the defects in the cooking and it is certainly worth casting your eye over the hors d'oeuvre trolley.

Trattoria Torna is in my opinion better for lunch than dinner.

Hours: 11 a.m. to 2 a.m. **Cuisine:** Italian. **Telephone:** 247-9506. **Reservations:** No. **Prices:** Medium ı. **Credit:** Most major cards. Except Nacional.

TROISGROS ★ ★ ★ ★ ★
Rua Custodio Serrão, 62 — Jardim Botanico.

Chef Claude Troisgros brought an impressive track record to his restaurant which is hidden away at the top end of the Lagoa.

He, himself, is from one of France's most traditional families of French chefs who hail from Roane — the name of his first restaurant in Rio — close to Lyon; he worked with Paul Bocuse and came to Brazil to head Gaston Lenotre's team at Le Pré Catelan in the Rio Palace for four years. Now, rightly and justifiably so, he has found success with his own name both in Rio and with his latest venture in São Paulo.

As his own boss, Troisgros followed Celidonio at Club Gourmet in perfecting the marriage between the French school of cooking and 'the ingredients, many of them unknown in France, which are to be found in Brazil.

Troisgros' menu is small, small enough for Troisgros to handle personally and always holds a few surprises including a full set meal which really is a surprise for the diner. That is a chef with confidence.

Troisgros also had the confidence to locate his restaurant away from Ipanema in a pretty house in a back road at the Botafogo end of the Lagoa, a road nobody normally uses.

The easiest way to find Troisgros is by taking Rua Jardim Botanico, heading in the direction towards Botafogo. Before the end of Rua Jardim Botanico you cross the lights with Rua Maria Angelica, take the next right and you will find Troisgros located on the first corner on the left. If you are coming from Botafogo you should go along the Lagoa and turn up Rua Maria Angelica and into Rua Jardim Botanico.

As long as Claude Troisgros has the stamina as a foreigner to run a restaurant in Rio and another in São Paulo he will constantly produce some of the city's best and most delightful dishes. The opening of Laurent Suaudeau's restaurant Laurent can only help keep Troisgros on his toes. The friendly rivalry of these two great French chefs is an unexpected bonus for all in Rio who like to eat out and eat well.

Hours: 7:30 p.m. to midnight. (Closed on Sunday). **Cuisine:** French. **Telephone:** 226-4542 and 246-7509. **Reservations:** Yes. **Prices:** Expensive. **Credit:** A limited number of major cards.

UN, DEUX, TROIS ★ ★ ★
Rua Bartolomeu Mitre, 123 — Leblon.

Dining at Un Deux Trois should be part of a two part evening, although it does not have to be.

Comfortable if a shade conventional, Un Deux Trois serves a palatable level of international cuisine that can be enjoyed quietly before moving upstairs where an orchestra plays music for dancing.

Un Deux Trois can take a double reservation for the restaurant and nightclub, although each option is available separately.

Un Deux Trois is a short walk from the Marina Palace and Marina Rio Hotels.

Hours: 7 p.m. to 4 a.m. (Lunch served from noon to 4 p.m. at the weekend). **Cuisine:** International. **Telephone:** 239-0198. **Reservations:** Yes. **Prices:** High. **Credit:** All major cards.

VALENTINO'S ★ ★ ★ ★
Rio-Shearton Hotel — Vidigal.

The dinner only Valentino's is the restaurant that the Rio-Sheraton always deserved to give itself and its guests. A restaurant that is slowly becoming ever more popular with the residents of Rio and the guests of this fine hotel.

One of the city's most attractive and comfortable restaurants, and now complimented by the hotel's new lobby and the One-Twenty-One Bar, Valentino's offers a menu of North Italian and international dishes of the highest standards, dishes that cross the border to the *nuova cucina*. And in Sidney Marzullo they have one of Rio's most brilliant dinner pianists.

Last year I said that Valentino's was unlucky not to hit the magic five stars and the same is true this year. Valentino's problem, ironically, is that it is too good for its own good. By that, and this is the feedback I get from the readers, I mean that the menu is just a little bit too complex and sophisticated for the average palate, and average of course means the majority, even among the visitors who come to Rio or the foreign residents who are here the year round.

While I would never normally ask a chef to drop his standards I can't help thinking that Valentino's could and would be enjoyed by more people if the menu was just a little bit more accessible.

If you are a serious gourmet and like to experiment then Valentino's should be close to the top of your list of restaurants to try while in Rio

Hours: 7 p.m. to midnight. **Cuisine:** Italian/International. **Telephone:** 274-1122. **Reservations:** Yes. **Prices:** Expensive. **Credit:** All major cards.

VARANDA ★ ★
Inter-Continental Hotel — São Conrado.

The Varanda restaurant of the Inter-Continental Hotel received a smart facelift in 1986 and now faces a year when it will be challenged by the hotel's outstanding Monseigneur and the newly inaugurated Alfredo di Roma.

Unlike its "competition", Varanda is an open air restaurant by the poolside where daily one of the city's best hot and cold buffets is served at both lunch and dinner. Sadly the price freeze meant that the barbecue selection had to be dropped from the buffet selection but barbecued steaks and seafood can still be ordered separately. For Saturday lunch the buffet is complimented by a traditional *feijoada*.

A must if you are having a lazy day around the hotel pool.

Hours: Noon to 3 p.m. and 7 p.m. to 11 p.m. **Cuisine:** International. **Telephone:** 322-2200. **Reservations:** No. **Prices:** Medium. **Credit:** All major cards.

VIA FARME ★ ★
Rua Farme de Amoedo, 47 — Ipanema.

One of the most satisfactory new restaurants to open in Rio during 1984 was Via Farme.

Proving that appearances can be deceptive, you would never imagine from the road that Via Farme was not just one more of the mediocre Italian restaurants to be found in every corner of the city. In fact Via Farme serves good medium priced Italian dishes which are highlighted by the excellent and interesting seafood selections.

Due to its position, just two blocks back from Ipanema Beach, Via Farme is a popular call for a late lunch or early dinner after time spent on the beach.

Via Farme should rate highly on everyone's list of good medium priced restaurants.

Hours: Noon to 2 a.m. **Cuisine:** Italian. **Telephone:** 227-0743. **Reservations:** No. **Prices:** Medium. **Credit:** All major cards.

VICE REY
Av. Mons. Ascaneo, 535 — Barra da Tijuca.

I give up with Vice-Rey, just when I think it might be a reasonable restaurant I go there and have a terrible meal with joke service and get presented with a wine list that smacks of being a rip off.

At times Vice-Rey is one of Barra's better restaurants, which in all honesty is not saying much, and is the area's only passable seafood restaurant with an image that dates back to Colonial days despite only being constructed in 1976.

Vice Rey promises so much and delivers nothing. Let's hope it changes that in 1987 or its owners pass the restaurant on to somebody who cares.

Hours: Noon to 2 a.m. **Cuisine:** Seafood/International. **Telephone:** 399-1683. **Reservations: No. Prices:** High. **Credit:** No.

LE VIEUX PORT
Rua Souza Lima, 37 — Copacabana.

As Copacabana needs a better selection of better restaurants I was delighted to hear that a new smart seafood restaurant had opened in Souza Lima.

At the time of going to press it was too soon to judge just how bad or good Le Vieux Port is. The day I went it still smelt new and for all I know their regular chef may not have even arrived, the food served being passable but nothing worth noting on your postcards home.

If you are in the area you could do worse and I for one will give it another chance in 1987.

A seafood restaurant with all the suitable nautical effects.

Hours: 1 p.m. to 1 a.m. **Cuisine:** Seafood. **Telephone:** 267 5049 **Reservations:** No. **Prices:** Medium to high. **Credit:** No.

14 BIS
Aeroporto Santos Dumont — Centro.

A lick of paint and some new upholstery would not go amiss at this airport restaurant which should be an interesting option for a lunch and dinner but won't be until the decor is upgraded.

Food is not too bad for an airport but could be better.

Hours: 11 a.m. to midnight. **Cuisine:** International. **Telephone:** 262-6511. **Reservations:** No. **Prices** Medium to high. **Credit:** All major cards.

Oriental Cooking

The best oriental cooking in Brazil is to be found in São Paulo. In Rio there is little to choose and each person seems to have their own favorites amongst the city's Chinese restaurants the most classy of which is Mr. Zee (see review) in General San Martin.

Generally the Japanese restaurants in Rio are of a higher standard than the Chinese and this is especially so of the Edo group and the sushi-bar Mariko in the Caesar Park Hotel.

The city's one Vietnamese restaurant, Le Viet Nam, is excellent but was being refurbished as I went to press with no signs of it re-opening so call them first.

CHINESE

Centro China — Rua Alice, 88 — Laranjeiras (225-5398).
Centro China — Av. Epitacio Pessoa, 1164 — Lagoa (287-3947).
China Town — Av. N.S. de Copacabana, 435 — Copacabana (257-6652).

Chinese Palace — Av. Atlantica, 1212 — Copacabana (275-0145).
Chon Kou — Av. Atlantica, 3880 — Copacabana (287-3956).
Grande Muralha — Rua São Clemente, 409 — Botafogo (266-4402).
Grande Muralha — Barra Shoppoing — Barra da Tijuca (325-2388).
Grande Muralha — Casa Shopping — Barra da Tijuca.
Huang — Rua Souza Lima, 37 — Copacabana (276-5049).
Kong Hwa — Av. N.S. de Copacabana, 1434 — Copcacabana (267-3844).
Mr. Zee — Av. Gen. San Martin, 1219 — Leblon (294-0591).
New Mandarin — Rua Olegario Maciel, 71 — Barra da Tijuca (399-5140).
Oriente — Rua Siqueira Campos, 16-B — Copacabana (255-3446).
Oriente — Rua Souza Lima, 37-A — Copacabana (267-5049).
Oriento — Rua Bolivar, 64 — Copacabana (257-8765).
Pretty China — Rua Siqueira Campos, 12 — Copacabana (235-3157).

JAPANESE

Akasaka — Rua Joaquim Nabuco, 11 — Copacabana (287-3211).
Edo — Estrada da Gavea, 698 — São Conrado (322-4063).
Edo Garden — Av. das Americas, 2578 — Barra da Tijuca (325-3319).
Edo Port — Barra Shopping — Barra da Tijuca.
Haku San — Rua Buenos Aires, 45 — Centro (263-2719).
Mariko (Caesar Park) — Av. Vieria Souto, 460 — Ipanema (287-3122).
Miako — Rua do Ouvidor, 45 — Centro (222-2397).
Miura — Av. Rio Banco, 156 — Centro (262-3043).
Tatsumii Sushi-Bar — Rua Dias Ferreira, 256 — Leblon (274-1342).

VIETNAMESE

Le Viet Nam — Av. Afranio de Melo Franco, 131 — Leblon (239-4491).

Vegetarian/Macrobiotic/Natural/Health Foods

Not so long ago the health conscious gourmet would have had little to choose from in Rio besides the "Natural" chain. Today a number of restaurants and bars claim to look after vegetarian, macrobiotic, and health food tastes. Amongst the best known are:

Le Bon Menu — Rua Araújo Porto Alegre, 71 — Centro.
Health's — Rua dos Beneditinos, 18 — Centro (253-0433).
Greens — Rua do Carmo, 38 — Centro.
Greens — Rua Senador Dantas, 84 — Centro.
Natural — Rua 19 de Fevereiro, 118 — Botafogo (226-9898).
Natural — Rua Barão da Torre, 171 — Ipanema (267-7799).
Sabor Saúde — Av. Ataulfo de Paiva, 630 — Leblon (239-4396).
Vida e Saúde — Rua do Rosário, 142 — Centro (252-3998).
Zan — Travessa do Ouvidor, 25 — Centro (252-6983).

Cheap & Cheerful

Even on a restricted budget you can eat out in Rio and eat well.
The best value in Rio is offered by the pizzarias and cheap Italian restaurants which can be found spread across the city. Their surroundings are normally pleasant and most of the menus stretch to a.

number of international dishes. Nearly all of this type of restaurant open early for lunch. stay open all day, and only close very late at night as well as offering a home delivery service to their immediate neighborhood. Here is a brief guide:

BOTAFOGO

Bella Blu — Rua da Passagem, 44 — 295-9493.
La Mole — Praia de Botafogo, 228 — 235-3366.

COPACABANA & LEME

Bella Blu — Rua Siqueira Campos, 107 — 255-0729
Bella Roma — Av. Atlântica, 928 — 275-2599.
La Mole — Av. N.S. de Copacabana, 552 — 257-5593.
Pizza Pino — Rua Constante Ramos, 22 — 255-4558.

IPANEMA

Pizza Palace — Rua Barão da Torre, 340 — 267-8346.
Raul — Rua Vinicius de Moraes, 71 — 247-5799.
Rio Napolis — Rua Teixeira de Melo, 53 — 267-9909
Romano — Rua Jangadeiros, 6.
Trattoria Torna — Rua Maria Quitéria, 46 — 247-9506.

LAGOA (IPANEMA SIDE)

Gattopardo — Av. Borges de Medeiros, 1426 — 274-7999
Pizza Pino — Av. Epitácio Pessoa, 980.

LEBLON

Bella Blu — Rua General Urquiza, 107 — 274-7895.
Guanabara — Rua Ataulfo de Paiva, 1228 — 294-0797.
La Mamma — Rua Turiba, 43 — 274-7747.
La Mole — Rua Dias Ferreira, 147 — 294-0699
Pronto — Rua Dias Ferreira, 33, 259-7898.

BARRA DA TIJUCA

La Mole — Av. Armando Lombardi, 175 — 399-0625
Tarantella — Av. Sernambetiba, 850 — 399-0995.
Trago Longo — Av. Sernambetiba, 1976 — 399-4668.

Galetos

If you are hungry and want a quick cheap meal that is a bit more nourishing and tasty than the usual junk food you should stop by at one of the many Galetos to be found in Copacabana and Centro.

A Galeto is basically a small churrascaria (barbecue house) where the patrons sit around a center counter from where you can see the meats being cooked.

The cheapest meal, and the house's speciality, is chicken but these small restaurants also serve steaks and other barbecued dishes.

The prices are low and the food usually extremely well cooked.

Fast Food

Junk food in Rio is anything but junky and you can find a hamburger or sandwich bar on just about every corner.

Since opening their first branch a few years back McDonald's have slowly taken over the city and you can now find the golden arches and genuine "Big Macs" in just about every corner of the city, including most of the big shopping centers.

The big Brazilian chains are Bob's and Gordon's and for pizzas the fast growing Mister Pizza chain.

My personal favorite is none of the above but Bonis who have just three branches in Rio serving good snacks and other meals at very reasonable prices. Bonis can be found in Copacabana on the corner of Av. N.S. Copacabana and Rua Siqueira Campos; in Ipanema on the corner of Rua Visconde de Pirajá and Rua Henrique Dumont; and in Barra Shopping.

Another location serving above average snacks is Chaika which is found in Rua Visconde de Pirajá close to Praça da Paz.

Tea for Two, or Three, or Four

In recent years the habit of taking tea in the afternoon has been growing, especially among the women of Rio's high society.

Tea in Rio is served between 4 p.m. and 6 p.m. Among the favorite locations are:

Café de la Paix — Meridien Hotel — Copacabana.
Chá e Simpatia — Rio Palace Hotel — Copacabana
Colombo — Rua Gonçalves Dias, 32 — Centro
Colombo — Av. N.S. de Copacabana, 890 — Copacabana
Lord Jim — Rua Paul Redfern, 63 — Ipanema.
Tiberius — Caesar Park Hotel — Ipanema.

SUGAR LOAF
IT'S MORE THAN YOU IMAGINED

Sugar Loaf is more than a mere symbol of Rio.
It provides not only a dazzling view of the city but also
a complete entertainment center.

Just take the cable car up to the top where a vast array
of services is at your disposal. Facilities include a top-notch
restaurant with a panoramic view, snack bars, and an
amphitheater where musical shows and weekly
presentations by "samba schools" are held.

You can also take a pleasant walk through the tropical
gardens, and don't forget to see the exhibits of
paintings and local arts and crafts.

Call your travel agent and leave a whole day to fully
enjoy the pleasures of the Sugar Loaf.

AO LÁPIS

SUGAR LOAF TOURISM

Av. Pasteur, 520/Praia Vermelha
Informations and Reservations · Phone:
(021) 541-3737 · Telex: (021) 32-896 · PCET-BR

Do you know anyone in Rio?

Maybe you do, or maybe you don't, but whichever is the case you can count on Lloyds Bank's *carioca* branch. Whether you are here as a tourist or on business, or to take up residence we can assist you with our full range of banking services including currency exchange transactions. You are most welcome to visit us at our address below conveniently located in the heart of the City's business centre or just give us a call at (021) 211-2331. We look forward to being of service to you.

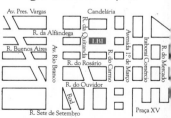

Lloyds Bank

Lloyds Bank in Rio: Rua da Alfândega, 33. Roger R. Seggins, Principal Manager

Entertainment and Night Life

SHOWS — THE BIG NAMES

Musically Brazil is one of the strongest nations in the world and were it not for the language barrier it is certain that Brazilian singers and musicians could give their North American and British counterparts a run for their money on a global scale.

Brazilian music covers an immense spectrum of styles which includes forms as diverse as Brazilian country and western, samba, frevo, all the way to good old rock'n'roll and even Brazilian New Wave.

As Rio is the nation's musical capital you can normally catch some live action even if you are only in town for one night.

Like any musical form Brazilian music of whatever style, takes a little bit of time to get used to but the following "Big" names should be enjoyed by any visitor even if they don't understand the lyrics.

Male: Guilherme Arantes — Jorge Ben — João Bosco — Chico Buarque — Erasmo Carlos -- Roberto Carlos — Djavan — Eduardo Dusek — Fábio Jr. — Fagner — Gilberto Gil — Pepeu Gomes — Gonzaguinha — Leo Jaime — Tom Jobim — Ivan Lins — Ney Matogrosso — Moraes Moreira — Milton Nascimento — Zé Ramalho — Ritchie — Lulu Santos — Toquinho — Alceu Valença.

Female: Amelinha — Maria Bethania — Nana Caymmi — Baby Consuelo — Gal Costa — Fátima Guedes — Nara Leão — Rita Lee — Elba Ramalho — Simone.

Groups: Barão Vermelho — Boca Livre — Cor do Som — Kid Abelha — Legião Urbana — MPB 4 — Paralamas do Sucesso — Roupa Nova — RPM.

Although Brazil has many top samba stars the ones that are most compatible with the "gringo" ear are Beth Carvalho, Alcione, Martinho da Vila and João Nogueira.

Where to See and Hear the Big Names

Despite being the country's music capital Rio is ironically not that well served when it comes to locations for live shows although matters have improved in recent years.

Rio's number one location for shows is Canecão. Inaugurated in 1967 it attracts the top names in the national and international music scene. Canecão can accomodate up to 2400 people sitting at individual tables with full bar service. Tickets for the shows range from $5 up to a maximum of $30 for top international acts although James Taylor, in 1986, did manage to hit the $100 mark, about $50 on the "black market" at the time. Tickets normally go on sale Monday for the coming week's shows, it is rare for Canecão to sell tickets more than seven days in advance.

During 1986 Canecão offered a much greater variety of shows than in past, on some weekend nights as many as three different acts would be performing which, although chaotic at times, did seem to work remarkably well.

Taking over Canecão's mantle, as the showhouse which features lengthy seasons from the top Brazilian stars, is the Scala showhouse in Leblon. Scala is expected to offer a more varied diet in the coming year including several international attractions..

Expected to rival Canecão and Scala in 1987 is the amphitheatre on Morro da Urca, the half-way stage for Sugar Loaf, which is to be totally reformed during the year. Shows take place every Thursday,

Friday and Saturday evenings on Morro da Urca and unlike the past the emphasis is now firmly on the live music and not the disco. Show time, which had been as late as 3 a.m., is now set around 10 p.m. Sugar Loaf offers a full bar and restaurant service.

An excellent location for shows, and one which is tragically under used, is the theatre of the Hotel Nacional which since 1985 has housed the Free Jazz Festival, one of the world's most important gatherings of jazz musicians. Outside the jazz festival the Nacional only normally hosts a couple of international shows a year plus the film festival in November.

On occasions the really big names in Brazilian and international music have to play the Maracanãzinho Gymnasium (capacity — 20,000) to cater for ticket demand and for those fans who can't afford to pay the "high" prices at Canecão and Scala. In 1986 the Praça da Apoteose, where the samba schools parade, was also made good use of for outdoor shows with crowds of over 50,000 present on a number of occasions including memorable concerts by James Taylor and RPM.

The biggest shows of all though are "Rock in Rio" which can attract in excess of 300,000 fans to its purpose built site in Barra da Tijuca which is only likely to be used again in January 1988.

A full list of who is playing where and when can be found in the entertainment sections of *O Globo* and *Jornal do Brasil* under "Show".

The following are the main locations for shows in Rio:

Asa Branca — Rua Mem de Sá, 17 — Lapa (252-4428).
Canecão — Av. Venceslau Braz, 215 — Botafogo (295-3044).
Casa da Cultura Laura Alvim — Av. Vieira Souto, 176 — Ipanema (227-2444).
Casa Grande — Av. Afrânio de Melo Franco, 290 — Leblon (239-4046).
Circo Voador — Largo da Lapa — Lapa.
Estadio do Remo — Av. Borges de Medeiros, 1424 — Lagoa (274-6546).
Golden Room — Av. Copacabana, 327 — Copacabana.
João Caetano — Praça Tiradentes — Centro (221-0305).
Made in Brazil — Av. Armando Lombardi, 1000 — Barra (399-2971).
Maracanãzinho — Rua Prof. Eurico Rabelo — Maracanã (264-9962).
Nacional — Hotel Nacional — São Conrado (322-1000).
Paço Imperial — Praça XV — Centro.
Parque Lage — Rua Jardim Botânico, 414 — Jardim Botânico (226-1879).
Praça da Apoteose — Rua Marquês de Sapucaí — Centro.
Scala II — Av. Afrânio de Melo Franco, 296 — Leblon (239-4448).
Sidney Miller — Rua Araújo Porto Alegre — Centro.
Sugar Loaf — Av. Pasteur, 520 — Urca (541-3737).
Teatro de Arena — Rua Siqueira Campos, 143 — Copacabana (235-5348).
Teatro da Galeria — Rua Senador Vergueiro, 93 — Flamengo (225-8846).
Teatro Ipanema — Rua Prudente de Morais, 824 — Ipanema.
Teatro do Planetário — Av. Padre Leonel França, 240 — Gávea (274-0096).
Teatro Vanucci — Rua Marquês de São Vicente, 52 — Gávea (274-7246).
Teresa Raquel — Rua Siqueira Campos, 143 — Copacabana (235-1113).

For the addresses of Rio's other theatres see "Theatre".

JAZZ AND MUSIC BARS

Brazilian jazz is only one of the strong branches that go to make up the whole musical tree that has made Brazilian music the force it is today, a force that has been felt within the U.S. with the success of amongst others Airto Moreira, Flora Purim, Eumir Deodato, Azymouth and Marcio Montarroyos, and in Europe with Egberto Gismonti and Hermeto Paschoal.

In 1984 the music scene in Rio changed dramatically with the opening of a number of excellent new bars dedicated to presenting jazz and other musical forms in an intimate setting. 1986 saw many news bars join the list while several restaurants, and Equinox and Le Flambard — now The Cattleman — come to mind, put more emphasis on music and less on the food they were serving. Where restaurants have the space you can now find a musician.

This rapid change in Rio's nightlife makes it very difficult to pin-point where you will hear the best music, to say you should play it by ear would probably sound a bit flippant but that is really the best answer.

Of the bars listed below the most important in terms of jazz are Jazzmania in Ipanema and People in Leblon. To give you some idea of the calibre of musician we are taking about Jazzmania staged shows by Pat Metheny, Wynton Marsalis and Wayne Shorter during 1986, the Brazilian talent on offer throughout the rest of the year was their equivalent.

Most of the other bars listed are bars which offer excellent live music but not the big names. The most popular are Chiko's Bar on the Lagoa, an institution in Rio; Alô Alô, Double Dose and Mistura Fina Studio, if it re-opens, in Ipanema; and the Rond Point in Copacabana.

The following all have daily musical programmes in comfortable surroundings. What and who is playing can be found in the entertainment sections of *O Globo* and *Jornal do Brasil* under "Show (Para Ouvir — Bares e Restaurantes)".

Alô Alô — Rua Barão da Torre, 368 — Ipanema (521-1460).
Bateau Mouche Bar — Av. Rep. Nestor Moreira, 111 — Botafogo (295-1997).
Beco da Pimenta — Rua Real Grandeza, 176 — Botafogo (266-5746).
Biblo's — Av. Epitácio Pessoa, 1560 — Lagoa (267-0113).
The Cattleman — Av. Epitácio Pessoa, 864 — Lagoa (259-1041).
Chiko's Bar — Av. Epitacio Pessoa, 1560 — Lagoa (267-0113).
Double Dose — Rua Paul Redfern, 44 — Ipanema (294-9791).
Equinox — Rua Prudente de Morais, 729 — Ipanema (267-2895).
Existe Um Lugar — Estrada das Furnas, 3001 — Barra (399-4588).
Gig Saladas — Av. Gal. San Martin, 629 — Leblon (294-3545).
Horse's Neck Bar — Rio Palace Hotel — Copacabana (521-3232).
Jakui — Hotel Inter-Continental — São Conrado (322-2200).
Jazzmania — Rua Rainha Elizabeth, 769 — Ipanema (227-2447).
Let It Be — Rua Siqueira Campos, 206 — Copacabana.
Mistura Fina Studio — Rua Garcia d'Ávila, 15 — Ipanema (259-9394).
One-Twenty-One — Hotel Sheraton — Vidigal (274-1122).
People — Av. Bartolomeu Mitre, 370 — Leblon (294-0547).
Rond Point — Hotel Meridien — Copacabana (275-9922).
Le Sete — Rua Maria Angelica, 43 — Lagoa (266-1494).
Tiger — Av. Sernambetiba, 4700 — Barra (385-2813).
Un, Deux, Trois — Av. Bartolomeu Mitre, 123 — Leblon (239-0198).
O Viro do Ipiranga — Rua Ipiranga, 54 — Laranjeiras (225-4762).
Vogue — Rua Cupertino Durão, 173 — Leblon (274-8196).
Zeppelin — Estrada do Vidigal — Vidigal (274-1549).

When major international jazz artists are touring Brazil they normally prefer the concert setting of the Sala Cecilia Meireles in

Largo da Lapa or the Sala Sidney Miller in Rua Araújo Porto Alegre.

The Teatro Municipal has also been used for concerts which has seen performances as diverse as Oscar Peterson and Jean-Luc Ponty.

Rio's now famous "Free Jazz Festival" is based on the theatre of the Hotel Nacional and in 1987 is set for September 2 through 7. For more information contact Dueto Productions at Rua Visconde de Pirajá, 146/2° in Ipanema.

PIANO BARS

There are a number of elegant locations in Rio where you can drink and enjoy live background music. If some of the bars located below are also listed under jazz and music bars that is because during the week they tend to place the music in the background rather than in the foreground as they do at the weekend.

Amongst the most popular piano bars are:

Antonino — Av. Epitácio Pessoa, 1244 — Lagoa (267-6791).
Caligola — Praça General Osório — Ipanema (287-1369).
Clube I — Rua Paul Redfern, 40 — Ipanema (259-3148).
Equinox — Rua Prudente de Morais, 729 — Ipanema (247-0580).
Horse's Neck Bar — Rio Palace Hotel — Copacabana (521-3232).
Lobby Bar — Hotel Inter-Continental — São Conrado (322-2200).
Nino's — Barramares — Barra da Tijuca (399-0018).
Palace Club — Rio Palace Hotel — Copacabana.
Petronius — Caesar Park Hotel — Ipanema (287-3122).
Les Relais — Rua Gen. Venâncio Flores, 365 — Leblon (294-2897).
Rio's — Parque do Flamengo — Flamengo (551-1131).
Rive Gauche — Av. Epitacio Pessoa, 1484 — Lagoa (521-2645).
Rond Point — Hotel Meridien — Copacabana (275-9922).
Skylab Bar — Othon Palace Hotel — Copacabana (255-8812).
Valentino's — Hotel Sheraton — Vidigal (274-1122).

VIDEO-BARS

A number of bars and restaurants in Rio have joined the video generation screening everything from films to pirated tapes of MTV.

The most classy, and best organized, location to view videos is Neal's the American bar and restaurant in Botafogo.

Crepusculo de Cubatão — Rua Barata Ribeiro, 543 — Copacabana (235-2045)
Gig Salads — Rua General San Martin, 629 — Leblon.
Jazzmania — Rua Rainha Elizabeth, 769 — Ipanema (227-2447).
Neal's — Rua Sorocaba, 695 — Botafogo (266-6577).
Vídeo-Bar Club — Rua Teresa Guimarães, 92 — Botafogo.

KARAOKÉ

The entertainment — for want of a better word — craze to hit Rio and São Paulo at the end of 1985 was karaoké.

Karaoké, in case you have never heard of it, is where the audience provides the entertainment by going on stage and performing.

A number of bars, namely Canja, Manga Rosa and Limelight, specialize in karaoké while others programme karaoké nights.

If you fancy yourself as a singer — and you are sure to be a hit singing in English — then the following bars should be of interest.

Canja — Av. Ataúlfo de Paiva, 375 — Leblon (511-0484).
Limelight — Rua Min. Viveiros de Castro, 93 — Copacabana (542-3596).
Manga Rosa — Rua 19 de Fevereiro, 94 — Botafogo (266-4996).
Vogue — Rua Cupertino Durão, 173 — Leblon (274-4145).

ROCK IN RIO

1985's "Rock in Rio" was one of the largest, if not the largest, musical festival ever staged. Many of the top names in Brazilian music performed over the festival's ten days alongside such international stars as AC/DC, George Benson, B-52s, GoGos, Iron Maiden, Al Jarreau, Queen, Scorpions, Rod Stewart, James Taylor and Yes.

Most of the shows attracted crowds in excess of 150,000 to the purpose built festival site next to Riocentro in Barra da Tijuca. On the first Saturday of "Rock in Rio," January 12, 1985, the crowd numbered 340,000 to see Ivan Lins, Elba Ramalho, Gilberto Gil, Al Jarreau, James Taylor and George Benson perform.

At the time of going to press it is expected that "Rock in Rio II" will take place in Rio during January 1988. Amongst the names mentioned for "Rock in Rio II" are Elton John, Lionel Ritchie, Duran Duran and Dire Straits as well as the return of Queen and James Taylor.

For more information about "Rock in Rio II" contact the organizer, Artplan, at Rua Fonte da Saudade, 329 in Rio (Telex: 021 30686).

DANCING A LA FAME, FLASHDANCE AND FOOTLOOSE.

A disco is a disco in anybody's language although in Rio you will find the international hits intermixed with the most danceable and up-to-date Brazilian sounds.

A few of the town's top dance spots like Hippopotamus, the Palace Club, Regine, and Studio C are private clubs but if you are staying at one of the five star hotels they should be able to arrange a temporary membership for you. The other chic discotheque in Rio is Calígola, below the Le Streghe restaurant in Ipanema.

Less formal, and appealing to a younger crowd, are Help on the beachfront in Copacabana and La Dolce Vita in Barra da Tijuca. In São Conrado the favorites are the nightclubs of the Inter-Continental (Papillon) and Nacional (Apocalypse) hotels and Zoom.

The "darks" and other new wave groups have as their temple Crepusculo de Cubatão in Copacabana (part owned by the British train robber Ronald Biggs) and the Robin Hood Pub in Alto da Boa Vista, while a more singles orientated disco is Bibo's on the Lagoa.

Other popular discos in Rio are Circus and Mikonos.

The following locations offer dancing for the young and young at heart. * denotes a private club.

Apocalypse — Hotel Nacional — São Conrado (322-1000).
Biblo's — Av. Epitácio Pessoa, 1484 — Lagoa (521-2545).
Caligola — Praça General Osório — Ipanema (287-1369).
Champagne — Rua Siqueira Campos, 225 — Copacabana (256-7341).
Charles Max — Rua Barão da Torre, 344 — Ipanema (227-9836).
Circus — Rua General Urquiza, 102 — Leblon (274-7895).
Crepusculo de Cubatão — Rua Barata Ribeiro, 543 — Copacabana (235-2045).
La Dolce Vita — Av. Ministro Ivan Lins, 80 — Barra (399-0105).
Help — Av. Atlântica, 3432 — Copacabana (521-1296).
Hippopotamus* — Rua Barão da Torre, 354 — Ipanema.
Metropolis — Praça de São Conrado — São Conrado.
Miami City — Av. Sernambetiba, 646 — Barra (399-4007).
Mikonos — Rua Cupertinho Durão, 177 — Leblon (294-2298).
Mistura Fina — Estrada da Barra da Tijuca, 1636 — Barra (399-3460).

Palace Club* — Rio Palace Hotel — Copacabana (267-5048).
Papillon — Hotel Inter-Continental — São Conrado (322-2200).
Regine * — Hotel Meridien — Copacabana (275-9922).
Robin Hood Pub — Av. Edson Passos, 4517 — Alto da Boa Vista (268-8357)
Studio C * — Hotel Othon Palace — Copacabana (236-0695).
Zoom — Praça São Conrado, 20 — São Conrado. (322-4179).

DANCING A LA FRED ASTAIRE AND GINGER ROGERS

There are a number of locations in Rio which cater for those of a more geriatric disposition who would like to trip the light fantastic and perhaps dine out at the sametime.

Asa Branca — Mem de Sá, 15 — Lapa (252-4428).
Bateau Mouche — Av. Reporter Nestor Moreira, 111 — Botafogo (295-1997).
Carinhoso — Rua Visc. de Pirajá, 22 — Ipanema (287-0302).
Rive Gauche — Av. Epitácio Pessoa, 1484 — Lagoa (247-9993).
Sobre As Ondas — Av. Atlântica, 3432 — Copacabana (521-1296).
Un. Deux, Trois — Av. Bartolomeu Mitre, 123 — Leblon (239-0198).
Vinicius — Av. N. S. de Copacabana, 1144 — Copacabana (267-1497).

SAMBA

You can't come to Rio without coming into contact with Samba It would be like going to New York and not going to Broadway , or going to London and not visiting a pub, or even worse going to Paris and avoiding French restaurants.

If you come to Rio at Carnival your immersion into samba will be complete. You will eat, sleep and even make love to its incessant beat. It takes over the entire city until at the end of all the madness even the most straight-laced and stilted visitors samba their way back on to the plane. Samba has a magic spell. Samba is an art form, a complete art form.

Samba is music, literature, and dance all rolled into one. The music and literature is easy to explain, simply every samba tells a story, be it told by one solitary *sambista* or by the 4000 that go to make up one of the samba schools that parade during Carnival.

And the dance?

Let's just say for the moment that once you have heard a true samba you will know the answer, or at least your feet and body will.

Martinho da Vila, one of Brazil's greatest *sambistas* once told me about the importance of the dance. "It takes over when language is no longer sufficient to express feeling," says da Vila. "It is fundamental to the spirit of the body."

If you arrive in Rio just before or during Carnival them samba will neatly fall into place. But what if you are one of the vast number of tourists and visitors who won't be in Rio at this time. What should you do?

Basically a visitor has a choice. Either he can head for one of the tourist shows which offer a little bit of every Brazilian flavor or he can go in search of the genuine article.

In the past the "real thing" required travelling deep into the *zona norte* to the samba schools themselves, but since 1983 this has changed.

The biggest change is what is known as "Clube do Samba" to be found at Estrada da Barra da Tijuca, 65 in Barra. Operated and organized by the top names in samba. "Clube do Samba" offers a full programme Wednesday through Sunday with major stars appearing at the weekend.

If you haven't got a car go by cab or get the hotel to organize a radio cab to take you and return to pick you up at a later hour. Make sure it is much later though. For details of what is happening at ''Clube do Samba'' call 399-0892 or look in the newspaper.

The other weekly samba happening, and the city's most popular, is the performance of the Beija-Flor samba school up Morro da Urca on a Monday night. What more could you ask for than for one of Rio's top samba schools to have as its backdrop one of the world's most spectacular views. A unique experience I promise you.

With Beija-Flor you are only seeing a small core of what you would see at Carnival but it does help to give an idea of the feeling and color that goes in to making Carnival one of the modern wonders of the world.

During the year Beija-Flor presents its show every Monday night starting with a video presentation at around 9 p.m. which is followed by the show itself at 10:30 p.m. Dinner is served in the Cota 200 restaurant from 8 p.m.

You can either visit the Beija-Flor show as part of an organized evening excursion or go by yourself by cab or car. Reservations on 541-3737.

In the high season Beija-Flor also normally perform on Thursday evenings and is set to appear next to the drive-in cinema on the Lagoa on Saturday from 9:30 p.m.

You may of course be the type of traveller who has to see the real thing, and so you should if you are going to stay in Rio for any length of time.

Most of the big samba schools are delighted to welcome visitors but it is wise to check their programme in advance, they may wish to rehearse in secret for Carnival for example.

Nearly all of Rio's samba schools are situated deep in the *zona norte* so ask the advice of your hotel receptionist or a resident about which would be the most convenient for you to visit. The three nearest will amost certainly be Mangueira, close to the Maracanã stadium, Salgueiro in Tijuca and Vila Isabel in Vila Isabel.

Beija Flor — Rua Wallace Paes Leme, 1652 — Nilopolis (791-1571).
Caprichosos de Pilares — Rua dos Saleiros — Pilares (233-4489).
Estácio de Sá — Rua Miguel de Frias — Cidade Nova (273-3644).
Imperatriz Leopoldinense — Rua Professor Lace, 235 — Ramos.
Império Serrano — Av. Min. Edgar Romero, 114 — Madureira (359-4944).
Mangueira — Rua Visconde de Niteroi — Maracanna (234-4129).
Mocidade Independente — Rua Cel. Tamarindo, 38 — Padre Miguel (332-5823).
Portela — Rua Clara Nunes, 81 (Portelão) — Madureira (371-0083).
Salgueiro — Rua Silva Teles, 104 — Tijuca (246-8604).
União da Ilha — Rua Copiuva, 120 — Ilha do Governador (351-3132).
Vila Isabel — Rua Barão de São Francisco, 236 — Vila Isabel (268-7052).

If you want to take photos of sambistas them go and see Beija-Flor at Sugar Loaf, that is what they are there for. If you go to a samba school proper leave the ''tourist'' in you back at the hotel and go for the fun and experience.

SHOWS FOR THE VISITOR

Besides the shows of Beija-Flor at Sugar Loaf, Rio offers three other major productions that are aimed at the visitor to Rio be they

Brazilian, South America, European or North American, and language is not a barrier to their enjoyment.

Rio's richest show, and one that covers carnival and the folklore of Brazil, is "Brasil de Todos Os Tempos" (Brazil Throughout the Ages) at Plataforma 1 above the Churrascaria Leblon in Leblon. Both Plataforma and the show have been completely reformed in the last twelve months. Show times is 11 p.m.

Rio's other major show, which opened in 1984, is "Golden Rio" at the Scala in Leblon.

Featuring Watusi, a Brazilian singer who made her name in Paris, and Grande Othelo, one of Brazil's most famous actors who has over 150 films to his credit, this beautifully dressed show takes you on a musical tour of Rio and Brazilian folklore, including Carnival, Gafieira, Rio by night, Bahia, bossa nova, plus Rio's famous mulatas and the *bateria* (percussion section) from the Mangueira samba school.

The Scala itself is one Rio's most elegant and comfortable showhouse. If you want, you can enjoy dinner before the show or just go for the show which normally gets underway around 11 p.m. Dancing continues after the show through until 4 a.m.

I can't see any visitor or resident not enjoying "Brazil Throughout the Ages" or "Golden Rio", which can easily hold their own with anything presented at Radio City in New York.

Rio's most traditional show is found at Oba-Oba who in 1984 moved from Ipanema to larger premises at Largo Humaita at the top end of the Lagoa.

Oba Oba's show is aimed at an older audience, or rather not for children, and features mulatas samba and Carnival.

If you have got the time you should try and catch all three shows plus Beija-Flor, and as they are presented nightly that should not be a problem.

Most of the tour companies run night tours to Scala, Plataforma and Oba-Oba, or you yourself can make a reservation and go by cab, none of the showhouses being far from the main hotel areas.

Oba-Oba — Rua Humaitá, 110 — Botafogo (286-9848).
Plataforma 1 — Rua Adalberto Ferreira, 32 — Leblon (274-4022).
Scala — Av. Afrânio de Mello Franco, 292 — Leblon (239-4448).

THE MORE ERUDITE ARTS

For the lovers of ballet, opera and classical music, Brazil, and particularly Rio, is no cultural backwater boasting its own very fine ballet and opera companies and a number of top rate orchestras and soloists. Rio is also on the tour circuit and attracts the top names in all the afore mentioned art forms.

Dance fans should head to the Teatro Municipal which is home to the city's fine ballet troupe under the direction of Dalal Achcar and her ballet master Desmond Doyle. The company performs not only a standard classical repertoire but also presents new works which include ballets based around the classics of Brazilian literature such as, *Gabriela*.

The Rio company attracts guest soloists of the very highest caliber to dance with them, and you will be more than pleasantly surprised at how accessible ticket prices are for an evening of world class entertainment.

The Teatro Municipal also hosts the city's opera company who normally perform six or more works during the year. Like the ballet company the opera company attracts top names from around the world to compliment its own talents.

The world of classical music has two main homes in Rio; the Teatro Municipal for large orchestral presentations and the smaller

Sala Cecilia Meirelles for chamber orchestras and soloists.

Rio has several orchestras, the main ones being the Brazilian Symphony Orchestra (OSB) and the Orchestra of the Municipal Theatre. The work of these two are complimented by visits from such diverse talents as Jean Pierre-Rampal, the New York and Vienna Philharmonics.

The following are the main theatres involved in the erudites arts:

Teatro Municipal (Ballet, Opera, Classical and Erudite Music) — Praça do Florinao — Centro (210-2463).
Sala Cecilia Meirelles (Jazz, Classical and Erudite Music) — Largo da Lapa, 47 — Centro (232-9714).
Teatro João Caetano (Ballet, Opera, Classical and Erudite Music) — Praça Tiradentes — Centro (221-0305).
Teatro Villa Lobos (Ballet and Dance) — Av. Princesa Isabel, 430 — Leme (275-6695).
Teatro Nelson Rodrigues (Ballet and Dance) — Av. Chile, 230 — Centro (212-5695).
Nacional (Ballet) — Hotel Nacional — São Conrado (322-1000).
Teatro Dulcina (Classical and Erudite Music) — Rua Alcindo Guanabara, 17 — Centro (220-6997).
Paço Imperial (Classical and Erudite Music) — Praça XV — Centro.
Casa Laura Alvim (Classical and Erudite Music, Dance) — Av. Vieira Souto, 176 — Ipanema (227-2444).

The full programme for what is going on in the "Erudite World" can be found in the entertainment sections of *O Globo* and *Jornal do Brasil* under "Dança", "Opera" and "Musica".

In 1987 we can expect a repeat of the very successful International Ballet Festivals which packed the Teatro Municipal throughout the months of April and May in 1985 and 1986.

THEATRE

Brazil has been blessed with many fine actors and actresses, a few of whom, such as Sonia Braga, Marilia Pera, and Claudia Ohana, have made a name for themselves in the U.S. and Europe through Brazilian films. But Brazilian drama is more than film and television, it is also live drama.

Unfortunately for the short term visitor it is impossible to learn enough Portuguese to understand a local production, but for those who stay longer it is worth devoting the occasional night to the theatre even if you start with a translated work or musical.

The main theatres in Rio for live drama are:

Arena — Rua Siqueira Campos, 143 — Copacabana (235-5348).
Cacilda Becker — Rua do Catete, 338 — Catete (265-9933).
Candido Mendes — Rua Joana Angelica, 63 — Ipanema (227-9882).
Clara Nunes — Gavea Shopping — Gavea (274-9696).
Copacabana — Av. Copacabana, 313 — Copacabana (257-0881).
Copacabana Palace — Av. Copacabana, 327 — Copacabana (255-7070).
Delfim — Rua Humaitá, 275 — Humaitá.
Dulcina — Rua Alcindo Guanabara, 17 — Centro (220-6997).
Galeria — Rua Senador Vergueiro, 93 — Flamengo (225-8846).
Ginastico — Av. Graça Aranha, 187 — Cnetro (220-8394).
Glauce Rocha — Av. Rio Branco, 179 — Centro (220-0259).
Glaucio Gil — Praça Cardeal Arcoverde — Centro (237-7003).
Gloria — Rua do Russel, 632 — Gloria (245-5527).
Ipanema — Rua Prudente de Morais, 824 — Ipanema (247-9794).

Lagoa — Av. Borges de Medeiros — Lagoa (274-7999).
Maison de France — Av. Pres. Antonio Carlos, 58 — Centro.
Mesbla — Rua do Passeio, 42 — Centro (240-6141).
Nelson Rodrigues — Av. Chile, 230 — Centro (212-5695).
Paço Imperial — Praça XV — Centro.
Parque Lage — Rua Jardim Botanico, 414 — Jardim Botanico (226-1879).
Praia — Rua Francisco Sá, 88 — Copacabana (267-7749).
Quatro — Gavea Shopping — Gavea (239-1095).
Senac — Rua Pompeu Loureiro, 45 — Copacabana (256-2641).
Serrador — Rua Sendor Dantas, 13 — Centro (220-5033).
Teresa Raquel — Rua Siqueira Campos, 143 — Copacabana (235-1113).
Vanucci — Gavea Shopping — Gavea (274-7246).
Villa Lobos — Av. Princesa Isabel, 430 — Leme (275-6695).

A full list of what is being performed around the theatres can be found in the entertainment sections of *O Globo* and *Jornal do Brasil* under "Teatro".

TELEVISION

Brazil has one of the highest standards of television anywhere in the world, a fact that is reflected by TV Globo being the fourth largest network behind only the big American three.

In Rio we currently have six stations, these being TV Educativa (Canal 2), TV Globo (Canal 4), TV Manchete (Canal 6), TV Bandeirantes (Canal 7), TV Record (Canal 9) and TVS (Canal 11).

All television is in the Portuguese language except when somebody is singing, or a film is left with its original soundtrack and subtitles added. You may, however, wish to catch a sports programme, the local coverage is excellent, or a news programme to check that the world is how you left if.

The channel whose news is easiest to follow for the non-Portuguese speaker is that of TV Globo (7:45 p.m. to 8:20 p.m.).

All channels compete furiously in their sports coverage with soccer, motor racing, basketball, volleyball and tennis all being particularly popular.

RADIO

Rio has far too many radio stations to list but it is fair to note that the best are to be found on the FM wave band. The most popular FM stations in Rio, which play the latest hits from the American and Brazilian charts are 98 (98,1 Mhz) and Cidade (102.9 Mhz). What you hear on 98 and Cidade is what the zone sul are buying. Other popular stations include Manchete (89.3 Mhz), Globo (92.5 Mhz), and FM 105 (105.1) while the heavy rock fans prefer to tune to Fluminense (94.9 Mhz).

For those of more erudite tastes your choice should be Radio Jornal do Brasil (99.7 Mhz) whose daily programme is listed in the *Jornal do Brasil*.

One third of all the music played by any station must be Brazilian, which is no hardship considering the amount of musical talent Brazil has as its disposal. However the not so good news for the non-Portuguese speaker is that all stations have to broadcast the government's news programme. "Agencia Nacional", between 7 p.m. and 8 p.m. during the week.

If you have a Short Wave radio, you will be able to tune in to other stations around the world including the Voice of America and the B.B.C. World Service. The B.B.C. can be picked up in Rio on 15.26 Mhz, 12.04 Mhz, 11.75 Mhz, 9.91 Mhz, 9.60 Mhz, and 6.00 Mhz.

CINEMA

As one of the world's major movie markets — ninth to be exact — the big American and European releases quickly find their way to Brazil where, I am happy to report, they are left with their original soundtracks, only Portuguese subtitles being added.

Foreign movies are popular in Brazil, especially in Rio and São Paulo, so expect to stand in line at the weekend for the week's big release. There are no cinemas in Rio that accept advance bookings.

To check what is showing around town look in the daily entertainment section of either *Jornal do Brasil* or *O Globo* under "Cinema". The names are clearly given in English.

The best cinemas in Rio in terms of comfort and sound are: —

Downtown: Metro Boavista.
Flamengo and Botafogo: Largo do Machado I & II — São Luiz I & II — Veneza.
Copacabana: Condor Copacabana — Roxy — Ricamar — Studio Gaumont.
São Conrado: Art, I, II, III & IV.
Barra da Tijuca: Art I, II & III — Barra I, II & III.

CINEMAS/MOVIE HOUSES

DOWNTOWN

Metro Boavista — Rua do Passeio, 62 (240-1291).
Odeon — Praça Mahatma Gandhi, 62.
Palácio I & II — Rua do Passeio, 40 (240-6541).
Pathé — Praca de Floriano, 45 (220-3135).

FLAMENGO & BOTAFOGO

Botafogo — Rua Voluntários da Pátria, 35 (266-4491).
Cineclube Estação Botafogo — Rua Voluntários da Pátria, 35 (286-6149).
Coper Botafogo — Rua Voluntários da Pátria, 88.
Coral — Praia de Botafogo, 316.
Largo do Machado I & II — Largo do Machado, 29 (205-6842).
Lido I & II — Praia do Flamengo, 72.
Ópera I & II — Praia de Botafogo, 340 (552-4945).
Paissandu — Rua Senador Vergueiro, 35 (265-4653).
São Luiz I & II — Rua do Catete, 307 (285-2296).
Scala — Praia de Botafogo, 320 (266-2545).
Studio Gaumont Catete — Rua do Catete, 228 (205-7194).
Veneza — Av. Pasteur, 184 (295-8349).

COPACABANA

Art-Copacabana — Av. Copacabana, 759 (235-4895).
Bruni Premier — Rua Barata Ribeiro, 502 (266-4588).
Cinema I — Av. Prado Júnior, 281 (295-2889).
Condor Copacabana — Rua Figueiredo Magalhães, 286 (255-2610).
Copacabana — Av. Copacabana, 801 (255-0953).
Jóia — Av. Copacabana, 680.
Rian — Av. Atlântica, 2964 (Under Construction).
Ricamar — Av. Copacabana, 360 (237-9932).
Roxy — Av. Copacabana, 945 (236-6245).
Studio Gaumont Copacabana — Rua Raul Pompeia, 102 (247-8900).

IPANEMA, LEBLON & GÁVEA

Bruni Ipanema — Rua Visc. de Pirajá, 371 (521-4690).
Cândido Mendes — Rua Joana Angélica, 63 (227-9882).
Lagoa Drive-In — Av. Borges de Medeiros, 1426 (274-7999).
Leblon 1 & II — Av. Ataulfo de Paiva, 391 (239-5048).
Rio-Sul — Gávea Shopping (274-4532).

SÃO CONRADO

Art. I, II, III & IV — São Conrado Fashion Mall (322-1258).

BARRA DA TIJUCA

Barra I, II & III — Barra Shopping (325-6487).
Art I, II & III — Casa Shopping (325-0746).

INTERNATIONAL FESTIVAL OF FILM, TV AND VIDEO

In 1984, Rio staged its first "International Festival of Film, TV and Video" (FESTRIO), which was such a success that it has now been confirmed as a yearly event. It is one of the world's most important festivals ranking alongside Cannes, Venice, Berlin, Montreal and Moscow.

FESTRIO, which screens over 300 films in ten days, is based on the convention center of the Hotel Nacional, while another 20 theatres around the city are used for parallel screenings

In 1987, FESTRIO is scheduled to take place in November.

For more information about FESTRIO contact the organizers who are based at the Hotel Nacional — Av. Niemeyer, 769 in São Conrado. Tel. 322-1000. Telex: 021 23615.

FOR HIS EYES ONLY (WHERE THE BOYS ALL GO ON A SATURDAY NIGHT)

This is the part of the guide a lot of you have been waiting for where I deal with man's indiscriminate lust for women and even man's indiscriminate lust for man. If you don't want to know more about what can be a fairly touchy subject in some households I suggest you avert your eyes and skip on to the next section of the book, that way nobody gets hurt or offended.

Rio has several areas which can loosely be described as "red light districts." Some, for example, around the docks, you would not wish upon your own worst enemy, while others, Copacabana for instance, can be a source of endless late night entertainment.

As Copacabana is the only area that should attract you, let us start and end there.

The raunchier fun sports of Copacabana can be found in a compact area that runs from Rua Duvivier through to Av. Princesa Isabel, or as you look from the beach from behind the Hotel Lancaster up to the Hotel Meridien.

Unlike most large cities, Rio's raunchier side is kept fairly discreet, at least from the street, so that a walk through the area, even at night, is unlikely to upset anyone including women and children. As a matter of fact a large school is located in Praça Lido which makes up the heart of Copacabana's "red light district."

Most of the clubs have fairly innocuous names, no windows, and certainly no lurid posters or such like. Remember we are in Catholic Brazil!

"Step into my parlour"

Most of the clubs clearly state at their doors that nobody under 18 can enter and keep it that way to protect their license.

Individually the clubs bill themselves as offering all manner of entertainment. Some would like to be listed as discotheques, others as night-clubs or bars with music, even cabarets, although the more honest admit to offering erotic shows and strip tease.

The easiest way to find out what is happening around Praça Lido — officially Praça Bernardeli — is to experiment, especially as the live entertainment tends to change with the fashions.

Most of the clubs are used to dealing with foreigners so you will normally find one member of the staff who has a little bit of English. It is important before sitting down to order a drink to find out exactly, what you will be paying for. Agree a price and stick to it The price includes the artistic cover and a certain number of drinks, probably two. The price for your "two" drinks will be the same whether you drink water or vodka.

It is difficult to quote a price for you to go by because the clubs invariably try and charge what they think they can get away with, but in dollar terms it won't be high. At the end of 1986 a Portuguese speaking foreigner would have been paying around $10. That includes the show and two drinks. Hardly a fortune to spend!

If you don't like the sound of the deal you are being offered, leave, there are plenty of other places in a short distance you can try, and they know it. You, however, should know what your limits are, both financially and otherwise and stick to them.

The shows in Copacabana run the whole spectrum of erotic entertainment from the simple strip down to live sex acts.

Here is a quick guide to the area, most of these clubs offer a show of one kind or another but a few just have taped music and you make your own entertainment!

Working from Rua Duvivier to Av. Princesa Isabel the clubs are:

Rua Duvivier: Baccara — Munich — Don Juan, **Av. Atlântica:** Holliday, **Praça Bernardeli (Lido)** — Sherazade — Golden Club — Lido — Pussy Cat — Barman, **Av. Prado Júnior:** Erotika — Sunset — Plaza — Malvina's Bar; **Av. N. S. de Copacabana:** Bataclan; **Av. Princesa Isabel:** Night and Day — New Scotch — Frank's Bar — Barbarella — Boite Hi-Fi; **Rua Gustavo Sampaio (Behind the Meridien):** Swing.

Most, or to be honest all, of the bars mentioned above are filled with "friendly" young girls. Happily the girls in Rio are not pushy. The girls will strike up a conversation at your table or wait until you make the first approach. Virtually all are engaged in the world's oldest profession so don't be unfair and monopolise the goods all evening unless you are going to "buy" them. In most of the bars the girls will be willing to give you thirty minutes or more of their time to see if you are interested. Many of the girls speak English. The cost of the girls varies but if you budget what it costs to fill the gas tank of a Monza you won't be far wrong. (**Note:** To save General Motors being inundated with further phone calls the capacity of the Monza tank is 62 litres, which is about 16 1/2 gallons.)

Rio's "red light" bars are what you make of them. If you want to go in and score quickly that is up to you, but if you want to go in with a group and be entertained by an erotic and normally humorous show and enjoy a few drinks with some extremely attractive young ladies, then that is also possible.

Those bars which offer a show and the Holliday comes to mind, also welcome wives and girlfriends, although unaccompanied women would be advised to stay away.

If you leave one of the bars with your new "lady friend" you would do as well to remember that most of the respectable hotels will not look kindly on your behaviour, it is therefore advisable to ask the young lady for some suggestions as to where to go, I am sure she will not be short of ideas! If you have a car there are of course the motels to go to, and I will deal with them separately below.

While on the subject of "steppin' out" I do advise any gentlemen who enjoys purchasing women to avoid picking "goods" up from the side of the road. You will get a very nasty shock when you get to your final destination to discover the "she" is a "he" as most of them are "travesties". If you want a real genuine lady stick to the Copacabana bars or the saunas (*termas*) and escort agencies that advertise in most of the "tourist" press.

Gay Rio

Those of a less heterosexual nature should head for the opposite end of Copacabana, to the bars around the mouth, and in, the Galeria Alaska (Av. N.S. de Copacabana, 1241). The Galeria Alaska houses the Teatro Alaska which normally has a gay, transvestite show as does the Teatro Brigitte Blair in the Travessa Cristiano Lacorte off Rua Miguel Lemos. Opposite the Teatro Brigitte Blair is the popular bar called "The Club."

Another popular "gay" night spot, but only on Friday nights, is the Papagaio Disco at Av. Borges de Medeiros, 1426, next to the Drive-In cinema on the Lagoa.

The most popular gay part of the beach in Copacabana is in front of the Copacabana Palace Hotel while in Ipanema it centers around Rua Farme de Amoedo and runs down to Rua Vinicius de Moraes.

Saunas (Termas)

Rio's commercial saunas, as advertised in the "tourist" press, are well run and well equipped and the male and female receptionists will cater for your *every* need. The only problem for the patron seems to be in discovering which of the saunas are heterosexual and which are gay. To avoid unnecessary embarrassment ask your hotel porter for his recommendation.

Motels

The motels of Rio could have been included in the "Typically But Uniquely Brazilian" section of this guide, because indeed they are unique.

Brazilian motels are designed not for the weary traveller but for lovers. And if you think there is something tacky about that you could not be more wrong.

Motels sprang up in Rio about twelve years ago, Brazil's answer to the permissive society. The original demand came from young couples who found it difficult to leave the confines of their family home before marriage.

While the motels are still predominantly used by young couples they are also frequented by married couples looking for a bit of piece and quiet away from the children, the maid and the telephone, and let us be honest, couples who are indulging in a little extra-marital sex.

Most of the motels in Rio are situated on the access roads to the city, the most popular area for the *zona sul* being Barra da Tijuca and the Joá area. Rio's most famous motel is VIP's located on the Av. Niemeyer between the Sheraton and Nacional hotels. VIP's is five star luxury all the way as is the Hawaii at Estrada da Barra da Tijuca, 3186. Both motels have exceptionally luxurious suites which cost around $30 for six hours or $70 for 24 hours. The suites all feature private swimming pools and sauna.

A standard apartment in one of the better motels will cost you around $18-a-day, but before you rush to move from your hotel let me warn you that they really won't be that happy to see you after the first 24 hours.

Other well known Rio motels in the Barra area are King's, Mayflower, Playboy, Duna's and Orly, and in the city, Ebony in Rua da Glória, 46, which even gives you a mask to wear in the elevator as the apartments don't have separate garages as in Barra.

1985 saw the introduction of perhaps the ultimate motel/sauna, "Ilha da Fantasia" (Fantasy Island).

Fantasy Island is located in Barra at Av. Armando Lombardi, 20. For more information call 252-8742, 232-1314, or 399-1293.

If you are in Rio for any length of time do yourself, your girlfriend, or even your wife (!) a favor and visit a motel, preferably in a suite. You will have a lot of fun and some rather unique memories of Rio.

Carnival

Rio de Janeiro's Carnival is larger, livelier, louder and more incredible than anything one can possibly imagine.

Even living in Rio for the eleven months prior to Carnival is no preparation for what happens in the weeks surrounding it and despite appearances, or what you may have read in magazines and newspapers, Rio's carnival is not an event designed to attract foreign tourists nor is it violent or dangerous. Carnival is a genuine national celebration which for the Brazilians is more important than Christmas, New Year and Easter all rolled into one.

It is probably the size of Carnival that first over-whelms the foreign visitor. It is not an event that is restricted to one area of the city, or one social group, but is a celebration, party if you like, that takes over the entire population of a city that is one of the ten largest in the world.

To survive Carnival in Rio you are going to need an awful lot of stamina, a fair amount of money, and a touch of good humour.

But what is Carnival?

Well other than the general air of madness that pervades the city, Carnival has three main ingredients and they are the parade, the balls, and the street.

Officially Carnival is scheduled to run from the Saturday before Ash Wednesday through to mid-day on the Wednesday. Today the reality is different however with the first major ball of the season taking place on the Friday of the proceeding week at the yacht club.

Non-stop Carnival activity starts on the Thursday before Carnival with the "Black and Red Ball" at the Flamengo soccer club and continues uninterrupted through Wednesday which has now become a day of rest and recuperation for the following weekend when the winners parade takes place on Saturday night through to late Sunday morning.

In 1987 Carnival proper will run from Thursday, February 26 through Wednesday, March 4, with the winners parade on Saturday, March 7. In 1988 the main Carnival dates are February 11 through Wednesday, February 17.

CARNIVAL BALLS

As it is the balls that get Carnival underway let us have a look at them first.

Rio's Carnival balls are elaborate costume parties which start around 11 p.m. and carry on through until 5 a.m. or later. The balls are propelled and driven by the never ending samba beat supplied by live groups who continuously change personnel to insure that the music never stops.

Don't be at all surprised if at your first ball the music all sounds the same because by your second you will begin to recognize the individual songs and even have your own favorites.

Every club or suitable hall holds a Carnival ball but the city, as you would imagine, does have a definite circuit of "fashionable" balls and these are the ones the foreign visitor should head for.

The Yacht Club: It is the traditional "Hawaiian Ball" of the Rio Yacht Club (*Iate Clube do Rio de Janeiro*) that gets Carnival activities underway on the Friday the week before Carnival. February 21 in 1987 and February 6 in 1988.

Set around the club's large swimming pool, under a moon-lit sky and gently swaying palm trees, the "Hawaiian Ball" is one of the most lavish and beautiful of all the balls and in recent years one of the best behaved.

Tickets can only be purchased from the Yacht Club itself in Av. Pasteur in Botafogo.

Flamengo: Flamengo is Rio's most popular soccer team and they hold a series of balls over Carnival in their gymnasium close to the Lagoa.

Flamengo's most important ball is the "Black and Red" (team colors) which takes place on the Thursday before Canival, February 26 in 1987 and February 11 in 1988.

Over the last few years the "Black and Red" has been the most frenetic of all the balls with the behavior at times bordering on double X or worse. If you are at all prudish this is the one Carnival event to stay away from.

Because the "Black and Red" is the opening event of uninterrupted Carnival activity it is a big event for the media who get their first opportunity to see which celebrities are in town, a Miss World or two perhaps, and almost certainly a number of top names from the rock world and a few from Hollywood for good measure.

Tickets from the club are reasonably priced at $30-a-couple with the lesser balls at around $ 15.

Pão de Açucar (*Sugar Loaf*): Sugar Loaf's Carnival ball may be one of the most expensive — $75-a-head — but it is also one of the most spectacular when the truly beautiful people of Rio get together in one of the city's most lovely settings.

Organized by Guilherme Araujo, the "Sugar Loaf Ball", of which this will be the ninth, traditionally takes place on the Friday, in 1987 that will be February 27 and in 1988, February 12.

Tickets for the ball are sold from Araujo's office in Rua Visconde de Pirajá, 414/909 in Ipanema. Tel. 287-7749.

Scala: Chico Recarey very astutely picked up a number of Carnival balls in 1984 to help launch the Scala which in just a few years has become one of the main centers of Carnival activities.

As of going to press it is still unclear which balls the Scala will host, although it is certain that it will host one everynight.

Tickets and more information are available from the Scala box-office. Scala is located at Av. Afranio de Mello Franco, 292. Tel. 274 9148.

Champagne Ball: One of the big hits of Carnival is the *Baile do Champagne* organized by Humberto Saade, the carismatic owner of the exclusive Dijon chain of shops. It is likely that the *Baile do Champagne* in 1987 will take place at the Scala on February 25.

Tickets and information from the Dijon stores or from the world headquarters in Rua Farme de Amoedo.

Monte Libano: A large private club on the Ipanema shore of the Lagoa, Monte Libano, like the Scala, holds a series of important balls nightly during Carnival.

At the time of going to press it was probable that the "Atlantic Ball" would take place on the Saturday while the famours "One Night in Baghdad" would be Carnival's last major ball on the Tuesday night.

Reservations and information from the club at Av. Borges de Medeiros, 701 on the Lagoa. Tel 239-0032 or 239-2399.

Hotel Celebrations: Most of the top "five star" hotels will have their own Carnival celebrations of one kind or another be it a ball or a breakfast. Celebrations at the hotels tend to be more "civilized" than the others around town, but no less fun for the visitor. The Hotel Nacional traditionally holds a large ball on the Monday of Carnival, while on the Tuesday the Copacabana Palace presents the "Golden Ball" in the hotel's Golden Room.

Two of Carnival's best dressed, and most up-market celebrations, take place at the private clubs of the Meridien and Rio Palace hotels.

Tickets and information from the hotels.

Gay Balls: Our less heterosexual friends are not overlooked during Carnival and a number of Gay Balls are scheduled nightly across the city attracting charter groups of gays from the U.S. and Europe.

The most famous of the balls is the "Grande Gala Gay", which is likely to be held at the large Help disco on Copacabana Beach.

COSTUMES AND COSTS

Imagination is everything at Carnival and you can always find something to use as the base for your costume which should be as skimpy as possible to help cope with Rio's summer heat that in the enclosed atmosphere of a Carnival ball can get fairly oppressive at times.

Costumes don't have to be elaborate — although many of the local residents will spend months in the preparation of their "fantasia" — you can pick up garlands of flowers and other accompaniments to help dress up your costume at every street corner.

Although many of the balls state "Costume or Black Tie" you will do yourself and your heart a big favor if you stick with a costume because as a visitor you will have no chance of surviving the heat in a long dress or jacket and tie.

For the locals who get paid in cruzados Carnival is anything but cheap, the tourist, however, will find it relatively cheap especially if you compare it with a night on Broadway, and I promise you a night of Carnival is a lot more entertaining.

In dollar terms you can expect to pay at the better balls anywhere between $15 and $90-a-head.

STREET CARNIVAL

Street carnival is the main afternoon and early evening attraction of Rio's Carnival, and easily the most spontaneous.

Street carnival, and the *bandas* (bands) which are such an integral part, are one of the most traditional aspects of Carnival, and not something you will want to miss. Even the parade of the main samba-schools was in the past and still technically is part of street carnival.

Street carnival is impetuous and impulsive fun and the most truly democratic aspect of Carnival. It attracts the rich and the poor, the black and the white, the young and the old, and most importantly for you, the Brazilians and the foreign visitors.

In the crowds that follow the *bandas* as they slowly snake their way through the different neighborhoods you will find a reversal of roles. You find men impersonating women, children acting as adults, and adults like children. It is an infectious madness which should not alarm you, it is all being done in good humor and the last thing anyone wants to do is upset a visitor.

To join in the fun you will of course have to find yourself a *banda*. Most of the *bandas* go out around 4 p.m. although some start as early as 2 p.m., and go on until the early hours. or at least until they have an audience.

If you are staying in Copacabana you will have no problem in finding a *banda*, there is normally a small one on just about every corner or junction with the beach. Copacabana also has a number of larger and more famous *bandas* which during their ''walk-about'' attract a following of many thousands of people who help bring the area to a complete stand still. In Carnival the *banda* has the right-of-way so keep to the back roads if you are in a hurry.

Following a *banda* is not over taxing. You dance when you want and sing when you want, and there are always plenty of bars along the route where you can stop off for a cooling chopp.

Some of the larger and more famous Copacabana *bandas,* and their routes are:

Banda do Leme. Gustavo Sampaio — Aurelino Leal — Av. Atlântica.

Banda da Sá Ferreira. Sá Ferreira — Bulhões de Carvalho — Francisco Sá — Raul Pompéia — Francisco Otaviano — N.S. de Copacabana — Xavier da Silveira — Av. Atlântica.

Banda da Miguel Lemos. No set route but the *banda* leaves from Rua Miguel Lemos between Av. Atlântica and N. S. de Copacabana.

Banda da Vergonha do Posto 6. Bar Bico (Francisco Sá) — Av. Atlântica — Joaquim Nabuco — N. S. de Copacabana — Sousa Lima — Raul Pompéia — Bar Bico.

Banda do Arroxo. Belford Roxo — Barata Ribeiro — Inhangá — N.S. de Copacabana.

Copacabana is not the only area to have *bandas*. A number can be found snaking through the roads of Ipanema and Leblon including perhaps the largest and most famous of all *bandas*, the *Banda de Ipanema*, which traditionally starts from Praça General Osório, better known to the foreign visitors as the Hippie Square.

If you are staying up in the city look out for the *Banda da Glória* which bases its activities around Rua Cândido Mendes.

RIO BRANCO AND THE BLOCOS

Part of street carnival is also considered to be the goings on around Av. Rio Branco in Centro. Here you find the parades of the Clubes de Frevo, the Blocos de Enredo, the Blocos de Empolgação, which includes the famous rivalry of Cacique de Ramos and Bafo da Onça, each likely to be numbering 10,000 participants, and the group II-A and II-B samba schools.

It is worth noting that in recent years the area surrounding Av. Rio Branco and its parades has been the Carnival ''black spot'' for foreign visitors. Now that does not mean, as some foreign periodicals have been known to write, that you are going to be gunned down, stabbed to death, and then trampled on by a rioting crowd.

Far from it, the worst that is likely to happen to you is petty pilfering, but how petty will depend on you so don't take your camera, unless it is one you don't mind losing, nor do you want your passport, jewelry, travelers checks, etc. Leave them back at the hotel in the hotels safe-deposit box.

Go to the Rio Branco area to have fun. You won't be able to if you are worrying about your belongings.

The quickest and safest way to get down to Rio Branco at Carnival is by metro (subway). Take a taxi to the metro station in Botafogo and then take a train as far as Cinelândia or Carioca.

THE GREATEST SHOW ON EARTH

The best known ingredient of Carnival in world terms is the Sunday and Monday night parades of the large group 1-A samba schools (working class social clubs) which takes place on March 1 and 2 in 1987 and February 14 and 15 in 1988 along the purpose built Passarela do Samba, inaugurated in 1984 on Av. Marquês de Sapucaí.

To many people the parade of samba schools is just that, a parade. Which is a pity because it is so much more. It is a competition, a story, an historical lesson, dance, song, movement, in fact the ultimate theatre performed over two nights by more than 50,000 players, the vast majority of whom are amateurs.

If you take the time to read what follows you will learn a little about the riches of the parade, what to look for and when. So let's start with the basics and the simple facts that are often overlooked.

If you can accept for starters, that you are not watching a parade but theatre, all-be-it on the move, you will be a long way to appreciating the spectacle.

Many months before Carnival each of the schools meet to decide what the theme of their particular school's presentation would be at Carnival. As each school chooses individually it is quite possible that more than one school will choose the same theme.

Once a school has chosen its theme it is up to the members of the school, to write the song, the *samba-enredo* that fits the theme, *enredo*.

Around the beginning of November the schools finally select their samba for the coming year's parade. Today the deadline is tougher than in the past because a major source of revenue for the samba schools is the sale of the record with all the year's sambas, and that needs to be in the stores to take advantage of the Christmas market.

By the end of December each year we know what the themes of the competing schools are and what their sambas sound like.

Going back in time, to the day when the school chose its theme, rather than the final *samba-enredo*, I must introduce the most important figure of any school's carnival activity, the *carnavalesco*. Carnavalescos are a cross between a director and a set designer, only this set has to move with the action.

So while the school's writers start putting together their competing *samba enredos* the carnavalesco is already sketching the costume designs for the dancers, the floats and everything else that goes into making the parade one of the wonder's of the world.

So what have we got at this stage?

We have got a school. We have a theme. We have a song. And we have a man who is coming up with ideas of how the school should parade and what it should look like.

But what then is the actual parade made up of?

Starting at the Beginning — The Parade

Starting once against at the beginning, you will be greeted as the school comes down the avenue by the *abre-alas*. A literal translation.

would be "opening-wing" and each similarly dressed group which follows in the school will be known as an *ala* (wing).

The *abre-alas* is the school's title page, and the float will normally represent an open book or scroll. Somewhere on this float should appear the name of the school and before it the letters G.R.E.S. which stand for "Grêmio Recreativo Escola de Samba" (Samba School Recreational Guild):

Close to the *abre-alas* comes the *Comissão de Frente* which holds an important position in the parade as it counts points for the final result, and as a couple of points out of two hundred can mean the difference of one place, a bad or good *Comissão de Frente* could make the difference between winning and losing.

In the past the *Comissão de Frente* was considered to be the "board of directors" of the school, or at least distinguished looking gentlemen that could pass for being one.

In recent years the image of the *Comissão de Frente* has changed. Beija-Flor introduced more complex choreography while in 1983 Salgueiro presented a *Comissão de Frente* composed entirely of actresses from TV Globo's popular soap operas. In 1985 Beija-Flor's *Comissão de Frente* was made up from the stars of the top Brazilian women's volleyball teams; Mocidade Independente's featured children; while Império Serrano paraded a *Comissão de Frente* dressed as waiters in keeping with the schools theme that beer is the fuel that drives carnival.

But the *abre-alas* and *Comissão de Frente* are just the start, behind them comes the school.

The bulk of the school is made up of the various *alas*, the wings, or blocks of people in similar costume who are linked to one part of the theme. Salgueiro in 1985, for example, had over 3,000 people split between 34 different *alas* and that is not counting the 300 people in the percussion section, *bateria*, or the 120 women in the *Ala das Baianas*.

Some of the *alas* will be present just to give color and movement, as it has not been lost on the *carnavalescos* that people view the parade from above. In the old days you would have viewed it from the street level.

So what is the present state of play?

We have the school, the theme, the song, and the man who is directing the operations. We also now have the *abre alas* and the *Comissão de Frente*, and the *alas* which make up the bulk of the school.

In passing I have not clearly explained that every school has to parade with an *Ala das Baianas*. This consists of hundreds of older women, normally black, dressed in the traditional flowing white dresses of Bahia. Their presence in the parade honors the earliest history of the parade which was brought to Rio from Salvador in 1877.

When the *baianas* all twirl together it is a memorable sight and one of the best sights to film from the stand because even though the movement blurs the photo you will be more than happy with the result, especially when enlarged.

The Parade's Individual Components

I now come to the more individualistic components of the parade.

The most famous, and like the *Comissão de Frente*, a points scorer, is the *Mestre-Sala* and *Porta-Bandeira*, the dance master and flag bearer.

This couple dress in lavish 18th century formal wear, regardless of the school's theme, and are expected to carry on a complex series of dances as they move up the avenue. The couple present one of the truly artistic presentations of the parade. The girl, the *porta-*

bandeira, has the honor and responsibility of carrying the school's symbol and for this reason her presentation must be dignified and at the same time beautiful.

Due to the popularity of the *porta-bandeira* and *mestre-sala* most of the schools have subsidiary couples who are placed throughout the school who dream of one day being the school's number one choice.

The *porta bandeira* and *mestre sala* are not the only important figures in the parade though, there are also the *Figuras de Destaque*, prominent figures. These are usually famous personalities or people dressed in the extremely rich costumes that Rio's Carnival is famous for. In recent years they decided to put these figures on their own floats or cars. The reasoning for this was two-fold. First the people in heavy costumes were slowing the schools down; one has to remember the weight of the costume, the heat, and the distance that has to be covered. Second, by putting the person on a float you could push them at the speed you want but also they will have direct eye contact with the public in the stands who they can work to get the school the maximum possible crowd response.

Finally in this section we have the *passistas*, the most individual aspect of the parade, normally the best samba dancers and the most lively. The girls will be dressed in the bare minimum while the men will usually carry some percurssion instruments and perform various gymnastic feats along the way.

The Driving Sound

The sound that drives the school comes from the *bateria*, an army of percurssion players, all in the same costume, who beat their way from one end of the avenue to the other. If you stand on the road next to the *bateria* the force of the sound will literally move you back.

Despite being over 300 or more strong the *bateria* still finds it difficult to get its beat to carry over the whole school. For this reason it come about a quarter of the way through the school. Three quarters of the way down the avenue it will turn off from the school between sectors 9 and 11. Here it will stay while the rest of the school passes, before joining on at the end.

The song itself is driven by the *puxador de samba* who travels down the avenida on a truck surrounded by sound equipment. Normally each school has at least four or more *puxadores*.

In the past the school employed a system of runners who would run from the sound truck back down the school keeping everyone in time with the *puxador*. Today, in the era of radio mikes etc., things are a little simpler and the speaker systems stretches from one end of the avenue to the other.

Finally, we come to the *Alegorias* or the gigantic floats which are the main set pieces of the parade. A float hardly needs a detailed description but you may be surprised by their size and complexity, as well as their beauty and attention to detail.

Like the smaller floats which carry the *figuras de destaque*, the larger *alegorias* have a big part to play in the contact the school makes with the public in the stand and are normally filled with people, mainly girls, to produce the desired response from the crowds.

According to the rules each school is only allowed a set number of floats but happily until now the judges have overlooked this matter, choosing to judge the quality and forgetting the quantity which they allow the schools to decorate their parade with.

THE PARADE

The parades in 1985 and 1986 were the best organized, especially as far as foreign visitors were concerned, be they tourists or members of the press, and I have no reason to doubt the capabilities of the Rio Tourist Board, Riotur, to repeat this in 1987 or even go one better.

In 1987 the parade of Group 1-A samba-schools will start at 7:30 p.m. on Sunday, March 1 and Monday, March 2, with eight schools parading on the Sunday and eight on the Monday. Each school must parade, according to new regulations, for a minimum of 85 minutes and a maximum of 95 minutes and their floats can be no wider than eight metres and no higher than 10 metres. For the statistically minded the length of the parade ground, the Passarela do Samba, is 1700 metres or 1860 yards.

Tickets for 1987 went on sale back in October 1986 and as in every Carnival the result is certain to be a sell out.

Foreign visitors have two stands especially reserved for them-stands seven and nine — and while at $80-a-night the tickets are more expensive than any other stand it must be said that the amenities on offer are better and more comfortable.

In my opinion, the best place to see the parade, other than dancing in it, are the *cadeiras de pistas*, the ring-side seats, which consist of a table and four chairs.

Tickets to the "Tourist Stands" should be available from your travel agent but if you have any doubts or worries you should contact Riotour on 232-4320. All the other stands, boxes, and *cadeiras de pista* have been sold through the state bank, BANERJ. BANERJ's central ticket office can be found at Av. Nilo Peçanha, 175 in Centro (Tel. 224-0202).

As in the past, 1987 will see the weakest schools parade first, that is Unidos do Jacarezinho, Império da Tijuca and Estácio de Sá on the Sunday and São Clemente, Unidos da Ponte and Unidos do Cabuçu on the Monday. This means that is unlikely that any of the top schools will parade much before 1 a.m. on either of the nights, that said, Carnival, like any other competition, can see the triumph of the underdog.

The full draw for the main Carnival parades in 1987 made by Riotur and the League of Samba Schools resulted in the following:

Sunday, March 1, 1987
Unidos do Jacarezinho
Império da Tijuca
Estácio de Sá
Caprichosos de Pilares
Salgueiro — *Winner in 1960, 1963, 1965, 1969, 1971, 1974 & 1975.*
Beija-Flor — *Winner in 1976, 1977, 1978, 1980 & 1983.*
Imperatriz Leopoldinense — *Winner in 1980 & 1981.*
Mangueira — *Winner in 1940, 1948, 1949, 1950, 1954, 1960, 1961, 1967, 1968, 1973, 1984 & 1986.*

Monday, March 2, 1987
São Clemente
Unidos da Ponte
Unidos do Cabuçu
Império Serrano — Winner in *1948, 1949, 1950, 1951, 1955, 1956, 1960.*
Império Serrano — *Winner in 1948, 1949, 1950, 1951, 1955, 1956, 1960, 1972 & 1982.*
Vila Isabel
União da Ilha
Portela — *Winner in 1935, 1939, 1941, 1942, 1943, 1944, 1945, 1946, 1947, 1951, 1953, 1957, 1958, 1959, 1960, 1962, 1964, 1966, 1970 & 1980.*
Mocidade Independente de Padre Miguel — *Winner in 1979 & 1985.*

CARNIVAL SUNDAY TO THE YEAR 2000

In case you want to make plans to come to Rio for Carnival in the coming years here are the dates of Carnival Sunday — the first night of the big parades — till the year 2000.

February 14, 1988 / February 5,. 1989 / February 25, 1990 ./ February 10, 1991 / March 1, 1992 / February 21, 1993 / February 13, 1994 / February 26, 1995 / February 18, 1996 / February 9, 1997 / February 22, 1998 / February 14, 1999 / March 5, 2000.

If you are going to be travelling within Brazil make sure you purchase a Brazilian "Air Pass" when you buy your ticket to Brazil.

You can't buy the "Air Pass" in Brazil and internal air travel is not cheap.

D

Sugar Loaf
Corcovado
Author's Tour
The Beaches
Things to See
The Art World
Rainy Days

Two Landmarks

Rio de Janeiro hasn't got one outstanding landmark, it's got two: Sugar Loaf and Corcovado.

Both offer spectacular but quite different views of the city, and each has its own distinctive atmosphere. Strangely though neither could be said to hold pride of place in the Carioca heart, coming a poor second to the beach, but if you want my opinion the residents take these two natural wonders a little bit too much for granted.

A friend of mine who had travelled to every corner of the world and seen every site finally made it to Rio. On getting to the top of Corcovado he was overwhelmed. After all his travelling he had finally found a sight that not only lived up to, but surpassed all expectations. For him the view from Corcovado was the single most inspiring sight in the world, a fact I think you will agree with when you get to the top.

In terms of size Sugar Loaf is just a little shorter than the World Trade center in New York at 1300ft, but Corcovado is nearly double its size topping out at 2326ft and making a mockery of New York's claim to have the world's highest open air viewing platform.

Sugar Loaf

Sugar Loaf is more than a landmark. It is a complete entertainment center which offers spectacular views and pleasant walks, the top names in Brazilian and international music live, some of the best samba in town, one of carnival's most brilliant balls and even a reasonable restaurant.

Sugar Loaf's name comes from the Portuguese *Pão de Açúcar* and is presumed to have been given to the mountain because of its shape which resembles a cone of sugar, or sugar loaf. This could be wishful thinking however because it is far more likely that the name *Pão de Açúcar* came from the language of the Tupi indians who called it *Pau-nh-Acuqua*, "high hill, pointed and isolated."

Man's first contact with Sugar Loaf dates back to 1817 when Henrietta Carstairs, an English woman, first successfully scaled the summit and planted the British flag for all to see. In the subsequent years a series of other British and Brazilian climbers conquered the mountain, and each time the flag changed to the appropriate nation's. In 1851 the first collective climb took place made up from American and British climbers, including one women and a ten year old boy. It is recorded that the group spent the night on the mountain and celebrated with a display of fireworks for the city to see.

Today climbing Sugar Loaf is a popular sport and each weekend a group can usually be seen clinging to its sides, it was however only in 1972 that four Australians finally conquered the North Wall, the last unclimbed route.

Going Up in Style

The majority of visitors do not climb Sugar Loaf today, but take the modern cable car which links Praia Vermelha with the summit in two stages in less than six minutes.

The idea for a cable car was first thought about in 1908 by the engineer Augusto Ramos. Along with industrialist Manuel Galvão, Ramos signed an agreement on June 30, 1909 with the then mayor of Rio, Serzedelo Correia, to start work on the project. It should be noted that the mayor was so sceptical of the project that he gave Ramos 30 years in which to complete the project, Ramos needed less than four.

The first stage between Praia Vermelha and the Morro da Urca was inaugurated by 50 members of the press on October 9, 1912 and by the public on October 12. That Sunday 577 people rode to the top of Morro da Urca and the mayor gave permission for the company to raise the number of journeys made by the car to five in the morning and four in the afternoon.

On January 18, 1913 the second stage to the top of Sugar Loaf was inaugurated and Cariocas could finally gaze down on the city and appreciate its beauty from above.

The first cable car system, of German construction, operated for 60 years and transported Rio's many famous visitors of the time to the top. But the cars which took six minutes to complete each stage, could only carry 24 people, or 112 in an hour.

As the years passed it became clear that Sugar Loaf's cable cars could not cope with demand yet only as recently as 1969 was anything concrete done to plan for the future, and on May 5, 1970 the then Governor, Negrão de Lima, gave permission for a project which could cope with demand until the year 2000.

Work on the new cable car system, which was to cost 1.3-million dollars, got underway on July 13, 1970. Two years later on October 29 1972 the new Italian cable car system went into action and the old one which had served Rio faithfully for 60 years and three weeks made its last journey.

The new system raised the number of passengers that could be carried in one hour from 112 to 1360; the new cars could carry in an hour what the old cars took a day to do.

Carrying up to 75 passengers in each car, the new system is one of the safest in the world and despite what you may have seen being done to it in the James Bond movie *Moonraker* there has never been an accident on the system.

The Facts You Will Want to Know

Sugar Loaf (Pão de Açúcar) is a short cab ride from Copacabana and not that far from Ipanema. All the major tour companies run excursions and not surprisingly every cab driver knows how to find it.

Sugar Loaf's cable cars run daily from 8 a.m. to 10 p.m. The longest you will ever have to wait for a car in the low season is 30 minutes but normally it is less because the cars go as soon as they are full.

There are two stages in your trip to the summit. The first links Praia Vermelha to Morro da Urca.

Morro da Urca is the main entertainment center and is where the outdoor theater and restaurant are located and where the Carnival ball takes place.

On Urca you will be approached by photographers who snap away. Smile, they don't bite and you are under no obligation to buy the photograph. One of the most popular souvenirs is to have your picture mounted on a plate. If you are clever you will ask the photographer to take your photo with Sugar Loaf as the backdrop. Again if you don't like the photo at the end you don't have to buy it. The photos are developed and mounted while you travel up the second leg to the top of Sugar Loaf itself.

Remember to take a map up with you, you will also want one for Corcovado, although the maps at the back of this guide will help.

At the top explore: there is a beautiful walk-way through the gardens at the back that many tourists miss. From here you have the most spectacular views of the harbour mouth and along the coast to Itaipu.

On your return to Morro da Urca you should think about stopping for lunch at the Cota 200 restaurant which offers an international menu of adequate quality, and surprisingly for a major tourist attraction, at very moderate prices. Both Morro da Urca and Sugar Loaf have snack bars for the junk food addicts.

One last bit of advice, don't rush Sugar Loaf. You can stay up it all day if you want. Far too many visitors dash straight up and down without ever really appreciating it. I have been up the mountain a hundred times and never tire of it, I will even travel up for lunch or a walk and fresh air.

Sugar Loaf "At-A-Glance"

Height: Sugar Loaf Mountain — 1300 ft. Urca Mountain — 705 ft.
Cable Car Hours: The cable cars run daily from 8 a.m. to 10 p.m. and later when there is a show on Morro da Urca or Beija-Flor are performing.

Live Shows: Live shows, featuring top name from Brazil and abroad, take place on Morro da Urca most Thursday, Friday and Saturday evenings. Dinner is served from 8 p.m. with the shows starting around 10 p.m. or later. The restaurants and bars then stay open through until 2 a.m. To find out who is performing at Morro da Urca you can either look in the entertainment section of *Jornal do Brasil* or *O Globo* or call the box office on 541-3737 or 295-2397.

Samba: Beija-Flor, one of Brazil's most famous samba schools, performs every Monday evening at 10:30 p.m. and is preceded at 9 p.m. by a film explaining a little of the history of samba and carnival. The cost at the end of 1986 was just US$12 for dinner at the Cota 200 restaurant and Beija-Flor's show or US$10 for the show. During the high season the programme is normally repeated on Thursday evening. Reservations on 541-3737 and 295-2397.

Restaurant: The Cota 200 restaurant is open daily from noon through to 7 p.m. and later when there is a show or Beija-Flor are performing.

Children's Programme: A free show and discotheque especially for children takes place every Saturday and Sunday from 4 p.m. till 5:30 p.m. on Morro da Urca.

Discover Brazil: A spectacular 180° audiovisual presentation entitled "Discover Brazil" will be introduced during the second half of 1987. The show will last about 15 minutes with tickets on sale from a special box office. As the soundtrack is musical, there are no language difficulties in "discovering Brazil."

Carnival Ball: Sugar Loaf's Carnival Ball is traditionally held on the Friday of Carnival, which means February 27 in 1987. One of the year's most glamorous occasions, tickets cost about US$70.

Corcovado

Gray Bell in his book "The Beautiful Rio de Janeiro" published in 1914 considered: "To go to Rio and not go up Corcovado is a folly" Today it would be sheer stupidity.

One of the first people to scale the peak was no lesser a personage than Dom Pedro I accompanied by his Empress Leopoldina. At the time you reached the summit on a road that cut across the hills from Alto da Boa Vista.

On January 7, 1882, Brazil's second emperor, Dom Pedro II, gave permission to two enginners, Francisco Passos and Teixeira Soares, to build a railroad to the peak so that all of Rio could enjoy the magnificent view.

By 1884 the new train line was inaugurated as far as the stop by the old Paineiras Hotel a building which today stands empty waiting for a decision as to it's fate.

One year later in 1885 the train reached all the way to Corcovado, 2180 feet above sea level. 130 feet below the summit. According to Bell you would have found at the summit a small open pavilion known as Corcovado's Cap, built in 1824, plus a stone balcony which had been built to overlook the southern drop, a sheer 1,000 feet.

In case you are wondering, Corcovado is the name of the actual mountain and not the statue of Christ we see today, this is a fact that many visitors confuse. The name Corcovado means hunchback and describes the physical appearance of the mountain.

The idea of the Statue of Christ first came to light in 1921 when the country was planning to celebrate the 100th Anniversary of its Independence. A popular magazine of the day suggested that a competition be run to chose a national monument. The competition was won by Heitor da Silva Costa who proposed a giant statue of Christ with his arms outstretched to embrace the city.

The idea was greeted with unanimous enthusiasm, unlike a project in 1888 to put a huge statue of Christopher Columbus on top of Sugar Loaf. Money for the new project was raised in collections taken in churches throughout Brazil.

Work Begins on the Statue

Work on the statue began in Paris where engineers, designers, and sculptors met to decide how to tackle the problems of mounting a statue that would last on a wind swept peak open to the elements, 2,400 feet above sea level.

While the body and arms of the statue were left to the architects and engineers, French sculptor Paul Landowski started work on the head and hands of Christ. The head at the end would stand 12 feet high and weigh nearly 35 tons while each hand would weigh nine tons and make up the measurement of 75 feet from fingertip to fingertip.

The sculpture was brought to Rio from Paris and faced in soapstone before being hauled up the mountain to be attached to the supporting pillars.

The monument was officially inaugurated on October 12, 1931 by Guglielmo Marconi who threw the switch that lit the statue. Marconi was not in Rio though, but aboard his yacht in Genoa harbour.

In 1965 Pope Paul VI inaugurated a new lighting system in much the same manner from Rome, and on October 12, 1981 Pope John Paul repeated the act to mark the 50th Anniversary of South America's most famous landmark.

The View from the Top

From the balcony in front of the 100ft statue which stands on a 22ft pedestal you have a comprehensive view of the city.

To Christ's left the panorama sweeps from Maracana, with the *zona norte* stretching behind, round to the International Airport on Ilha do Governador and the full dimensions of the bay with the *Serra dos Orgãos* mountain range in the far distance, home of Petropolis and Teresopolis.

In front of Christ the city center looks like a toy town. The visitor can appreciate from the Corcovado the full sweep of the bay and how the beaches join one another. From Corcovado Rio is no longer a confusion of roads.

Sugar Loaf sits directly in front of Corcovado and behind it the open sea. To the right. Copacabana and Ipanema, and below the Lagoa, Jockey Club and Botanical Gardens, and through to São Conrado.

In truth the view is beyond description, words and even photographs are not enough Seeing is believing.

Getting to the Top

Getting to the top of Corcovado is not as difficult as you may imagine. It can be reached either on an organized tour, by car, or by train.

For the first time visitor I would recommend the organized tour, because without a guide to point out the sites you will lose a lot. Some of the tours use buses to get to the top, others the train. The cost is $20, a figure which I imagine will remain constant throughout the year.

The train is the second easy way for a visitor to see Corcovado for the first time. New trains of Swiss design were recently inaugurated and make the 3.5 kilometer climb through the mountain greenery, some of it reminiscent of the jungle, in just 20 minutes. The trains run from their own station at Rua Cosme Velho, 513 from 8 a.m. to 6:40 p.m. The station can be reached easily by cab from any point in the city, just ask for Rua Cosme Velho, it is in the road which runs down from the center of the Rebouças Tunnel to Laranjeiras.

If you have time while waiting for your train walk up Cosme Velho towards the tunnel, the first road you come to on the right is the Largo do Boticario an extremely pretty square which although looking colonial isn't, but the friends back home won't know this when you show them your photos.

If you are really adventurous you will take a car up Corcovado, and I will come to my own special tour in a moment but first the basics. The easiest way to get to Corcovado is to drive through the Rebouças Tunnel from the Lagoa and turn off in the middle following signs to Corcovado.

It's that simple. In recent years they have introduced a small toll charge for cars to continue from the Paineiras Hotel, pay it and continue on up, and keep going despite what anyone tells you on the way, only obey the police. This warning is not for your safety it is just that the parking attendants like visitors to park as low down the hill as possible to leave room at the top. Forget it, it's a long walk. If the top really is full the police wont' let you up.

Parking is normally chaotic but you will find a place, especially during the week.

The Author's Tour

I have been up Corcovado so often that I have lost count but I'm still overcome by the view, everytime I get to the summit. It all seems unreal and impossible in a city of Rio's size.

Over the years I have developed a special tour which has never yet disappointed any of my visitors and I don't expect it will disappoint you.

The aim of the game is to get underway at around 10:45 a.m., it is not in my opinion too civilized to be moving much before this time in the morning, especially if you have done justice to the Rio night life.

Set out and take the standard route to Corcovado through the Rebouças Tunnel at the top end of the Lagoa, turning off in the middle and following signs to Corcovado. Should the sign to Corcovado be missing, and believe me it has been known to happen, take the steeper of the hills to your right as you come off the Rebouças in to Cosme Velho.

As you wind your way up the hill you come across signs marked for "Corcovado", "Alto", and "Mirante Dona Marta". It is the "Mirante Dona Marta" that you are heading for first, which will be well posted to your left. Taking the left turn — watch which side of the road you are on as it can get a little bit confusing at this intersection — follow the road along. Soon you come to a car park and the Dona Marta viewing platform located 1200 feet above sea level. This offers a third different view of the city than the ones you get from Sugar Loaf and Corcovado, and from here you can take a nice series of photos using Rio's two most famous landmarks, Sugar Loaf and the statue of Christ on Corcovado, as the backdrop.

Back in the car you will find that you have to return down the road the way you came and join up with the Corcovado road which you now follow to the summit.

You should reach the top between 11:30 a.m. and noon. Time is what you make of it in Rio, so take as long as you want up Corcovado. You should never feel rushed in Rio.

When everyone in your party has had enough, drive back down the mountain and when you reach the intersection, just after the toll-gate, turn left following signs to "Alto". You will pass almost immediately on your left the old Paineiras Hotel. You are now on route for a fairly lengthy drive through the Tijuca National Park, or as you look up at Corcovado from below, the greenery that surrounds it.

A Drive Through the Forest

The drive is very pretty and lots of fun, with plenty of spectacular views of Rio en route. Just keep going on and on, there is only one turn off and you ignore that, following any signs to "Alto" or "Alto da Boavista". Eventually you come to an intersection with a major road, by major I mean it has got traffic on it. Turn right and within a couple of hundred yards you come to what in England would be the village green — it does perhaps need a little imagination on your part, but there is a bar called "Robin Hood" and a British phone box. Go round the green — posted "Floresta da Tijuca" — and enter the Tijuca Forest (See "Tijuca Forest").

In the forest you will pass the Cascatinha de Taunay, a small waterfall, and further up the road the delightful Mairynk Chapel.

Just around the corner from the chapel you come to a fork in the road, the two roads go either side of a large picnic area, and both take you to different restaurants which are clearly signposted, in the heart of the park.

While neither restaurant has any culinary pretensions, they are an ideal choice for a lazy lunch when time is on your side. The left hand fork takes you to the "posher" choice, the "Os Esquilos", while the right fork takes you to "A Floresta" which I prefer for its rustic charm — although I have had it referred to as "of dubious charm" on first sighting — and the humming birds which dart in and out of the rafters as you eat. Whichever restaurant you choose you won't be disappointed. What they lack in the culinary arts they more than make up for in atmosphere. You will find it difficult to believe that you are still in the "city" of Rio.

Coming Back to Rio

To get back to Rio you want to take the Estrada do Açude. From "A Floresta" you must return to the fork in the road and head for "Os Esquilos". You then take the first left. From "Os Esquilos" you come back down the road and turn first right.

After a short drive through the forest you come to the gate by a pretty pond. You now have a choice of returning via Barra da Tijuca, São Conrado or the Lagoa by way of the Chinese View.

If you wish to return via the Lagoa or São Conrado you turn left after the park gates. Follow the road down to the main road. At the main road turn right and immediately fork to the left of the old-fashioned lamp post. To your left will be the "Centro Educacional do Sagrado Coração" You are now on the Estrada da Vista Chinesa.

Following the road along you come to a fork in the road after 2 km, there is in fact a 2 Km post in the middle of the fork. The Estrada da Vista Chinesa is the left hand fork and this takes you back down to the Lagoa past the Emperor's Table and Chinese View. You will come out eventually in Rua Jardim Botanico alongside the Botanical Gardens.

If you take the right hand road at the 2 Km post you will be on the Estrada da Gavea Pequena. Continue along until you come to the inter-section with Estrada Pedra Bonita, Turn left, it is clearly posted to "São Conrado" You will wind your way down to Praça de São Conrado close to the restaurant El Pescador.

The more adventurous of you, and those that don't mind taking the risk of getting lost, should turn right as you come out of the park gates. Continue to the top of the hill where you find a tree in the middle of the road forming a small roundabout. Stop here for a spectacular view over Barra da Tijuca. Now take the left hand exit from the roundabout, going down the lane in front of the gates with "N° 21" and "Praça Martins Leão" on them. This winding lane offers many spectacular views over Barra and the surrounding countryside. You will eventually emerge on the Estrada Tijuacu. Turn right. Carry on down to the main road and turn right again. You should have "Supermaçado Rio" to your left. You are now on the Estrada da Furnas which takes you down to Barra. Keep an eye out for the bar "Existe Um Lugar", you will probably have seen its name in the local papers and always wondered where it is. Now you know.

Just after the Hollywood motel you meet the Estrada da Barra da Tijuca. Turn left and follow signs to "Barra". You will have the Itanhanga Golf Club on your right (see Map 11). Over the bridge turn right, you can now chose to explore Barra da Tijuca, or if you prefer, return to Rio by taking the "retorno" opposite the Esso garage.

If you are new to Rio, follow signs to Avenida Niemeyer, this will take you past the Inter-Continental, Nacional and Sheraton hotels before dropping down to Leblon and Ipanema.

Whichever route you take, if you follow these directions I can promise you a lazy, relaxed day you will remember for a long time.

Rio's Finest

The Leading Hotels of the World®

The Rio Palace is Rio's finest hotel. And Rio, as everyone knows, is the world's most beautiful city, thanks to its people, its climate, its easy-going fashion, its poetic lands-cape and its tropical flavor. The finest hotel in Rio also has the best location. Overlooking Copacabana and just steps from Ipanema you have the world's two most famous beaches virtually at your doorstep. The Rio Palace offers top quality throughout in its facilities as well as its services. This is the Rio Palace. Rio's finest - specially designed for guests like you.

ЯR
RIO PALACE
★★★★★

Rio de Janeiro: Av. Atlântica, 4.240 - Phone (021) 521-3232 - Telex (021) 21.803
Consult your travel agent or our representatives
The Leading Hotels of the World or Nikko Hotels, Utell International

N° Reg. Embratur-01564-00-21-4

Standard

Through London you can reach the world.

BRITISH AIRWAYS
The world's favourite airline.

The Beaches of Rio

Seeing really is believing when you are talking about the 90 kilometers of golden sand that goes to make up the beaches of Rio which stretch from the Bay of Guanabara in the east to the Bay of Sepetiba in the west.

It doesn't matter if you are visiting Rio for four days or four years, as you will find a good percentage of your time is spent enjoying Rio's beaches be it for sport, a barbecue, a business meeting, or just to catch the sun.

Rio has many beaches and these should be the ones that interest you most; starting from Flamengo in the Bay of Guanabara and working west.

FLAMENGO

Flamengo is a residents' beach, the only hotels close by being the Gloria, Novo Mundo and Flamengo Palace.

About a kilometer long Flamengo is the result of Brazil's largest landscaping project which reclaimed the whole Flamengo Park area from the bay.

Without any firm tradition within the community, Flamengo is a beach for sport and sun bathing, swimmers preferring the beaches along the sea coast away from the polluted waters of the bay.

BOTAFOGO

Similar characteristics to Flamengo, this 600 meters of curving sand is more popular with residents of the area than outsiders.

VERMELHA

Its thick yellow sand, not found on other beaches in the city, gave this beach its name, *Vermelha* (red).

Little more than 100 meters long, Praia Vermelha is situated below Sugar Loaf facing the sea. Normally sheltered by the headland from the South Atlantic the beach is popular with swimmers.

LEME

To all intent and purpose Leme and Copacabana are the same beach, there is no physical break like the canal which separates Ipanema and Leblon, but for all this the "Leme end" of the beach retains its own distinct characteristics.

Leme is more tranquil than its more famous neighbor, helped by the fact that the residential area behind only goes back three blocks while in Copacabana it stretches to six or more. Parking is also easier in Leme as there are fewer hotels and many less bars. Leme's most famous hotel is the magnificent Meridien but others of renown such as the Leme Palace and Luxor Continental are also in the area.

COPACABANA

Copacabana, the world's most famous beach, stretches for more than three kilometers from Av. Princesa Isabel in the east to Copacabana Fort in the west.

The center of Rio's tourist trade, both national and international, Copacabana comfortably accommodates not only the thousands of visitors who lie on it each year but also the 300,000 residents who live in the 109 streets behind.

Avenida Atlântica, which runs along the top of the beach, is alive 24 hours-a-day and landmarked by three very special hotels: the towering Meridien in the east (strictly speaking on Leme Beach); the 30 story Othon Palace in the middle; and one of Rio's most luxurious hotels, the Rio Palace, in the west. In between come other splendid hotels such as the world famous Copacabana Palace, a landmark in its own right, and the Ouro Verde.

Then there are the beach front bars which line the avenue from one end to the other and offer every type of international and ethnic cuisine all available without even changing from your beach clothes.

Wider than any other beach in Rio, Copacabana is the home of beach soccer, an event which can usually be viewed at any time of the day, and volleyball, the nation's latest passion. It is also home to a thousand or more beach salesman who will tempt you with their wares be it a simple ice cream or one of Copacabana's famous bird kites.

ARPOADOR

A thin strip of 400 meters of sand Arpoardor is tacked on to the eastern end of Ipanema. The sea is always rougher here and because of this Arpoador is the domain of the *zona sul* surf set. Worth visiting to watch those surfers at play but keep an eye out for flying surf boards!

IPANEMA

Nearly two-and-a-half kilometers long, Ipanema is the beach of Rio's beautiful people, and for me that little bit more civilized than all the others.

Less crowded, except at weekends, Ipanema is the beach to set the trends that all the other beaches follow. The bikinis are a little bit smaller, the girls that little bit lovelier.

While the sun is up the beach at Ipanema comes alive as the residents of Rio's top district lap up the sun and take to the cooling waters of the South Atlantic. At night the beach goes to sleep except for the occasional game of soccer or the joggers that never seem to stop.

Unlike Copacabana few hotels line the beach and only two bars face it, instead the avenue is lined by expensive apartment blocks taken straight from the pages of *Vogue* magazine.

Ipanema is truly residential, so when hunger calls the residents don't mind losing sight of the beach as they go in search of the area's more intimate restaurants where lunch will be played out into the early evening.

Spending a day on Ipanema Beach is not an experience you will forget.

LEBLON

Separated from Ipanema by the canal at Jardim de Alah which links the Lagoa to the sea, Leblon stretches a further one-and-a-half kilometers to the west. With many of the same characteristics of Ipanema, Leblon is even more residential although no less crowded at the weekend, with one solitary bar, Canecão 70, overlooking the beach, and few hotels.

VIDIGAL

A small pretty beach of some 500 meters, Vidigal has become the private beach of the Rio-Sheraton Hotel which sits directly behind it.

SÃO CONRADO

São Conrado, or Pepino as it is better known, is home to two of Rio's main resort hotels, the Inter-Continental and Nacional, as well as being the landing area for the city's hangliders who pack the sky each weekend with their colorful kites. Pepino is also home to the beautiful Gavea Golf Club.

BARRA DA TIJUCA

At over fifteen kilometers long Barra is Rio's longest beach.
While serving the new residential area of Barra in its first four miles, a mini-Copacabana, it becomes more deserted as you go along the coast where you will always find a spot for your own beach barbecue, even at the weekend. The lack of buses keep most of the people away from Barra, and that will include you if you don't get a car.
Expect to find a cooling breeze on Barra at any time of year.

RECREIO DOS BANDEIRANTES

A huge rock marks the end of Barra and here starts a stretch of sand of just over one kilometer known as Recreio.
Deserted during the week, Recreio fills up at the weekend as it is the end of the line for a number of bus routes.
During the week Recreio makes a pleasant change from Ipanema and Copacabana and an enjoyable meal can be had at reasonable prices at the Ancora restaurant overlooking the beach. Ancora is open daily from 9 a.m. to midnight.
Because of the large rock, Recreio is sheltered for swiming. Do not try and swim around the rock however, as you are likely to join a number of others at the bottom of the sea who have discovered that the rock is larger than it looks.

PRAINHA

150 meters long Prainha is a surfers' beach like Arpoador. Inhabited at the weekend by the young surfers and their followers, deserted in the week.

GRUMARI

A thirty minute drive along the beaches of Barra from Ipanema will take you to one of Rio's most unspoilt beaches, Grumari. During the week Grumari is practically deserted, even at the height of the summer season, but fills up at the weekend with Cariocas looking for a variation from Ipanema and Copacabana.
A couple of shacks on the beach serve drinks and snacks but otherwise the area is unspoilt. If you visit Grumari you will have to go by car. Take the opportunity then to drive on up the hill at the end of the beach. Just over the brow of the hill you will come to a little shack restaurant, *Vista Alegre* (Happy View), on a tight bend in the road. Stop here to appreciate the excellent *Caipirinhas* and a magnificent view over the Marambaia sandbank which stretches below far into the distance. Don't bother to go in search of this

virgin sand though as it belongs to the navy. *Vista Alegre* is open seven days a week from 8 a.m. to 10 p.m.

If you think you have seen Grumari before, that could be because it was the featured beach in Michael Caine's popular comedy, "Blame It On Rio".

Grumari is so deserted during the week that "Blame It On Rio" could be filmed without any interference from outsiders, a remarkable fact when you realise how close the beach is to the center of Rio.

BEACH WARES

On every beach in Rio but especially on Copacabana, Ipanema, Leme and Leblon, you will be surprised by the sophistication and number of wares on sale. Ice Creams, sun oil, natural sandwiches, clothes, hats, kites, and even beer, can all be bought without ever leaving your towel.

Beach salesmen are some of the most interesting characters you will meet during your stay in Rio so take full advantage of them and their good humor. Remember the beach, and their patch of it, is their livelihood. Prices, therefore, are normally fair and the products of good quality. If they weren't the local Carioca population would soon put them out of business.

SURVIVING ON RIO'S BEACHES

There is only one trick to having a good time on the beach and that is being *sensible*. If you are sensible and stop and think before you act, I promise you you will keep out of harm's way.

Swimming: When you arrive on the beach stop and look around you. Are other people swimming? Is the red flag up? How large are the waves?

Generally in Rio the waves are quite large, although even this can be deceiving as often they are breaking over a sand bank further out and are, in reality, only a couple of feet high. Look and see where people are standing, this will show you where the sandbank is, if there is one. Once through the waves you only have to contend with a gentle swell, but watch the currents. The currents in Rio tend to take you down the beach and not away from it. This is important to know because you will invariably end up coming out of the water further down the beach than you entered. Remember therefore to line up where you went in, and presumably where your towel and friends are, with a building at the top of the beach, buildings don't move!

If you are unlucky enough to get into trouble in the water don't panic. Rio has an excellent lifeguard service which keeps a constant watch on swimmers from points along the beach, from support boats and helicopters. If you get into trouble they will come and help you.

Sun: Don't forget that Rio is a tropical city, a fact that can easily be forgotten when you are being cooled by a pleasant breeze from the sea. If you end up burning yourself in your first few days believe me you will ruin your holiday and could end up in hospital. Listen to people who know, the residents, and stay in the shade for your first few days making sure to cover the top of your head when the sun is at its highest.

Keeping What is Rightfully Yours: The easiest way to lose your belongings in Rio is to take them to the beach.

You will often hear it said that Rio is a city with a high crime rate, while this is true I blame the visitor for eight beach robberies out of ten. It may seem incredible but every day in Rio a number of visitors go to the beach laden down with cameras, *walkmans,* all their holiday money, passports and plane tickets! They sit on the sand for awhile showing all the world and his brother exactly what they have then go in swimming leaving all their valuables unguarded on top of a towel. And surpise, surprise when they get back the valuables have gone for a walk never to be seen again.

Now I ask you, would you put your wallet and camera down in a busy street in New York, London, or Paris, then walk round the block and still expect them to be there when you get back? Of course not, so why do you do it in Rio? Is it hardly surprising that the staff at hotels and the local police force show little sympathy to such people.

Two times out of ten though the robbery is premeditated and you are set up as the white skinned tourist sticking out like a flashing beacon on the golden sands.

This is how the "sting" works.

Early on you will be spotted by a band of youths, the same band who helped take your camera and wallet for a walk the day before. But today you are smart, or so you think, you have hidden your valuables in your bag. But you forget, they saw the camera when you used it to take a photo of the bronzed beauty who went by, and didn't you show them your wallet when you bought the ice cream?

If you are sitting in a group you will most likely be quite safe, but once left alone, ironically to mind the bags while the others swim, you will be approached by a friendly looking lad who will normally try one of three aproaches. They are: A. Ask you the time. B. Ask for a light. C. Comment on what you are reading. Your first reaction will be panic – you don't think you can answer the youth and you have forgotten the phrase "I don't speak Portuguese". During your panic another youth will have approached from the other side where the bag is – get the picture? – grabbed it, and run. Simple but sweet, it rarely fails.

I appreciate that you don't want to be paranoid about every friendly Brazilian who comes along, so avoid problems by keeping your bag in view at all times.

Of course the solution to the problem is so simple it is ridiculous. Don't take valuables to the beach.

If you want to take photos fine. Go to the beach and take photos and then return to the hotel. This way you won't have your camera stolen nor will you get sand in it. Take your *walkman* if you wish, if it's always round your neck you won't lose it, will you?

And money. What do you really think you will buy on the beach that costs $1000. You would be lucky in a group to spend more than $10 so why take more? Rio is so cheap that it is highly unlikely that you will need to take anymore to the beach than you will mind losing, and that includes if you are going on to lunch.

Remember the byword is "be sensible", look around and see what the local Carioca takes to the beach.

Get the point?

Things To See and Do

BATEAU MOUCHE

At some stage during your visit to Rio you will almost certainly be overcome by the urge to explore the bay of Rio (Guanabara Bay) by boat. Now if you are not up to America or Admiral's Cup standard don't worry, the answer is the Bateau Mouche.

Bateau Mouche is a private company operating out of Botafogo who have built a solid reputation of giving value for money and looking after visitors well.

Bateau Mouche offer, every day but Monday, a morning and afternoon cruise, or a combination of both. The morning, cruise leaves at 9:30 a.m. and covers the lower half of the bay stopping for lunch and a swim at Piratininga.

Depending on the conditions of the sea this tour also takes in Copacabana Beach. The cruise ends at 1:30 p.m. and costs $25.

The afternoon cruise covers the top half of the bay including the Niteroi Bridge and a visit to Paqueta. Leaving at 2:30 p.m. and returning at 6:30 p.m. the afternoon cruise costs $17. Both tours can be combined for $30.

My personal suggestion would be to incorporate a cruise on the Bateau Mouche with a visit to near by Sugar Loaf. Go up Sugar Loaf early morning, around 9 a.m., and spend the morning there. Take an early lunch at either Cota 200 on Morro da Urca, the half way stage of Sugar Loaf, or at Sol e Mar which is from where the Bateau Mouche sails; then take the afternoon cruise at 2:30 p.m. which covers the most interesting part of the bay and has the benefit of coming back as Rio is starting to light up, an impressive sight from the water.

Bateau Mouche can be found at Av. Repórter Nestor Moreira, 11 in Botafogo (Sol e Mar Restaurant). Telephone: 295-1997 or 295-1947. Reservations can be made with the reception desk of your hotel in Rio who will also have the color brochure which describes the cruises further. The prices above include the transfer from your hotel to the Bateau Mouche.

THE BOTANICAL GARDEN

Rio is blessed with one of the world's most important Botanical Gardens, a paradise of plants and trees from the four corners of the earth tucked away off Rua Jardim Botanico behind the Jockey Club.

Founded by Dom João on June 13, 1808, Rio's Botanical Garden spreads over an area of about 340 acres, half of which is natural forest.

Over 5,000 species of plants live in the garden as well as innumerable types of birds and animals. The most impressive plants from a layman's point of view are the avenues of palms planted when the Garden first opened.

The time you spend in the garden, which is open from 8:30 a.m. to 5 p.m. or 6 p.m., will depend on your mood. You can take a quick stroll, sit and read a book, or take all day exploring the hidden secrets of the gardens. The area of the garden is well patrolled and totally safe so this is the time to go wild with creative photography.

The Garden can be entered in Rua Jardim Botanico either at number 920 or 1008 where the car park can be found. The library of the Botanical Garden is also situated at Rua Jardim Botanico, 1008 and it is more likely that you will find literature in English about the Garden here than at the smaller, although more famous, entrance at 920.

The Botanical Garden is a must for any visitor to Rio who likes nature.

HELICOPTER TOUR

One of the most impressive and spectacular tours you can undertake in Rio is unquestionably the 20 minute helicopter tour organized by Gray Line.

Leaving from the Jacarepaguá Airfield in Barra da Tijuca your helicopter will whisk you over the mountains and the *favelas* of Rocinha and Vidigal, down to the beaches of Leblon, Ipanema and Copacabana before circling Sugar Loaf and returning past Corcovado and the statue of Christ. The route is subject to alterations due to the prevailing weather conditions and other Rio air-traffic.

The cost of the helicopter tour is $48 and this includes the transfer to-and-from the airfield and your hotel. Reservations should be made in advance with Gray Line on 294-1444, 294-1196 or 274-7146.

Don't forget to take your camera and your nerve!

Note: Gray Line can modify the flight plan if there is a specific part of Rio you wish to fly over or to.

HIPPIE FAIR

The last thing you will see in the Hippie Fair is a hippie. Whoever named the fair obviously couldn't spell artisan.

Rio's Hippie Fair is located in Praca General Ososrio in Ipanema at the Copacabana end of Rua Visconde de Piraja and runs every Sunday from 9 a.m. to 6 p.m.

Hundreds of booths sell every imaginable type of arts and crafts, mostly of a very reasonable price and quality.

If you can't find a souvenir at the Hippie Fair you never will. You can buy beautiful paintings of Rio and Brazil, key rings, jewelery musical instruments, kites, hammocks, toys and even food. A particularly popular item are the leather goods at prices you won't believe, and that includes well made leather bean bags.

Prices in the Fair range from less than one dollar up into the hundreds but make sure you bargain. Everyone else does, especially if you are buying more than one item.

Rio's Hippie Fair is so well established that it is a popular weekly event even with the local Cariocas who go in search of shoes, bags, belts and other knicknacks.

You will not want to miss the Hippie Fair so make sure you plan for it early in your stay. If you are doing nothing your first Sunday go down to Ipanema and get it out the way since who knows what you will have planned for your second Sunday. Even if you don't buy anything on your first visit you will know what is available and that allows you to make a quick visit on your last Sunday if you have things that you want to pick up.

Many of the vendors speak English or at least understand it.

JEWELRY TOUR

Brazil is world famous for its gemstones and while you are in Rio you should not miss the opportunity of learning more about them, even if they are out of your budget.

A traditional attraction in Rio for many years has been the tour of H. Stern's workshops which since 1983 has been located in Ipanema at Rua Visconde de Piraja, 490.

The building, H. Stern's world headquarters, it is worth noting, is the largest space ever built exclusively for the production and sale of jewelry.

The tour itself is located on the third floor of the Stern building, is free, and can be taken anytime during normal shop hours.

The tour, which takes about 15 minutes, takes you through every aspect of the jeweller's work, from discovery to preparation and design, on to the final finished product. Your "tour guide" will be a Sony Walkman which comes in nine different languages. You can chose from English, Portuguese, Spanish, French, Japanese, German, Italian, Arabic and even Chinese.

Besides the actual tour you will be able to visit the Stern museum which currently houses the world's largest uncut gemstone, an aquamarine. On the floors below you will be able to see and hold fabulous examples of the finished product (Stern has 150,000 individual pieces of jewelry in stock in Rio) and can ask multi-lingual staff any questions the tour did not answer.

The H. Stern complex also houses a number of other jewelry showrooms, as well as a gift shop and an excellent handicraft and souvenir store. Information on 259-7442.

Another Rio jeweller to offer a tour of their workshops is Roditi. Roditi's tour is based at Av. Rio Branco, 39 (15th floor) in Centro.

(See "Shopping — Jewelry).

JOCKEY CLUB

Rio's Jockey club runs one of the most beautiful courses in the world which is easy and cheap to visit for any visitor to Rio. (See "Sport-Horse Racing").

Situated on the Gavea side of the Lagoa the race course sits between the glassy waters of the Lagoa and the greenery of the Botanical Garden and the mountains beyond. The magnificent view from the stands is capped by Corcovado and the statue of Christ the Redeemer.

Races at the course take place four times a week, 52 weeks of the year, and for a visitor to get into the palatial members' stand costs less than a dollar.

Racing in Rio dates back to June 12, 1825 when the course was in Botafogo, the present track only being inaugurated on July 11, 1926.

The most important race of the year is the Brazilian Grand Prix which takes place on the first Sunday in August and attracts horses from all over South America and sometimes from the U. S. A. and Europe. The first Grand Prix was raced in 1933 and attracted a crowd of 60,000, which is more than twice the capacity of the stands. Today the crowds are restricted on the big race day to an elegant 35,000; and in one afternoon Rio manages to combine its Derby and Royal Ascot in one.

For the record the Jockey Club boasts five separate stands, a paddock, a turf track of 1.34 miles, a sand track of 1.26 miles, and an Equestrian Village with more than 1,600 stalls.

During your visit to Rio you should spend sometime at the track; for a complete change I suggest the less crowded night time programme run on Mondays and Thursdays when the races take place under floodlights on what will be one of Rio's many balmy tropical nights. Can you ask for more?

MARACANA

Rio is the home of the Maracana Stadium. The largest of its kind in the world, it can hold a capacity crowd of close to 200,000.

Built for the 1950 World Cup, its' capacity has only been tested once when 199,854 turned up to see Brazil lose 2-1 to Uruguay in the final of the 1950 competition. Crowds of over 130,000 are far from rare at Maracana though, particularly when it is a classic between two local teams such as Flamengo and Vasco.

In 1983 and again in 1984 the big game turned out to the the final of the National Championship which attracted crowds in excess of 160,000 while 180,000 turned out to see Frank Sinatra play a memorable concert a few years back, a fact that is recorded in the Guinness Book of Records as the largest crowd ever for a single artist. Sinatra has now been followed by Kiss and the Pope no less, as well as the Brazilian and Russian volleyball teams.

If you are any sort of sports fan Maracana has to be visited during your stay in Rio. The week's most important game is played on Sunday afternoon, kicking off at 5 p.m. (See "Sports — Soccer"), but if you don't like crowds you can visit the stadium during the week. Maracana is open Monday to Friday from 9 a.m. to 5 p.m. and entry is through gate 18 in Rua Prof. Eurico Rabelo. Inside the stadium you can see a small, but interesting, sports museum and travel up in an express elevator to see the view from the Presidential Box. The rest of the tour, which normally includes the playing field and changing rooms, will depend on what is scheduled for the stadium on the day of your visit.

The best way to reach Maracana is by car or taxi, and the stadium is well sign posted.

A number of surprises lie in store for the first time visitor to Maracanã. The first, and major surprise, is just how advanced the stadium's design was for 1950, leaving many of the more modern stadiums in its shadow. For example, despite its size it is only 375 feet from the playing field to the very furthest viewing point. The playing area is large, by the way, measuring 120 by 82 yards.

The second surprise is that Maracana, or the Mario Filho Stadium to give it its' proper name, is more than just a soccer stadium.

The whole complex in fact boasts an athletics stadium and an Olympic swimming pool. Maracana is also the home of the Maracanazinho Gymnasium ("Little Maracana") with a capacity of 20,000. Maracanazinho is used for obvious sporting activities such as volleyball and basketball and is also the venue for most of the major concerts hosting in recent years: The Police, Van Halen, Joe Cocker, Genesis, Barry White, Earth Wind and Fire, Rick Wakeman, Peter Frampton, the Rio Jazz Festival plus most of the top names in the Brazilian music world.

MUNICIPAL THEATRE

Rio's historic Municipal Theatre, modelled on the Paris Opera and inaugurated on July 14, 1909, introduced guided tours of the building during 1985.

At the time of going to press it was expected that special tours for non-Portuguese speaking visitors would be started in 1987. For more information ask somebody who speaks Portuguese to call the theatre on 210-2463 (Ramal: 182).

NITERÓI

It's not very kind, although not far from the truth, to say that the best thing about Niterói are the views across the bay to Rio.

A visit to Niteroi though, is certainly worthwhile and if you are British you are sure to find yourself heading across the bridge one weekend to catch a game of rugby or cricket at the Rio Cricket and Athletic Club founded in 1872.

To visit and appreciate Niteroi properly you need a car. Cross the Rio-Niteroi Bridge, an experience in itself, and once through the toll gate follow signs to *Centro/Icaraí*. Turn off at the Shell Garage several miles down the road following signs to *Icaraí*, the wall to your right is the Rio Cricket Club, on emerging at Praia de Icaraí turn left and follow the coast along Estrada Leopoldo Froes. Now you will understand about those magnificent views of Rio.

Sticking to the coast road you will páss the Rio Yacht Club, not to be mistaken for the *late Clube do Rio*, and come to Praia São Francisco.

If you are getting hungry by this time you have several options ahead on the coast road.

On Praia São Francisco itself you will find a branch of Porcão, the excellent churrascaria *rodizio*, while further along at the end of Enseada de Jurujuba, where the road climbs to go round the headland, is the Hotel Samanguaia which serves an indifferent lunch that is saved by the tranquil setting of the hotel's varanda which overlooks the bay.

If tranquil settings are not your scene drive on into the village of Jurujuba where you will find the restaurant Bicho Papão which specializes in sea food. Lunch in this small fishing hamlet is never lazy with the constant flow of clients from Niteroi and Rio who are looking for something different at the weekend.

Continuing on through Jurujuba along the coast will bring you to the Fortaleza de Santa Cruz (The Fort of Santa Cruz) which guards the entrance to the bay of Guanabara.

Parts of the fort date back to the XVI century, to the time when Villegaignon first colonized Rio for the French in 1555. Since that time the fort has expanded and today is considered architecturally the most important historic fortification in the country.

The times the fort is open to the public vary. As of going to press it opened daily from 8 a.m. to 4 p.m., but this could easily change, so have someone who speaks Portuguese ring the fort on 711-0166 or 711-0462. The alternative is to take the Gray Line tour of Niteroi (See — Organized Sightseeing) which will show you the bridge, the beaches and the fort.

NORTHEAST FAIR

In complete contrast to the middle-class ambience of Ipanema's Hippie Fair is the Fair of the Northeast (*Feira do Nordeste*) which takes place every Sunday from 6 a.m. to 6 p.m. at the Campo de São Cristóvão, not far from the National Museum.

The Northeast Fair is a fair of the people, which offer thousands of booths of every size selling everything from a hammock and the beautiful lace wear of the Northeast, to a pig's head or a box of nails. You name it and the fair seems to have it, and at a very low price.

To get to the fair take a cab, as it is not far through the Rebouças tunnel from the zona sul. You will find plenty of cabs in the area to bring you back and if you have a car, parking is not difficult.

Be warned that the Fair of the Northeast is usually very hot and fairly dusty and some of the sights, especially the meat stalls, are not for the squeamish.

A visit to the fair is definitely an education into Brazilian ways. See it, if you can, but if time is short, make sure you see the Hippie Fair and not this one.

After a visit to the Fair of the Northeast you will know that you have been abroad.

PAQUETA ISLAND

Personally I consider Paqueta to be Rio's most overated tourist attraction, an attraction which is a throw back to the early 1960s when Rio still had to discover its full tourist potential.

Paqueta is a small, unassuming island tucked away at the top end of Guanabara Bay. Its charm in the 20th century is that no motorized transport is allowed on the island, the only method of getting about being horse-drawn carriages or the good old-fashioned bicycle.

As a tourist attraction it used to be "the" island to visit, a quiet tropical paradise, but that in retrospect seems ridiculous with the unspoilt beauty of hundreds of deserted islands easily accessible from Itacuruçá less than one-and-a-half hours drive from Rio.

As something to do, as a way to pass a day in Rio, Paqueta can be a very pleasant experience, if just for the boat ride up the bay. Boats leave regularly throughout the week from Praça XV — at the time of going to press the times were 5:30 a.m., 7:10 a.m., 10:15 a.m., 1:30 p.m., 3 p.m., 5:30 p.m., 7 p.m. and 11 p.m. — and take about an hour-and-a-half to cruise their way up the bay at a cost of less than 50 cents.

Hydrofoils do the same journey in less than 25 minutes sailing at the weekend on the hour from 7 a.m. to 4 p.m. and during the week from 8 a.m. to 5 p.m. The cost by hydrofoil is about $1 and the ideal is to go one way by hydrofoil and the other by boat.

The other method of visiting Paqueta is to take the afternoon cruise on the Bateau Mouche (See Above) which calls in to Paqueta late in the afternoon.

Once on Paqueta your time is your own, the choice a horse-drawn carriage or a bicycle made for one, two, three and even four. All are available close to where the boat docks.

It is unlikely that you would want to stay on Paqueta but if you do, the best hotel is the Flamboyant on Praia Grossa (Tel.: 397-0087) which also has the island's best restaurant.

PARKS

Rio is blessed with a multitude of pleasant parks for you to discover during your stay, two of which, the Tijuca National Park and the Botanical Garden, I have dealt with separately.

Rio's most famous park is **Flamengo** which is transversed every week day by a large percentage of the population on their way to-and-from work in the city.

Flamengo is the result of Brazil's largest landscaping project that reclaimed the whole park area from the bay. Today the park is a sportsman's paradise with tennis courts, football pitches, basketball and volleyball courts, as well as the beach. On Sunday one of the expressways that cuts through the park is closed to give even more space for recreation. Flamengo is quite safe to walk in during the day as long as you stick to the beaten track. I would not however recommend it at night when you are likely to be the only person in the park.

Other sites to be found in the Flamengo Park are the city's yacht Marina, the Monument to the Dead of World War II, the Modern Art Museum, the Carmem Miranda Museum and the excellent restaurant Rio's.

Rio's best kept park, and my personal favourite, is the **City Park**. Situated on the Estrada Santa Marina in Gavea. The City Park offers 10 acres of sloping lawns and romantic ponds to picnic by, and the small but interesting, City Museum. The City Park is open daily from 8 a.m. to sunset.

Rio's other parks include: **Quinta da Boa Vista**, home of the National Museum and Zoo. You will certainly visit this well laid out park during your stay in Rio, but stay away at weekends; **Campo Santana**, where the Republic was proclaimed in 1889; **Parque da Catacumba**, a small park on the Epitácio Pessoa side of the Lagoa which has a permanent outdoor exposition of sculptures; **Parque do Catete**, or rather the grounds of the Museum of the Republic; Passeio Publico, situated in front of the Mesbla department store downtown which was Rio's first park. These are just a few of Rio's parks. I have not mentioned Parque Lage (Rua Jardim Botanico, 414), Parque Garota de Ipanema (Arpoador) and many others. But I don't think you need to be told what a park is, search them out and explore, that is half the fun.

In the parks remember to "be sensible", and don't go wandering off into the bushes. In tropical Rio you never know what you might find!

PLANETARIUM

Rio has a modern Planetarium which you will pass to your right when heading out to São Conrado and Barra via the Dois Irmãos tunnel.

Built in 1970 the Planetarium was totally reformed in 1976 and now offers a varying programme throughout the year including musical presentations which use the Planetarium's unique facilities for special effects. The majority of the educational programmes are in Portuguese unless otherwise stated. If you speak Portuguese you can ring 274-0096 for more information.

The Planetarium which is situated in Rua Padre Leonel Franca in Gavea also has its own theatre and amphitheater.

SANTA TERESA AND THE BONDE (STREETCAR)

Santa Teresa is one of Rio's prettiest residential areas, an area where time has stood still. Houses dominate rather than the tall apartment blocks which have sprouted elsewhere, and even the old street cars continue to run.

If you want to visit Santa Teresa (see "Art and Antiques — Chacara do Céu Museum") go by car or get a cab, on no account use the **bonde**. (streetcar). In writing this book I have been told time and time again by hotels and consulates to emphasize that the *"bonde"* is Rio's tourist "black spot." Gangs of youths literally strip tourists clean on the bonde and nobody, including the driver, will come to their aid. To stop the assaults, which are also directed against the local population, the streetcar company has enclosed some of the cars.

Should you be the macho type who still insists on riding the *bonde* because you want to tell your grandchildren you went across the arches in Lapa then please leave all your valuables, including your camera at the hotel and carry very little else. For your next trick I suggest you ride the subway in New York through Harlem at night with a carrier bag full of dollars and a big sign saying "rob me", it amounts to the same thing.

TIJUCA FOREST

Rio's largest park is the Tijuca National Park of which the Tijuca Forest is one small part.

As you look up at Corcovado from the Lagoa the mass of greenery you see clinging to the edge of the mountain is the Tijuca National Park, and despite what would appear to be almost dense jungle it is quite accessible, with roads running through its entire length allowing visitors to enjoy its many natural wonders.

The most famous part of the park is situated in the heart of the mountains at a place called Alto da Boa Vista. Alto da Boa Vista can be reached from any part of the city. The prettiest route for visitors is to take the Lopes Quintas turning off Jardim Botânico, two roads before the edge of the Botanical Garden, that links with Estrada Dona Castorina, which takes you past the famous Chinese View and Emperor's Table. The other attractive route is to take the Estrada da Canoas which climbs up the mountains from Praça de São Conrado; first right past the El Pescador Restaurant..

At Alto da Boavista you will find the entrance to the Tijuca Forest off Praça Afonso Vizeu. A short distance into the forest you come to the Cascatinha Taunay, an attractive waterfall which falls over 100 feet. In the car park opposite you will see a plan of the forest, including the park's two restaurants, "Os Equilos", and "A Floresta."

Both restaurants are open for lunch and an early dinner (last orders at 7 p.m.), what they lack in gourmet cooking they more than make up for in atmosphere and moderate prices.

The forest is currently open from 7 a.m. to 9 p.m. and can be reached in about 30 minutes from anywhere in the city.

If you go for a walk in the park try and keep to the main paths otherwise you may get disorientated and lose the way back to your car.

However long you stay in Rio you will always have something new to discover in this beautiful forest which is unique for a major city.

TIVOLI FUNFAIR

Rio has a permanent funfair which is located on the shores of the Lagoa in front of the Jockey Club and next to the Drive-In Movie.

Tivoli, as the fair is called, is adequate for children although the people at Disney are not likely to lose any sleep over it as competition.

Tivoli is open Thursday and Friday from 2 p.m. to 8 p.m. Saturday from 3 p.m. to 11 p.m. and Sunday from 10 a.m. to 10 p.m.

VILLA RISO — COLONIAL TOUR

To revisit a little piece of Rio's Colonial past you need to head for the Villa Riso in São Conrado.

The tour of the Villa Riso, which lasts from 12:30 p.m. until 4 p.m., includes a look at the historic gardens and house which date from the early 18th century; a presentation of Brazilian musical theatre from 1860 through 1914; and a buffet lunch where a traditional *feijoada* and barbecue are served.

The tour has been organized by the Brazilian pianist Cesarina Riso whose family has owned and restored the Villa Riso since 1932.

At the time of going to press the Villa Riso tour takes place every Tuesday although more days will be added during the high season. To reserve your place on the tour you should call 322-1444, 322-0899 or 274-1708 in advance. The tour, including lunch, costs around US$22 and they can arrange to pick you up from your hotel.

The Villa Riso is located at Estrada da Gavea, 728 (next to the Gavea Golf Club) in São Conrado.

THE ZOO

Rio's zoo takes a lot of stick but really it's not that bad. Not one of the world's great zoos it is still a pleasant place to spend a sunny afternoon and see a wide variety of animals and an excellent bird collection.

A visit to the zoo can be combined with a look at the National Museum (See "Museums") which is located nearby.

Rio's zoo is open from 8 a.m. to 4:30 p.m. but closed Monday. Entry is virtually free.

ORGANIZED SIGHTSEEING

A variety of tour companies operate in Rio and their tours can be booked at most hotel receptions or through the better travel agents.

While all tours may seem equal on paper, some are more equal than others.

A company with an excellent reputation the world over, and one it upholds in Brazil, is Gray Line. As a major ground operator Gray Line offers more than just the usual tours and claims to be able to look after every demand a tourist could possibly make. So if you don't see a tour that takes your fancy go and speak to them. If time is limited, and money is not, then this is certainly the way to see the sites. Gray Line's main office is in the Rio-Sheraton Hotel but reservations can be made on 274-7146, 294-1444 or 294-1196.

Another operator with an excellent and growing reputation is Rio Sightseeing who can be contacted on 542-1393 or 541-5696. Other major operators in Rio are Lup Tour (541-4747), Combratur (541-6599) and Sul America (257-4732 or 257-4235).

Pamphlets describing the tours can be found in all hotel lobbies, with most of the tour companies covering the following.

- Corcovado/Tijuca Forest (Duration: 4 hours. Cost $17).
- Sugar Loaf/Botanical Gardens (Duration: 4 hours. Cost: $18).
- Rio By Night (Duration: 6 hours. Cost: $40).
- Petrópolis (Duration: 6 hours. Cost: $20).
- City Tour (Duration: 4 hours. Cost: $13).
- Paradise Island (Duration: 9 hours. Cost: $36).
- Soccer Game (Duration: 4 hours. Cost $17).
- Samba (Duration: 4 1/2 hours. Cost: $40).
- Macumba (Duration: 5 hours. Cost: $38).
- Santa Cruz Fort/Niterói (Duration: 4 hours. Cost: $15).
- Helicopter (Duration: 20 minutes. Cost: $48).
- Búzios (Duration: 11 hours. Cost: $40).
- Shooting the Rapids (Duration: 9 hours. Cost: $50).
- Museums of Rio (Duration: 4 hours. Cost: $15).

The Art World of Rio de Janeiro

MUSEUMS

It is difficult to believe that *any* visitor comes to Rio specifically to see the city's museums and that is why I can never understand the attack of culture which hits most tourist the moment they leave their own back yard. These "tourists" are the very same people who would never dream of entering a museum in their own country, yet for some reason they are content to waste what precious time they have on holiday plodding around exhibitions which hold the minimum of interest for them.

Basically if you don't like museums stay out of them. If, however, you have an historical interest, and time is on your side, then there are a number of museums in Rio which are worth tracking down.

National History Museum

Praça Marechal Ancora (near Praça XV de Novembro) — Centro. Open Tuesday through Friday from 10 a.m. to 5:30 p.m., and Saturday, Sunday and holidays from 2:30 p.m. to 5:30 p.m. Tel.: 240-7978.

The National History Museum was only founded as recently as 1922 during the celebrations for the 100th Anniversary of the Declaration of Independence but for all that it is located in one of the city's oldest buildings, parts of which date back to 1603 when it was the Fortaleza de São Tiago (São Tiago Fort).

The building alone is worth visiting the National History Museum for, a museum which covers the history of Brazil from its discovery in 1500 to the Proclamation of the Republic in 1889. The National History Museum is considered to be Brazil's most important historical museum.

Itamaraty Palace (Diplomatic Museum)

Av. Marechal Floriano, 196 — Centro. Two minutes walk from Presidente Vargas metro station. Open Tuesday through Friday from 11 a.m. to 5 p.m.

The Itamaraty Palace was the first of Rio's museums to be fully restored and therefore outstanding in comparison with the others.

Only re-opened in the second half of 1983 the museum has expanded from four small rooms to take over the whole Itamaraty Palace, home to the Brazilian Foreign Service from 1899 until its move to Brasilia in 1970.

The Palace itself dates back to 1854 and was home to Brazil's first Presidents from 1889 until 1897 when the President's official residence moved to the Catete Palace (Museum of the Republic).

The Palace's most distinguished resident however would have been the Barão do Rio Branco, an outstanding statesman, who as Brazil's Foreign Minister helped shape the whole of South America as we know it today.

To get the most out of the Itamaraty Palace you should plan your visit in advance to guarantee a guide (Portuguese, English and French are available). For more information about guided tours call the Palace on 291-4411 and ask for Ramal (extention) 71.

Note: At the time of going to press the museum was closed for further restoration work.

Museum of the Republic

Rua do Catete, 179 — Flamengo. Next to the Catete metro station.

A visit to the Museum of the Republic, which first opened in 1960, would complement a visit to the National History Museum in that the Museum of the Republic picks up the story of Brazil from the Proclamation of the Republic in 1889 through to 1960 when the capital of Brazil changed to Brasilia, but sadly the museum has been closed for several years due to a lengthy restoration programme which began back in July 1984.

The museum itself occupies all three floors of one of the most impressive buildings of the Empire — The Catete Palace — which was built to a German design between 1858 and 1866.

In 1896 the Palace was purchased by the Government and served as the official residence of the President of the Republic hosting every Brazilian President from Deodoro da Fonseca until Getulio Vargas who committed suicide there on August 24, 1954.

At present the ground floor contains furniture, paintings and other objects pertaining to the first nine Presidents of the Republic, while the lavish second floor conserves the Palace's original decor. The third floor features the bedroom in which Vargas was found dead; exhibitions relating to Presidents Epitacio Pessoa, Juscelino Kubitschek and Castelo Branco; and the bedroom occupied by Cardinal Eugenio Pacelli in 1934 before he became Pope Pius XII.

While the Palace is being restored two tours of the building have been organized each month. To reserve a place on one of the tours, or to check if the museum has re-opened, you should call 265-9747.

The City Museum

Est. Santa Marinha (Parque da Cidade) — Gávea. Open Tuesday through Sunday from 12 noon to 4:30 p.m. Tel.: 322-1328.

Located in the city's best kept park, the City Museum has occupied the residency of the Marques de São Vicente, built in the second half of the 19th century, since 1948. In this pretty two-story house you will find objects and furniture set out in chronological order tracing the history of Rio de Janeiro and the part it played in the overall history of Brazil. Although small, a visit is worth combining with a stroll in the park or even a picnic.

The National Museum

Quinta da Boa Vista — São Cristóvão,: Open Tuesday through Sunday from 10 a.m. to 4:45 p.m. Tel.: 264-8262.

If you visit one museum during your stay in Rio, the National Museum will be the one. Not only is it featured on most of the organized tours but it also sits next to the city's Zoo and Fauna Museum (open noon to 5 p.m.).

Founded by Dom João VI on June 6, 1818, the National Museum is the country's oldest Scientific Institute. Starting as the House of Birds it has subsequently been called the Royal Museum and the Imperial Museum before becoming the present National Museum.

Although dedicated to the sciences and featuring over one million items including Brazil's most complete archeological, zoological, paleontological, botanical, ethonological, mineral and classical antiquity collections, it is the actual home of the museum that is of great historical importance.

Built in 1803 this impressive palace was given as a gift by its wealthy Portuguese owner, Elias Antonio Lopes, to Dom João VI when he came to Brazil in 1808. It acted as the residence of the King during his time in Brazil, and afterwards served the same purpose for the Emperors Pedro I and Pedro II and as the seat of the Imperial Government up until the Proclamation of the Republic in 1889.

The house became the National Museum in 1892. But sadly there are no traces of its historical past to be found in the museum.

Of special interest to the foreign visitor will be the Bendego meteorite to be found on the ground floor. The metorite discovered in the State of Bahia in 1888 is the largest ever found in the Southern Hemisphere. On the second floor the South American and Brazilian Archaeology rooms should be of interest as well as the rooms dedicated to Indian ethnology and Brazilian folk exhibits.

Situated close by at the entrance to the zoo you will find the Fauna Museum displaying stuffed birds and mammals from the country's different regions including the Amazon, the Pantanal of Mato Grosso, and the Tocantins River in Goias.

To get to the National Museum, Zoo and Fauna Museum follow signs to Maracana until you find Quinta da Boa Vista posted, which is reached by crossing the São Cristóvão Viaduct between Praça da Bandeira and the Maracana Stadium. I advise you to visit the area during the week when it is less crowded than the weekends.

Carmem Miranda Museum

Av. Ruy Barbosa — Parque do Flamengo. Open Tuesday through Friday from 11 a.m. to 5 p.m. and on Saturday and Sunday from 1 p.m. to 5 p.m. Tel: 551-2597.

This small well kept museum, opened in 1976, is worth a quick visit if you are passing. Dedicated to one of Brazil's most famous exports, the singer and actress Carmem Miranda, the museum features the late star's clothes, jewels, awards and costumes.

ART & ANTIQUES

Brazil has a vibrant art world which won't be found in any stuffy museum or formal art gallery, instead it will be found in the small private galleries which abound in both Rio and São Paulo, galleries like the *Galeria de Art Jean-Jacques* in Urca which specializes in the primitive school of Brazilian art.

The art of Brazil is something to be appreciated but above all enjoyed by the visitor, it is art that you will want to buy as a reminder of time spent in Brazil and *Cidade Maravilhosa*. Leave the great Masters to the formal galleries of Europe and the U.S., they are not of the Brazilian spirit.

Art galleires are a Brazilian way of life. You pass one, you enter, you appreciate. If you like something and have the money, you buy it. Simple but that is what art is all about.

As you walk around Rio you will come across many galleries but to save you some shoe leather I suggest you head for either the Gavea Shopping Center (Rua Marques de São Vicente — Gavea), the Cassino Atlantico center under the Rio Palace Hotel in Copacabana or the Itanhanga Art Center at Estrada da Tijuca, 1636, almost opposite the Itanhanga Golf Club. All the centers have a number of art and antique stores which cover a wide range of Brazilian styles. Enter and appreciate, you are under no obligation to buy and you will learn far more than by sticking to the more formal galleries.

One gallery which it is worth going out of your way to visit is the *Galeria de Arte Jean-Jacques* located in a house at the entrance to Urca, a short walk from Sugar Loaf (Rua Ramon Franco, 49 — first right as you head away from Sugar Loaf). *Jean-Jacques* specialize in Brazilian primitive art, the most popular art form with visitors and a style that is now catching on in the U.S. and Europe. The gallery has its own full programme of shows planned for the year. Prices vary from $60 to $600 for a medium size painting although you can pick up a good lithograph for $20. The gallery is open Tuesday to Saturday from 11 a.m. to 8 p.m. To contact Jean himself, who speaks perfect English, call 542 1443.

Hippie Square Art

If you see something you like at the Sunday Hippie Fair in Ipanema (Praça General Osorio) or in the daily exhibition in front of the Othon Palace Hotel on Copacabana Beach don't be ashamed, it has happened to others before you.

The only criticism that can be levelled at the art to be found at the Hippie Fair or in Copacabana is that it is painting to formula.

Basically, the customers at these two fairs are visitors, not just foreign visitors but visitors from all over Brazil, so it is likely that they are seeing the works for the first time as thousands have done before. The artists therefore produce scenes that have sold well in the past, scenes that have proven popular with the visitors that came before. Don't misunderstand me: the artists are good but they are also businessmen, they paint to demand.

If you see a particular painting or piece of art that you like, and there is every chance you will, buy it. The prices are not high and it is unlikely that you will see the likes of it hanging on your friend's wall, unless, of course, they visited the Hippie Fair or Copacabana when they came to Rio!

Antique Fairs

As the artists have their fair at the Hippie Square on Sunday it is the turn of the antique dealers on Saturday, when they meet at Praça Marechal Ancora, close to Praça XV, and on Sunday when they meet at Casa Shopping in Barra. Open from 10 a.m. to 6 p.m., the fair has over 60 stalls which offer smaller antiques from china to guns, from silver picture frames to rugs. Both fairs offer options for a lazy lunch. Albamar, in Praça Marechal Âncora, and Rodeio, in Casa Shopping.

Antique Auctions (Leilão)

If you are in Rio for any length of time, and know what you are looking for, you will find that the local auctions can be both an interesting and profitable pastime.

The main auctioneers normally announce their up-and-coming auctions in the weekend editions of *O Globo* and *Jornal do Brasil*.

The main auction houses in Rio are:

Leone — Av. Francisco Otaviano, 132 — Copacabana. Tel: 287 4758.

Banco das Artes — Rua das Laranjeiras, 540 — Botafogo. Tel: 265 0123.

Ernani — Rua São Clemente, 385 — Botafogo. Tel: 286 3246.

Galeria de Arte Ipanema — Rua Anibal Mendonça, 27 — Ipanema. Tel: 239-2032.

Investirarte — Cassino Atlantico Shopping Mall — Copacabana. Tel: 521-1442.

THE FORMAL GALLERIES

Rio is not blessed with any outstanding art galleries in the traditional sense of the word. It is explained that the weather is to blame, for not only does Rio's tropical weather attack the paintings but it also keeps the general public away on the beach. If you want to see paintings and are Brazilian you go to São Paulo, like Paulistas come to Rio for the beach.

Rio does however have two locations that attract art lovers of whatever nationality or background: the National Museum of Fine Arts and the Chacara do Céu Museum.

National Museum of Fine Arts

Rio's most important art collection is to be found at Av. Rio Branco, 199, almost opposite the Municipal Theatre. Boasting more than 10,000 pieces, the museum splits the display between Brazilian artists of the colonial period and 19th century, Brazilian artsits of the 20th century, and foreign artists.

One of Rio's best run museums, the National Museum of Fine Arts is open Monday, Wednesday and Friday between noon and 6 p.m., on Tuesday and Thursday from 10 a.m. and on Saturday and Sunday and holidays from 3 p.m. to 6 p.m.

Chacarà do Céu Museum

The Chacarà do Céu ("Little House in Heaven") is a unique museum hidden away in the heights of Santa Teresa at Rua Murtinho Nobre, 93.

Opened in 1972, Chacará do Céu was the residence of the late Brazilian industrialist Raymundo Ottoni de Castro Maya who left the house and his magnificent collection of art to the nation. The house has been left as it was when Castro Maya lived and this is what gives the place its extraordinary charm. The collection on display covers paintings, sculptures, silverware, furniture and other objects which reflect the good taste of their owner. Outstanding amongst the collection are works by Candido Portinari, one of Brazil's most important artists, but also on display are works from Monet, Matisse, Picasso and Salvador Dali. Chacara do Céu is open Tuesday through Saturday from 2 p.m. to 5 p.m. and on Sunday from 1 p.m. to 5 p.m. The museum is best reached by car or taxi, but make sure it waits for you, or you can take the 206 or 214 bus to the Cuvelo stop from the Menezes Cortes bus terminal. Despite what you may be told, avoid the Santa Teresa streetcar.

Modern Art Museum (MAM)

MAM is not what it should be, nor is it ever likely to be after a fire in 1978 destroyed its entire collection. With no collection of its own MAM now relies on staging diverse exhibitions throughout the year; while some of these are quite outstanding the general standard is pretty mediocre. Avoid unless raining. Open Tuesday through Sunday from noon to 6 p.m.

Rainy Days and Cloudy Afternoons

Even tropical Rio gets the odd day of rain, especially towards the end of the year, and you may get a cloudy day or two to contend with.

Although not designed for rain Rio, as a major city, does offer several options for the day you can't lie on the beach topping up your golden tan.

The following are a few suggestions, and anything that can be done on a rainy day can of course be done on a cloudy afternoon.

RAINY DAYS

— Window shopping in Rio Sul or Barra Shopping.
-- Take H. Stern's jewelry tour in Ipanema.
— Visit the museums and art galleries.
-- Go bowling or ice-skating!
— Play a game of squash.
-- Take a sauna.
— Go to the movies.
— Visit the Jockey Club and go racing.
— Spend four hours over a leisurely lunch.
— Go for tea at the Lord Jim or Rio Palace.
— Try your luck in the video game arcades.
— Write your postcards and letters.

CLOUDY AFTERNOONS

-- Shopping in Ipanema.
— Visit Maracana.
-- Visit the Zoo.
— Walk around the Botanical Gardens.
— Tour the historical points of downtown Rio.
-- Play golf or tennis.
— Hire a boat and go for a sail in the bay.

- Visit Tivoli funfair.
- Go for a walk in the Tijuca Forest.
- Take the Bateau Mouche or hydrofoil up to Paqueta Island.
- Take a tour to Petropolis.
- Hire a car and explore Rio.

Tourist Timetable

Certain events only take place on specific days in Rio so here is a timetable to help you plan your visit.

Monday
- Beija Flor (Sugar Loaf)
- Horse Racing (Jockey Club)

Tuesday
- Villa Riso Colonial Tour

Thursday
- Horse Racing (Jockey Club)

Friday
- Shows up Sugar Loaf.

Saturday
- Horse Racing (Jockey Club)
- Feijoada (Most hotels and restaurants)
- Shows up Sugar Loaf.
- Antiques Fair (Centro)

Sunday
- Hippie Fair (Ipanema)
- Northeast Fair (São Cristóvão)
- Horse Racing (Jockey Club)
- Soccer (Maracanã)
- Antiques Fair (Casa Shopping)

You should also note that golf, as a non-member of a club, can only be played Tuesday through Friday, while H. Stern's jewelry tour is open Monday through Saturday during normal commercial hours.

There is no secret to surviving in Rio de Janeiro you just have to be sensible.

E

**Sport
Recreation
Clubs**

Sport and Recreation

BALLET

Ballet in Rio has become immensely popular over the last decade, both to watch and to learn. If you are in Rio long enough and want to take lessons the best schools are those run by Dalal Achcar, director of the Rio Ballet Company, who uses the methods of Britain's Royal Academy of Dancing.

The Ballet Dalal Achcar can be contacted on 247-6974, 322-9794 or 274-8169. The schools are found in Ipanema at Rua Visconde de Piraja, 233; in Gavea at Rua das Oitis, 20; and in São Conrado in the Fashion Mall.

BILLIARDS/SNOOKER

While a number of private clubs, like the Yacht Club and Paissandu, have their own tables there are very few locations around town open to the visitor. Two locations which are open, and offer tables at a reasonable price, are the *Clube do Taco* at Rua Barata Ribeiro, 655 in Copacabana and the *Pé de Vento* in Estrada da Canoa in São Conrado (see "Bowling").

BOAT HIRE

Rio de Janeiro should be a yachtsman's paradise but unfortunately the high cost of imported boats and parts has kept the sport limited to a small group of rich enthusiasts. The exception is dinghy sailing where Brazil has produced a number of world and Olympic champions.

The opening of Rio's own marina gave the sport a more democratic appeal taking it from behind the hallowed and sacred walls of the Rio Yacht Club and throwing the sport open to more people who could afford the boat but not the yacht club share!

Visitors who wish to hire a boat also benefited from the move to the marina in Gloria where you can hire all manner of vessels from a windsurfer at around $5 an hour to a luxury motorcruiser which will set you back several hundreds of dollars for the day. In the middle would be a 32' motor cruiser for about $100 or a yacht of the same size for $120. Reservations should be made in advance at the marina which it is wise to visit early in your stay to check on craft availability, especially as a number of the rental firms are not on the phone.

If you wish to call for more information try 265-0797 (Marina da Gloria), 285-2247 (SP Nautica) or 285-3097 (Escola de Vela). Two Rio based companies that organize boat hire, fishing expeditions and diving are Ponto Mar (266-6066) and Atlantic (551-5988).

If you wish to visit or use the elegant late Clube do Rio de Janeiro (Rio Yacht Club) and are already a member of a recognized club I suggest that you write to the Commodore in advance at Av. Pasteur, Botafogo explaining the situation. If you have already arrived in Rio, and have your yacht club membership card with you, ask the hotel to ring the club secretary on 295-4482 to see if the club will extended to you a temporary membership.

If you wish to hire a *saveiro* (Brazilian schooner) in the Angra dos Reis area, to the west of Rio, call Mauro Dantas at A.C. Dantas

Transpórtes Maritimos, on 259-2599, or Sepetiba Turismo on 237-5119.

BOWLING

Bowling is not and never has been a popular sport in Brazil and the only electronic alley in the country is located in São Paulo.

If however you bowl for fun then you should be able to amuse yourself at Rio's two bowling alleys which are both situated in São Conrado. To be more specific, Estrada da Canoa which is the first right having passed the restaurant El Pescador.

Pé de Vento and *Strike* are open Monday through Friday from 6 p.m. to 2 a.m. and at the weekend from 2 p.m. to 2 a.m.

CAMPING

Camping in Brazil is organized by the *"Camping Clube do Brasil"*, who are members of the "International Federation of Camping and Caravaning".

In Rio the *"Camping Clube do Brasil"* can be contacted at Rua Senador Dantas, 75 (29th floor) in Centro or by calling 262-7172.

The club has organized camp sities throughout Brazil, including twelve in the State of Rio which are located in Cabo Frio (two sites), Friburgo, Araruama (two sites), Paraty, Araial do Cabo, Itatiaia, Muri, Barra da Tijuca, Recreio das Bandeirantes, and Atafona, while there are at least a further 50 privately owned sites scattered throughout the state.

DARTS

If you are looking to throw a few arrows during your stay in Rio you should head for the city's two main pubs which are both situated in Rio's zona sul.

Rio's most famous and British pub is The Lord Jim located in Rua Paul Redfern in Ipanema, Darts are popular here so come early and be prepared to wait your turn. The Lord Jim is open from 5 p.m. through to 1 a.m. (closed on Monday).

The other home for darts in Rio is The Queen's Legs at the top (Botafogo) end of the Lagoa at Av. Epitacio Pessoa, 5030. Open daily from 6 p.m.

FISHING

The best way to go fishing in Rio is with one of the members of the yacht club (Tel. 295-4482) who has his own boat. If this is not possible go to the marina in Gloria where you can hire boats with all the necessary equipment, including a skipper to take you to the main fishing grounds.

The cost of such an outing is going to depend on what sort of fish you are after. If you want to go game fishing for Marlin, whose season runs November through January, then you can expect to pay up to $1,000 for a boat that will take five people fishing comfortably; this price you will be glad to know includes lunch!

For more information visit the marina (265-0797) or call Ponto Mar (266-6066), Navega (717-0295) or Atlantic (551-5988).

GOLF

Golf remains an almost exclusively foreign sport in Brazil, dominated by the American, European and Japanese communities. Little or no golfing equipment is made locally and the high price of land around Rio and São Paulo has restricted the number of courses in both cities.

The city of Rio has just two courses and both belong to private clubs with a high percentage of foreign members, the clubs however welcome visitors during the week from 7 a.m. until sunset. Green fees in Rio are relatively high in comparison to the cost of anything else in the city, and at the end of 1986 a round of golf with caddy was averaging out at $25 plus another $5 for the hire of clubs.

Rio's two golf clubs are Gavea Golf and Country Club (Tel. 322-4141) to be found at Estrada da Gavea, 800 in São Conrado, next to the Hotel Inter-Continental, and the Itanhanga Golf Club (Tel. 399-0507) which is located in Barra da Tijuca at Estrada da Barra, 2005. Itanhanga boasts both an 18 and 9 hole course.

Two other golf options can be found close to Rio. The Hotel do Frade, just past Angra (See "Trips — Green Goast"), has its own 9 hole course where they charge hotel residents green fees of approximately $15 for 18 holes. The other choice takes you in the opposite direction and up to the mountains and Teresopolis where you will find the tricky 9 hole Teresopolis Golf Club. Green fees in Teresopolis are around $10, and if you wish to stay the night you can do no better than the Hotel Alpina overlooking the course.

GYMNASTICS

Gymnastics is an obsession with the Carioca population that has caught on with the foreign community. If the "gymnasts" are not working out on the beach they will be found tucked away in one of the hundreds of clubs around the city. Choice is bound to be personal and linked to where your friends go and its convenience to your work and home. Two of the most popular locations with both short and long term visitors are the well equipped gymnasiums of the Rio-Sheraton Hotel (Tel. 274-1122) and Hotel Inter-Continental (Tel. 322-2200).

HANG GLIDING

A popular local sport, Brazil has already produced its own World Champion.

The center for hang gliding in Rio is the Pedra Bonita, a mountain which sits behind São Conrado where the flyers can be seen landing on the beach. If you want to get involved with the sport I suggest you go out to the landing area on Praia do Pepino.

Because of the money involved in this fairly expensive sport a good number of the pilots speak English and will be able to tell you how you learn the ropes or who can take you as a complete novice on a tandem flight. For more information call the *Associação Brasileira de Vôo Livre* (Tel. 220-4704) or Mauricio Barrelos (208-1625), Casimiro Clonowski (511-1500), and Rui Marra (226-6045 and 226-5207) who organize tandem flights.

HORSE RACING

Horse racing is a passion with a sizeable number of Cariocas and it is a passion that they can indulge in four days a week, 52 weeks of the year.

Rio is lucky enough to have one of the world's most beautiful racetracks, situated between the vibrant greenery of the Botanical Garden and the calm glassy waters of the Lagoa, a short cab ride from anywhere in the zona sul. (See "Things to See — Jockey Club").

Because of its arduous timetable the standard of racing is not as high as it might be, although only a real expert can tell. What is remarkable however is that the Jockey Club can offer a full programme of eight to ten races every Saturday and Sunday afternoon and every Monday and Thursday night. For the exact time of the races and for a few tips try the *Jornal do Brasil* which has excellent coverage of what is going on at the track.

Entry to the course is cheap, as of going to press you could get in to the public stands for the cruzado equivalent of 20 cents and the members enclosure for less than a dollar, and this to one of the best equipped and most civilized courses in the world.

I personally would recommend that you go for the members' enclosure which you are admitted to if you are a visitor to Brazil. Give the man at the main gate, situated in Praça Santos Dumont, your name and country of origin. The luxurious members' enclosure has a very well appointed bar and you can have a reasonable lunch or dinner at a table overlooking the course, a real taste of the good life! Reservations on 297-6655 or 274-0055.

Dress in the members enclosure should be smart casual, except for the big race day in August when the Grand Prix is held and collar and tie are the norm. In 1987 the G.P. Brasil will be held on Sunday, August 2 when a crowd of over 35,000 will be expected.

Betting at the track is relatively simple once you get the hang of it. Basically because of the small fields, normally between 8 and 16 horses, the Jockey Club only pays out on the first two horses.

For any race you can choose a horse to win (*vencedor*) or place (*placé*) — in the first two — or they have an extraordinary bet called a double (*dupla*). On the race card you will see that the runners for each race are broken into four equal groups. For the *dupla* you are predicting who the first two horses will be, but not by number, rather by group. If therefore you think that horse number 2 who is in group 1 will be one of the first two and horse number 9 who is in group 3 will be the other, then you bet *dupla* 13. It does not matter which way around the horses finish, it could be 2-9 or 9-2 you will still get paid. Your bet also covers all the other horse in those groups, probably 1, 2, 3 and 4 in group one and 9, 10, 11 and 12 in group three. Your chances of winning are therefore quite good. Of course if you think the first two horses across the line will both be from group one then you must bet the *dupla* 11. It sounds more complicated than it is.

In front of the main stand you will find a large totaliser board which gives you the up-to-the-minute account of how much money has been bet on each horse and *dupla*.

HORSE RIDING/ SHOW JUMPING/ POLO

Perhaps because most of Rio's greenery clings precariously to the side of the mountains, and the only other open spaces are taken up by the beach, there is little or no horse riding in Rio outside the private clubs.

The main clubs involved with horse riding in Rio are the *Sociedade Hipica Brasileira* on the Lagoa and the *Fazenda Clube Marapendi* in Barra.

The *Sociedade Hipica Brasileira* at Av. Borges de Medeiros, 2448 (Tel. 246 8090) will offer temporary membership to any visitor with an interest in horses but it is better to get your hotel to call in advance to confirm the situation or to write to the secretary of the club before leaving your own country.

All the horses at the *Hipica* are privately owned but many of the owners speak English and may be happy to lend you their mount if you know what you are doing. The club organizes regular show jumping competitions which are open to the public to watch.

The *Fazenda Clube Marapendi* revolves round its large equestrian center. Like the *Hipica*, the horses are privately owned but a simple telephone call might be all that is needed to organize a mount. The club is located almost opposite Barra Shopping on the Av. das Americas (Tel. 325-2440).

The only other club with horse riding in Rio is the *Itanhanga Golf Club* at Estrada Barra da Tijuca, 2005 (Tel. 399 0507). Itanhanga has a large stable of privately owned horses, many of which are involved in the polo played at the club over the weekend. Again, if you are interested in horses and know what you are doing, a call to the club would not go amiss. They would probably be delighted to greet you as a polo player and you will be following in the footsteps of Prince Charles who played there as a non-member during his visit to Brazil in 1978.

Your situation will of course be greatly helped at Itanhanga if you get your own home polo club to write to the club in advance of your visit.

ICE SKATING

Sounds like one for Ripley's "Believe It or Not", but yes you can ice-skate in tropical Rio de Janeiro.

Rio's one rink — the city used to have two — is located in Barra Shopping, out in Barra da Tijuca, and is open from 10 a.m. to midnight seven days a week.

MARATHON

Befitting a city of world renown, Rio has its own Marathon, a Marathon that is run over the most beautiful city course in the world.

Organized by the *Jornal do Brasil*, TV Manchete, and the running magazine *Viva*, the Rio Marathon attracts runners not only from all over South America, but also the top names from the U.S., Europe, Africa and Australasia. The record for the course is 2h.14m.13.S. set by Bill Rogers in 1981.

At the time of going to press the date of the 1987 Rio Marathon has been set for Saturday, August 22. It will be the eighth running of the Rio Marathon, a Marathon that attracted only 1,000 runners in 1980 but which quickly grew to 3,000 in 1981, 5,300 in 1982, 6,800 in 1983, 7,500 in 1984 and 9,000 in 1985 and 1986.

For more details about the Marathon, drop a note to the *Jornal do Brasil* at Av. Brasil, 500 or by telex to 021 23690 for the attention of the "Rio Marathon."

MOTOR RACING

At the Interlagos circuit in São Paulo on March 30, 1972, Brazil held its first Formula 1 Grand Prix. That same year a local boy by the name of Emerson Fittipaldi driving a Lotus won the World Championship, winning five of the season's 12 races. Two years later, in 1974, Fittipaldi won the World Championship for a second time, on this occasion in a McLaren.

In the years that have past since Fittipaldi's success Brazil has not let its hold on the world of Formula 1 slip.

At Long Beach in 1980 a relative newcomer from Brazil, Nelson Piquet, won his first Grand Prix. The following year, 1981, Piquet won his first World Championship, and like Fittipaldi he repeated the feat two years later. Brazil had won the world title four times in the space of twelve years and in the process become the third most successful motor racing nation of all time behind only Britain (ten titles) and Argentina (five titles for Juan Manuel Fangio).

The 1986 Formula 1 season was one of the most exciting ever with four drivers disputing the title for most of the season. Of the four drivers one was French, Alain Prost, the eventual champion, one was British, Nigel Mansell, and two were Brazilian, Nelson Piquet and Ayrton Senna.

Piquet and Senna, along with Prost, will be the favorites for the 1987 season which opens in Rio de Janeiro on April 12. Piquet will be driving the Williams-Honda in 1987, the car which won the constructors championship in 1986 by a large margin, while Senna will be behind the wheel of the familiar black and gold Lotus John Player Special which in 1987 will sport the Honda engine in place of the Renault turbo.

Rio de Janeiro hosted its first, Brazil's seventh, Grand Prix in 1978 at the then brand new circuit out in Barra da Tijuca by Jacarepagua. The Brazilian Grand Prix only moved to Rio quasi-permanently in 1981, and 1987 sees the seventh consecutive running of the race.

As of going to press the Formula 1 calendar for 1987 consists of 16 races with Brazil's sixteenth Grand Prix set to open the season on April 12.

The base of operations for the Grand Prix is the Inter-Continental Hotel and hotel rooms in Rio at this time are at a premium, even harder to find at the top hotels than during Carnival. Tickets for the race though are fairly easy to come by.

To get out to the Rio circuit you will need to hire a car, although during the time of the Grand Prix there are special bus services as well as tours for the enthusiasts.

The circuit (*Autodromo*) is well sign posted and parking plentiful.

Other live motor racing takes place throughout the year at the circuit and is listed in the sports pages of the local newspapers.

TV Globo (channel 4) will take coverage, live and in full, of the entire Formula 1 season which, in 1987, is set to run from April 12 through November 1, while TV Bandeirantes (channel 7) will cover the Formula Indy series in the U.S. from April 5 through November 1.

NATIONAL SPORTS: CRICKET, SOFTBALL, ETC.

Just because I do not mention a sport in the section of the guide does not mean that it is not played in Rio.

A lot of sport is played by the various national communities at an amateur level, and in Rio you can find such sports as badminton, cricket, hockey, softball, etc., and even an English language soccer team.

Because of the high cost of land in Rio's zona sul few of the sports have their own ground or club house and this tends to make them a little nomadic in their existence.

The easiest way of tracking down these wandering sportsmen and women, people who are usually delighted to welcome visitors into their fold be they here for four days or four years, is to contact the consulate of the countries you know to play the sport. For example if you want to find out how to contact the cricket playing community in Rio, you could ask at the British, Australian or South African consulates. Joining one of the local foreign community sports clubs in Rio is the quickest way for newcomers to make friends in the English speaking community.

RUGBY UNION

It may seem unlikely for a city as warm as Rio but the local rugby scene is fairly active, although always short of players of whatever calibre.

In Rio there are just three teams, Rio Rugby, Niteroi and Guanabara, of which Rio Rugby is seen as the "Ex-pats" team and basically English speaking.

The teams play most weekends between April and November and receive regular visits from the 20 or so clubs that are active in São Paulo. Recent years have seen visits from teams from Argentina, Bermuda, Botswana, Canada, the Cayman Islands, Chile, France, Uruguay, U.S.A. and Britain in the shape of such teams as the Penguins, Richmond and Edinburgh.

More information about Rugby Union in Brazil is available from the President of the "Associação Brasileira de Rugby" (Rua Prof. Vania de Abreu, 189) in São Paulo or in Rio you can contact Rio Rugby through the Lord Jim Pub.

SAUNA

Strange as it may seem, saunas are popular in tropical Rio and can be found at most private clubs and all the top hotels.

If you choose to go to one of the many commercial saunas (*"Termas"*) advertised in newspapers and tourist magazines expect to get a little bit more than you bargained for from the lovely "receptionists", but then this might be what you had in mind.

SKINDIVING

In recent years a number of companies have sprung up in the state of Rio de Janeiro which offer diving at all levels in the Rio, Búzios and Angra regions. The companies are able to rent you both the necessary equipment and a boat.

Contact in Rio the *Centro de Atividades Subaquáticas* (Marina da Gloria); *Ponto Mar* (Rua Prof. Alfredo Gomes 3, Tel. 266-6066); *Transamar* (Av. Alm. Barroso 63. Tel. 240-6325); *Atlantic* (Tel. 551-5988); *Subshop* (Rua Barata Ribeiro 774, Tel. 235-5446); or *Femar* (Rua Marquês de Olinda 18, Tel. 551-7597).

SKYDIVING

If you should be overcome by the urge to throw yourself out of a plane above Rio then the place to go is the Jacarepagua Airfield (Av. Alvorado, 2541) where the city's skydivers meet every Saturday and Sunday. At the same location you can hire your own plane to go sightseeing from the *Aeroclube do Brasil*. For more information ask somebody who speaks Portuguese to call 325-5301 or the *Academia Imagem* on 390-0978.

SOCCER

Brazil and soccer are synonymous.

Brazil is quite simply the world's most successful soccer nation which has as its high altar the Maracanã stadium in Rio, the world's largest stadium, capable of holding crowds of up to 200,000 people. (See "Things to See — Maracanã.")

Brazil can stake its claim to the number one spot by being the only nation to compete in all thirteen World Cup finals, having a record of playing 62 games, winning 41, drawing eleven and only losing ten since the first cup was played in Uruguay in 1930. Brazil has won the cup outright on three occasions, a feat matched only by Italy, Brazil's moments of glory coming in Sweden in 1958, Chile in 1962, and Mexico in 1970. The country was second in 1950, when the finals were held in Brazil; third in 1938 and 1978; and fourth in 1974. The World Cup finals are expected to be hosted by Brazil for the second time in 1994.

While Brazilians restrain their nationalistic tendencies for the World Cup, regional and club tendencies come to the boil every week in a display of sheer joy that is unknown in most of the so called civilized soccer playing nations. Going to see a game in any stadium, in Brazil but particularly Maracanã, is pure fun. Violence is rare between Brazilian soccer fans. Everything is done in good humor and visitors welcomed with open arms to join this celebration of national passion.

In Rio, and probably throughout Brazil, the most popular team is Flamengo. The Brazilian champions in 1983, Flamengo won the South American Cup in great style in 1981 and then went on to destroy Britain's Liverpool in a game played in Japan to decide the World Champion, a title which returned to Brazil in 1984 through the Porto Alegre team of Gremio.

Each year in Rio, Flamengo, Fluminense and Vasco alongside Bangu, Botafogo, America and several other smaller clubs, compete for two regional titles. The winners, which are usually from the clubs mentioned, then play-off to decide who is the champion of Rio for that year.

The rest of the year is filled up with the all important Taça de Ouro (Gold Cup), the Brazilian championship, which boils down to a series of sudden death semi-finals and finals to decide the national champion.

In Rio the big clubs share the use of Maracanã where the main game of the week can be found on Sunday afternoon kicking off at 5 p.m.

A visit to a game is a must for any sports fan. You can either make your own way to the stadium by bus, taxi or car — the stadium is well sign-posted — or join an organized tour which purchases your ticket in advance and takes you to the game by air-conditioned coach with accompanying guide. This is an expensive way of seeing the game but the safest if you want to play tourist rather than soccer fan.

For the world's greatest soccer playing nation it is surprisingly difficult for a temporary visitor to find a game in which to play.

If you are working in Brazil you will very likely find that your company has a team, although you may find yourself struggling to reach the grade, a grade which becomes frighteningly clear when watching a simple beach game on the sands of Copacabana. If they invite you to join their game though do. It does not matter if you make a fool of yourself because I can promise that it will be an experience to cherish. After all we can't be a Pele everyday of our lives!

SQUASH

Squash as a sport has been developed over the last few years by the foreign community living in Brazil, especially those of the British Commonwealth, and while it has not caught on as much as expected the number of courts and players is ever on the increase.

The main squash club in Rio, and one with a large number of English speaking members, is the Rio Squash Club at Rua Candido Mendes, 581 (Tel. 242-0642) in Gloria which boasts six championship courts, the best in Brazil.

In the same area of the town as the Rio Squash Club is Speed Squash at Rua Senador Pompeu, 78 (Tel. 233-1578) in the city, and Smash Squash to be found at Rua Couto Fernandes, 210 (Tel.: 245-3758) in Laranjeiras.

Out Barra way, and the closest courts to the Inter-Continental, Nacional, and Sheraton hotels, are the six courts at the KS Academy at Av. Armando Lombardi, 663 (Tel. 399-8543) in Barra da Tijuca. Other squash courts in Barra can be found at Lob Squash in the Itanhanga Center opposite the Itanhanga Golf Club.

A number of private clubs, such as the Paissandu Athletic Club, now have their own courts.

TENNIS

You can't talk about tennis in Brazil without mentioning Maria Esther Bueno who captured the Wimbledon crown for Brazil in 1959, 1960 and 1964, and did the same at the U. S. Open in 1959, 1963, 1964, and 1966. Bueno took the Ladies doubles title at Wimbledon in 1958, 1960, 1963, 1965 and 1966 and in the U. S. in 1960, 1962, 1966 and 1968, to go down in the record books as one of the greatest female tennis players of all time and voted "Female Athlete of the Year" in America's Associated Press poll for 1959.

Brazil is still looking for a successor to Bueno, be it male or female, and perhaps because of this, a large proportion of the middle and upper classes play tennis at their private clubs which in Rio include the super exclusive Country Club, the Caicaras Club, Leme Tennis Club, Paissandu Athletic Club, and the Naval Club. The visitor to Rio should however have no trouble finding a court to play on, especially during the week.

Rio's three resort hotels each have courts which are bookable and open to non-residents. The hotels are the Hotel Inter-Continental (322-2200), the Rio-Sheraton Hotel (274-1122) and the Hotel Nacional (322-1000).

Other courts are available at a number of tennis centers to be found in Rio. In Barra da Tijuca the most established center is *Clube Canaveral* at Av. das Americas, 487 (399-2192) while in Jacarepagua the best choice is the *Centro Carioca de Tenis* at Rua Timboacu, 765 (392-7009). Closer to Ipanema and Copacabana is *Lob Tenis* in Laranjeiras at Rua Stefan Zweig, 290 (205-9997 and 225-0329).

ULTRALIGHTS

If you have tried your hand at hang gliding and skydiving you may like to try the thrill of flying an Ultralight.

There are a number of Ultralight clubs in the state of Rio but the main one is the *Clube Esportivo de Ultraleves* at the Fazenda da Aeronáutica close to the motor racing circuit. For information call 342-8025

WINDSURFING AND SURFING.

Ever growing in popularity most local windsurfers invest in their own boards which can be picked up fairly cheaply. If you can't find somebody with a board to lend then contact the *Escola de Vela* at the marina in Gloria or call them on 285-3097.

The same story is true of surfing, which is not a sport to be recommended without proper supervision. Information about what is happening in the surf world in Rio can be obtained from *Waimea Surf Shop* in Rua Vinicius de Moraes, 129 in Ipanema.

PRIVATE CLUBS

If·you are planning to stay in Rio for any length of time you will find that membership to a sports club becomes indispensable to your life style, unless you·are going to live in one of the luxury condominiums in Barra which have their own facilities.

Clubs are joined in the majority of cases by the purchase of a club share which remains your property to sell. Monthly dues are paid for the up keep of the Club, but these are usually relatively low.

Rio's main sports clubs are:

Caicaras

Av. Epitácio Pessoa
Lagoa — 259-6262
Tennis, swimming, dinghy sailing.

Fazenda Club Marapendi

Av. das Américas
Barra da Tijuca — 325-2440
Horse riding, showjumping, swimming, basketball, volleyball.

Flamengo

Rua Mario Ribeiro
Lagoa — 274-2946
Swimming, tennis, soccer, water polo.

Gávea Golf and Country Club

Estrada da Gávea, 800
São Conrado — 322-4141
Golf and swimming.

Iate Clube do Rio de Janeiro

Av. Pasteur
Botafogo — 295-4482
Yachting, fishing, swimming, snooker.

Itanhanga Golf and Country Club

Estrada Barra da Tijuca, 2205
Barra da Tijuca —399-0507
Golf, polo, horse, riding, swimming

Jockey Club

Praça Santos Dumont
Jardim Botânico - 274-0055
Horse racing, tennis, swimming, downtown club.

KS Academy

Av. Armando Lombardi, 663
Barra da Tijuca -399-8540
Squash, gymnastics, judo, sauna.

Monte Líbano

Av. Borges de Medeiros, 701
Lagoa — 239-0032
Tennis and swimming

Naval Club

Av. Borges de Medeiros, 2363
Lagoa — 294-5992
Tennis, swimming, dinghy sailing, downtown club.

Paissandu Athletic Club

Av. Afrânio de Melo Franco, 330
Lagoa — 294-8482
Tennis, squash, bowling, snooker, swimming.

Rio Country Club

Rua Prudente de Morais, 1597
Ipanema — 239-3332
Tennis and swimming

Rio Squash Club

Rua Cândido Mendes, 581
Glória — 242-0642
Squash

Sociedade Hípica Brasileira

Av. Borges de Medeiros, 2448
Lagoa — 246-8090
Horse riding and showjumping

Teresópolis Golf Club

Caixa Postal: 92.600
Teresópolis — 742-1691
Golf, tennis, horse riding and
swimming.

Besides these private clubs the
two major resort hotels, the Hotel
Inter-Continental (Tel.322-2200) and
the Rio-Sheraton Hotel (Tel. 274-
1122), offer special memberships so
that Rio residents can use the hotel
facilities which include tennis and
swimming. For further information
contact the respective hotels.

SIGHTSEEING

RIO DE JANEIRO

- ijuca/Corcovado
- ugar Loaf
- etrópolis
- aradise Islands
- io by Night
- eija Flor
- cala
- ba-Oba

- Macumba
- Soccer
- City Tour
- Airport Transfers
- Stately Home
- Museums
- Helicopter
- White Water Rafting

- Ultralights
- Búzios
- The Fort of Santa Cruz
- Bus Charter
- Private Tours
- Schooner Hire
- Multilingual Guide Service
- Chauffeur Driven Limousines

Call us for advice on tours and sightseeing anywhere in Brazil.

INFORMATION & RESERVATIONS

274 7146 • 294 1196 •
294 0393 • 294 1444

Rio-Sheraton Hotel —
Av. Niemeyer, 121 —
Suite 214
Caixa Postal 5133 — Rio
de Janeiro — 22.072
Telex: (021) 32514 ATOZ
BR

The *Insider's* Guide to

São Paulo

For the Business Executive

Christopher Pickard

A Streamline Publication

Available from April 1987

F

Shopping
Shopping Centers
Jewelry
What to Buy

Shopping in Rio de Janeiro

Rio de Janeiro is one of South America's main shopping centers topped only by its larger and more sophisticated neighbor, São Paulo.

Cariocas are a strange breed though when it comes to shopping and only in the 1980s, with the opening of the massive shopping complexes of Rio Sul and Barra Shopping have their habits started to change.

To understand how a Carioca shops you have first to appreciate that Rio is a tropical city. Nobody wants to walk any distance when the temperature is in the hundreds, thus you find groupings of stores at every corner, especially in the main residential areas, but as parking became more and more difficult in Copacabana so the problems of shopping in Rio started to become an aggravation.

The answer at first was Ipanema. Parking was easier and a number of large air-conditioned galleries sprung-up, each holding a selection of small boutiques and stores. Everything you wanted was, and still is, found in the length of Rua Visconde de Pirajá, the fashion center of Rio de Janeiro.

Carioca women started to devote the morning to the beach and the late afternoon to shopping as the temperature dropped. It is common therefore for people in Rio to shop as late as 10 p.m.

At the start of the 1980s things began to change with the opening of Rio Sul a massive shopping complex which sits on the main artery that links Copacabana with Botafogo and the city. Centrally located, Rio Sul is no more than twenty minutes drive from any point in the zona sul.

For the first time Cariocas were offered with Rio-Sul plentiful free parking, all the top stores under one roof, and climatic conditions that could be controlled.

Rio discovered that it could now shop comfortably rain or shine. At first the city stuck to its habit of only going out in the late afternoon but this quickly changed so that Rio Sul is now busy from the moment it opens at 10 a.m. to the time it closes its doors at 10 p.m.

Rio Sul was joined in October 1981 by the even larger Barra Shopping which is located in the new and fast growing residential area of Barra da Tijuca which also attracts customers from São Conrado and Ipanema.

Personally I still prefer to stroll through Ipanema which retains its more distinct character and charm, but for shopping made easy, and this can be important if you are only in town for a few days, Barra Shopping, Rio Sul and the smaller gallieries of Fashion Mall and Gavea Shopping, are a dream come true.

BARRA SHOPPING
Av. das Américas, 4666 — Barra da Tijuca.

Thirty minutes drive from Ipanema you come to Barra Shopping which is billed as Latin America's largest and most complete shopping complex where a massive car park accommodates the thousands of daily shoppers who come from all over the city to make the center Rio's busiest, especially in the afternoon and at weekends.

Hundreds of boutiques and larger stores are found under one roof at Barra Shopping, as well as branches of the Mesbla and Sears department stores and C&A.

Barra Shopping offers just about every top name in Brazil, both in terms of stores and products, and alongside Rio Sul it is unquestionably the simplest way to shop in Rio.

Besides shopping, Barra Shopping offers three cinemas, a large children's playcenter, an ice rink, and numerous restaurant and snack bars.

Stores in Barra Shopping are open Monday through Saturday from 10 a.m. to 10 p.m. while the leisure areas operate seven days a week from 10 a.m. to midnight.

CARREFOUR
Av. das Américas, 5150 — Barra da Tijuca

Next door to Barra Shopping is the massive hypermarket Carrefour, Rio's best supermarket by a large margin.

A favorite with the foreign community, despite the drive, Carrefour offers excellent quality and value for money, a fact that is reflected in its popularity.

If you can't find what you are looking for at Carrefour, the likelihood is you never will, and that goes as much for food and drink as household and electrical goods.

Carrefour is open Monday through Saturday from 8 a.m. to 10 p.m. For refreshment there is a branch of McDonalds and the churrascaria "Panipa"

CASA SHOPPING
Rua Alvorado, 2150 — Barra da Tijuca.

The latest edition to shopping in Rio, and one that closes the circle so to speak with Barra Shopping and Carrefour, is Casa Shopping.

Designed to supply everything you want for the house, be it for the do-it-yourself freak or the interior decorator, Casa Shopping is a little different to any other center in Rio thanks to its design which is aimed to cut operating costs to a minimum.

In reality Casa Shopping is almost a small village. All the shops are at ground level and open on to the street. There is plentiful free parking and the center is well served for refreshments ranging from snack bars through Rio's best and most up-market churrascaria, Rodeio, to a Chinese restaurant, Grande Muralha

Casa Shopping boasts three cinemas, Art I, II & III, which sit above the center's center piece, the 4000 m2 Tok & Stok. Depending on the part of the world you come from Tok & Stok is the Brazilian equivalent of Conran's or Habitat.

On Sunday Casa Shopping hosts the Antique Fair.

CASSINO ATLANTICO
Av. Atlântica, 4240 — Copacabana. (Below the Rio Palace Hotel).

Cassino Atlântico has a long way to go before it can compete with Rio's other malls despite being one of the city's most attractive centers.

Cassino Atlantico has two main strengths and those are the art and antique shops which spread throughout the center and the souvenir shops that attract visitors from all over town.

FASHION MALL
Auto Estrada Lagoa-Barra — São Conrado. (Behind the Inter-Continental Hotel).

The Fashion Mall established itself in 1983, attracting the top names in Rio's "young" fashion world to create one of the city's most pleasant shopping enviroments.

The emphasis at the Fashion Mall is on fashion, from clothes to shoes and bags and on to sportswear, with just a few present shops interspersed with local handicraft stores.

Fashion Mall has a large number of snack bars and a cheap and cheerful Italian restaurant which overlooks the Gavea Golf course to the sea.

The mall has five cinemas and plentiful free parking.

Fashion Mall is open Monday through Friday from 10 a.m. to 10 p.m. and on Saturday until 8 p.m.

Note: There are always legitimate taxis waiting for fares outside the Fashion Mall and the line is organized by the police. This can be a pleasant change from some of the less reputable taxi drivers who prey off the tourists staying at the nearby hotels. This is a fact worth considering if you are staying at the Nacional or Inter-Continental hotels.

GAVEA SHOPPING
Rua Marquês de São Vicente, 52 — Gávea

A short cab ride from Ipanema and Leblon, Gavea Shopping was one of Rio's first major shopping centers. Gávea has found it difficult to find its' niche however. First it tried fashion and then just about everything else. Today Gavea has settled for a mix of high quality, privately owned stores, which sit alongside the big fashion chains of Fiorucci, Benetton, Dimpus, Loop, Cantão 4 and Atoba.

Gavea is particularly strong in respect to household goods featuring a number of top furniture designers as well as kitchen and bathroom showrooms. The center has several of the city's top art galleries as well as John Somers' main pewter showroom.

The center is kept busy at night by its three theatres and the Rio Sul cinema.

Open Monday through Friday from 10 a.m. to 8 p.m. Saturday from 10 a.m. to 1.00 p.m.

RIO DESIGN CENTER
Av. Ataulfo de Paiva, 270 — Leblon

Spreading over one block in Leblon, the Rio Design Center is the place to go if you are setting up home and have money to burn. The words "exclusive", "plush" and "expensive" come to mind when trying to describe the shops located in the Rio Design Center, an interior decorator's paradise.

Furniture, tiles, ceramics, kitchens, bathrooms, decorations, lamps, material, and even wallpaper are all to be found in the Rio Design Center, as well as several present shops, including Rachel, and the Nobili restaurant.

The entrance to the center's car park can be found in Av. Afranio de Melo Franco.

RIO SUL
Av Lauro Muller, 116 — Botafogo

The Rio Sul was the first major shopping complex to really work in Rio. Opening with all its stores already functioning it has never looked back and today is firmly established as a Rio landmark.

With branches of all the major fashion, electric appliance and gift shops as well as Mesbla, C&A, Lojas Americanas and a large and well stocked supermarket, Rio Sul offers all your shopping needs under one roof and with plentiful free parking.

Rio Sul has a number of snack bars and restaurants including the very good churrascaria T-Bone.

Rio Sul is a short cab ride from anywhere in the zona sul and a free bus service operates to-and-from most of the major hotels.

Open Monday through Saturday from 10 a.m. to 10 p.m.

DEPARTMENT STORES

Rio has tended towards large shopping galleries in preference to department stores and it is notable that Brazil's largest chain, Mesbla, has opened branches in both the big galleries in Rio.

Rio's most important department stores are:

Mesbla
Rua do Passeio   Centro.
Rio Sul   Botafogo.
Barra Shopping   Barra.

Sears.
Praia do Botafogo   Botafogo.
Barra Shopping   Barra.

C&A
Rio Sul   Botafogo.
Av. N. S. de Copacabana, 749   Copacabana.
Barra Shopping   Barra.

IPANEMA

Ipanema is not only the fashion center of Rio and Brazil but also holds that exalted position throughout the rest of Latin America, especially as far as summer fashions go.

Shopping in Ipanema, depending on the weather and the crowds, can either be a joy or a nightmare. It is certainly never dull.

If you want to "do" Ipanema properly take a cab to the start of Rua Visconde de Pirajá at either the cross roads with Henrique Dumont (Leblon end) or Praça General Osorio (Copacabana end), and walk the road from end to end.

On Friday a large food and flower market takes over Praça da Paz. This can be a fascinating experience for the visitor but please note that it snarls up the traffic and makes the whole area very congested. In other words if you want to shop calmly, don't chose Friday.

The highlights of Ipanema starting from the Leblon end are as follows:

Henrique Dumont — Anibal Mendonça: Billboard (records and videos), Myral (lingerie), Roupas A. B. (uniforms), Smash (women), Yves Saint Laurent, Vitrine de Ipanema (shopping center), Vídeo Shack, Hélio Barki (linens), Pé do Atleta (sports' shoes), Ipanema 2000 (shopping center), and Top Center (shopping center).

Anibal Mendonça: Towards the beach you will find Carmen (bags), Walk (men's shoes and shirts), Erowena Campbell (wallpaper and material), Wana Just (women) and Chands (women) while in the direction of the Lagoa are branches of La Bagagerie (women) and Chocolate (women).

Anibal Mendonça — Garcia d'Avila: The jewel center of Rio with the splendid H. Stern building, the world's largest jewerly store, dominating. Other major jewellers such as Amsterdam Sauer and Roditi also have branches on the block. Other attractions are

Siciliano (books), Disco (supermarket), Lojas Americanas (Brazil's Woolworth), Folic (women), Toulon (men), Soft Machine (women), Dom Saci (souvenirs), Eduardo Guinle (men), Georges Henri (women), Mr. Wonderful (men) and a branch of the very fashionable bag store, Victor Hugo.

Garcia d'Ávila. Rio's most fashionable street boasting on the Lagoa side branches of Krishna (women), Spy Great (women), Gregório Faganello (women), Oggi (men), Elle et Lui (men, women and gifts), Quorium (women), Target (women), Twiggy (women), Artecidos (material and wallpaper) and Dijon (men and women). On the beach side you can find the main branch of Company (men, women and children), Celeste Modas (women) and Carroussel (toys).

Garcia d'Avila — Praça da Paz (Rua Maria Quitéria): Post office, Studio Livros (books), Galeria 444 (small exclusive gallery), Cantão 4 (men and women), Van Gogh (men), Roberto Simões (gifts), Vasp, Marcas & Manias (merchandise), Gabriela (records), Rakam (material and cangas), New Gipsy (women), Red Green (women), Beneduci (shoes), Manfredo (material), Galeria 437 (bikinis including a branch of Bum Bum), Aspagus (knitwear) and Benetton (men and women).

On the corner of Maria Quitéria and Prudente de Morais — one block down to the beach — is a branch of Vivara, one of the better traditional gift shops.

Praça da Paz (Ruas Maria Quitéria and Joana Angélica): The heart of Ipanema both for fashion and travel. Home to Dimpus (women and children), Richards (men), Twiggy (women), Elle et Lui (men and women), Georges Henri (men), the "Quarter Ipanema" which houses Varesse (sports clothing and equipment), and the impressive "Forum" gallery with La Bagageria (women), Alice Tapajos (women), Roland Rivel (shoes and bags), Yes (women), Marcia Pinheiro (women and children), Mariazinha (women), Soft Shoes (shoes), Ruti Muti (children), La Bicoke (wedding), Pilar Rossi (women), Suely Sampaio (women), Toot (women), Picoli (children), Tonique (women), Bon Bon Dor (luxury chocolates), Pé do Atleta (sports' shoes) and Hallmark Cards.

Praça da Paz is also home to the exclusive Hippopotamus nightclub as well as the Sal & Pimenta, Negresco and Pizza Palace restaurants.

On the travel front you can find two big travel agents, Soletur and Casa Piano, as well as a Varig-Cruzeiro office. Casa Piano runs a very good *bureaux de change* on the basement level, where you will be payed the parallel rate for your foreign currencies, while for normal banking transactions a branch of Banco do Brasil can be found in the square.

Two blocks back from Praça da Paz towards the Lagoa on Joana Angélica is located the large material and linen store, Formatex, and the boutique by Tonny.

Praça da Paz (Rua Joana Angélica) — Vinicius de Moraes: Ulli Proença (wedding and cocktail dresses), Galeria 330 (shopping center), Dimpus (women), Celeste Modas (women), Casa Alberto (materials), Smuggler (children), Formosinho (shoes), Movie (women), Natan (jewels), Rachel (gifts), and Lutz Ferrando (photographic). The block is very strong for traditional men's fashion with all the main chains represented in close proximity including Tavares, Adonis, José Silva, Adamo, and d'Alessandro.

Vinicius de Moraes: Lagoa side boasts an impressive array of small boutiques including New Gipsy (women), Luli R. (women),

Veguti (women), Blu Blu (women), Avant Premiere (shoes and bags), Tropic (shoes and bags), Canga (shoes and bags), Rose Benedetti (jewels), Maison D'Elas (women), Dakar (women), Libera (women), Fofucha (women), Waimea Surf, Oliver (men), and Bum Bum (bikinis).

Towards the beach is a large branch of Red Green (women).

Vinicius de Moraes — Farme de Amoedo: Vip Center (shopping center), Smuggler (women), Kopenhagen (chocolates), Le Jardim (gifts), Monah (women), Gloria Modas (women), Owy (men), Ruban Bleu (women), Tapetes (hand made carpets), Blu 4 (women), Filippo (men), Etoille Modas (women), Unilivros (books), and McDonalds.

In Farme de Amoedo, towards the beach, you can find the world headquarters of Dijon, one of Brazil's largest and most fashionable chain of stores for both men and women.

Farme de Amoedo — Praça General Osório: Wrangler, Pituca (children), Toulon (men), Cabana (women), Anatur (travel agent and *bureaux de change*) and Casa Mattos (stationery).

Praça General Osório: Hippie Fair on Sunday, post office, American Denim (men and women), Mala Moderna (suitcases and bags), Formosinho (shoes), Vanderbilt (surf and sport), Bonita (children), Moto Discos (records), plus two excellent newsstands which carry a large range of English language magazines.

COPACABANA

The glory days of Copacabana as Rio's main shopping area closed with the opening of luxurious Rio Sul shopping center in Botafogo. Today shopping in Copacabana caters for the 300,000 residents of the area and the tourists who prefer to shop within a short walk of their hotels.

The main shopping area of Copacabana is restricted to seven blocks between Rua Paula Freitas and Rua Constante Ramos with Rua Santa Clara at its heart. Here you will find the main boutiques, although not as fashionable as Ipanema, and other related stores.

Copacabana has however kept its hold on the souvenir trade which dominates the area from Rua Paula Freitas up to Praça Bernardeli.

DOWNTOWN (CENTRO)

Stores downtown cater for the working man and woman who prefer to shop during their lunch hour rather than waste the weekend in a shopping center. Most fashions are offered, although traditional men's wear is particularly well represented.

If you are a tourist, rather than resident, it is unlikely that you will shop downtown but it is certainly worth a visit, especially as a number of streets are pedestrian precincts.

The classiest shopping areas downtown run either side of Rio Branco from Presidente Vargas down to Av. Alm. Barroso. Especially worth visiting is Rua Goncalves Dias which has the flower market at one end and Largo da Carioca at the other.

The further you move away from Rio Branco the cheaper the shops become both in terms of appearance and price. If you are in the mood stroll down either Rua Senhor dos Passos or Alfandega, which run parallel with Av Presidente Vargas away from Rua Uruguaiana. Here you enter the heart of the Rio "rag trade" where clothes of all types are sold at ridiculously low prices.

Shopping Guide

Rio is one of the world's major cities so like London, New York, Paris and Tokyo its stores offer every imaginable item, most of which have been manufactured in Brazil.

Foreign visitors find Rio a very cheap place to shop so you may discover yourself returning home not with the normal tourist trinkets but with beautiful and fashionable clothes, bags, shoes and even sportswear.

Brazil is of course one of the major centers for precious and semi-precious stones, and its jewellers and their designers are some of the best in the world. You are sure to visit a jeweller in Rio if only to look, but I think you will find it difficult to resist the many bargains on offer.

Don't expect to leave Rio empty handed!

The following is a guide to where to buy certain products in Rio:

JEWELRY

Brazil, and Rio in particular, has not built its image as the jewel center of the world without offering top class gemstones at honest and competitive prices.

In Brazil you can trust the top jewellers totally, there is too much competition for them to risk damaging their names just to get "one over" on a passing tourist. In any case Brazilian jewellers don't survive on sales to tourists, they prosper through sales to local Brazilians.

Rio has more jewelry stores than any other city in the world and some of them are obviously better than others. While I have no wish to dismiss every small jeweller in Rio as not being up to scratch, I do find myself advising visitors to stick to the tried and trusted names that have been looking after tourists and other visitors for decades.

The top name in Brazilian jewelry is H. Stern who can rightly call themselves jewellers to the world with 150 stores in 12 countries, including shops on Fifth Avenue in New York and in several other U.S. cities, as well as Argentina, Colombia, Chile, Ecuador, Peru, Venezuela, France, Germany, Portugal and Israel.

H. Stern was founded with $200 in capital back in 1946 by Hans Stern. Today Mr. Stern is still the very active chief executive of a company that has grown to become the fourth largest jeweller in the world, its annual dollar volume only bettered by Bucherer of Switzerland and Harry Winston and Tiffany & Co. of the U.S.

Next to H. Stern, and normally their stores literally are, come Amsterdam Sauer, another international jeweller with world wide connections. The third big name in Brazilian jewelry is Roditi with stores throughout Brazil and in New York and Geneva. Other well known Brazilian jewellers are Masson, M. Rosenmann, Natan, Sidi, Moreno, Gregory & Sheehan, Ernani & Walter, and Frank. This is not to say that all the other smaller jewellers are not reputable, but they survive on the personal service they give to long term customers.

There is no secret to buying jewelry, it is much the same as anything else in that you pay for what you get. Yes, there are bargains to be had in the Brazilian jewel world, but if you don't know what you are looking for you stand to lose a great deal of money. And if what you have found in a back street is such a bargain, how come the big jewellers with their vast resources and manpower don't know about it?

Brazil is blessed with huge deposits of precious and colored gemstones, and in some cases, aquamarines for example, the country holds more than 90% of the world's total supply. These large and varied deposits allow the jewellers to offer jewelry to fit every taste and budget. The jewellers of Brazil are highly professional, winning awards across the world, and it is probably the best organized Brazilian industry Brazilian jeweilers know how to look after the foreign visitor and rarely, if ever, rush or push you into a purchase you don't want. If they do, it is a sign that you are in the wrong jeweller.

Brazilian jewellers delight in showing their beautiful works to the public, even if they know it is quite out of your price range, but at least they allow you to feel like a millionaire for an hour or so.

Because the jewellers in Rio are so well organized I have no need to go into an in depth description of Brazilian gems. You will find that in your first few days in Rio you are supplied by the jewellers with enough information to turn you into a minor Brazilian gem expert. But to give you just a little taste of what's to come, you can expect to learn about aquamarines, tourmalines, emeralds, topazes, amethysts, diamonds, rubelite, golden beryl, lapis lazuli, and a host of others. As the jewellers are the experts I will leave the detailed descriptions to them, as you should. You should also let the jeweller know what you are looking for, tell him if it is a present you want or an investment, they can normally advise what is the best buy for your country.

You won't need any guide to find the jewellers, they are impossible to miss. H Stern and Amsterdam Sauer have stores in most of the hotels, they are also present in all the shopping centers, including Rio Sul and Barra Shopping, and in case you forgot that last minute gift, you will find them at the airport.

If Rio has a jewel center then I would have to say it is Rua Visconde de Pirajá in Ipanema, between Rua Garcia d'Ávila and Rua Anibal Mendonça, where you will find H. Stern's world headquarters, the largest jewelry store in the world, which offers on the third floor a free 15 minute tour through the world of Brazilian gems (see "Things To Do — Jewelry Tour"). Close to H. Stern's headquarters you can find a wide selection of other jewellers including large branches of Amsterdam Sauer and Roditi.

U.S. residents visiting Brazil may be interested to know that gems and jewelry purchased in Brazil may be free of duty. The official release of the Jewellers Association of Rio de Janeiro states: "U.S. Government executive order 11888 of November 24, 1975 regarding exports under the general system of preferencies states that Brazil is entitled to export gemstones and jewelry duty free, if 35% or more of the contents and labor of items is of Brazilian origin."

If you are outside of Brazil, and want to know more about the world of Brazilian gemstones, write to H. Stern at Rua Visconde de Piraja, 490 in Ipanema; Amsterdam Sauer at Rua Mexico, 41 in Centro or Roditi at Av. Rio Branco, 39 in Centro.

ANTIQUES

There is no one area for antiques in Rio, although Copacabana is stronger than most.

A good selection of top level stores can be found in the Cassino Atlantico center under the Rio Palace Hotel. For cheaper and smaller antiques try the Antique Fair which takes place every Saturday from 9 a.m. to 6 p.m. in Praça Marechal Ancora, close to Praça XV, and on Sunday in the car park of Casa Shopping, from 10 a.m. to 7 p.m.

Another popular road for antique dealers is Rua Siqueira Campos in Copacabana which includes the Shopping Center Copacabana that houses a number of stores.

Most of the foreign community in Rio purchase their antiques at the regular auctions (*Leilão*) held around the city. The auction houses advertise in the weekend editions of the *Jornal do Brasil* and *O Globo*.

BUFFET (HIRE SHOP)

Buffet Ltda.
Rua Rodrigo de Brito, 14 A
Botafogo — 295-1843

Buffet Ltda.
Rua da Passagem, 109
Botafogo — 295-5158

Carreira Banquete
Rua São Luiz Gonzaga, 1869
São Cristovão — 248-1031

Mercadão da Festa
Rua Dona Romana, 198
Engenho Novo — 201-3598

BUTCHERS

Most of the foreign community in Rio use, perhaps surprisingly, the frozen meat stores located between the large Sendas supermarket in Rua Adalberto Ferreira and the Cobal fruit and vegetable market.

For more specialized cuts of meat the number one choice is Wessel at Rua Marques de São Vicente, 67 in Gávea (opposite the Gávea Shopping Center). Tel: 259-2898. Wessel are open Tuesday through Friday from 10 a.m. to 8 p.m.; Saturday from 9 a.m. to 2 p.m. and on Monday from 2 p.m. to 8 p.m.

CAMPING EQUIPMENT RENTAL

Camping Tur
Rua Bolivar, 86-D
Copacabana — 235-5316

CHILDREN'S CLOTHES

Stores specializing in children's clothing can be found in the Rio Sul and Barra· Shopping centers as well as the "Forum" center in Ipanema· (Praça da Paz).

CIGARETTES

Brazil is not only one of the world's largest producers of tobacco and cigarettes but it also has one of the largest internal markets.

Amongst the international brands manufactured and available locally are John Player Special, Marlboro and Camel. The largest local brand, which is also one of the world's largest, is Hollywood. Other big names are Carlton, Minister, Free, Advance, and Galaxy. Cigarettes are cheap in Brazil and normally available from every corner bar.

COMPUTERS

Brazil has a growing market for small personal computers a good selection of which, including software, is to be found in Info-Shopping in Largo do Machado in Laranjeiras.

DELICATESSENS

Among Rio's better delicatessens are:

Bordeaux
Barra Shopping
Barra da Tijuca.

Casa dos Sabores
Rua Prof. Manuel Ferreira, 89
Gávea — 274-3595

Gourmandise
Rua Visconde de Pirajá, 44
Ipanema.

Wonder Food
Rua Real Grandeza, 76
Botafogo — 266-2299.

DRINK·

Spirits, wines, beer and soft drinks can be purchased at all supermarkets and there are no set licensing laws as in some countries.

There will be a deposit to pay on beer and soft drink bottles, and this can sometimes be more that the value of the liquid content!

If you are having a party you may find it better to order direct from the manufacturers who also deliver. For a full list of drink companies look in the Yellow Pages under *Bebidas*. One wholesaler, Kombinado, who is conveniently located for both Copacabana and Ipanema can be found on the right at the Lagoa end of Rua Pinheiro Guimarães in Botafogo, Tel. 266-0277, 266-0845 and 286-1598.

DRUGSTORES/CHEMISTS (FARMACIAS)

By the number of drugstores you pass in Rio you could be forgiven for thinking that the city is filled with hypochondriacs. I would rather believe that the Cariocas are a health conscious community.

In the day you will never be far from a drugstore, most of which stay open late, but it is always important to know where the 24 hour drugstores are located.

Copacabana (Meridien end): Farmacia do Leme — Av. Prado Junior, 237 (corner of Viveiro de Castro). — Tel. 275. 3847.

Copacabana (Othon Palace area): Farmacia Piaui — Rua Barata Ribeiro, 646 (corner of Constante Ramos) — Tel. 255 7445.

Copacabana Palace (Rio Palace end): Drogaria Cruzeiro — Av. N.S. de Copacabana, 1212 (corner of Souza Lima). — Tel. 287 3694.

Ipanema/Leblon: Farmacia Piaui — Av. Ataulfo de Paiva, 1283 (corner of Rita Ludolf) — Tel. 274 7322.

Barra da Tijuca: Drogaria Atlas — Estrada da Barra da Tijuca, 18 — Joa. Tel: 399 5421

DRY CLEANING

Rio's dry-cleaners are indifferent to say the least so it is no surprise to learn that the city's best cleaners send the clothes, shoes, or anything else you want cleaned to Belo Horizonte in Minas Gerais. The cleaners in question, Eureka and Zaz-Traz, have branches in Copacabana (Djalma Ulrich, 110 and Constante Ramos, 34), Ipanema (Maria Quitéria, 68), Leblon (Ataulfo de Paiva, 135), Gávea (Marques de São Vicente, 188) Laranjeiras (Laranjeiras, 21) and Barra Shopping.

ELECTRONICS

The widest range of electronic goods is possibly to be found in Carrefour, the large hypermarket situated along Av. das Americas in Barra. Other major appliance shops which can be found in Barra Shopping and Rio Sul are Garson and Ponto Frio. Branches of Garson, Tele-Rio, Arapuã, and Ponto Frio can also be found in Copacabana, Ipanema and Centro.

FANCY DRESS COSTUMES

Most Brazilians prefer to make their own costumes for Carnival and the city's costume balls but if you want to go wild try Mundo Teatral at Rua Sara, 24 in Santo Cristo behind the docks. Other costumes are sometimes available from Só a Rigor at Av. N.S. de Copacabana, 71, close to Av. Princesa Isabel. Tel. 275 4999.

FLOWERS

Rio, despite Brazil's wealth of flora and fauna, does not boast a sophisticated set up of flower shops as the local street markets tend to cater for most of the demand.

For special arrangements try Imperial Flores in Praça da Paz in Ipanema or the flower shop of the Copacabana Palace Hotel in Copacabana. Downtown you should visit the small, but impressive, flower market in Praça Olavo Bilac, at the top end of Rua Gonçalves Dias and Rosario close to the metro station at Rua Uruguaiana. A number of the flower market's stalls are linked with Interflora.

To order flowers by phone, call Clube das Flores (Rua do Lavradio, 206) on 242-0201 or 242-5485.

Brazil is also famous for its arrangements of dried flowers — the country's main center being Brasilia and in Rio you can find an excellent selection at Zuhause who have shops in the Rio Design Center and São Conrado Fashion Mall as well as Rua Barata Ribeiro, 303 and 458.

FOOD, FRUIT AND VEGETABLE MARKETS

Rio's food, fruit and vegetable markets are a way of life and will come part of your way of life if you come to live in Rio. The markets are worth visiting even as a tourist and worth avoiding if you are in a hurry. All the markets tying up the traffic in their area. The main markets in Rio are:

Monday: Ipanema (Av. Henrique Dumont), Leme (Rua Gustavo Sampaio) and Botafogo (Rua Vicente de Souza).

Tuesday: Ipanema (Rua Jangadeiros and Praça General Osório) and Botafogo (Rua Barão de Macaubas).

Wednesday: Copacabana (Rua Domingos Ferreira), Botafogo (Praça Nicaragua) and Humaitá (Rua Maria Eugenia).

Thursday: Copacabana (Rua Belford Roxo and Rua Ronald de Carvalho), Leblon (Rua General Urquiza) and Gloria (Rua Conde Lage e Taylor).

Friday: Ipanema (Praça da Paz), Botafogo (Rua Rodrigo de Brito) and Gávea (Praça Santos Dumont).

Saturday: Lagoa (Rua Frei Leandro), Botafogo (Rua Paulo Barreto and Rua 19 de Fevereiro) and Laranjeiras (Rua Prof. Ortiz Monteiro).

Sunday: Copacabana (Rua Décio Vilares), Barra (Av. Arquiteto Afonso Reidy), Gloria (Av. Augusto Severo) and Urca (Praça Tenente Gil Guilherme).

FOREIGN NEWSPAPERS AND PERIODICALS

Most newsstands carry a selection of foreign periodicals but an exceptionally strong selection can be found at the newsstands in Praça Serzedelo Correia and the corner of Av. Prado Junior and Av. N.S. de Copacabana in Copacabána; Praça General Osório and Praça da Paz in Ipanema; at the corner of Av. Ataulfo de Paiva and Rua Rita Ludolf in Leblon; Carrefour; along Rio Branco; and at most of the city's and hotel's better book shops.

For subscriptions to foreign publications, payable in cruzados, contact South American Distribution Services at Av. N.S. de Copacabana, 605/1106 (Tel. 255-6125).

FORMAL WEAR HIRE

Só a Rigor
Av. N.S. de Copacabana, 71
Copacabana   275 4999

Wilmar
Rua Alcindo Guanabara, 17/605
Centro - 220-0041

FURNITURE, LIGHTS, ETC...

The furniture industry in Rio was revitalized in 1984 with the opening of the Rio Design Center and Casa Shopping as well as the steady improvement in the shops at the Gavea Shopping Center.

For designer furniture and household accessories, and when money is not a problem, you can do no better than the Rio Design Center and Gavea. Both have a wide selection of shops catering for the top end of the market.

For "younger" and cheaper furniture and accessories try Casa Shopping which contains not only the 4,000 m2 Tok & Stok but also a branch of the very popular Gelli chain. Gelli is also represented in Rio Sul while Tok and Stok operate a branch in the Cassino Atlantico below the Rio Palace Hotel.

For cheap, basic furniture try the big department stores Sears and Mesbla.

GIFTS

Cariocas love to give presents so gift shops abound. Good groupings of gift shops can be found at Rio Sul, Barra Shopping and Ipanema. The top names in presents, in the traditional sense, are Roberto Simões, Rachel and Vivara. Try also H. Stern in Visconde de Piraja in Ipanema.

HAIRDRESSERS

All the top hotels have their own beauty parlors and barber shops and because of the language barrier

these are the best — and safest! — option for the non-Portuguese — speaking visitor.

If you are living in Rio you will soon discover which are the best hairdressers. From experience it seems to be a matter of taste and no one hairdresser dominates in the foreign community although Lennart at Toriba (Av. Bartolomeu Mitre, 553, Tel.: 259-2447 & 274-4347), Gerrard at the Meridien Hotel (Tel.: 275-0045 & 275-8295), David at the Copacabana Palace Hotel (Tel.: 255-7070, Ramal 389) and Jean-Claude in the Terrasse Center in Leblon (Rua Conde Bernadotte, 26. Tel.: 294-1696) are all popular and speak English.

HAMMOCKS

Brazil makes very beautiful and inexpensive hammocks which you will find being sold on the beach, on street corners near the major hotels, at the Sunday Hippie Fair in Ipanema, and at the Fair of the Northeast in São Cristóvão.

HI-FI

The top names in hi-fi can be found in the shopping centers of Rio Sul and Barra Shopping. Look for Brenno Rossi, Garson and Ponto Frio. For more specialized equipment try Josias on Av. Francisco Otaviano, which runs alongside the Cassino Atlantico gallery by the Rio Palace Hotel.

Carrefour carries a large range of sound equipment at competitive prices.

IMPORTED FOODSTUFFS

The better supermarkets such as Carrefour in Barra and Sendas in Leblon have imported food and drink sections, however, the most diverse range of goods will be found downtown at Lidador and Laticinios Pomerode on the corner of Rua da Quitanda and Rua da Assembleia behind the bus station.

Lidador can be contacted by phone on 221-4613 and delivers to all parts of the city. Imported and luxury food and drink stores can also be found tucked away in a number of shopping galleries in Copacabana and Ipanema, as well as the Cobal in Leblon.

LIQUOR

Most brands and types of liquor are available in Brazil and the majority are manufactured in the country. The one big exception to the rule however is whisky, be it Scotch, Canadian or Bourbon.

Because of Brazil's strict import controls you can except to pay up to $30 for a genuine bottle of Whisky, and far more if you are drinking in a bar or restaurant. For considerably less money you can buy a local equivalent of Scotch that has been transported in bulk and bottled here. Examples of Brazilian bottled Scotch are Bell's, Long John, Teacher's and Vat 69. Most other liquor in Brazil is cheap, with a bottle of Barcardi Rum costing around $2 a bottle in the supermarkets.

Imported liquor can be purchased, at a price, from the same locations as imported foodstuffs and it is worth remembering that on arrival in Rio you are allowed to purchase up to $300 worth of imported liquor. I repeat, in case you thought it was a printing error, three hundred dollars worth of liquor and other goods.

LOBSTERS

Lagosta Viva
*Rua Cardoso de Morais, 384/202
Bonsucesso — 230-5799.*

Home delivery of fresh and live lobsters, fish and other crustaceans. Lobsters from $10 a kilo

MARBLE AND STONE TOP TABLES

Fritz
*Rua Sorima, 130
Joá.*

MEN'S CLOTHING

Traditional: Traditional men's fashion is available in every part of Rio especially Centro, Copacabana, and Ipanema (between Praça da Paz and Vinicius de Moraes) as well as the big shopping centers, Barra Shopping and Rio Sul.

Names to look for in traditional fashion are Tavares, Adonis, Temper, José Silva, Di Dom, Via Vento, Oggi, Aramis, Quinta Avenida, Van Gogh, Borelli, Adamo, d'Alessandro and C&A.

Boutiques (Casual): The top names in male casual fashion can be found in Ipanema and also Fashion Mall, Rio Sul and Barra Shopping.

Names to look for are Company, Fiorucci, Dimpus, Cantão 4, Wrangler, Levi's Chomp, Boys & Girls, Benetton, Toulon, and Phillipe Martin.

High Fashion: High fashion stores differ from boutiques in that the clothes they offer are chic and on the expensive side for Brazil, although not for the U. S. or Europe.

High fashion stores are restricted to Ipanema, Rio Sul, Barra Shopping and Fashion Mall.

Names to look for in high fashion are Richard's, Oliver, George Henri, Elle et Lui, Dijon and Yves Saint Laurent, Fillipo, Mr. Wonderful, Eduardo Guinle, Polo By Kim.

Sports Wear: Sports shops can be found all over Rio offering famous marks at very reasonable prices. Among the best known chains are Varese and for shoes Pé do Atleta (Athlete's Foot).

Shoes: There are no major chains of shoe stores in Rio, except Formosinho and Sapasso, but the shopping centers all have a good variety of stores offering different designs to suit every pocket.

Shoes are cheap in Brazil, but if you want them to last invest in the more expensive marks which you will still find inexpensive in relation to what you pay at home.

Fashion Mall is particularly strong for men's shoes but Rio Sul, Barra Shopping and Gavea all have a good selection as does Ipanema in general.

MOTORCARS

Chevrolet, Fiat, Ford, General Motors and Volkswagen all operate on a large scale in Rio. For a full list of authorized dealers see the Yellow Pages (*Lista Telefonica Classificada*) under *Automoveis*.

If you want to buy a second-hand car I suggest you go to a reputable dealer. Most of the major dealers advertise in the classified section of the *Jornal do Brasil* and *O' Globo*. Amongst the best known are Dirija (Rua Edgard Werneck, 1313 — Jacarepagua. Tel. 342-4277); Gatão (Av. Itaoca, 362 — Bonsucesso. Tel. 270-6349); Mesbla (Rua General Polidoro, 80 — Botafogo. Tel. 295-8887); and Pavão (Av. Itaoca, 464 — Bonsucesso. Tel. 270-9191).

MOTORCYCLES

Honda and Yamaha are the most popular makes in Rio. Their showrooms can be found all across the city, for a full list of authorized dealers see the Yellow Pages under *Motocicletas*.

MUSICAL INSTRUMENTS

There are no outstanding musical instrument stores in Rio although in Copacabana you can try Casa Milton at Hilario Gouveia, 88 (off Praça Serzedelo Correia) and in Ipanema, Clave in Praça Toledo (Jardim de Alah end of Rua Visconde de Pirajá)

OPTICIANS

Opticians are to be found all over Rio. To find the closest to you look in the Yellow Pages under *Otica*. If you want an English speaking optician ring the Rio Health Collective on 551-0940 between 9 a.m. and 2 p.m.

PEWTER

Strange as it may seem, Brazil's is one of the top pewter makers in the world, producing what is widely regarded as the "Rolls Royce" of pewter, the John Somers' collection.

Brazil's top pewter, including that of John Somers, is crafted in the historic town of São João del Rey in Minas Gerais. There you can visit the pewter factories and the Somers' museum.

The pewter of John Somers is on sale in most good gift shops, branches of H. Stern, and their own shops in the Inter-Continental and Gavea Shopping.

PERFUMES AND COSMETICS

The major department stores, Mesbla and Sears, carry a full range of the top names in cosmetics as do a number of the better drug stores. You should also find what you are looking for in terms of perfumes and cosmetics in Rio Sul, Barra Shopping, Fashion Mall and Ipanema.

PHOTOGRAPHIC

Cariocas are big on photography so you will never be far from a shop which can develop your films. The service in Brazil is high quality, fairly cheap, and can normally be done in one or two days. The big names in developing are Colocenter and Curt; you will find their stores in Centro, Ipanema, Copacabana as well as Rio Sul, Barra Shopping, Fashion Mall and Cassino Atlantico.

If your films are especially urgent a shop in Rio Sul offers a one hour developing service.

Should your requirements be more technical try Lutz Ferrando who have stores all over Rio including in Copacabana at Av. N.S.

Copacabana, 462 and in Ipanema at Rua Visconde Piraja, 261. Another very reliable choice·is Delacroix at Ataulfo de Paiva, 725 (close to Praça Antero de Quental) in Leblon. Delacroix ·himself is a top photographer whose work is often featured in the *Latin America Daily Post* and other publications. Delacroix speaks English and the shop can be reached on 239-6394.

For just about every imaginable type of film or camera battery go to the Centro Comercial Copacabana, 581 (close to Praça Serzedelo Correia). Downtown try the gallery at Rio Branco, 156, just up from the Municipal Theatre.

PRINTS OF RIO

Prints of Rio, both old and modern, make a lovely souvenir of Rio. The best selection are to be found in the Kosmos books stores of Rua do Rosario, 155 in Centro and in front of the Copacabana Palace Hotel.

RECORDS

For such a musical nation the general standard of record stores in Brazil is fair at best.

The largest chain in Rio is Gabriella who have stores in just about every shopping area of Rio including the major galleries. I however prefer Hi-Fi Billboard in Rio Sul; Billboard and Modern Sound in Barata Ribeiro, corner of Santa Clara, in Copacabana; and Gramaphone in Gavea Shopping.

If you know what you are looking for you can't beat the prices at Disco do Dia, upstairs at the Centro Comercial Copacabana in Av. N.S. de Copacabana next to Praça Serzedelo Correia. The gallery has a number of other cheap record stores.

If you want to chose a good selection of Brazilian music to take home, and think you will require the help of a shop assistant, shop early in the morning when the stores are empty and the staff have more time.

The average price of an album in Brazil is around $4. The quality of pressings are equal to those of the United States although in general the standard of tapes is poor. If you can carry them, buy records.

SOUVENIRS

Taste and budget dictate that a city such as Rio must offer souvenirs that are acceptable to the widest possible market. Some of the souvenirs on offer I am sure you will find quite distasteful but others will fit the bill perfectly.

The best area for souvenir shops is Copacabana and for some reason they have bunched themselves in Av. N.S. de Copacabana between Rua Paula Freitas and Praça Bernardelli. Looking from Copacabana Beach that means from behind the Hotel Trocadero to behind the Hotel Ouro Verde. Numerous stores offer every imaginable souvenir from leather goods to precious and semi-precious stones, as well as dolls, t-shirts, key rings, stuffed spiders and fish, etc.

Other concentrations of souvenir shops are to be found in the Cassino Atlantico under the Rio Palace Hotel, and in the area surrounding the H. Stern building in Ipanema (corner of Visconde de Piraja and Garcia d'Avila) which has its own very high quality souvenir shop.

The other major source of souvenirs is the Hippie Fair which takes place every Sunday in Praça General Osorio. (see "Things to See – Hippie fair").

The most tasteful of the souvenir t-shirts can be found in the Rio Sul shopping center and if you totally run out of ideas of what to take home you can always give everyone a copy of "The Insider's-Guide to Rio de Janeiro"!!!!

SPORTS EQUIPMENT

Rio's climate makes the city a paradise for sports enthusiasts and because of this you can find a sports store on every corner. Well known marks like Adidas, Nike and Le Coq Sportif are manufactured locally and exported to the rest of the world, as are the big local marks such as Topper.

Barra Shopping, Rio Sul, Fashion Mall, Gavea Shopping and Cassino Atlantico all have sports shops as do Ipanema, Copacabana and Centro. One of the biggest chains for sports' goods is Varese, and for running shoes, Pé do Atleta.

Rackets can be restrung at Ataulfo de Paiva, 135 in Leblon (Tel.: 294-0145) and at the Pro Shop in the Terrasse Center (Rua Adalberto Ferreira) opposite the large Sendas supermarket in Leblon.

STATIONERY

Stationery shops are not widely in evidence in Rio. In Centro, Rio's most famous office supply and stationery store is União at Rua do Ouvidor, 77. Designers and artists should go to Meira S.A. at Av.

Erasmo Braga, 227 opposite the Castelo bus terminal.

Mesbla department stores have adequate stationery sections as do most of the major shopping centers. In Ipanema try Casa Mattos in Visconde de Pirajá, close to Praça General Osório, who also have branches in Copacabana at Av. N.S. de Copacabana, 690 and Centro at Rua Ramalho Ortigão, 22.

The best selection of birthday cards and wrapping paper can be found in Marie Papier in Vitrine de Ipanema at Rua Visconde de Piraja, 580 (between Henrique Dumont and Anibal Mendonça) and at Hallmark Cards in Forum, which is located in Praça da Paz in Ipanema.

UNICEF, who specialize in Christmas Cards, have their showroom at Rua Mexico, 21/9º (Tel.: 240-5758) in Centro.

SUPERMARKETS

Perhaps I am strange but I have always found walking around supermarkets in foreign countries to be more interesting than the local museums. It really does give you the feeling of being abroad to see row upon row of products and names that you never dreamt about in your own country.

Rio has several big chains of supermarkets the best known being Sendas, Peg Pag, Disco and Casas da Banha. If you are staying in the Copacabana or Botafogo area the best supermarkets to visit are Pão de Acucar in Av. N.S. de Copacabana, just past Praça Serzedelo Correia, and the Peg Pag in Rio Sul. In Ipanema and Leblon the preference of the foreign community living in Rio is the giant Sendas supermarket on the corner of Rua Adalberto Ferreira in Leblon, in front of the permanent fruit and vegetable market, Cobal.

Many members of the community choose to drive out to the two huge hypermarkets situated in Barra along Av. das Americas. The first you come to is Freeway and a little further down the road beyond Barra Shopping, Carrefour.

A name known throughout the world, Carrefour was one of the first companies to invest in the Barra area and lead the way to the future.

In Rio most supermarkets are open from 8 a.m. until 10 p.m., Monday through Saturday, although Casas da Banha at Rua Siqueira Campos, 69 in Copacabana is open 24-hours-a-day.

TICKETS

Travel: Rio has many travel agents who can make reservations for any on — going journey you have outside or within Brazil, including the bus services. Two travel agents who are popular with the foreign community are Marlin Tours at. Av. N.S. de Copacabana, 605 (suite 1204). Tel: 255-4433 and Avipam at Av. Rio Branco, 251 in Centro. Tel: 240-9628.

All the major airlines have offices in Rio, a full list of which is given in the General Information section of the guide under "Airlines"

Theatre: A ticket booth is located on the ground floor of the Rio Sul shopping center and in Praça da Paz.

Maracana/Maracanazinho/Teatro Municipal: Tickets for events of any kind to be held at the Maracana sports complex can be purchased in advance from Guanatur Turismo at Rua Dias da Rocha, 16 in Copacabana (between Constante Ramos and Santa Clara). Tickets for Maracana and the Teatro Municipal are also on sale from the box office of the Teatro Municipal.

Motor Racing (Formula 1 Grand Prix): Tickets for the Grand Prix go on sale at a number of locations around the city including a chain of banks.

Rock In Rio: Tickets for the first "Rock In Rio" were on sale at branches of Banco Nacional and Barra Shopping.

If coming from abroad for the second "Rock In Rio" you can write in advance to Artplan, Rua Fonte da Saudade, 329 — Lagoa.

Free Jazz Festival: Tickets for Rio's annual jazz festival go on sale in the month. leading up to the event and are well advertised. In 1986 the price per night was around $15.

Carnival: Tickets are on sale at branches of BANERJ throughout Rio for the majority of the stands. Tickets for the tourist stands are available from travel agents, or closer to Carnival, in the foyer of most of the major hotels.

Canecão: Tickets for shows at Canecão normally go on sale the Monday of the week of the shows. Tickets from the Canecão box office in Av. Venceslau Braz, 215 in Botafogo (Tel.: 295-3044).

Plataforma: Reservations for the shows at Plataforma should e made at the box office in Rua Adalberto Ferreira, 32 in Leblon (Tel.: 274-4022).

Scala: Tickets for shows at Scala 1 and 2 are on sale from the theatre box office in Av. Afranio de Mello Franco, 292 in Leblon (Tel.: 274-9148).

Sugar Loaf: Tickets for Beija-Flor and the shows on Morro da Urca are available in advance from the Sugar Loaf box office at Av. Pasteur, 520 (Tel.: 295-3044) from where the cable cars depart from.

TOYS

For a country where children can do no wrong the selection of toys available is to say the least disapointing and quite expensive when compared with other products. If you have to buy a toy you will find the best choice in Barra Shopping, Rio Sul and Ipanema.

TV RENTAL

Televisions can be bought in most of the main shopping areas of Rio including Rio Sul, Barra Shopping and Carrefour. If you want to rent contact:-

Colortel
*Rua Mena Barreto, 165
Botafogo — 286-3522*

Kentv
*Rua Arnaldo Quintela, 56
Botafogo — 286-8398*

VIDEO FILMS

Video has boomed in Brazil, as in the rest of the world, in the last few years. Brazil now manufactures a number of excellent machines locally including by Philips, Philco and Sharp (all VHS), as well as Sony (Betamax).

The Brazilian machines are compatible with both the Brazilian (Pal-M) and American (NTSC) television systems but *not* the European.

All video clubs stock films in the American system (NTSC), which is also the system used by nearly all the video tape manufacturers in Brazil, and predominatly work with the VHS format, only a few stocking Betamax.

Some of the better video clubs in Rio, each offering several thousand films are:

New Video
Av. Rio Branco, 156/221
Centro — *220-2120*

Vídeo Clube do Brasil
Rua General Urquiza, 156
Leblon — *259-8594*

Video Clube do Brasil
Fashion Mall
São Conrado — *322-3816*

Vídeo Clube do Brasil
Rua Frei Leandro, 20
Jardim Botânico — *246-9003*

Video Clube Nacional
Rua Visconde de Pirajá, 365
Ipanema — *247-1972*

Video Shack
Rua Visconde de Pirajá, 595
Ipanema — *259-3291*

WINES

Brazilian and imported wines can be found in most good supermarkets as well as the more specialized foodstores (see "Imported Foodstuffs"). A listing of Brazilian wines can be found in the "Eating Out" section of this guide.

WOMEN'S CLOTHING

Traditional: Traditional women's fashion stores are concentrated in Copacabana, Ipanema, and the big shopping centers of Rio Sul and Barra Shopping.
Names to look for in traditional fashion are Alice Tapajos, Cabana, Celeste Modas, Etoile, Gloria Modas, Korigan, Mademoiselle, Marcia Pinheiro, Piu Bella, Quorom and C&A.

Young Fashion (Casual): Young fashion stores differ from boutiques in that the clothes they offer are less individual and avant-garde while still being up-to-date.
The main concentration of young fashion is in Ipanema but most of the stores have branches in Fashion Mall, Rio Sul, Barra and Gávea Shopping.
Names to look for in young fashion are American Denim, Bee, Blu Blu, Cantao 4, Company, Gang, Levi's Maria Bonita, Marie Claire, Monah, New Gipsy, Newspalan, Pants Shop, Spy Great, Smuggler and Wranglers.

Boutiques: Ipanema is the center not only of the Rio fashion trade but the Brazilian as well. The following boutiques have been chosen for the quality and individuality of their goods. Most have branches in Fashion Mall, Rio Sul, and Barra Shopping: — Aspargus, Benetton, By Tonny, Dimpus, Fiorucci, Krishna, La Bagagerie, Luli R., Mariazinha, Movie, Pandemonium, Twiggy, Yes, Zoomp and the "Forum" gallery in Ipanema generally.

Classics: Top and classic women's fashions are concentrated in exclusive boutiques in the Ipanema area although a few examples can be found in Rio Sul, Barra Shopping, Fashion Mall and Gávea Shopping.
Names to look for in classic women's fashion are Dijon, Elle et Lui, Georges Henri, Yves Saint Laurent, and the "Forum" Gallery in Ipanema generally.

Lingerie and Nightwear: A number of stores specializing in lingerie can be found in Ipanema and Copacabana as well as at all the shopping centers. Names to look for are Amor Perfeito, Make Love and Myral.

Stockings: Because of the weather most Brazilian women forget about stockings and tights. A good selection though can be found at Casa Olga who have branches around town. The Ipanema store is located at Av. Visconde de Piraja, 550; in Leblon at Av. Ataulfo de Paiva, 320; in Copacabana at Av. N.S. de Copacabana, 632, 777, 891 and 1088; and in Barra Shopping

Maternity Wear: Maternity wear stores can be found in Ipanema and Copacabana as well as Gavea Shopping, Fashion Mall, Barra Shopping and Rio Sul.

Shoes and Handbags: Brazil is famous throughout the world for its fashion shoes and handbags which can be seen in Rio in most of the main shopping areas as well as all the top galleries.
No one chain of shoe stores dominates in Rio although the prices at Formosinho are hard to beat.
Most of the top boutiques carry a line of shoes.
For bags the names to look out for are Victor Hugu, Beltrami, and Carmen.

Bikinis: Brazilian bikinis are in a class of their own. Women love them and men love them even more.

Because of Rio's climate virtually every boutique carries a line of bikinis. although the most popular and fashionable are to be found at Bum Bum in Ipanema (Rua Visconde de Pirajá, 437 and Rua Vinícius de Moraes,), Barra Shopping and Rio Sul and Cantão 4 who have branches all over town.

In Ipanema a large selection of bikini and swimwear boutiques, including Bum Bum, can be found in the gallery at Rua Visconde de Pirajá, 437 while in Copacabana the place to look is the Centro Comercial Copacabaná at Av. N. S. de Copacabaná, 581. In Rio Sul look for the fourth floor, believe me the center does have four and not three floors, and in front of the Peg Pag supermarket you will find an excellent selection of swimwear shops.

Bikinis make an excellent present for men to take home to their wives or girl friends, but be warned, once they have seen a true Brazilian bikini they may never let their man come back to Rio alone again.

G

History
Historical Tour
Uniquely Brazilian

The History of Rio de Janeiro

As *The Insider's Guide to Rio de Janeiro* is essentially a guide I do not feel the need to go into a lengthy narrative about the historical and political growth of Brazil, these matters being best left in the hands of the experts whose accounts you will find at your local library, or at worst in the pages of the better encyclopedias. I do believe however, that a short history of Rio will be of help to you in your enjoyment and appreciation of the city.

Discovering Rio de Janeiro

While it is generally agreed that Pedro Alvarez Cabral discovered Brazil, first named Vera Cruz (True Cross), on April 25, 1500 for the King of Portugal, there seems to be some disagreement as to exactly when Rio itself was discovered.

One version credits the discovery of Rio to the navigators Andre Gonçalves and Americo Vespucci. Vespucci, an Italian by birth, was one of the great explorers of his time, undertaking a number of voyages for the King of Spain to discover more about the "new world". He first visited what we now know as the Caribbean in 1497 just four years after Columbus, and it is probable that he landed in the north of Brazil as early as May, 1499.

Vespucci's most important voyage for this story was his third, undertaken at the request and expense of the Portuguese King Dom Manuel. Sailing from Lisbon on May 13, 1501 the fleet of three ships commanded by Gonzalo Coelho and navigated by Vespucci were given the task of inspecting Cabral's new discovery of Vera Cruz. It took the fleet until the August of 1501 to reach the north coast of Brazil after a long and dangerous crossing.

From here on the facts get rather misty with the passing of time. What is known for certain is that the fleet made its way down the east coast of South America, going far enough south for Vespucci to realize that they were dealing with a new continent and not an extension of Asia as Columbus had assumed.

As the story goes, part of the fleet, and perhaps all of it, with Gonçalves and Vespucci navigating, stopped off in Guanabara Bay on January 1, 1502. Presuming to have discovered the mouth of a great river they christened it *Rio de Janeiro*, or River of January. No attempt was made to land at this time, although records show that the fleet returned in 1503 and set up camp for some time at Cabo Frio, slightly east of Rio, and one can presume that they must have visited the bay again.

I note that the discovery of Rio was disputed because Alured Gray Bell in his book "The Beautiful Rio de Janeiro", published in London in 1914, said of its discovery: "….we have no record of the Bay of Rio being known to Europeans before 1519, when Fernan de Magellan anchored in the harbour for fourteen days. In 1531 Martin Affonso remained three months in the bay, but apparently failed to appreciate its strategical importance."

The First Settlers Arrive

What is agreed by all is that the first colonists in Rio were French.

In 1555, 600 men under the command of Admiral Villegaignon disembarked at a little, low lying island to which they gave the name of Coligny. Today that island is called after Villegaignon and has virtually become part of the mainland with the landfill that has gone to make the Santos Dumont airfield. Villegaignon built a fort on the.

island and started to explore the bay, reinforcing his position with the arrival of a further thousand settlers in 1557.

The Portuguese Government offended by the establishment of this French colony on what was after all Portuguese soil, ordered the Governor General of Brazil, Mem de Sá, then resident in Bahia, to expel them. Mem de Sá's fleet entered the harbour on February 21, 1560, and in two days took control of the garrison. His job done, Mem de Sá returned to Bahia without taking the precaution of establishing his own garrison. With Mem de Sá's departure the French returned, this time to set up camp on the mainland close to what is now Catete.

In 1565, the Portuguese returned under the command of the Governor General's nephew, Estácio de Sá, who landed on March 1 of that year just west of Sugar Loaf. A bitter two year struggle ensued with the French defeated by the arrival of Mem de Sá himself with reinforcements on January 18, 1567. Two days later on January 20, Estácio de Sá was mortally wounded by an Indian arrow while in combat with the French settlers and their native allies. With the death of his nephew, who is credited with the founding of Rio de Janeiro, Mem de Sá moved the site of the new town to Morro de Castelo (Castle Hill), an area in front of what is today the Santos Dumont airfield.

The Portuguese Dig In

Securing their position at the base of Morro de Castelo, the Portuguese settlers slowly started to reclaim the marshy land which lay between them and the Morro de São Bento where in 1617 the Benedictine monks would start work on the construction of their church and monastery. But the growth of Rio was basically slow, by 1648 consisting of only three roads of which the main one was Rua de Misericordia.

The turning point in the development of Rio came in the 1690s when gold was discovered in nearby Minas Gerais. As the nearest seaport to the gold fields Rio became the logical point for the Portuguese to base their taxing and control operations. News of the gold spread and in 1710 the city was put under siege by the French; 12,000 inhabitants stood firm and repelled the 1,000 strong force under the comand of Du Clerc. The following year, 1711, Rio was not so lucky. With a fleet of 18 ships and over 5000 troops the French under Duguay-Trouin tried again. Entering the harbour on September 12 and forcing their way into the city they sacked Rio and almost left it totally destroyed. After a heavy ransom had been paid, the French departed.

Little is recorded as to what happened between 1711 and 1763 except that during this time the population swelled to over 30,000. To cope with the demands of the growing population work started on the *Aqueducto da Carioca* (the Carioca Aqueduct), or simply Arcos as it is known, in 1724. The Arcos was built to bring water from the forest of Santa Teresa to the public fountain in what is now Largo da Carioca. Today, and since 1896, those same arches have served as the base for a viaduct which links the "bondinhos" (small street cars) from the hill of Santo Antônio to that of Santa Teresa.

The Capital Moves to Rio

As Rio had outgrown Bahia it was given the honor in 1763 of being named as the capital of the Vice-royalty of Brazil. The wealth attracted to Rio by the continuing gold-rush brought with it the first trappings of European civilization. The most important streets were paved, marshy areas were drained to form Largo de Carioca and the city's largest lagoon was filled in to create Rio's earliest park, the Passeio Publico.

Rio now started to snake its way southward to Gloria, Catete, Laranjeiras and Botafogo, and northward to Estacio, Tijuca and São Cristóvão. The city comprised of forty-six streets and nineteen squares.

As the 19th century dawned events were taking place in Europe, rather than Brazil, that were going to turn Rio into one of South America's great cities. Napoleon was on the move and in 1808 Dom João VI of Portugal was forced to abandon his country to the invading forces and set sail for his colony, Brazil; had he not, Brazil would probably have gone the way of all of Spanish America and become a republic in the first quarter of the 19th century. As it was the monarchy would last until 1889 and leave the city with its respectable antiquity intact.

João VI arrived in Rio on March 7, 1808 at what is now Praça XV, bringing with him an entourage of over 15,000 Portuguese nobles. Rio became the capital of the Portuguese empire and a European nation was ruled from an American nation for the first time.

Rio's European Development

The effect of the arrival of the Portuguese court can be seen in the developments which took place between April and November 1808 when João created the Supreme Military Court, the Law Courts, the Naval Academy, the Powder Factory, the Commercial Tribunals, the School of Medicine and Surgery, the Royal Printing Works, the first Brazilian newspaper, the Botanical Gardens, and the Bank of Brazil. The ports were opened and the economic boom in Rio continued.

João VI's time in Brazil was crucial to the growth of Rio; in his thirteen years the city was tranformed from an unimportant, fairly detestable little town into an outpost of European civilization, the capital of the newly created kingdom of Brazil which formed part of the United Kingdom of Portugal, Brazil and the Algarve.

With the defeat of Napoleon at Waterloo in 1814 the pressure began to mount on João to return to Portugal, if he didn't the mother country itself would be lost.

As the revolutionary climate in Europe spread, João realized he could stall no longer and in 1821 returned to Portugal leaving behind his son Pedro as Prince Regent with instructions to make Brazil an independent nation. In the 13 years of João's reign Rio's population had grown from 30,000 in 1808 to what the official census recorded as 112,695 inhabitants in 1821.

Brazil and Rio As One

The history of Rio now becomes almost indistinguishable from that of Brazil as Pedro declares independence for Brazil on September 7, 1822 to become Emperor Pedro I.

With the death of Dom João VI in Portugal in 1826 a similar problem arose over the Portuguese and Brazilian thrones. Due to his increasing unpopularity in Brazil, and his desire to return and rule Portugal, Pedro I chose to abdicate in favour of his five year old son, Pedro II.

What followed for Brazil was a ten-year regency period which allowed the nation to experiment with republicanism. During this time the city of Rio continued to evolve and in 1832 Charles Darwin went on record as proclaiming Rio "... more magnificent than anything any European has ever seen in his country of origin."

With Brazil ruled by a council of Regency a number of areas pushed for their own independence from Rio, but the solution was found in 1831 with the crowning of Pedro II, then 15 years old, as Brazil's second emperor. With the legitimate heir to the throne as the visible head of the nation again, the traditional sectors of society fell into line, and slowly peace was established.

The new Emperor showed at an early stage that he was of a totally different character to his father, for one he was Brazilian born, and besides he was considered to be scholarly and tolerant.

The long reign of Pedro II (1831-1889) was to see a great increase in the importance of Rio as the nation's capital.

As Pedro's administration turned to the problems of the country so Rio turned on its own troubles which in 1849 included the first major outbreak of yellow fever which for a time would destroy the reputation of Rio as a health resort and tourist center. In fact Pedro himself led the exodus in the summer months to the cooler and healthier climate of nearby Petropolis.

Yet progress in Rio was rapid. Reforestation programmes were introduced to recover the Tijuca Forest. In 1851 steam navigation was introduced between Rio and Europe; the city was lit by gas in 1854; the first railway opened in 1858 and the first tramway in 1868; and in 1874 the residents of Rio were in direct contact with Europe for the first time thanks to the trans-Atlantic telegraph which linked "Posto 6" in Copacabana with London.

In 1876 Pedro, by then a renowned traveler, made a historic journey to the United States where he covered 10,000 miles in three months and in the process met up with Alexander Graham Bell at an exhibition in Philadelphia. Bell presented the Emperor with one of the first working models of the telephone, which when installed between Rio and Petropolis became the first telephone line in the world outside of the U.S.A.

Although Pedro was now only in his fifties the country seriously started to consider who his successor should be. By right of accession the crown would go to Pedro's daughter Isabel, but she was married to a Frenchman, the Count d'Eu, and as Pedro grew older Brazilians feared the possibility of a Frenchman ruling Brazil.

The End of the Empire

In the end it was going to be another of Pedro's journeys that brought his downfall.

In 1888 while Pedro was in Europe and Isabel was regent she decided to tackle the problem of slavery, a problem that had been a thorny political issue dating back to 1815. On May 13, 1888 Isabel took it upon herself to sign the decree emancipating the remaining slaves, but crucially without compensation to their owners. That one action wiped out the crown's principal source of support; the price of the freedom of millions of African slaves throughout the country was the almost immediate overthrow of the Empire and the declaration of the republican form of government.

While Pedro was in Petropolis on November 15, 1889, the leaders of the conspiracy met in Campo de Santana (Praça da República) there, Deodoro da Fonseca declared himself to be the interim leader of the new Republic of Brazil. Within twenty-four hours the monarchy had collapsed, and within forty-eight hours Dom Pedro II and the entire royal family had been shipped "bag and baggage" out of Brazil to exile, where Pedro died in 1891.

From the turn of the century Rio started to take on the shape we know today. A tunnel cut in 1892 opened the way to Copacabana, and another in 1904 did the same for Leme. But the most radical improvements were happening downtown. On March 8, 1904 work started to demolish 590 buildings to make way for a new central avenue. Six months later Rio had Av. Rio Branco — so named in 1912 which was to become the Champs-Elysee of Brazil. A mile and a half long, it was the focal point of the city with outdoor cafés lining the elegant pavement, Rio Branco was the Ipanema of its day, and people came to see and be seen.

In 1905 work began on Rio's magnificent Municipal Theatre. Built from various marbles it was modelled on the Paris Opera. At a cost at the time of over two million pounds sterling it was Rio's most luxuriously and extravagantly constructed building. It was also the most costly.

The other major project of the time was the building of Av. Beira Mar, then a bay-side drive, that stretched from the city center all the way to the distant and sparsely populated area of Praia Vermelha, where from January 19, 1913 you could take the cable car to the top of Sugar Loaf.

Rio also started to clear up its health problems thanks to the eminent Dr. Oswaldo Cruz who by 1906 had managed to control deaths by yellow fever and smallpox to less than sixty.

To the Present and on to the Future

Besides the general expansion and modernization of the city with the passing of time, three further projects in the middle of the century shaped Rio as we know it today, and all concerned the reclamation of land from the sea.

The first project in the 1940s included the removal of a hill in downtown Rio whose earth was poured into the bay to make what is now the Santos Dumont airfield, inaugurated in 1944.

The second scheme, and one on a much larger scale, required earth and mud dredged from the harbour, as well as earth brought from the hill of Santo Antonio where the city's new Cathedral stands. The result was Flamengo Park; 12 million square feet of land reclaimed from the sea, which gave the city not only a huge new leisure area but perhaps more importantly, two expressways to relieve the congestion of traffic from the new residential areas to the city center. Flamengo Park, the country's largest landscaping project, was concluded in 1960.

The final landfill concerned Copacabana beach and helped change a narrow beach, with a two lane road, into what we see today, one of the most impressive beaches in the world backed by a six lane highway, lined by wide sweeping sidewalks decorated with their famous mosaic designs that are known throughout the world. This project finished in 1971.

The final chapter in Rio's historical and political past was closed on April 21, 1960 with the dedication of Brasilia as the new capital of the Republic of Brazil; by then Rio's population numbered over four-and-a-half million.

Somehow I don't think Rio minds not being the political capital, it is not an essentially political city, no, it far better fits its mantle of being the nation's capital of culture and tourism, for which it can be guaranteed a glorious future.

A Pictorial Souvenir

If you wish to see how Rio de Janeiro has changed over the years you can do no better than get hold of a copy of "O Rio Antigo do Fotógrafo Marc Ferrez" (The Old Rio of Photographer Marc Ferrez). This beautifully produced book contains over 200 rare photos of Rio between 1865 and 1918. Photos which show quite clearly what Rio has grown and expanded from. "O Rio Antigo" was first published in 1984 and is available in most good Brazilian book shops.

Historically Speaking: The Center of Rio

As you will have now read, Rio is not only a city of the future, but also a city of the past; an honorable past which has left reminders of its former glories in the narrow streets of downtown, Centro, where Rio was born and from where it has since grown.

Today Centro is the business heart of Rio which hustles and bustles Monday through Friday and sleeps during the weekends. It is an area you will want to visit while in Rio.

Because of severe traffic congestion, no tour company offers an adequate tour of downtown Rio. This guide has perhaps shamed some of the companies into improving the situation, but it is still not good. What is certain though, is that the only way to see downtown is to walk. The distances, you will be happy to hear, are not that great, and if you do get tired or hot you can always take a cab to your hotel.

The walking tour I suggest takes about three hours to complete without stops for lunch or shopping.

But before you set out, a few words of advice.

Make sure you dress appropriately, that means flat shoes ladies and expect the city to be hotter than the beach. No shorts though, if you want to enter the São Bento Monastery.

Surprising as it may seem, the best time to walk about downtown is during the week and not at the weekend. The sheer volume of people milling around downtown make assaults rare during the week. At the weekend the place is deserted after noon on Saturday so you become an easy isolated target. It is also true to say that you won't get the real flavor of the city center if you visit it over the weekend.

Plan your tour to start around 10 a.m., this way you will miss the rush hour and be able to split the walk by taking lunch somewhere along the route. It is also worth noting that along the way you pass close by the National History Museum, the National Museum of Fine Arts and the Teatro Municipal while being a short cab ride from the Itamaraty Palace, the Museum of the Republic, and Modern Art Museum.

Finally, if you have any questions you want to ask your airline company take your ticket along with you, during your walk you will be near most of their main Rio offices.

Getting Downtown

The easiest way to get downtown from the zona sul is by metro from Botafogo or by the air-conditioned buses marked "Castelo" which take you to the Meneses Cortes Bus Terminal in the very heart of Centro. (See "Information — Buses").

If you go by bus you will be taken through Flamengo Park and along Praia do Flamengo. On your left you will see the Gloria Hotel and behind, the beautiful octagonal church of Nossa Senhora da Gloria built in 1714. Dom Pedro II was married in the church and his daughter, Isabel, baptized. N.S. da Gloria is open Monday through Friday from 8 a.m. to noon and 1 p.m. to 5 p.m.

Coming up immediately to your right will be the monument built in memory of all those who died in World War II, including the Brazilians who fought alongside the allies in the Italian campaign. The monument houses a small museum depicting Brazils participation in the war.

The monument itself represents two arms raised with the hands outstretched beseeching God in prayer. Since its inauguration in 1960 the monument has been visited by all visiting dignitaries, including Pope John-Paul who celebrated mass from its steps in 1980 for over two million people.

The bus will continue up Av. Beira Mar, or Artero, watch out for the U.S. Consulate General to your left in Av. Presidente Wilson, and turn into President Antonio Carlos. This is where you should disembark from the bus. By choice alight in front of the

Church of Saint Luzia, blue in color at present, built in 1721 on a spot where a chapel has been located since 1582 on what was then the seashore.

If you are coming up to town by metro (subway) you should take a bus or cab to the metro station in Botafogo. Take the train as far as Cinelandia, and leave the station via the exit nearest the rear of the train. Once through the turnstile follow signs to "Sta Luzia", you will emerge on the corner of Rua Santa Luzia and Av. Rio Branco which is marked by the Air France office.

Walk down Rua Santa Luzia, passing the aeronautical building to your right, home to La Tour, the city's only revolving restaurant. From here you will be able to see the Church of Saint Luzia at the end of the road.

The Walk Begins

From the church of Santa Luzia cross over President Antônio Carlos, keep alert as this is one of the city's busiest roads. Having crossed head up Av. Santa Luzia which is marked on the corner by the Petrobrás garage, the street comes out alongside the National History Museum (see "Museums").

The entrance to the museum, which was recently restored, faces on to the main highway which you will be able to see in front of you. From the end of Av. Santa Luzia, you can see the white side wall of the museum, parts of which date back to 1603 and 1762.

From in front of the museum you can see under the overpass the green octagonal tower that is today the Albamar restaurant (see "restaurants"). The tower, one of four, is all that remains from the city's old market and has been a restaurant since 1933 offering some of the best seafood in town. From the Albamar you will see an unusually shaped island fortress in the bay. This is the Ilha Fiscal where on February 19, 1889, Dom Pedro II attended his last ball as Emperor of Brazil. On November 15, 1889 the monarchy was overthrown and Brazil became a republic.

Behind the Ilha Fiscal, in the distance, is the Rio-Niteroi bridge, or to give it its official title the "President Costa e Silva Bridge". The bridge is over nine-and-a-half miles (15.5 km) long, nearly 200 feet high at its highest point, and 90 feet wide. Over 10,000 workers and 60 engineers were involved in its construction.

To continue our walk you should follow the overpass along, away from the National History Museum. Shortly you will come to Praça XV, the historical center of Rio.

Today the water front is the home of the frequent ferry services to Niteroi and Paqueta but in 1808 it witnessed the arrival of Dom João VI of Portugal who had fled from Europe in the face of Napoleon's advancing armies. Eighty one years later, in 1889, Dom João's grandson, Pedro II, would sail from the exact same spot on his way to exile in Europe after Brazil had been declared a republic.

In the days of the Empire the sea shore did not stretch as far as it does today, so to tread the cobblestones of the original Praça XV, or Largo do Paco as it was, you must take the walkway to the main square.

Within Praça XV there are a number of important historical buildings, the most important of which was the House of the Viceroy, a colonial style building constructed in 1743, which became the Royal Palace with the arrival of Dom João. The building has just undergone a massive restoration programme which restored the authentic visual outline of the time when Dom João was in residence. The building served as the headquarters of the Post and Telegraphic Department from the proclamation of the republic in 1889 until the early 1980s. Today the building hosts art exhibits and the occasional erudite concert.

Also to be found in Praça XV, by crossing the busy Av. 1º de Marco, is the old Metropolitan Cathedral built in 1761 which served as the Royal Chapel and saw the coronation of Pedro I in December 1822.

On the outside wall of the Cathedral is a plague commemorating the first mass to be held in Rio. The date was March 1, 1565. Next door to the old Cathedral is the prettier Church of the Carmo Convent built in 1755.

To leave Praça XV cross over Av. 1 de Marco and go through the Arco do Telles (Telles Arch) located on the opposite side of the square to the House of the Viceroy. The Arco do Telles dates back to the eighteenth century and since then has survived a major fire that destroyed the old Senate House which it linked to another similar building.

A Break For Lunch

The Arco de Telles leads into a tiny street called Travessa do Comercio. Time has stood still here and the street is a quiet pedestrian precinct lined by the original houses, one of which, "The English Bar" no less, is a pleasant watering hole if lunch is approaching and one of Centro's best restaurants.

The first street crossed by Travessa do Comercio is Rua Ouvidor, one of the city's most important commercial centers and home to many of the top international banks which dominate the street after crossing Av. 1 de Março. Before Av. 1 de Março it is the city's fishing industry — including tackle stores — that rules the roost.

As you turn left from Travessa do Comercio into Rua Ouvidor you will come immediately on your left to the minute Church of Our Lady of Merchants which despite its size, or perhaps because of it, is worth a visit. The church dates from 1750.

Carry on along Ouvidor, where you will catch the atmosphere of the working city, until it crosses Rua de Quitanda where you turn right. In three short blocks you come face to face with the Church of N. S. de Candelaria one of Rio's most noble churches. This is a landmark in its own right, sitting in the center of the enormous Av. Presidente Vargas, once the widest avenue in South America and for many years the setting for the famous Carnival parade of samba schools.

A church has stood on this site since 1705 although the present structure only dates from 1775 and the dome from 1877, rebuilt in 1894 after being hit by a stray cannon-ball. The inside is magnificent. Candelaria is open for viewing from 7 a.m. to noon and 2 p.m. to 4 p.m. during the week with Sunday Mass at 10 a.m., 11 a.m. and noon.

You now move on to the São Bento Monastery. To reach it you must walk towards the bay away from Candelária and take the second left which will be our old friend, Av. 1º de Março. The monastery is situated at the end in Rua Dom Gerardo and on the way you will pass through the main naval district, on your left you will find many stores specializing in military uniforms and flags. To reach the monastery from the road you take the elevator located in number 40, Rua Dom Gerardo. São Bento is one of the city's most historic buildings and has remained structurally untouched since being built between 1617 and 1641. The inside is richly decorated and the monastery and grounds are a haven of tranquility in the hustle and bustle of downtown Rio.

Walking to the end of Rua Dom Gerardo brings you Av.Rio Branco; turn left. This area has little of interest unless you want to change your dollars. It is the center of the "parallel" market operations. On the corner of Rua Visconde de Inhaúma you should make note of the old Brazilian Mint, Casa da Moeda. If you think the building, with its majestic balconies, would be more befitting of a Presidential Palace, you would be right. As the story goes, a French architect was commissioned to design the Brazilian Mint and the Presidential Palace in Santiago, Chile. At this stage *Murphy's Law* came in to play and the plans got sent to wrong cities. The result was that Rio ended up with a Presidential Palace as its' Mint and Santiago, to this day, has a Mint, the Casa de la Moneda, as its' Presidential Palace.

By the time you get to the crossroads with Av Presidente Vargas you should be able to see the War Memorial which was positioned to be seen through the whole length of Rio Branco.

Rio Branco, it is interesting to note, only dates from 1904 when 590 buildings were demolished to make way for the new Central Avenue which was later named Rio Branco in 1912 after the death of the country's foreign minister, Barão de Rio Branco.

Cross Av. Presidente Vargas and continue up Rio Branco on the right hand side, taking the third right into Rua do Rosario. You are now in the main shopping area of Centro.

In Rua do Rosário besides taking in the general flavor of the area look out for number 155, Kosmos, where you will find a fine selection of prints of old Rio at very reasonable prices.

Further up, on the corner of Gonçalves Dias, you come to the small but impressive flower market. The variety here is staggering.

Turning into Gonçalves Dias, away from the flower market, you come, on your left, to Colombo (N° 32) which has been serving elegant lunches and teas for more than 90 years.

Go inside, if only for a fruit juice from the counter. A cheap and reasonable lunch can also be had at Colombo but expect to stand in line. (See — "Restaurants").

At the end of Gonçalves Dias is Largo da Carioca. Largo da Carioca has been an active part of the city since the early 17th century and today is the meeting place of the old and the new. The old sits sublimely a top a low hill overlooking the square represented by the Church and Convent of Saint Anthony, built between 1608 and 1620, and the richly decorated Church of Saint Francis which dates from the 18th century. Both churches have recently had their façades restored thanks to a grant from Citibank and the Fundação Roberto Marinho.

Metropolitan Cathedral

In Largo da Carioca itself you will find a mass of traders and street performers who stretch all the way down the side of the Teatro Municipal to Praça Floriano and Cinelândia. You however should walk away from Rio Branco and head up Av. República do Chile past the cubic, futuristic headquarters of Petrobrás, the state oil company, to the new Metropolitan Cathedral.

Still seemingly far from finished, the first stone was laid on January 20, 1964, the Cathedral itself was inaugurated on November 16, 1976 to celebrate the 300th anniversary of the Diocese of Rio.

The Cathedral stands on a spot which used to be the hill of Saint Anthony. Today all that remains is the small hill overlooking Largo da Carioca, the rest was excavated and used for the landfill which became Flamengo Park.

Work continues on the Cathedral and it is hoped that eventually it will have a sacred Art Museum and a method of taking visitors up to the roof to get a panoramic view of the Cathedral and city.

For those who like statistics the Cathedral is 83 meters high externally and 68 meters internally with no internal columns to support the structure. The church has a diameter of 106 meters and a capacity for 5,000 sitting and 20,000 standing, a figure that was surpassed on August 2, 1980 when Pope John-Paul visited the Cathedral.

The inside of the church is dominated by four huge stained glass windows each measuring more than 20 by 60 meters.

Each window has a predominant color scheme and they represent the ecclesiastical (green), the saintly (red), the Catholic (blue), and apostolic (yellow).

From the Cathedral you can stroll down to the Largo da Lapa crossing beneath the 36 arches of the Aqueduto da Carioca (Carioca Aqueduct), one of Rio's best known landmarks.

Work started on the aqueduct in 1724 and it was designed to bring fresh water from the "forest" of Santa Teresa down to the public fountain in Largo da Carioca. In 1896 the arches became the base for the viaduct which links the Santa Teresa streetcars with the city center, a service which still runs today but one that should be avoided by any visitor who is carrying valuables.

The aqueduct and the surrounding Lapa area make an interesting back drop for photographers. In one direction you have the aqueduct and behind it the futuristic Cathedral and Petrobras headquarters backed by some of the city's tallest skyscrapers, while in the other direction you have the original houses dating back to the last century that have been painstakingly restored in their original colors. One of the, the Asa Branca Nightclub, was opened by the King of Spain no-less.

At the turn of the century this area, and Lapa, which stretches away beyond the arches, was the center of the city's nightlife full of bars, cabarets, and clubs.

If you are a classical music fan you will find yourself coming to Largo da Lapa to hear recitals at the Sala Cecilia Meirelles. It is time to move on though, and your feet may be pleased to hear that the end is almost in sight.

Taking the road opposite the Sala, Rua do Passeio, you will pass on your right Passeio Publico, the city's oldest park, landscaped in 1789. The sea used to come up to the far wall of the park which could only be reached by boat. On your left you have Mesbla, one of the city's largest department stores.

If you follow Rua do Passeio along you will come again to Rio Branco and the area known as Cinelândia from the movie houses that were built here in the 1930's. In front you have the magnificent Teatro Municipal built in 1905 and modelled on the Paris Opera. At the time of building it was Rio's most luxuriously and extravagantly constructed edifice, and almost the most costly.

Inaugurated on July 14, 1909, it remains today the center of Rio's cultural activities. Tours of the theatre are at present infrequent, so treat yourself to returning in the evening to see one of the theatre's many presentations or for a small flavour of the theatre you can enjoy an excellent lunch or drink in the Café do Teatro (See — "Restaurants") located in the building's basement.

To conclude our tour of downtown Rio you must cross Rio Branco by the Teatro Municipal where on the opposite side of the avenue you will find the National Museum of Fine Arts, Rio's most important art collection.

I leave you here, in the very heart of downtown Rio. To return to the zona sul, and your hotel, you can either catch the metro from Cinelandia or Largo da Carioca to Botafogo, or by walking up Rio Branco, away from the War Memorial, you will discover the bus terminal to your right in Rua São José where you can catch the air-conditioned bus. If you are totally exhausted take a cab back to your hotal or apartment, it won't cost much.

Typically But Uniquely Brazilian

THE BEACH

Life in Rio revolves around the beach, be it Copacabana, Ipanema, Flamengo, or one of the many others that go to make up the city's 90 kilometers of golden sand.

No other city of Rio's size has such perfect, beautiful and clean beaches on its doorstep. It is impossible to spend 24 hours in Rio without passing one of them.

The importance of the beach to Rio can't be over emphasized. It is the city's playground, park, sports facility, meeting place, bar and office all rolled into one.

Because it is so easy to get to the beach, even if only for twenty minutes, they are always full of life, you could even be forgiven for thinking at times that the Carioca never works.

The beach is the life blood of Rio. Babies are taken to the beach in their first few weeks. They learn to walk and play there, they grow up there. As the children get older the beach becomes their meeting place, at first under the watchful eye of Mum and Dad and then alone. Carioca boys first discover Carioca girls on the beach and vice versa. Romances blossom and fade on the beach but one day grow to marriage, and with the children from the marriage the cycle begins again.

There is nothing "touristy" about the beaches of Rio, they are a microcosm of Brazilian life. I have never met anyone who has been bored on a Rio beach, there is just too much to watch, and it is on the beach that it comes home that you really are one of the very few lucky foreigners to have had the chance of sampling the delights of *Cidade Maravilhosa.*

THE BIKINI

The bikini was born in Rio and has been growing up here ever since. A Brazilian bikini is in a class of its own, often copied but never equalled.

Brazil leads the fashion world when it comes to bikinis, which is not all that surprising when you consider the amount of time the average Carioca girl spends on the beach. Most European and American designers would throw their hands up in horror at the thought of trying to set a new fashion each year with only the size of the bikini to work with, but Brazilian designers somehow seem to manage.

Each summer there is a subtle change in shape and the introduction of new colors which date previous costumes as "last year's thing."

One year designers tried to bring back the one piece costume but the girls from Ipanema, with a little bit of encouragement from the boys no doubt, weren't having it and the bikini continued to reign supreme.

Your first sight of a Brazilian girl in her bikini will be one of the many memorable views you take back from Rio, perhaps even more memorable than the one from the top of Corcovado!

THE CANGA

Complementing the bikini is a large square of material called a *canga*. Not so much in fashion as it was a couple of years back, the *canga* is still a familiar sight on the beaches of Rio.

Although no more than a piece of material which the girls lie on top of instead of using a towel, the *canga* is transformed by the girls into many differing styles of dress to walk to and from the beach in. With a *canga* imagination is everything.

Specially cut *cangas* with beautiful Brazilian scenes can be found at Rakam in Ipanema and Copacabana.

CAIPIRINHA

The perfect accompaniment to *feijoada* is a *caipirinha*, in my humble opinion Brazil's greatest contribution to mankind.

Caipirinha is a wonderful drink, prepared very simply by chopping a lemon into a glass, peel and all, which you then crush the juice out of using a little wooden mortar. To the crushed lemon add ice, sugar and a dose of *Cachaça*. Simple but believe me effective.

The secret ingredient, *Cachaça*, is made from crushed sugar cane and not unlike rum, although with a flavor that is quite distinctly its own. *Cachaça* comes in varying strengths and qualities and somehow remains one of Brazil's best kept secrets.

Some people who find *Cachaca* to be a little too potent prefer to base their *Caipirinha* on either rum or vodka but just once make sure you try the real thing, ask for a *Caipirinha de Cachaça*.

COFFEE

If Brazil is known for one product, that product is coffee.

Still today one of Brazil's most important exports, coffee has taken the name of Brazil into countless homes around the world.

Once you arrive in Brazil you will quickly realize that the songwriter who wrote: "There is an awful lot of coffee in Brazil" was not joking.

Brazilians drink an enormous amount of coffee, an amount that is taken in small "doses" throughout the day known as *cafezinho* (literally "small coffee").

On an average working day a Brazilian will expect to drink anything from 10 to 20 of these little demitasses, regardless of being rich or poor.

You will quickly discover that wherever you go a *cafezinho* is waiting. At first you may find it rather stronger than expected but you will soon get used to it and realize what real coffee is all about.

Brazilians rarely have milk with their coffee or drink out of a big cup, the exception being at breakfast. After every meal coffee is served as part of the courtesy of the restaurant. The perfect end to what I hope will have been a perfect meal.

Locally people take their coffee very sweet. Some say it is the Brazilian sugar that makes the coffee so special, and normally you are offered the sugar to put in to your cup before the coffee is served. In offices, supermarkets and other places you may find the sugar has already been added to the coffee, if so ask for your coffee *sem açucar* ("without sugar").

If you want to take some coffee back with you the easiest place to buy it is the supermarket where you can see a wide variety, all of good quality. Ground coffee comes in sealed packs but for an extra long life try the Melita coffee which comes vacuum packed. If you can't get to a supermarket though don't worry, because both beans and powder are on sale at the international airport in specially designed travel boxes.

Sets of the small Brazilian coffee cups are on sale in most good gift shops and can certainly be found in all the major shopping centers.

FAVELAS (SHANTYTOWNS)

Rio's *favelas* are very pretty, picture postcard pretty in fact, but from a distance, a distance the visitor should maintain.

Favelas are Rio's main areas of poor housing which have grown up on hill sides where nobody else had an interest in the land. Today the big established *favelas* have complicated infrastructures and the government supplies them with electricity and water.

95% of the people who live in *favelas* have only committed one crime, they are poor. Most are law abiding citizens who work in low paid jobs in the *zona sul*. There are however a small element who live in the *favela* who are hardened criminals. Foreigners, no matter how long they have been in Rio, or how well they speak Portuguese, should never venture into the *favelas* however enticing they look.

No Brazilian will think you are brave because you have walked through a *favela*, they will just think you are mad.

FEIJOADA

Rio's contribution to the national cuisine is *feijoada*, a dish which although served throughout Brazil is never found better than in Rio.

Not the most attractive of dishes, *feijoada* is based on black beans, a staple item in every Brazilian diet.

A type of stew the ingredients of *feijoada* are many and include dried meats, bacon, salted pork and ribs, various types of sausages, and most importantly the ear, tail and trotter of a pig. The above will be served with white rice, *farofa* (fried manioc flour), kale, sliced oranges, and a hot pepper sauce.

Because *feijoada* is a heavy meal by any standards it is traditionally served for Saturday lunch, this tradition holds true today with many restaurants, and nearly all the hotels, making special Saturday presentations.

The visitor, would be well advised to try his first *feijoada* at one of the top hotels where the ingredients are presented separately and there is somebody on hand to explain what goes where.

Feijoada is a fun dish, wonderfully Brazilian in character, which is likely to be quite different from anything you have tried before.

It's worth noting that many foreigners who live in Brazil find on leaving that the thing they miss most is their Saturday *feijoada* after a morning spent on the beach.

Note: Most hotels and restaurants although specializing in *feijoada* on Saturday offer other dishes for those who find *feijoada* a little too much to handle.

FESTAS JUNINAS

June sees the celebration of the feasts of Saint Anthony (June 13), Saint John (June 24) and Saint Peter (June 29) which are honored by the *festas Juninas*.

The parties held by both rich and poor are steeped in folklore which have the participants dressing up as typical peasants from the interior, the boys in checked shirts and jeans with a neckerchief and straw hat, the girls in their "best" dress and hair tied up in bunches. The music played is from the interior and the parties normally take place around a large bonfire or barbeque where hot drinks are served.

The sky during the time of the *festas Juninas* is lit up by huge balloons which carry below them elaborate patterns of burning candles that invariably drift safely out to sea.

Rio's top clubs all hold *festas Juninas*, but try to get invited to the one held at the Gavea Golf Club.

FIGA

Every country has its good luck charm and Brazil's is the *figa*.

A clenched fist with the thumb extended between the second and

PARADISE HAS A NAME

Búzios

Búzios

Búzios

POUSADA NAS ROCAS

When the top *Cariocas* choose to leave Rio for the weekend or their holidays the place they head for is Buzios, 170 km from Rio, where the number one choice for de-luxe accommodation and service is the Pousada nas Rocas on Ilha Rasa.
If you are looking for Paradise in Paradise your choice has to be Pousada nas Rocas.

Reservations and Information. *Rio de Janeiro*: Rua da Quitanda, 191. Tel.: (021) 253-0001. Telex. (021) 34033. ***Búzios***: Tel.: 2303.

THE INSIDER'S VIDEO

NOW SCREENING AT THE BEST HOTELS IN RIO

third finger, a *figa* should be received as a gift. You should never buy one for yourself.

Figas come in all sizes and are made of every sort of material, from wood to gold. Most jewellers carry a full range of *figas* made from gold or precious and semi-precious stones that look good hung around the neck on a gold chain.

Once you are given a *figa* it stores up all the luck you haven't used, but be careful not to break or lose it, that will end your store of luck.

GUARANA

Although you may have never heard of *guarana* it is destined to become a major world seller.

Guarana in its natural form is a Brazilian shrub, the berries of which can be ground down to form a powder with "magical" qualities.

Containing 5 percent caffeine, *guarana* has similar properties to coffee in that it is a nerve stimulant and restorative. Many Brazilians dilute the *guarana* powder and use it as a pick-me-up while the vast majority of Brazilians drink the commercialized soft drink which retains the *guarana* flavour but little else.

Guarana, Brazil's Coca Cola, is served at every restaurant and bar and you should find it a refreshing and stimulating soft drink that you will be looking out for at your own supermarket when you get home.

JEWELRY

Brazil is blessed with deposits of pratically every kind of gemstone and precious metal, and in many cases holds over 90 percent of all the world's known supplies.

Brazilian jewels and jewellers are known the world over, only at the time you may not have recognized them as Brazilian.

Rio offers the chance for the visitor to feel like a millionaire because even the smartest looking jewellers have stones and settings to fit every pocket. Prices for even the top gemstones are normally only a fraction of what you would expect to pay in other countries.

For their intrinsic beauty or their value as an investment Brazilian jewels should not be missed during your stay.

JOGO DO BICHO (GAME OF THE ANIMALS)

Brazilians love to gamble but don't ever get the chance legally except for the weekly soccer pools and a game called *loto*. Out of illegality has grown the *Jogo do Bicho*.

Invented by Baron Drummond in the 1870s to raise money for improvements to the zoo, it was based around the idea of giving each visitor a ticket with a certain animal on it. At the end of the day a winning animal was drawn and those holding corresponding tickets would receive a cash prize. The result was announced by the hoisting of a flag above the zoo depicting the winning animal.

The *Jogo de Bicho* was so successful that the zoo paid off its improvements and scrapped the game, but the *Jogo de Bicho* was not to die and today, although clandestinely, the game thrives on just about every street corner helping to finance Carnival.

MACUMBA

Macumba appears both exciting and romantic to the foreign visitor, but many of these forget that Macumba is a religion to a large proportion of the Brazilian population and should be treated as such.

To explain Macumba would need a book and not a chapter.

Loosely Macumba has its roots in various African and Indian rituals but it has developed over time to become characteristically Brazilian, a religion that is followed by young and old, rich and poor, the educated and the uneducated.

The belief in Macumba is that all aspects of our lives are influenced by spirits both good and evil, many of these spirits carry the same names as Catholic saints and it is interesting to note that the Catholic church in Brazil must "tolerate" Macumba or risk losing many Catholics who would move totally over to it.

Macumba rites are performed in a location called a *terreiro*. *Terreiros* can be found all over Rio but please remember they are places of worship and not a tourist attraction.

There is no one *terreiro* that I can recommend in Rio although tour companies do arrange tours which are tourist orientated. If you are genuinely interested in finding out what goes on speak to someone at your hotel desk. The chances are that many people working at the hotel will be linked and worship at a *terreiro*. If they see your interest is genuine they will normally be delighted to take you along, but please leave your camera at home. If you want to take pictures go on an official tour.

One last word of advice, if you go to a *terreiro* try and wear white and don't cross your arms or legs, this is believed to interfere with the arrival of the spirits.

The most visual of all Macumba celebrations is the Feast of Iemanja held on December 31

MUSIC

Brazil is one, if not "the" most musical nation on earth. The people are musical, the cities vibrate to their own distinctive beat, and the most varied and diverse rhythms from north to south, east to west capture the heart and feet of the listener.

A visitor could be forgiven for thinking that Brazilian music is samba and nothing else. In truth samba is only one small Brazilian sound, a sound that has its roots buried deep beneath the city of Rio de Janeiro and Carnival.

But Brazil as a whole is about than samba. Could you have forgotten Bossa Nova already? And then there are the styles you may never have heard of: *frevo, baiao, coco, fote, tropicalismo, pastoril, maracatu*, and the *Jovem Guarda*, and that's just for starters.

In world terms, Brazilian music suffers from its Portuguese lyrics, but then if you speak Portuguese you soon realise that as a language it is more musical than English, so aren't the Brazilians right not to change? Why accept second best when you've got the best?

In Brazil, American and European music walk hand in hand with Brazilian, at once you realize that all have their distinct qualities. It is impossible to say which is the better.

During your time in Brazil you should take the opportunity to hear as much music as you can. Far too many foreigners who come to live in Brazil hide behind their national record collection and miss so much.

At any one time in Rio there are two or three big names performing and in the summer weekends this could climb to eight or ten.

From my experience samba, except during carnival, is the least compatible of all Brazilian musical forms to the foreign ear. So while you should certainly catch samba live you would be well advised to steer away from it on record and try something else.

Under "Entertainment — Shows" I have listed the top names in

Brazilian music, names which given the chance you should try and listen to.

NEW YEAR'S EVE

The celebration of New Year in Rio is an incredible and unique spectacle which most of the world knows little about.

December 31 is the Feast of Iemanja, the goddess of Sea, and one of the most important Macumba gods.

Macumbeiros start arriving on the beaches of Rio in their thousands early on December 31. By early afternoon Copacabana is a mass of people and glowing candles as the macumba rituals are played out.

As the evening wears on more and more people arrive to join in the celebrations on the beach, especially Copacabana, and by midnight more than one million people will be present, predominantly dressed in white.

For the macumbeiros the importance of midnight is to offer their gifts to Iemanja. At a few seconds to midnight they lay their offerings on the sea shore and if all goes to plan the waves will pluck their offerings away and drag them into the depths. Some macumbeiros send gifts on elaborately built rafts, a sight which is unique anywhere in the world.

Midnight is usually signalled by a spectacular firework display when the 36 storey Hotel Meridien, which holds one of the city's most chic parties, turns itself into a gigantic Roman Candle.

After midnight the city goes back to partying, and the year's first samba strikes up. New Year parties are held in the road, in beach front apartments, in hotels, in fact everywhere. And at dawn a large proportion of the party goers will be back on the beach to see the sun rise before going home or to one of the hotels for breakfast.

Regardless of what you choose to do next New Year if you are in Rio you should spend a little time on the beach and watch this incredible ritual at close hand.

PAU D'AGUA

Looking to be nothing more than a piece of dead stick the *pau d'água* (water stick) is a remarkable and miraculous plant which you will want to take back home to show the folks what funny things they have in the tropics.

This innocuous piece of wood sprouts and flourishes into life when stood in water and is difficult for even the most inept gardener to kill.

Pau d'água can be found in most good florists and should easily be able to withstand the journey home.

SOCCER

Brazilian soccer is unique; it is the most exciting brand of the sport found anywhere in the world. For more information about Brazilian soccer see ''Sports — Soccer'' and ''Things To See — Maracana''

H

Day Trips and
Longer
Air Pass
On From Rio
Brasilia
Foz do Iguaçu
Manaus
Minas Gerais

Day Trips and Longer

BUZIOS

Armação dos Búzios is one of Brazil's best kept secrets.

Situated less than 200 km from Rio on good roads, Búzios is a little bit of paradise which boasts 17 golden beaches, some of the nicest restaurants in Brazil, yet still manages to remain relatively unspoilt.

Basically a small, rustic fishing colony, Búzios was discovered by the wealthy and famous of Rio who were looking for a weekend retreat away from the hustle and bustle of Rio's beaches. A place if you like where the beautiful people could remain beautiful.

The rich and famous moved into Búzios constructing spectacular houses which all contained a certain built in rustic charm. Few hotels existed at this time and Buzios remained truly off the beaten track with the only access being a dust road which became impassable in certain conditions. To keep the area's "privacy" there were no signs to show you the way in. A newcomer could be lost for days on dirt roads looking for this mecca of the "in" crowd. The hoi polloi stayed away.

The influx of money into the Búzios region was bound to change things, and it did. More houses were built and the first of the *pousadas* (inns) began to spring up. The village of Búzios took on the challenge of catering to the whims and wants of the jet set, and as these were travelled people the village had to offer the best in terms of beach boutiques and restaurants.

Today Búzios still retains its air of mystery over the average Brazilian who prefers to keep away and stay down the coast in the larger resorts of Saquarema, Araruama, and Cabo Frio. Why the average Brazilian is scared of Búzios is a little difficult to say. Perhaps it's a question of class, or rather as I believe the question of price, that Búzios is beyond their means. In truth Búzios is no more expensive than anywhere else in Brazil, and that means cheap for the foreign visitor, but nobody is letting on.

Once visited, Búzios is difficult to forget. Tourists who are lucky enough to be taken there return to spend future holidays while the residents of Rio search out houses to rent for the whole year and return weekend after weekend to seek out the sounds of silence away from the office in Rio.

Getting to Búzios

Today getting to Búzios is fairly simple, and can be reached either by car, bus and taxi or plane. Personally I suggest this is the time to hire a car as a big part of the beauty of Búzios is exploring and hunting out new beaches.

To get to Búzios you must cross the Niterói Bridge and follow signs to *"São Gonçalo, Rio Bonito, Campos, Vitória"*, and then *"Manilha, Rio Bonito"*. 26km after having passed through the toll station, at the end of the bridge, you join the BR-101 which is sign-posted *"Itaboraí, Rio Bonito"*.

61 km after the Niterói bridge turn off the BR-101 by following the road to the right marked clearly *"Araruama/Cabo Frio"*. On the outskirts of Araruama the inland and coast roads join up and continue as the RJ-106. You will now be driving alongside the Lagoa de Araruama which you could be forgiven for thinking is the sea. Approximately 125km after having crossed the Niterói bridge you turn away from the Lagoa, still on RJ-106, following signs to *"Macaé*

or *Búzios.''* 16km up this road you come to the first marked turning to the right which is posted to Búzios. It is now only 19km more before you reach the village itself.

The drive is 170km from the end of the Niteroi Bridge to the center of Búzios and depending on the traffic conditions will take between two-and-a-half and three hours.

If you don't want to drive to Búzios you can take the bus to Cabo Frio from the Rodoviaria Novo Rio which runs every hour and costs about $2. From Cabo Frio it is a thirty minute taxi ride to Búzios, although many of the top inns will agree to meet you.

For those who wish to fly to Búzios, Costair offers a service from Rio to Búzios on Friday and Saturday with the return flights on Sunday and Monday. Reservations can be made in Rio on 253-0001.

Where to stay in Búzios

If you are not staying as a guest in a house Búzios still offers a number of picturesque and comfortable *pousadas* (inns) to stay at, most of which should be booked in advance especially during the high season which now stretches from late November through March.

None of the inns listed below has an address — when you get to Búzios you will see why — but all are well sign posted, and easy to find.

Auberge de l'Hermitage

More of a resort complex than an inn. l'Hermitage is one of Búzios top hotels, awarded four stars by the state-tourism board, Embratur.

Set on Manguinhos beach, 7 km before the village of Búzios. l'Hermitage offers 16 well appointed apartments all set at ground level around the main complex.

L'Hermitage has its own first class restaurant, considered one of the best in Búzios, which overlooks the sea and is open for lunch and dinner, including to non-residents.

* 16 Rooms
* Air Conditioning
* TV Room
* Room Service
* Restaurant
* Tennis Court
* Volleyball Court
* Snooker
* Sauna
* Games Room
* Conference Facilities
* On beachfront

Rates: From $85 per double.
Credit: American Express, Elo, and Dinners.
Reservations: In Rio at Rua da Assembléia, 10 — Sala 3420 (Tel. 222-8282 or 222-8385) or at the hotel (Tel. 224-6757).

Buzios Beach Club

Set at the top end of Geríba Beach, the Búzios Beach Club is a condominium of 34 privately owned houses of similar architectural styles which are rented out by the owners through the condominium management. The number of houses available for rent varies during the year from 14 to 34.

All the Beach Club houses come fully equipped and sleep up to eight, although the majority of houses have three bedrooms.

The club has its own pool and tennis courts as well as a restaurant and bar if you don't want to cook yourself. A maid service takes care of the household chores.

Prices at the Beach Club very wildly depending on the season, yet it usually works out cheaper for a group than staying in a pousada.

In 1986 the Beach Club inaugurated its own small pousada which has 17 rooms.

* 34 houses
* Full restaurant service.
* Bar
* TV Room and Vídeo
* Swimming Pool
* Tennis Courts
* Volleyball Court
* Sauna
* On beachfront

Rates: On request
Credit: None
Reservation and Information: In Búzios at the club on (0246)231193

Búzios International Apart Hotel

A rather strange time-sharing

project located behind the main street of Búzios, away from the beach, Búzios International Apart Hotel was purpose built and inaugurated in early 1984.

By far the largest housing project in Búzios, the Apart Hotel offers 136 apartments of one or two bedrooms, each with small kitchenette, living room, and bathroom.

The complex has its own restaurant, a large pool, volleyball court and games room.

* 136 Rooms
* Fully air-conditioned
* TV Room
* Games Room
* Volleyball Court
* Restaurant
* Snooker
* Sauna
* Swimming pool

Rates: From $50 for a one bedroom apartment.
Credit: All major cards
Reservations: With Farol Turismo in Rio on 233-3636 or in Búzios on (0246) 231430.

Cabanas de Búzios

Cabanas de Búzios is a leisure complex of 30 cabins close to Manguinhos Beach.

Each cabin has a living room, double bedroom, bathroom, and small bar with refrigerator, and can sleep from two to four.

The complex has two swimming pools, tennis and volleyball court, and complete restaurant service.

* 30 Cabins
* Fully air conditioned
* Full restaurant service
* Room service
* Bar
* Swimming Pool
* Tennis Court

Rates: From $50.
Credit: None
Reservations: In São Paulo on (011) 853-1077 or in Búzios on (0246) 231411.

Casas Brancas

Situated on top of a hill overlooking the village of Búzios, this elegant pousada offers just fourteen well appointed rooms.

The pousada has no dining facilities as such, due to its proximity to the village of Búzios, although it will prepare snacks for residents who wish to spend the day around the pool without leaving the inn.

* 14 Rooms
* Fully air conditioned
* TV Room with Vídeo
* Swimming Pool
* Bar
* Games Room

Rates: From $70 per double.
Credit: American Express, Elo, Visa and Nacional
Reservations: In Búzios on (0246) 231458

Casa D'Elas

More a house than a hotel, the small, just 15 rooms, comfortable Casa d'Elas in located alongside Casas Brancas, on Morro Humaitá, overlooking the village of Búzios.

* 15 Rooms
* Bar
* TV Room
* Games Room
* Swimming pool

Rates: From $40 to $55 per double.
Credit: American Express, Elo, Visa and Nacional.
Reservations: In Búzios on (0246) 231217.

Gravatás

While not as well appointed as the top Búzios pousadas like l'Hermitage, Casas Brancas and Martim Pescador, Gravatás is positioned on one of Búzios best beaches, Geribá, not far from the Búzios Beach Club.

The daily rate includes lunch which is served from 1 p.m. to 4 p.m. in the new restaurant block which also includes the sauna and games room.

* 56 Rooms
* Fully air conditioned
* TV Room
* Restaurant (lunch only)
* Bar
* Games Room
* Sauna
* On beachfront
* Pool (opening 1987)

Rates: From $50 per double.
Reservations: In Rio on 232-1601 or 242-3204 or in Búzios on (0246) 231218

Mandrágora

Mandrágora is one of Búzios' best appointed and equipped pousadas which over recent years has expanded its facilites to include squash and tennis courts. More improvements are planned.

Located on the main access road to Búzios, away from the coast, Mandrágora is a short drive from all the region's main beaches, you would however feel at a loss without your own transport.

* 18 Rooms
* Fully air-conditioned
* Mini-bar in every room
* Restaurant
* Bar
* TV Room
* Games Room
* Tennis and Squash Courts
* Sauna
* Pool (opening 1987)
* Conference facilities

Rates: From $60 per double.
Credit: Elo
Reservation: In Búzios on (0246) 231348 or by telex in Rio on 021 32989.

Martim Pescador

Like many of Búzios' pousadas, Martim Pescador is run by its owner which is reflected by its homely atmosphere and attention to detail in service. Set on the top of a hill, Martim Pescador offers a spectacular view of Manguinhos Beach which should not be missed at sunset by even non-residents who can enjoy a drink in the comfortable and well appointed bar.

* 10 Rooms
* Fully air-conditioned
* Restaurant service for guests
* Bar
* Pool (Opening 1987)
* Squash Court (Opening 1987)

Rates: From $60 per double.
Credit: Most major cards.
Reservations: In Búzios on (0246) 231449.

Ossos

Pousada dos Ossos is a comfortable and traditional pousada located in Praça Eugênio Honolds close to Praia dos Ossos.

Pousada dos Ossos has its own boat for day trips around the beaches of Búzios and can organize fishing and diving.

The owners have plans to open a new purpose built, 45 room hotel on Praia João Fernandes during 1986.

* 15 Rooms
* Fully air-conditioned

* Restaurant
* Mini-bar in every room
* TV Room
* Bar

Rates: From $50 per double.
Credit: Most major cards.
Reservations: In Búzios on (0246) 231108.

Rocas

A purpose built leisure center on its own private island, located 700 meters from the mainland, Pousada nas Rocas aims at the top end of the market which in its first two years of operation it has captured to become ''the'' pousada in Búzios.

A goumet restaurant, three bars, one on one of the island's beaches, tennis courts, games rooms, a volleyball court, a jogging track, organized fishing trips, sailing, windsurfing, archery, and live music are just some of the attractions of this sophisticated resort.

The rooms and suites, two to a chalet, are furnished to the highest international standards and are in keeping with the resort's relaxed and restful atmosphere.

The Pousada nas Rocas has in two years made its name nationally so reservations are a must even in the low season.

* 70 rooms
* TV and mini-bar in every room.
* 24-hour room service.
* Fully air-conditioned.
* Restaurants.
* Three bars.
* Swimming pool.
* Tennis court.
* Volleyball court.
* Archery.
* Vídeo and games room.
* Boat hire.
* Windsurfer hire.
* Own schooner.
* Jogging track.
* Helipad.
* Transfers between Rio and Búzios.
* Conference facilities.

Rates: Single from $120. Double from $160. (Full board).
Credit: Most major cards.
Reservations: In Rio on 253-0001 and in São Paulo on 284-7511.

Other Accommodation

Búzios offers umpteen other pousadas at varying prices and usually it is safe to say that you can drive to Búzios and find accommodation at one of these without too much trouble. Your travel agent or hotel though will be able to reserve accommodation for you before you set out to make sure you are not disappointed.

To help with your reservations other pousadas which accept bookings in advance in Rio de Janeiro are Atobá (242-9130)

Estalagem (246-0455)' Lagostim (267-0266), Moana (256-7592), Pousada dos Búzios (274-6608), and Pousada dos Sete Pecados Capitais (267-6030).

In Búzios try Pousada do⁸ Sol (0246-231490), Vila do Mar (0246-231298), Casa de Pedra (0246-231607), or La Coloniale (0246-231434).

Eating out in Búzios

Eating out in Búzios is sadly not what it used to be, and many of the leading chefs have packed their bags and returned to Rio, leaving behind good but not "outstanding" eateries.

Two restaurants to keep their standards are the French cuisine of "Au Cheval Blanc" and the Italian of "Le Streghe".

Other names to look out for in Búzios are VIP Club, Chez Michou, Oasis, Satiricon, La Nuance and Casa Velha, which serves fondue. The pousadas with the most consistent kitchens are the Pousada nas Rocas and Auberge l'Hermitage. But to list all the restaurants and bars is unfair and would take away the edge of discovery which is one of the particular joys of a weekend or week in Búzios.

All types of food can be found in Búzios in a varying degree of sophistication which stretches from beachside shacks offering grilled seafood all the way to the chic international restaurants, restaurants which would not be out of place in the center of Ipanema. One thing for sure though, all of Búzios restaurants have charm.

Búzios in essence defies a guide book, the fashions and moods of this small village change too quickly. It is difficult, therefore, to tell you where you can go and drink, or dance, or listen to music, but I don't believe you will have any problem finding these places once you find Búzios.

COSTA VERDE (GREEN COAST)

In striking contrast to Buzios and the *Costa do Sol* (Sun Coast) is the area known as the *Costa Verde* (Green Coast) which spreads over 280 km of some of the world's most beautiful coastline to the west of Rio de Janeiro, to a point where the states of Rio and São Paulo meet beyond the historic town of Parati:

As its name suggests, the *Costa Verde* is dominated by lush vegetation that covers the rolling hills which sweep down to the tropical beaches that separate them from the waters of the South Atlantic.

A drive in the region is a must for any visitor with time on their side and long term visitors should plan to make the drive from São Paulo to Rio along the coast road at least once during their time in Brazil, a drive of over 600 km compared to the 430 km of the more popular inland route via Resende.

So what does the *Costa Verde* offer the visitor besides spectacular scenery and how does it compare with Buzios?

In simple terms it doesn't. While Buzios is one tiny paradise tucked away in the corner of the *Costa do Sol*, the *Costa Verde* offers the visitor diverse options spread over a much larger area.

Gourmet Cooking

Part of the gourmet cooking of the *Costa Verde* is in the hands of two small restaurants to be found in the tiny fishing village of Pedra de Guaratiba less than an hours drive from Ipanema.

The restaurants in question are Quatro Sete Meia and Candido's, both of which attract the "in" crowd from Rio who drive out for leisurely weekend lunches, and to savour the best seafood in the Rio region.

Quatro Sete Meia, the more famous of the two restaurants, can cope with just 24 guests so reservations are a must. Owned and run by a Canadian, Eugene Moss, and a Brazilian, Antonio Moraes, Quatro Sete Meia has seen itself in the past featured in the pages of the hallowed *New York Times* which compared it favourably alongside the Meridien's "Saint Honoré" and Rio Palace's "Le Pré Catelan."

In the same road as Quatro Sete Meia, Rua Barros de Alarcão, is the larger but equally popular Candido's which offers a more diverse menu but of a similarly high standard of cuisine.

Pedra de Guaratiba is rustic and lazy so make a visit a whole day affair with plenty of time to lull over the food, much of it typically Brazilian.

A good suggestion is to hire a car and driver for the day and let him take you down the beaches of Rio (Barra, Sernambetiba, Prainha and Grumari). At the end of Grumari the road climbs inland; just beyond the brow of the hill on a tight corner you come to a little shack known as the *Vista Alegre* (Happy View) which is worth stopping at for a caipirinha, a plate of *camarão* (shrimp) and the magnificent view before dropping down to Pedra for lunch. Alternatively you can bear left into Guaratiba itself where the restaurant Tia Palmira attracts a number of the "in" crowd for lunch (310-1169).

Candido's is open all week from 11:30 a.m. until 7 p.m. (11 p.m. on Saturday and Sunday) with reservations a must at the weekend (395-1630 or 395-2007). Quatro Sete Meia opens only Friday through Sunday from 12 noon until 11 p.m., reservations are also essential (395-2716).

By car the quickest route to Pedra de Guaratiba is along BR-101, the Rio-Santos Highway, following signs to Santa Cruz. The turnoff to "Pedra" is clearly marked and about 45km from Rio.

Tropical Islands

One of the most popular day trips from Rio is a boat ride around the tropical islands of Sepetiba Bay, known in the organized sightseeing world as the "Paradise Island Tour"

Leaving from the fishing village of Itacuruçá, *saveiros*, a traditional type of Brazilian schooner, take you on an unforgetable voyage around unspoilt tropical islands. Forget Disney folks, this is the real thing!

The organized trips include a lunch stop at one of the islands and other tourist activities, but it is also possible to hire the schooners, with crew, for your own trip. This can be done by either contacting the tour companies direct or asking somebody who speaks Portuguese to call Mauro Dantas (325-7172 or 259-2599) or Sepetiba Turismo (237-5119) who have a number of schooners for rent in the area for day trips and longer.

Itacuruçá can be reached by car following the Rio-Santos Highway (BR 101) through Santa Cruz and then following signs to Angra. The turning to Itacuruçá, 88km from Rio, is clearly marked and driving time from Rio is about one-and-a-half hours.

If you have the urge to stay on one of the islands I would suggest the Hotel Ilha de Jaguanum, on the island of Jaguanum, or the Hotel Pierre on the island of Itacuruçá.

The Hotel Ilha de Jaguanum's own boat transports guests from the Yacht Club in Itacuruçá to the hotel, a 40 minute ride away. The hotel, set on its own private beach, consists of 12 apartments and seven bungalows which can be reserved in advance at Sepetiba

Turismo, Av. N.S. de Copacabana, 605/202 in Rio de Janeiro, Tel. 237-5119. Rates from $60 per double, full board.

In November 1986 the Hotel Pierre re-opened after being totally refurbished. The Pierre offers 51 apartments and three suites, restaurant, games room, swimming pool sauna, boat hire, and conference facilities. Reservations in Rio on 242-7545 or at the hotel on 788-1560. Rates from $90 per double, half board.

In October 1987, the area will be transformed by the opening of the 325 room, Mediterranée Vila das Pedras, the latest addition to the world of Club Mediterranée. The whole project is budgeted at more than $17-million.

A Weekend Away

The dramatic coastal scenery mentioned earlier only starts to come into its own past the turn off to Itacuruçá as you move into the heart of the *Costa Verde* and the Angra dos Reis (King's Cove) region. You should now be starting to think of the benefits of an overnight stop or weekend away.

The main group of hotels in the Angra region is run by the *Hotels do Frade* (Friar's Hotels) who offer the Hotel Frade Portogalo, 134km from Rio, and the Hotel Frade leisure complex, 62km before the historic town of Parati.

Between Portogalo and Frade you will find other options including in Angra dos Reis the Angra Inn and 164km from Rio the Hotel Porto Aquarius.

Portagalo
Km 71 Rio-Santos

Overlooking the bay of Ilha Grande, this comfortable resort hotel offers 80 rooms and 20 suites all with TV, mini-bar, air-conditioning and private bathroom.

The hotel's modern chair lift carries guests from the hotel's sun deck to the beach below where a nautical center offers fishing, diving, boat rental and schooner tours. The lower area also houses *Chez Todoroki*, an excellent French restaurant in the capable hands of Todoroki, the chef responsible for launching *Equinox* as one of Rio's outstanding restaurants.

* 80 rooms.
* 20 suites.
* TV and mini-bar in every room.
* 24-hour room service.
* Fully air-conditioned.
* Safe-deposit box.
* Three restaurants.
* Snack Bar.
* Bar.
* Chair lift to beach.
* Swimming pool.
* Tennis court.
* Games room.
* Sauna.
* Boat hire.
* Conference facilities.

Rates: From $60 per double.
Credit: Most major cards.

Telephone: (0243) 65-1022.
Reservations: Rua Joaquim Nabuco, 161 in Copacabana. Tel. 267-7375. Telex. 021-31034.
Distance from Rio by road: 134 km.

Angra Inn
Estrada do Contorno, 2629

Located 9km through the town of Angra dos Reis this purpose built apart-hotel has operated as a hotel since December 1985 aiming to cater for the less sophisticated traveller or the traveller with children.

Set on a quiet beach, the 100 room Angra Inn offers a swimming-pool, water sports, tennis courts and playground.

* 100 rooms.
* 5 suites.
* TV and mini-bar in every room.
* Room service.
* Fully air-conditioned.
* Restaurant.
* Snack Bar.
* Bar.
* Swimming pool.
* Tennis courts.
* Games room.
* Sauna.
* Playground.
* Boat hire.
* Conference facilities.

Rates: From $60 per double
Credit: Most major cards,
Telephone: (0243) 65 1299.
Reservations: Rua General Urquiza,

132 in Leblon. Tel. 294-4045. Telex. 011-30751.
Distance from Rio by road: 163km.

Porto Aquarius
Km102 Rio-Santos

Built in 1980 as a time sharing project, Porto Aquarius has transformed itself in recent years in to a chic leisure complex with the emphasis on water sports.

Located 10km on from Angra dos Reis — the turn off from the main highway is clearly posted — Porto Aquarius sits on the shores of one of the region's prettiest bays.

The hotel added 48 new rooms at the end of 1986 as well as a second pool and larger convention facilities.

Porto Aquarius' attractive waterfront restaurant has a distinctive Italian flavor while simple tastes are catered for by the snack bar and bar.

The location of the hotel is a yachtsman's paradise with its own pontoons, safe ancorage and boats for hire including saveiros.

* 96 rooms.
* TV and mini-bar in every room.
* Room service.
* Fully air-conditioned.
* Restaurant.
* Snack Bar.
* Bar.
* 2 swimming pools.
* Games room.
* Sauna.
* Boat hire.
* Conference facilities.

Rates: From $70 per double.
Credit: Most major cards.
Telephone: (0243) 65 1642.
Reservations: In Rio at Visconde de Pirajá, 650/213. Tel.: 294-8099. Telex. 021-21270.
Distance from Rio by road: 164km.

Frade
Km 123 Rio-Santos

Simplicity and comfort are the key to this ever growing resort complex located on its own private beach overlooking a bay that boasts more than 300 tropical islands.

Frade offers everything for an energetic weekend away including tennis courts, horse riding, volleyball, fishing, boat hire, diving and a 6500 yard nine hole golf course designed by Peter Allis and David Thomas.

For sustenance the complex offers three restaurants, including the well regarded *Chez Dominique*, as well as several snack bars and bars.

The hotel must, however, be careful not to expand too quickly as parts of the complex were looking decidedly shabby during most of 1986 while the staff seem to have forgotten that they are there to serve the customers and not the other way around.

I expect, and hope, that Frade will do better in 1987 if not they will find it impossible to compete with the new Club Mediterranée.

* 101 rooms.
* 17 suites.
* 16 houses.
* TV and mini-bar in every room.
* 24-hour room service.
* Fully air-conditioned.
* Safe-deposit box.
* Three restaurants.
* Snack Bar.
* Bar.
* Nine hole golf course.
* Two swimming pools.
* Volleyball and soccer.
* Horse riding.
* Tennis courts.
* Games room.
* Sauna.
* Boat hire.

Rates: From $60 per double.
Credit: Most major cards.
Telephone: (0243) 65 1212.
Reservations: Rua Joaquim Nabuco, 161 in Copacabana. Tel. 267-7375, Telex. 021-31034.
Distance from Rio by road: 186km.

PARATI

250 km, and over three hours drive from Rio, on the Rio-Santos Highway you come across the Costa Verde's main attraction, the historical town of Parati.

Inhabited since 1650, and officially recognized as a town ten years later, the town of Parati has changed little since its heyday as a major staging post for Brazilian gold passing from Minas Gerais to Portugal in the 18th century. With the construction of the inland Rio-São Paulo road in the 19th century Parati lost its strategical importance and was virtually ignored over the next hundred years until it was rediscovered as an authentic colonial town that had remained untouched right into the 20th century.

Today Parati is a National Monument preserved for all time, considered by UNESCO to be one of the most important examples of colonial architecture surviving anywhere in the world.

Parati is so genuine that it is difficult to believe it is not one large Hollywood film set, instead it is the genuine Parati that has played host to countless films, most notably the production of the Brazilian classic *Gabriela*.

Parati can be visited in a day, if you leave Rio early, but if you have time I suggest you spend the night in one of the town's many *pousadas* (inns) which are always ready to greet guests. Parati also has a large number of charming restaurants offering traditional and international cuisine.

Some of the top *pousadas*, which can be reserved in advance from Rio, are the Mercado de Pouso (267-7794) and the Frade Pousada Parati (267-7375), which is part of the *Hotéis do Frade* group, while in Parati you can call the Pardieiro (0243-71-1538) or Aconcheg (0243-71-1598).

Further information about Parati can be obtained from the tourist information center at the entrance to the old town (0243-71-1186) or the Flumitur (State of Rio de Janeiro Tourism Authority) desk in the old prison, Rua Santa Rita (0243-71-1256). Here you can pick up information about the town including a layout of the streets which it is interesting to note are paved with irregular stones forming a canal that drains off storm water and allows the sea to enter and wash the streets at full moon and high tides.

Direct bus services from Rio to Parati are run by the Eval bus company from the Novo Rio bus station in Rio. Buses depart every three hours.

PETRÓPOLIS

The most traditional of all the day trips from Rio is the one that takes you 66 kilometers into the mountains to the Imperial city of Petrópolis.

As a city itself Petrópolis is not that spectacular, but the one hour drive and the surrounding country side certainly are.

To get to Petrópolis drive out of Rio on the Avenida Brasil, past the airport turn off before taking the Rodovia Washington Luiz which is clearly marked to Petrópolis.

The roads to Petrópolis are excellent and most of the section that winds up the mountains is one-way, a second road having been built to bring you back down.

The scenery along the way is nothing short of magnificent at times so try to go when the cloud cover is not too low.

Just before Petrópolis itself you come around a bend to be confronted by the imposing sight of Quitandinha.

Once one of the world's "Grand Hotels" Quitandinha in all its splendour is only a parody of what it once was. Although today a rather down market sport and country club it is still worth stopping to have a look around. If ever a building has held its atmosphere it is Quitandinha. The building almost cries out for the better times when it hosted Kings and Queens and famous Hollywood movie stars.

The ruin of Quitandinha came about as a direct consequence of the decree in 1946 which outlawed gambling in Brazil. If gambling ever comes back though, I am certain so will the glorious days of this once noble hotel.

The center of Petrópolis is only a short drive from Quitandinha, you will enter the city on Rua Washington Luiz which along with Rua João Pessoa and Rua do Imperador has most of the city's better restaurants, although none of them can be considered gourmet class.

The main attraction in Petrópolis is the Summer Palace of Dom Pedro II which today houses the Imperial Museum.

The first Imperial visitor to Petrópolis was Dom Pedro I who visited the area in 1829 and was much taken by the natural beauty and its agreeable climate. In 1983 he bought a farm.

With the abdication of Dom Pedro I and his return to Portugal the farm and its land became the property of his son, Dom Pedro II.

The importance of Petrópolis became greater with the opening of a new road from Rio to Minas Gerais which passed close to the town. Shortly afterward Dom Pedro II passed a decree to initiate an agricultural colony in the town and on his farm was built the Summer Palace. The year was 1845.

With the deteriorating sanitary conditions in Rio and the outbreak of yellow fever in 1849 Dom Pedro II spent more and more time in his palace in Petrópolis which led to the top echelon of Carioca society following their Emperor's example, and this included most of the foreign diplomatic corps of the time.

The Imperial Museum is open to the public from Tuesday through Sunday from noon to 5:30 p.m. and amongst its many treasures are the crown of Dom Pedro, chiselled from gold and containing more than 600 diamonds and pearls: and the telephone presented to Dom Pedro II by Alexander Graham Bell.

Other sites worth visiting in Petropolis are the Cathedral, where the tombs of the Emperors and their wives can be seen; Santos Dumont's house (Rua do Encanto, 124); and the Crystal Palace (Rua Alfred Pacha).

If you are interested in plants and flowers you should take time to visit the nurseries of Floralia on Estrada do Alcobaca (open daily from 9 a.m. to 5 p.m.) and Binot at Rua Fernandes Vieira, 390 (open Monday through Saturday from 8 a.m. to 11 a.m. and 1 p.m. to 3.30 p.m.), which are both located close to Petropolis.

Another attraction of Petrópolis is its knitwear industry which is displayed at its best in Rua Teresa.

TERESÓPOLIS

If you are considering staying the night in the area, perhaps to explore the National Park of Serra dos Orgãos, then you should move on to Teresópolis which is located 54 kilometers from Petrópolis or 95 kilometers from Rio by the direct route.

Teresópolis has several acceptable hotels for the foreign visitor, including close by, at Km 22 of the road linking Teresópolis to Friburgo, the five star Rosa dos Ventos.

Closer to town is the Alpina, located in front of the tricky nine hole Teresópolis Gold Club, a club which is open to non-members.

Alpina ****
Rua Cândido Portinari, 837
Teresópolis — 742-5252

Rosa dos Ventos *****
Estrada Teresópolis-Friburgo, Km 22
Teresópolis — 742-8833

São Moritz ****
Estrada Teresópolis-Friburgo, Km 36
Teresópolis — 742-4360

All the hotels have a full bar and restaurant service plus swimming pool and sauna.

SHOOTING THE RAPIDS

A new and exciting day trip was added to the tourist calendar in 1984, one which should appeal to the adventurous resident and tourist alike.

Your trip takes you one-and-a-half hours past Petrópolis to the Paraibuna River near Levy Gasparian in the Três Rios region. Here you embark on large inflatable boats to ride the river 17 km downstream to Santa Fé.

The ride, which lasts a little over four-and-a-half hours, takes you over 23 falls that vary in height from 3ft to 15ft, as you are swept along past the rich vegetation typical of the area.

The cost of the tour, including transfers from your hotel, breakfast and lunch, costs $50. For more details call Gray Line in Rio on 274-7146, 294-1444, or 294-1196. At present the tour runs on Saturdays and Wednesdays.

Air Pass

If you are considering travelling on to explore the rest of Brazil, you should purchase a Brazilian Air Pass from your travel agent before arriving in Brazil. The air pass can only be sold outside Brazil and to non-residents.

The Brazilian Air Pass comes in two forms, and can be purchased for the flights of Transbrasil, Varig-Cruzeiro, and Vasp, each pass only being valid for the flights of the issuing carrier.

The most complete air pass sells for $330 and allows 21 days of unlimited travel within Brazil, although the same route cannot be flown twice in the same direction. The cheaper pass costs $250 and is valid for 14 days allowing visits and stopover at four cites in addition to your point of entry, which is likely to be Rio de Janeiro. Both passes start from the day of your first internal flight and the routing can be reserved in advance before you arrive in Brazil or at the time in Brazil.

Considering the size of Brazil, and the cost of internal flights, the air pass offers excellent value. It is also worth noting that if an air pass is unused it can be cashed in for a full refund, and so is a worthwhile investment even if you are not sure that you will want to travel.

On From Rio to the Rest of Brazil

Rio de Janeiro is just the opening chapter to the Brazilian story, a story that unfolds across 3.3-million square miles; a coast line of

4,500 miles of warm, white beaches; and a population of 140-million. Brazil is the story of the world's fifth largest nation in terms of area — surpassed only by the Soviet Union, U.S.A., Canada and China — and the sixth largest in terms of population. A nation that is destined to become in its entirety "the" tourist destination of the 1990s.

Our story began in Rio de Janeiro, South America's most important tourist destination, the gateway to Brazil through its modern international airport which connects visitors with flights to the furthest points of Brazil, on to the hidden treasures of a great nation: to the North and the natural wonders of the Amazon and its capital, the man made oasis of Manaus; to the Northeast and the beaches and history of Salvador, Recife, João Pessoa, Fortaleza, and São Luiz; to the Central-West and the contrast between the nation's futuristic capital, Brasilia, and the Mato Grosso savannah; and Southward to São Paulo, Porto Alegre, and one of the natural wonders of our planet, the falls at Foz do Iguaçu.

All of Brazil can be reached from Rio, and reached cheaply if you are smart enough to purchase a Brazilian Air Pass before you arrive in the country.

NORTHERN BRAZIL

The Amazon, a name that stirs the emotions of man. A natural wonder that supplies over half the planet's oxygen and pours enough water into the Atlantic each day to supply a city of 10-million inhabitants for a period of nine years. 4,200 miles of river that supports 1,500 types of fish, is overflown by 1,800 species of bird, and shadowed from its banks by 250 different mammals and many thousands of animals.

Even today the Amazon retains its mystery, a mystery which is greater to man than even the moon.

One mystery the Amazon holds which is no longer true, is its inaccessibility and un-hospitality to man.

Manaus can be reached daily from Rio on one of the many daily flights that connect the two cities, or at a more relaxed and leisurely pace by flying to Belém, at the mouth of the Amazon, and taking a luxury five day cruise up to Manaus passing through the very heart of the Amazon. It has also become popular in recent years for the large liners to call in on Manaus and treat their passangers to the wonderous sites of the Amazon. Your local travel agent should be able to tell you which ships will be calling this year.

For accommodation Manaus can boast the five-star, 358-room, Hotel Tropical, South America's largest resort hotel.

Manaus stands today proof positive that man could tame the "green Hell". The rubber barons have moved on, but its position as a "Free Port" has guaranteed Manaus its future. (See Manaus).

Manaus' Top Hotels

Hotel Tropical •••••
Estrada Ponta Negra
Manaus — Amazonas
Tel: (092) 238-5757
Telex: 092-2173

Novotel ••••
Av. Mandii, 4
Tel: (092) 237-1211
Telex: 092-2429

Hotel Amazonas ••••
Praça Adalberto Vale

Manaus — Amazonas
Tel: (092) 234-7679
Telex: 092-2277

Imperial••••
Av. Getulio Vargas, 227
Manaus — Amazonas
Tel: (092) 233-8711
Telex: 092-2231

Manaus' Top Amazon Lodges

Amazon Lodge and Village
P.O. Box 514
Manaus — Amazonas

Tel: (092) 232-1454
Telex: 092-2641

Pousada dos Guanavenas
Rua Ferreira Pena, 755
Manaus — Amazonas
Tel: (092) 233-5558
Telex: 092-1101

Amazon Cruises

ENASA
Rua Uruguaiana, 39
Rio de Janeiro
Tel: (021) 222-9149
Telex: 021-30217

Ecological Safari
Rua 10 de Julho, 695
Manaus — Amazonas
Tel: (092) 234-5014
Telex: 092-2225

Santarém's Top Hotel

Tropical ****
Av. Mendonça Furtado, 4120
Santarém – Pará

Tel: (091) 522-1533
Telex: 091-1647

Belém's Top Hotels

Hilton International *****
Av. Presidente Vargas, 882
Belém - Pará
Tel: (091) 222-5611
Telex: 091-2024

Equatorial Palace****
Av. Braz de Aguiar, 612
Belém — Pará
Tel: (091) 223-6500
Telex: 091-1605

Novotel Belém****
Av. Bernardo Sayão, 4804
Belém — Pará
Tel: (091) 226-8011
Telex: 091-1241

Selton Belém****
Av. Julio César, 1777
Belém — Pará
Tel: (091) 231-6222
Telex: 091-1585

NORTHEASTERN BRAZIL

Brazil's Northeast has everything to make it one of the world's major vacation centers, especially for people who demand perfect weather and even more perfect beaches and that perhaps is why it is the number one holiday destination for Brazilians.

From São Luis in the North to the Bahia Basin in the South, the Northeast has over 2,000 miles of virtually uninterrupted soft white beaches, while for the historically minded there is Salvador, the ex-Capital of Brazil with its 154 churches, most of which are treasured architectural masterpieces.

The Northeast is Brazil's most folkloric region, folklore that is waiting to be discovered and part of that folklore is the Bahian cuisine with its spicy dishes which have elevated the cooking of Brazil alongside that of France and China.

São Luiz's Top Hotels

Quatro Rodas *****
Praia do Calhau
São Luiz — Maranhão
Tel: (098) 227-0244
Telex: 098-2123

Hotel Vila Rica *****
Av. D. Pedro II, 299
São Luiz — Maranhão
Tel: (098) 222-4455
Telex: 098-2169

Fortaleza's Top Hotels

Esplanada Praia *****
Av. Presidente Kennedy, 2000
Fortaleza – Ceará
Tel. (085) 224-8555
Telex: 085-1103

Imperial Othon *****
Av. Presidente Kennedy, 2500
Fortaleza – Ceará
Tel: (085) 224-7777
Telex: 085-1569

João Pessoa's Top Hotels

Tropical Hotel Tambaú•••••
Av. Almirante Tamandaré, 229
João Pessoa — Paraiba
Tel. (083) 226-3675
Telex: 083-2158

Recife's Top Hotels

Hotel Miramar•••••
Rua dos Navegantes, 363
Recife — Pernambuco
Tel. (081) 326-7755
Telex: 081-2139

Quatro Rodas •••••
Av. José Augusto Moreira, 2200
Olinda — Pernambuco
Tel: (081) 431-2955
Telex: 081-1324

Recife Palace Hotel •••••
Av. Boa Viagem, 4070
Recife — Pernambuco
Tel: (081) 325-4044
Telex: 081-4528

Boa Viagem ••••
Av. Boa Viagem, 5000
Recife — Pernambuco
Tel: (081) 341-4144
Telex: 081-2072

Grande Hotel ••••
Av. Martins de Barros, 593
Recife — Pernambuco
Tel: (081) 224-9366
Telex: 081-1454

Jangadeiro ••••
Av. Boa Viagem, 3114
Recife — Pernambuco
Tel: (081) 326-6777
Telex: 081-1502

Mar ••••
Rua Barão de Souza Leão, 451
Recife — Pernambuco
Tel: (081) 341-5433
Telex: 081-1073

Recife Othon ••••
Av. Boa Viagem, 3722
Recife — Pernambuco
Tel: (081) 326-7225
Telex: 081-2141

Hotel Savaron ••••
Av. Boa Viagem, 3772
Recife — Pernambuco
Tel: (081) 325-5077
Telex: 081-1428

Hotel Vila Rica ••••
Av. Boa Viagem, 4308
Recife — Pernambuco
Tel: (081) 326-5111
Telex: 081-1903

Maceió's Top Hotels

Altesa Hotel Jatiuca••••
Praia da Lagoa de Anta, 220
Maceió — Alagoas
Tel: (082) 231-2555
Telex: 082-2302

Beira Mar ••••
Av. Duque de Caxias, 1994
Maceió — Alagoas
Tel: (082) 223-8022
Telex: 082-2202

Luxor de Alagoas••••
Av. Duque de Caxias, 2076
Maceió — Alagoas
Tel: (082) 223-7121
Telex: 082-2179

Salvador's Top Hotels

Bahia Othon Palace •••••
Av. Presidente Vargas, 2456
Salvador — Bahia
Tel: (071) 247-1044
Telex: 071-1217

Hotel da Bahia •••••
Praca 2 de Julho, 2
Salvador — Bahia
Tel: (071) 237-3699
Telex: 071-1136

Meridien Bahia •••••
Rua Fonte do Boi, 216
Salvador — Bahia
Tel: (071) 248-8011
Telex: 071-1029

Pousada do Carmo •••••
Lago do Carmo, 1
Salvador — Bahia
Tel: (071) 242-3111
Telex: 071-1513

Quatro Rodas •••••
Rua do Farol de Itapuã
Salvador — Bahia

Tel: (071) 249-9611
Telex: 071-2449

Salvador Praia •••••
Av. Presidente Vargas, 2338
Salvador — Bahia
Tel: (071) 245-5033
Telex: 071-1430

Itaparica Island's Top Hotels

Club Mediterranée ••••
Estrada Nazaré do Bom Despacho
Ilha Itaparica — Bahia
Tel: (071) 241-0033
Telex: 071-2143

SOUTHEASTERN BRAZIL

The Southeast is home to nearly half the Brazilian population and the cities of São Paulo, Belo Horizonte and of course Rio de Janeiro.

São Paulo, the business capital of Brazil, Latin America's largest industrial and commercial center, a city which covers an area five times larger than Paris, a city which offers international cuisine and nightlife of a variety and quality of New York and Paris, but at half the price. São Paulo, the counterbalance to the frivolity of Rio de Janeiro, a city that is covered in full in *The Insider's Guide to São Paulo for the Business Executive.* (Available March 1987).

Belo Horizonte, gateway to the historical state of Minas Gerais where you find the town of Ouro Preto, a historical monument that is protected and recognized by the United Nations. (See Minas Gerais).

São Paulo's Top Hotels

Brasilton •••••
Rua Martins Fontes, 330
Centro — São Paulo
Tel. (011) 258-5811
Telex: 011 25558

Caesar Park •••••
Rua Augusta, 1508
Cerqueira César — São Paulo
Tel. (011) 285-6622
Telex: 011 22539

Eldorado•••••
Av. São Luiz, 234
Centro — São Paulo
Tel. (011) 256-8833
Telex: 011 22490

Grand Hotel Ca'd'Oro •••••
Rua Augusta, 129
Centro — São Paulo
Tel. (011) 256-8011
Telex: 011 21765

Hilton •••••
Av. Ipiranga, 165
Centro — São Paulo
Tel. (011) 256-0033
Telex: 011 21981

Holiday Inn Crowne Plaza •••••
Rua Frei Caneca, 1360
Cerqueira César — São Paulo
Tel. (011) 284-1144
Telex: 011 33096

Maksoud Plaza•••••
Alameda Campinas, 150
Bela Vista — São Paulo
Tel: (011) 251-2233
Telex: 011 30026

Moffarej Sheraton Palace•••••
Al. Santos, 1437
Cerqueira César — São Paulo
Tel: (011) 284-5544
Telex: 011-34170

Transamerica •••••
Av. Nações Unidas, 18591
Santo Amaro — São Paulo
Tel. (011) 523-4511
Telex: 011 31761

Santos and Guarujá Top Hotels

Casa Grande•••••
Av. Miguel Stefano, 999
Guarujá — São Paulo
Tel: (013) 91900
Telex: 013 1746

Park Balneário Hotel •••••
Av. Ana Costa, 555
Santos — São Paulo
Tel. (0132) 34-7211
Telex: 013 1241

Campinas' Top Hotel

Royal Palm Plaza •••••

Praça Rotatoria, 88
Campinas — São Paulo
Tel. (0192) 2-9085
Telex: 0192-1028

Campos do Jordão's Top Hotels

Orotour Garden•••••
Vila Natal
Campos do Jordão — São Paulo
Tel: (0122) 62-1078
Telex: 0122-329

Vila Inglesa •••••
Estrada do Salto, 3500
Campos do Jordão — São Paulo
Tel. (0122) 63-1955
Telex: 0122-399

Belo Horizonte's Top Hotels

Othon Palace Hotel•••••
Av. Afonso Pena, 1050
Belo Horizonte — Minas Gerais
Tel. (031) 226-7844
Telex: 031 2052

Brasilton Contagem (Hilton)••••
Rod. Fernão Dias, Km 365
Contagem — Minas Gerais
Tel. (031) 351-0900
Telex: 031 1860

Del Rey ••••
Praça Afonso Arinos
Belo Horizonte — Minas Gerais
Tel. (031) 222-2211
Telex: 031 1033

International Plaza Palace ••••
Rua Rio de Janeiro, 109
Belo Horizonte — Minas Gerais
Tel. (031) 201-2300
Telex: 031-3048.

Real Palace••••
Rua Espirito Santo, 901
Belo Horizonte — Minas Gerais
Tel: (031) 224-2111
Telex: 031-2608

Ouro Preto's Top Hotels

Hotel da Estrada Real ••••
Rodovia dos Inconfidentes. Km 87
Ouro Preto - Minas Gerais
Tel. (031) 551-2122
Telex: 031 6133

Luxor Pousada ••••
Praça Antonio Dias, 10
Ouro Preto - Minas Gerais
Tel. (031) 551-2244
Telex: 031 2948

Quinta dos Barões ••••
Rua Pandiá Calógeras, 474
Ouro Preto Minas Gerais
Tel. (031) 551-1056

Chico Rey ••••
Rua Brigadeiro Mesquita, 90
Ouro Preto — Minas Gerais.
Tel.: (031) 551-1223.

São João Del Rey's Top Hotel

Porto Real •••
Av. Eduardo Magalhães, 254
São João Del Rey — Minas Gerais
Tel.: (032) 371-1132.

Tiradentes' Top Hotels

Solar da Ponte ••••
Praça das Meireces
Tiradentes — Minas Gerais.
Tel.: (032) 355-1255.

CENTRAL BRAZIL

Brazil's Central-West is an area of striking contrasts, that vary from the futuristic designs of the nation's capital Brasilia to the untouched backwaters of the Pantanal Matogrossense, the savannah of Mato Grosso.

Brasília, the dream city of the future, a city born to a nation's capital, a city to open up the untouched interior of Brazil.

The Pantanal Matogrossense, an area only recently discovered and explored by man. Once a vast inland ocean, it is today one of the largest and richest reserves of wildlife known to man, complimented by the Araguaia River, considered to be the world's most abundant source of fish, a river which contains the Island of Bananal, the largest river-island in the world. (See Brasilia).

Brasilia's Top Hotel's

Carlton •••••
Setor Hoteleiro Sul
Brasilia — D.F.
Tel. (061) 226-7320

Telex: 061-1981

Hotel Nacional •••••
Setor Hoteleiro Sul
Brasilia - D.F.
Tel. (061) 226-8180
Telex: 061 1062

San Marco *****
Setor Hoteleiro Sul
Brasília – D.F.
Tel. (061) 226-2211
Telex: 061 3744

Aracoara ****
Setor Hoteleiro Norte
Brasília – D.F.
Tel: (061) 225-1650
Telex: 061 1589

Eron Brasilia Hotel *****
Setor Hoteleiro Norte
Brasília – D.F.
Tel. (061) 226-2125
Telex: 061 1422

Garvey Park ****
Setor Hoteleiro Norte
Brasília – D.F.

Tel. (061) 223-9800
Telex: 061 2199

Phenecia ****
Setor Hoteleiro Sul
Brasília – D.F.
Tel. (061) 224-3125
Telex: 061 2254

Saint Paul ****
Setor Hoteleiro Sul
Brasília – D.F.
Tel: (061) 223-9420
Telex: 061 3721

Torre Palace ****
Setor Hoteleiro Norte
Brasília – D.F.
Tel. (061) 225-3360
Telex: 061 1905

SOUTHERN BRAZIL

Our Brazilian story comes to a close in the South, an area that is home to countless European immigrants who have flourished in their small communities that copy life as their forefathers knew back home in Europe. Germans, Italians, Swiss and Poles have all made their mark on the South, a region that is responsible for Brazil's fine wines.

The South is also home to the Brazilian cowboy, the "gaúcho", the man responsible for the country's superb meats.

The South's main attraction though is physical and can be found at a point close to where the borders of Brazil, Argentina and Paraguay meet, a place called Foz do Iguaçu. At Foz you will be treated to a spectacle of over 275 waterfalls, some more than 300 feet high, a natural formation five time larger than its more famous American cousin Niagara.

And as if to prove that man can take on the challenge set by nature, you can also visit close by the site of the Itaipu Dam, the largest hydroelectric plant in the world. (See Foz do Iguaçu).

Foz do Iguaçu's Top Hotel's

Hotel Bourbon *****
Estrada das Cataratas
Foz do Iguaçu – Paraná
Tel. (0455) 74-1313
Telex: 045 2247

International Foz *****
Rua Alm. Barroso, 345
Foz do Iguaçu – Paraná
Tel. (0455) 73-4240
Telex: 045 2574

Hotel das Cataratas ****
Rodovia das Cataratas, Km. 28
Foz do Iguaçu – Paraná
Tel. (0455) 74-2666
Telex: 045 2113

Mirante Hotel ****
Av. Rep. Argentina

Foz do Iguaçu – Paraná
Tel. (0455) 73-1133
Telex: 045 2296

Panorama ****
Rod das Cataratas, Km. 12
Foz do Iguaçu – Paraná
Tel. (0455) 74-1200
Telex: 045 2257

Rafhain Palace Hotel ****
Rod. BR-277, Km. 727
Foz do Iguaçu – Paraná
Tel. (0455) 73-3434
Telex: 045 2453

Salvatti ****
Rua Rio Branco, 577
Foz do Iguaçu – Paraná
Tel. (0455) 74-2727
Telex: 045 2237

San Martin ••••
Rod. das Cataratas, Km 27
Foz do Iguaçu – Paraná
Tel. (0455) 74-2577
Telex: 045 2248

Curitiba's Top Hotels

Hotel Iguaçu Campestre •••••
BR-116 – Km. 396
Atuba   Paraná
Tel. (041) 262-5313
Telex: 041 5943

Araucaria •••••
Rua Dr. Faivre, 846
Curitiba – Paraná
Tel. (041) 262-3030
Telex: 041 5548

Florianópolis Top Hotel

Florianópolis Palace Hotel •••••
Rua Artista Bittencourt, 26
Florianópolis – Santa Catarina
Tel. (0482) 22-9633
Telex: 0482-191

Laguna's Top Hotel

Itapiruba Tourist•••••
Praia Itapiruba
Laguna   Santa Catarina
Tel. (0486) 55 0022

Águas Mornas' Top Hotel

Águas Mornas Palace Hotel
Rua Cel. Antonio Lekmkuhl, 2487
Águas Mornas – Santa Catarina
Tel. (0482) 45-1312
Telex: 0482 427

Porto Alegre Top Hotel's

Plaza São Rafael •••••
Rua Alberto Bins, 514
Porto Alegre – Rio Grande do Sul
Tel. (0512) 21-6100
Telex: 051 1339

Center Park Hotel ••••
Rua Cel. Frederico Linck, 25

Porto Alegre – Rio Grande do Sul
Tel. (0512) 25-5388
Telex: 051 2737

City ••••
Rua José Montaury, 20
Porto Alegre – Rio Grande do Sul
Tel. (0512) 24 2858
Telex: 051 1609

Continental
Lago Vespasiano Julio Veppo, 77
Porto Alegre – Rio Grande do Sul
Tel. (0512) 25-3233
Telex: 051 2038

Everest Palace ••••
Rua Duque de Caxias, 1357
Porto Alegre – Rio Grande do Sul
Tel. (0512) 24-7355
Telex: 051 1650

Embaixador ••••
Rua Jeronimo Coelho, 354
Porto Alegre – Rio Grande do Sul
Tel. (0512) 21-5622
Telex: 051 1527

Plaza ••••
Rua Senhor dos Passos, 154
Porto Alegre – Rio Grande do Sul
Tel. (0512) 26-1700
Telex: 051 1339

Gramado and Canela's Top Hotels

Hotel Laje de Pedra •••••
Parque Laje de Pedra, Km. 3
Canela – Rio Grande do Sul
Tel. (054) 282-1530
Telex: 054 1844

Serra Azul ••••
Rua Garibaldi, 152
Gramado – Rio Grande do Sul
Tel. (054) 286-1082

Serrano ••••
Rua Costa e Silva, 1112
Gramado   Rio Grande do Sul
Tel. (054) 286 1329

Brasília

    I cannot lie. I am not impressed with Brasilia and if it really is an architects view of the future then God help us all.

    Brasilia is the reverse of the old cliché in that it is a nice place to live (or so I am told) but you would not want to visit it. Unless, that is, you can see it all in a day.

If you are on an air-pass and have a spare day Brasilia is best visited en route to Manaus, most of the flights from Rio to Manaus passing through Brasilia. And I can promise you, you won't need more than 24-hours to explore the Brazilian capital from top to bottom.

The headquarters of the Brazilian Government is about architecture and design, both of which have dated badly since the city's inauguration by the then President of Brazil, Juscelino Kubitschek, on April 21, 1960.

During your visit you will have the chance of viewing the Brazilian Congress and Senate, the Presidential Palace, Supreme Court, Foreign Office, ministries, etc., etc.

There is a City Museum, but it consists entirely of a few pertinent Portuguese sentences etched into marble and nothing else. For a fee they will even sell you an English, Spanish or Japanese translation! You can also visit the Cathedral whose interior at present is ruined by a monstrosity of a souvenir shop which the architect Oscar Niemeyer is trying to have removed, and the monument to President Kubitschek which is interesting if you are Brazilian or speak Portuguese but not if you aren't or don't.

The city is well mapped and due to its size you can cover most of the main sights on foot or by short taxi rides.

The hotels are reasonable and functional, aimed not at the tourist but the visiting businessman and woman, who dare I say it, can't get all their business done in one day.

All the most up-to-date information about Brasilia — times of opening etc. — and a good selection of maps can be found in the Brasilia telephone directory under "Achei!", or in the city's guide book. "Guia Oficial de Brasilia" which is on sale at the bookstore of Brasilia's modern airport.

If you want to avoid staying the night in Brasilia you will find a number of tours which operate from the airport itself. You can either go with a group or individually in a car. All the main tour operators have desks in the arrivals hall of the airport.

Note: For a full list of Brasilia's best hotels see "On From Rio — Central Brazil".

Foz do Iguaçu

Every country likes to claim that it has one of the wonders of the world, but in Brazil's case it is not an idle boast for at Foz do Iguaçu Brazil has one of the natural wonders of the world, the Iguaçu falls, and close by, one of the planet's man made wonders, the Itaipu Dam, the world's most powerful hydroelectric plant.

Even before the era of the air-pass or the Itaipu Dam, a visit to Foz do Iguaçu was a must to see the water falls, a formation five times larger than its more famous North American cousin, Niagara. Today with the air-pass and dam Foz should feature on every travellers routing around Brazil and South America.

Getting to Foz do Iguaçu is not a problem. All three of the major Brazilian internal carriers — Varig, Vasp and Transbrasil — have daily flights from Rio to Foz, normally via São Paulo, with a flight time of a little over one hour and 45 minutes. The cost of the return flight between Rio and Foz is about $130 if you don't have an air-pass.

While it is possible to do the falls in a day, I personally recommend that you plan to stay three days, two nights, in the area.

Your arrival in Foz, if you have not driven the 560 km from Rio, will be at the International Airport — Brazil's seventh busiest — located 15 km from the town of Foz and 10 km from the falls.

The airport is small but well organized and in the arrivals hall you will find the counter of the state tourist board, Paranatour, who can solve any last minute problems, including accommodation.

One of the myths which hangs over Foz is that there is only one hotel of merit, the Hotel das Cataratas, while in fact Foz has the fourth largest number of hotel beds in the country, offering something for every taste and budget.

Certainly the Hotel das Cataratas is a lovely hotel and the only one situated at the falls, but the new five star Internacional in the town of Foz should not be forgotten nor the four star Salvatti and Mirante. Other good hotels between Foz and the falls are the Bourbon, D. Pedro I Palace, Rafhain Palace, and San Martin. Paranatur or your travel agent will be able to advise on the best two and three star hotels.

At the airport there is a plentiful supply of taxis and buses all of which are paid for in advance at the airport. The executive bus, for example, from the airport to Foz costs around $1 and drops you close to most of the main hotels, if not at the door. Strangely, there is no bus between the airport and the falls, although the Hotel das Cataratas has its own bus for guests.

If you are not staying out at the Hotel das Cataratas you will find that most of the other hotels offer tours to the falls, Itaipu Dam, etc., although it can be just as easy, and cheap, to bargain with a taxi driver to take you around the sights.

Normal buses from the town of Foz to the falls run on the even hours and return on the odd hours costing about 50 cents, plus another 50 cents to enter the National Park. Make sure though that you get the bus going all the way to the falls (*Cataratas*) and not just to the gates of the National Park, which run every half hour, because they leave you with a little 7 km walk from the gate to the falls.

THE FALLS

It was Eleanor Roosevelt who proclaimed on seeing the falls at Foz do Iguaçu: "Oh, poor Niagara!", and even that was something of an understatement.

From the Brazilian side of the Iguaçu River (the opposite bank is Argentina) you view all 275 individual falls from right to left spreading over an arch of 2.7 km.

To view the falls there is a paved pathway starting from in front of the Hotel das Cataratas which cuts along the Brazilian bank for just over 1 km. For the walk wear flat shoes which grip. The spray from the falls and the generally damp atmosphere can make the route slippery underfoot in places.

There is no charge for viewing the falls except the 50 cents to enter the National Park.

Take as long as you want on the walk and make full use of the viewing platforms along the way. The most spectacular platform on the Brazilian side winds out over the Santa Maria Fall at the base of the Floriano and Deodoro Falls to give a straight view up the Iguaçu River to the most impressive fall, the Devil's Throat. The Argentine side has a viewing platform on the lip of this fall, which in terms of volume of water per second, is the largest such fall in the world.

Where the falls join the Brazilian bank, at the Floriano Fall, is an elevator to carry you from the base of the falls to the top. From the top of the elevator shaft's viewing platform there are memorable views of the falls from above.

You can now either walk back up the road to your left, back to the hotel, or by turning right walk along the river bank above the falls. It is from here that the buses wait for their return to the town.

If you are not immediately returning to the town you can return up the road to the hotel or take the elevator back down and retrace your steps along the river bank.

There is little else to say about the falls themselves because seeing them is everything. Photographs, however good, don't do the falls justice and words certainly cannot adequately describe their majestic power and beauty. The following notes may, however, help your enjoyment and understanding of the falls.

— The falls were discoverd in 1542 by the Spanish explorer Alvar Nunez Cabeza de Vaca during his voyage from the Southern Atlantic to Asunción in Paraguay.

— The name of Iguaçu comes from the Guarani indians who called the river and waterfalls "Great Water" (Igua, water; açu, great).

— The dry season, when the falls are at their least spectacular (10,000 cubic metres of water per second against 30,000 cubic metres per second in the rainy season) is April through July, which is also the winter months when Foz will be found to be considerably colder than Rio.

— In 1977 the falls dried up for the only time in their history while in 1983 a flood destroyed the walkways and viewing platforms on the Argentine side, now rebuilt, and stripped the falls of most of their vegetation which is only now growing back. Pictures of both the flood and drought can be seen in the Museum of the National Park to be found close to the entrance of the park. The park opens daily from 6 a.m. to 8 p.m. and the museum from 6 a.m. to 8 p.m. Guests of the Hotel das Cataratas can of course come and go as they please.

— The falls were used as the dramatic backdrop for Roland Joffe's *The Mission* which won the Golden Palm at the 1986 Cannes Film Festival.

— In front of the Hotel das Cataratas, to the right of the pathway, is the helicopter service which operates a six minute tour of the falls for $25. The helicopter service also offer a 50 minute tour for $100 covering the falls, the town of Foz do Iguaçu, the Itaipu Dam and lake, and a six minute tour, also costing $25, leaving from the international airport which covers just the Itaipu dam.

IGUAÇU NATIONAL PARK

The National Park which houses the waterfalls covers an area of more than 170,000 hectares (420,000 acres/656 square miles) between 25°05' S and 25°41' S and 53°40' W and 54°38' W.

The park's vegetation is predominantly sub-tropical and can be explored and appreciated on a number of set tours starting from the Hotel das Cataratas.

The two most popular tours take you to the Salto do Macuco, a small waterfall in the center of the forest close to the river bank, and Poço Preto, a 12 km drive through the forest in an open car to a tranquil spot on the Iguaçu River, up-stream of the falls.

More information about the tours is available from the hotel (Tel. 74-2666) while to learn about the park itself you should visit the park's museum.

THE ARGENTINE SIDE

At the end of 1985 a bridge opened between Brazil and Argentina which not only opened up an important new route between the two countries (RN-12 in Argentina and the BR-469 and BR-277 in Brazil) but also made the lives of tourists wishing to visit the Argentine side of the falls a lot easier.

Before deciding to visit the Argentine side of the falls it is best to check with your local Argentine Consulate to see if you are one of the nationals who require a visa to enter Argentina . In Foz do Iguaçu the Argentine Consulate is located at Travessa Vice-Consul Eduardo Ramon Bianchi, 26 and is open from 8:30 a.m. to 1 p.m.

The new bridge, named after the late Brazilian president Tancredo Neves, is located at km 09 of the Estrada das Caratas and cost $34-million to construct.

THE THREE FRONTIERS

The meeting of the frontiers of Brazil, Argentina and Paraguay is the non-event of visiting Foz de Iguaçu.

Unless you are the type of tourists who likes to visit a place just to say you've been there, there is little to recommend in going out of your way to view three obelisks sitting on the river banks of Argentina, Paraguay and Brazil where the Parana and Iguaçu rivers meet.

ITAIPU

By 1989 the eighteen turbines of the Itaipu Dam will be producing 12,600,000 kilowatts of energy, making it the largest and most powerful hydroelectric power plant in the world.

To even the simple layman the Itaipu Dam is an impressive piece of engineering and the statistics behind it could keep trivia freaks happy for years.

Between the start of construction in 1975 and the inauguration of the first two turbines on October 25, 1984, Itaipu became the largest construction site in the world with more than 40,000 workers involved directly in the project. To support these workers the population of the town of Foz do Iguaçu jumped overnight from 35,000 to 140,000.

To make room for the dam enough earth and rock was removed from the river to fill 25 silos the size of Maracanã stadium in Rio while the amount of concrete used in the dam itself is enough to pave a two lane highway between Lisbon and Moscow.

The total extension of the dam is 8 km, a dam which holds back a reservoir of 1,460 square kilometers containing 29 billion cubic meters of water, that is five times larger than Rio's Guanabara Bay.

At its completion the dam will have cost Brazil and Paraguay — it is a joint project — over $15-billion.

The Itaipu Dam is open daily for visits. You can either go on an organized tour from your hotel or take a taxi to the site.

In a specially built tourist reception area you are shown a 17 minute film explaining the construction of the dam and then taken on a tour of the site iself. The actual tour varies with the work taking place on the dam but lasts about one hour and includes a ride along the top of the dam. The tour is free.

Because the tours only start at certain times (8.30 a.m., 10 a.m., 2.30 p.m. and 4 p.m. as of going to press) you should call the public relations department of Itaipu in advance (Tel. (0455) 73-3133). The film is available in . various languages and I found the people most helpful even if it only meant showing the film for one or two people.

If you want any literature about the construction of the dam please ask the guides. They told me that when they gave pamphlets to everyone they spent most of their time picking them up from around the site.

For information in advance about Itaipu write to the "Assessoria de Relações Públicas" — Itaipu Binacional — Centro Executivo — C.J. Habitacional "A" — Foz do Iguaçu — Paraná — Brazil.

ITAIPU BOAT TRIP

The reservoir above the Itaipu Dam has become in recent years the world's largest man made lake on which you can take either a lunch or dinner cruise on the purpose built *Agua Viva Um*.

The cruises, which last about three hours, sail at 11 a.m. for lunch and 6 p.m. for dinner. Reservations should be made in advance with the Tropical Hotel Group, read Varig, which operate the Hotel das Cataratas in Foz do Iguaçu (74-2666). Reservations can also be made in the town of Foz do Iguaçu at Av. Juscelino Kubitschek, 800 (73-1535).

DUTY FREE

One of the big attractions for the Brazilians to go to Foz do Iguaçu is the duty free zone across the Paraná River in the city of Presidente Stroessner in Paraguay.

The duty free zone could have been in Foz do Iguaçu itself but I was told that without the money earned at Stroessner the Paraguayan economy would be very badly hit, the Brazilians therefore support their South American neighbors by not having a duty free zone on their side of the river.

To get from Brazil to Paraguay is simplicity itself, you simply cross the *Ponte da Amizade* (Friendship Bridge) either by taxi, bus, car, or even foot. The controls at each end of the bridge are fairly lax, although you should carry your passport while both US dollars and Brazilian cruzados are happily accepted in the stores.

The city of Presidente Stroessner is not very exciting in itself but will be of interest to foreigners to see the immediate differences between Brazil and Paraguay. The "famous" cassino is not however worth crossing the bridge for.

The shops in the duty free zone are well stocked and in South American terms the prices are low for imported goods. By chance I happened to visit the duty free zones of President Stroessner and Manaus in the same week and can tell you from what I saw that in Paraguay the prices were better and the selection greater. If you are worried about taking expensive items back across the bridge and border I am told that for an extra 10% the goods will be delivered anywhere in Brazil.

The stores in Presidente Stroessner stay open till 10 p.m., so no need to eat into your sightseeing time at the falls or dam, and for the foreign visitor, the market of Paraguayan goods offers cheap leather goods, especially bags.

FOZ DO IGUAÇU TIMETABLE

Due to the arrival and departure times of the main flights from Rio I would suggest the following timetable.

Day 1: Morning flight from Rio to Foz — Transfer to hotel — Afternoon visit to Itaipu Dam — Early evening visit to Presidente Stroessner in Paraguay.

Day 2: Full day at falls and National Park.

Day 3: Morning flight to Rio or any other Brazilian city.

Note: If you are touring by car you would probably travel out of Foz on the state's most important tourist route, the BR-277, which links Foz with Curitiba. At Curitiba train enthusiasts should not miss the opportunity of riding the Curitiba-Paranaguá railroad which dates back to 1885, a memorable journey of some 100 km from the city to the coast.

Note: For a full list of Foz do Iguaçu's best hotels see "On From Rio — Southern Brazil".

Manaus and the Amazon

Just the names of "The Amazon" and "Manaus" are enough to stir the emotions of most men and women. Forget African safaris or treks through the Far East, it is still the Amazon that is regarded as the unobtainable, the earth's final mystery.

As a whole, the Amazon basin spreads across two-fifths of South America, covering an area of 2.5 million square miles of which 580,000 square miles make up the Brazilian state of Amazonas which has Manaus as its capital.

Tourism, as such, is still relatively new to the region and not yet fully defined, but in the next five years I think we will see Manaus, and the areas of the Amazon closest to it, becoming more and more in demand from both serious travellers and tourists.

GETTING TO MANAUS

I don't think you should consider travelling to Manaus by bus or car which leaves you the option of air or river travel.

Manaus is linked to most Brazilian cities by daily flights. Flight time from Rio de Janeiro is just short of four hours with the most direct flights arriving via Brasilia, some two hours and 30 minutes away. As a point of interest, the city of Miami is only five hours and 15 minutes flying time from Manaus.

The cost of the simple economy return from Rio to Manaus is around $425 which is an ample demonstration of the value of both Brazilian air-passes at $330 and $250.

You can also fly in-and-out of Manaus via Belém on the Brazilian coast. This flight can act as your gateway to the Brazilian Northeast and the towns of São Luiz, Fortaleza, João Pessoa, Recife, Maceió and Salvador.

A number of tour companies operating charters make full use of Manaus in their routing of the $250, four city-air-pass. By entering Brazil via Manaus the companies have a cheaper and shorter flight from Europe and the United States than by entering via Rio. The client then has 14 days to visit four other Brazilian cities, other than Manaus, and can spend as much time as they like in Manaus and the Amazon region before and after their Brazilian tour.

You can also get to Manaus by boat. Each year a number of large cruise ships call in on Manaus while there is a regular service to-and-from Belém on the comfortable air-conditioned boats of ENASA (Emprèsa de Navegação da Amazonia S/A).

Flight time from Belém to Manaus is one hour and 45 minutes while the ENASA boats take five days to cover the same 1713km route by river and four days on the return cruise. The more interesting trip, it is generally agreed, is from Belém to Manaus when the boats hug the river bank to avoid the Amazon's strong currents.

The modern catamarans, Pará and Amazonas, specially designed for Amazon travel, hold up to 138 passengers. More details are available from ENASA's headquarters in Belém at Av. Presidente Vargas, 41. Tel. (091) 223-3011. Telex. (091) 2064.

Arriving by plane in Manaus brings you to the city's international airport, one of the most modern in South America.

As Manaus is a duty free zone you will find posted in the airport the dollar and current cruzado value of duty free goods that each adult can purchase and bring back into Brazil. At the time of going to press this amount was $600.

Although not important if you are just visiting Brazil, you should remember as a foreigner living in Brazil to register any items of value which you are bringing in to Manaus which could on your departure be mistaken for duty free purchases. I am thinking particularly about your camera equipment. The registration of goods is made at a desk in the baggage hall. You should also remember that the time in Manaus is one hour earlier than most of Brazil.

As at nearly all Brazilian airports, you can choose from buses and all types of taxis to get you to your final destination. All are paid for in advance in the airport which is about 15km from the center of Manaus.

If you are staying at the Tropical Hotel, 10km from the airport, you will find that the hotel has its own bus service costing around $2.

You now have to decide what you are in Manaus to see and do, because believe me there are three very different options which can be combined or done separately. I am talking about Manaus, the Amazon, and believe-it-or-not, the Tropical Hotel.

THE TROPICAL HOTEL AND OTHER ACCOMMODATION

Opened by the Brazilian President in 1976, the Tropical Hotel is the flag-ship of Varig's Tropical Hotels Group and with 341 rooms and 17 suites the largest resort hotel complex in South America.

By itself, even without Manaus or the Amazon, the Tropical Hotel would be worth visiting for a restful holiday at a world class resort hotel.

The Tropical boasts shops and restaurants, swimming pools and saunas, bars and cocktail lounges, a barber shop and beauty parlor, a discotheque, tennis courts, a games room, a travel agent, pool-side barbecues, extensive tropical gardens and even its own zoo.

Unfortunately, like any other country in the world you have to pay for five star luxury in Brazil. Room rates at the Tropical vary from $90 to $125 and suites from $160 to $725. Reservations can be made at any Varig office or direct with the hotel in Manaus at Estrada da Ponta Negra. Tel. (092) 238-5757. Telex. (092) 2173.

The Tropical Hotel also organizes most of Manaus' top tours which include cruises on the Amazon, Negro and Solimões rivers, the "Meeting of the Waters", fishing trips, city tours, and even overnight accommodation in their own jungle lodge, although this will cost you an extra $145 for a double room.

The hotel runs a courtesy bus service between the hotel and city of Manaus. The journey of 18km takes exactly 30 minutes, the buses leaving the hotel for Manaus on the hour and returning on the half hour.

Do not however be mistaken in to thinking that visiting the Tropical Hotel is visiting the Amazon, the two are completely different.

If you are going to Manaus to see the city or just stopping over before going on to a jungle lodge then the city of Manaus offers cheaper and more simple accommodation. The city has three four star hotels which are adequate, the Novotel being a favorite with businessmen due to its location in the industrial zone, and the Amazonas and Imperial in the city center. Other hotels include the three star Lord and Ana Cassia Palace, while the Central is a modern two star hotel in the center of town. In all Manaus has 1630 hotel rooms.

THE CITY OF MANAUS

Sadly with the passing of time since the rubber barons departed and the tourists returned, the city of Manaus has allowed much of its historic heritage to fall into disrepair.

Manaus, which is located just south of the equator at 3°8' and 60°61 W, started as the Fort of São José da Barra in 1669 and as a town took the name of Manaus in 1856. The famous Rubber Boom, which brought untold European wealth to the city, lasted from 1890 through 1911.

Manaus' new wealth and prosperity dates back to 1967 when the Brazilian Government made Manaus a duty free zone. The aim was two fold. Firstly to encourage Brazilians to visit Manaus and secondly, and more importantly, to encourage companies to set up factories which would be allowed to import certain component parts and then "re-export" to the rest of Brazil. The result is that most of Brazil's electronic industries, including video, hi-fi and television, are located in the area.

The most famous building in Manaus is the Teatro Amazonas built over 12 years — which opened in 1896 and was restored to full working order in 1974.

Seating 684 the theatre reflects the richness of the period of its construction. The tiles came from Alsace, the dome and furniture from Paris, the mirrors, porcelain and smaller chandeliers from Venice, the marble from other parts of Italy, the columns and banisters from England, and the central chandelier from France.

The theatre also has a luxurious ballroom featuring a floor made up of 12,000 pieces of wood that are secured without a single nail or drop of glue as well as the works of the Italian painter Domenico de Angelis.

The theatre, which dominates the center of Manaus, opens daily (except Monday) from 9 a.m. to 5 p.m.

The other main historical part of Manaus is the dock area, close to the duty free shopping zone, where the Customs House, prefabricated in England, floating dock, the largest of its kind in the world, and the Municipal Market, based on Paris' Les Halles, can be found. All three date from the turn of the century.

In the dock area you can also find what in my opinion is the city's most interesting museum, the Manaus Harbor Museum. The museum, at Boulevard Vivaldo Lima, 61 is open Monday through Friday from 8 a.m. to 11 a.m. and 2 p.m. to 5 p.m. The city's other museums, including Indian and Tiradentes, are not up to much.

Manaus is also of interest to Brazilians, South Americans, and foreigners living in Brazil for its duty free shopping.

The main zone of tax free stores is located between Rua Eduardo Ribeira (where the Tropical Hotel's bus stops) and Rua Dr. Moreira and Av. 7 de Setembro and Rua Marquês de Santa Cruz. An area four blocks by three.

Manaus as a duty free zone does not offer the selection of

President Stroessner, close to Foz do Iguaçu, with no alcohol and very little perfume. The main interest is therefore for Brazilian made electrical goods at tax free prices. These include CD machines, VCRs, hi-fis, and even washing machines and micro-wave ovens.

Strangely the stores in Manaus in the off-season close as early as 6 p.m. or 6.30 p.m.

In 1986 a new purpose built shopping mall started to operate. The idea of CECOMIZ, Centro Comercial da Indústria da Zona Franca de Manaus, is to be the shop window of goods manufactured in the area. The only problem CECOMIZ could face is its location in the industrial zone on the Estrada do Contorno close to the Bola da Suframa.

THE EXOTIC AMAZON

The Amazon, or rather the real Amazon, the Amazon as you imagine it, is not to be found on the outskirts of Manaus. If you want to discover the real jungle and some of its many secrets, you are going to have to put yourself out a little. All I can promise is that if you do you will have one of the experiences of your life, an experience which, having got all the way to Manaus, you would be a fool to miss. Then again if you are the type of traveller who just wants to go on a pleasure trip up a river to say that you have been on the Amazon or walk along a beaten path to say that you have been in the jungle, then so be it. But for those of you with a taste for adventure, adventure with comfort, there are a number of exciting options.

These trips will help open your eyes to the reality of the Amazon, its size and diversity. Just for starters contemplate the fact that in the rivers of the Amazon they have discovered more than 1500 species of freshwater fish. In Europe the number of species total 150. In Amazonas there are 1800 species of birds to look for, 250 different mammals, and literally thousands of animals, reptiles, amphibians and insects and that is not even talking about the plant life.

The trip I took into the Amazon region, a trip which I was told time and time again by people working within tourism in Manaus was the best, was to the Amazon Lodge located over 80 km from Manaus in the heart of virgin jungle and waters.

The Amazon Lodge tour costs around $200 to $250 depending on the season and lasts for three full days, two nights. The cost includes all meals and transport. The only other cost you have over the three days is your bar bill at the lodge!

In the early morning of Day One the Amazon Lodge pick you up from your hotel and take you through Manaus to the Agricultural Port where you board a boat for the 45 minute crossing of the Amazon, which depending on the season can be from 8km to 15km wide. Leave most of your heavy baggage back in Manaus at the office of the Amazon Lodge or in your hotel. All you will need for the tour should fit in an overnight bag.

During the crossing of the Amazon the boat passes the "Meeting of the Waters" where the rivers Negro and Solimões meet but refuse to mix. The two very different colored rivers stubbornly flow alongside each other for several kilometers. This is considered to be one of the sights of Manaus, however, as part of the Amazon Lodge tour it is hardly memorable.

The boat ends its journey at the small village of Careiro where you board the lodge's bus for a one hour 30 minute drive along the BR-319, a muddy highway that links Manaus to Porto Velho. At the crossing of the Araca River you swap transport again, this time from bus to high speed launch which takes you on a two hour cruise down the river to the lodge. As the journey progresses you

RECIFE PALACE
★★★★★

Follow the sun.
And spend the whole year in Recife.

RECIFE PALACE
HOTEL.
BOOK YOUR
PLACE IN THE
SUN.

Stay right on Boa Viagem
Beach, the most exciting
spot in Recife. Just five
minutes away from the
International Airport and
less than 15 minutes from
downtown, with all that
special Recife Palace service.
All this set in the heart of a
city that basks in the sun all
year round - with a special place
reserved just for you.

Address: Av. Boa Viagem, 4070 -
Recife - PE - 50.000 - Brazil -
Tel.: (081) 325-4044 -
Telex (081) 4528 REPH BR -
EMBRATUR 01564-00-21-4

Book directly with the hotel or
through BHB - Best Hotels of
Brazil.
Toll Free-SP (011) 800-8618 - RJ
(021) 800-6158
São Paulo (011) 258-8822
Tlx (011) 23826
Rio de Janeiro (021) 262-0107
Tlx (021) 34133

Standard

Carlton.Um raro prazer.

can feel the tension mount amongst your fellow travellers. The thought of "What am I doing here in the middle of nowhere? I must be nuts," runs through everyone's mind. The journey is exciting and interesting in itself, the incline to the top of the roller coaster and the unknown.

Arrival at the Amazon Lodge, your home for the next two days, dampens the worries. Greeted by the enthusiastic and friendly staff and other intrepid explorers like yourself who are about to take your boat back to "civilization". You are soon relaxed with a cold drink, lunch, and the fantastic stories and experiences of the other explorers' last two days.

The lodge itself only accommodates up to 10 people at any one time. Swiss owned and run, the whole operation ticks along like clockwork. The support infrastructure for the floating lodge is hidden away on a nearby island where the supplies etc. are stored. On the lodge the only noise and disturbance is from the surrounding jungle, even the electricity is silently powered by solar panels.

The lodge then is your base. You can go off and explore the immediate surroundings in small canoes. The local wildlife, including monkeys, parrots and even a friendly tapir, comes down to the riverbank behind the lodge, accustomed by now to the comings and goings of the human species. Tours to further afield are taken in larger motor-powered boats. Your itinerary will include a jungle walkabout, fishing for piranha, a visit to a riverside dwelling, and at night, a crocodile "hunt". Don't worry though, no harm comes to the crocodiles or any other wildlife. You will also have the chance to experience the sun rise and set over the jungle. Magic, pure magic, even for a city slicker like myself.

At the end of your time on the lodge you will have become the intrepid explorer and greet the "newcomers" to the lodge with your fantastic stories of a memorable three days. After lunch, all meals are served at the lodge, it is sadly time to return back down the rivers to Manaus.

Back at Manaus you can either return to your hotel or go to the office of the Amazon Lodge where there is a place to shower and change before going on to the airport.

The Amazon Lodge is not the only jungle lodge though, in fact the same company inaugurated the Amazon Village at the end of 1986. The Village consists of 18 wooden bungalows which sit on the river bank 100km from Manaus. There is also the purpose built Pousada dos Guanavenas, located 200km down river of Manaus, which can be reached by bus or sea-plane, and the Ecological Safari which is based on the 20 berth Tuna.

Tuna, which cruises the upper Negro River from Manaus, is accompanied by a supervisor who helps make a video documentary of your cruise, a physician from the Tropical Diseases Hospital in Manaus, and a scientist working for the National Institute for Research on the Amazon (INPA). Tuna's cruises last four days three nights or seven days/ six nights.

More lodges are due to open in the coming year. For more information you can contact the Amazonas State Tourism Authority (EMAMTUR) at Av. Taruma, 379 in Manaus. Tel. (092) 234-5414. Telex. (092) 2279. The Amazon Lodge and Village can be contacted directly at Transamazonas Turismo Ltda. at P.O. Box 514, Manaus. Tel. (092) 232-1454. Telex. (092) 2641.

LEAVING MANAUS

The only thing you have to remember about leaving Manaus is to check in at least two hours before your flight. The extra time is required to clear customs who will check your duty free purchases to make sure they are within the set limits. Because of the amount of goods purchased in Manaus the airlines normally allow an extra 10 kilos of luggage for free.

If you have time to kill before your flight the airport, for an airport, has an excellent restaurant.

Note: For a full list of Manaus' best hotels and lodges see "On From Rio — Northern Brazil".

Minas Gerais

If you are interested in history, art, architecture, or gemstones, you should visit the historical towns of Minas Gerais (General Mines) close to Brazil's third largest city, the capital of the state, Belo Horizonte.

Belo Horizonte, or Belo as it is known to its friends, is located 434 km inland from Rio, en route to Brasilia. To get to Belo you may choose to drive or go by bus via the BR-040. I however would recommend that you make use of the regular air service that links the two cities in 50 minutes and which will cost you about $70 return it not flying on an air-pass.

In Minas it does not matter how adventurous you are, or how much you loath organized tourism, you are going to have to accept that to fully appreciate the historical towns you will need a guide. The maps of the area are poor and what few books have been written in English about the towns and historical churches are totally inadequate.

You can choose to join a set tour run by one of the many excellent ground operators in Belo or if you have the money get the operator to supply a car and guide just for you.

As Minas is not a "touristy" destination the level of guides is high. The operators know that you are not likely to be visiting the region if you don't have a basic interest in the historic, the guides are therefore prepared to answer any questions.

One way to explore the historical towns is to base yourself on Belo Horizonte. The city has some very good hotels, none more friendly than the Brasilton Contagem run by the Hilton Group. From Belo you can strike out to visit the towns of Ouro Preto, Congonhas, Mariana, and Sabará, all dating back to the 18th century, and the caves at Maquiné, or further afield to the towns of Diamantina, São João del Rei and Tiradentes.

OURO PRETO

The most famous of the Minas towns is Ouro Preto which on September 2, 1980 was designated to be a world monument — "Cultural Patrimony of Mankind" — by UNESCO as one of the world's largest homogenous collections of baroque architecture, with 13 churches dating back to the early 18th century.

Ouro Preto, or Vila Rica (Wealthy Village) as it was known when the state capital, is also the home of the "School of Mine Engineering and Metallurgy", considered the best of its kind in South America, and its "Museum of Mineralogy" which attracts experts from around the world.

If you can, try and spend at least one night in Ouro Preto during your visit to Minas.

Ouro Preto was also the birth place in 1938 of the the artist and sculptor Antonio Francisco Lisboa, known as "Aleijadinho" (The Little Cripple), who incredibly produced some of his greatest works after an unknown disease had virtually crippled him. Much of his work was done with the hammer and chiesel strapped to what remained of his hands.

Aleijadinho's work can be found throughout the historical towns but none better, or more famous, than that at Congonhas where in the churchyard of the "Sanctuary of Good Jesus of Matozinhos" you can see his 12 prophets carved from soapstone, and below in six small chaples, 64 cedar sculptures carved by him between 1796 and 1799 and painted by Ataíde and Francisco Xavier Carneiro depicting the passion of Christ.

Another important historical town, and for a variety of reasons, is São João del Rei.

With an attractive selection of churches and other buildings dating back to the 18th century, São João del Rei at 375 km is the nearest of the historical towns to Rio de Janeiro and at 185 km the furthest from Belo Horizonte.

São João del Rei is not only famous for its architecture though and in the 20th century has become the Brazilian, if not world, capital of high class pewter. There are a number of pewter factories to visit in the town including the factory and museum of John Somers whose works can be seen from the top gifts shops of Rio all the way to the Victoria and Albert Museum in London.

São João del Rei also boasts an impressive sacred art museum and the Institute of Historic and Artistic National Patrimony.

The town figured heavily in the news in 1985 as the birth place and final resting place of the late Brazilian president, Tancredo Neves, a man whose popularity and tragic death has caused the town to become almost a shrine to the Brazilian people.

The historical towns can be visited in days or weeks, the choice is yours.

ORGANIZED TOURS

One of the most interesting packages is put together by Revetour and takes three days.

On "Day One" you leave Belo and drive 185 km through the area to São João del Rei. On the way you will visit Congonhas and see the works of Aleijadinho mentioned above. Overnight you stay in São João and in the morning take "Smokey Mary", an old steam train dating back to 1881, which carries you to Tiradentes a village where nothing new has been built since the 18th century, even the roads dating back to 1740. The train takes you on to Campolide, and then by coach to Barbacena, the rose capital of Brazil, and Ouro Preto.

After an overnight stay in Ouro Preto, "Day Three" gives you more time to explore the historic city before a visit to Mariana and the gold mine at Passagem. In the evening you return to Belo Horizonte.

Revetour also organizes special tours for people interested in minerals and precious stones which vary from three to eight days.

The main tour operators to contact in Belo Horizonte for the historical towns are:

Revetour
Rua Espírito Santo, 1892
Belo Horizonte — Minas Gerais
Tel: (031)337-2500
Telex: 031-2036

Unitour
Rua Tupis, 171
Belo Horizonte — Minas Gerais
Tel: (031) 201-7144

Kontik-Franstur
Rua Espírito Santo, 1204
Belo Horizonte — Minas Gerais
Tel: (031) 222-5988

Ouro Preto Turismo
Rua Alagoas, 1314
Belo Horizonte — Minas Gerais
Tel: (031) 221-1222

Note: For a full list of the best hotels in Minas Gerais and the historical towns see "On From Rio — Southeastern Brazil".

Airports
Airline Companies
Air Taxis &
Helicopters
Shipping Lines
Buses
Car Hire/Car
Rental
Motorcycle Rental
Taxis
Subway and
Railway
Leaving Rio

Airports

Rio de Janeiro International Airport (Galeão)
Ilha do Governador
Information: 398-6060 & 398-5050.
Cargo: 398-3450.
Flight Times: 398-4133, 398-4477 & 398-4134

Santos Dumont Praça Senador

Salgado Filho Centro.
Information: 262-6212.
Ponte Aérea: 220-7728.

Jacarepagua Av. Alvorada, 2541
Barra da Tijuca.
Information: 342-3305.

Airlines Companies

Aer Lingus
Tel.: 259-5198

Aerolineas Argentinas
Rua São José, 40 — Centro
Tel. 221-4255

Aeroperu
Praça Mahatma Gandhi, 2 — Centro
Tel. 240-1622. Telex: 22679
Airport: 398-3787

Air Canada
Av. Mar. Câmara, 160/1016 — Centro
Tel. 240-3539, Telex: 35780

Air France
Av. Rio Branco, 257 — Centro
Tel. 220-8661.
Reservations: 220-3666
Airport: 398-3490

Alitalia
Av. Pres.. Antônio Carlos, 40 — Centro
Tel.: 210-2192
Reservations: 262-5088
Airport: 398-3143

American Airlines
Rua Assembleia, 10/36 — Centro
Tel. 221-9455.

Austral
Av. N.S. de Copacabana, 500 — Copacabana
Tel. 255-6466¡ Telex: 33449

Avianca
Rua Mexico, 11 — Centro
Tel. 240-4413. Telex: 31492
Airport: 398-3775

British Airways
Av. Rio Branco, 108/21 Centro.
Tel.: 221-0922. Telex: 32473
Reservations: 242-6020
Airport: 398-3888
Toll Free: 021-800-6926

Canadian Pacific
Av. Rio Branco, 311 — Centro
Tel. 263-6675

Cathay Pacific
Av. Rio Branco, 181 — Centro
Tel. 220-1484. Telex: 24735

China Airlines
Av. Franklin Roosevelt, 115/603
Tel. 220-1711

Continental
Rua da Assembléia, 10/3311 Centro.
Tel. 222-5161. Telex: 30973

Ecuatoriana
Av. Alm. Barroso, 63/1908 Centro
Tel. 240-1075

El Al
Av. Rio Branco, 257 — Centro
Tel. 220-6098. Telex: 23060

Flying Tigers
Tel. 363-1524. Telex (011) 36471

Iberia
Rua Pedro Lessa, 41 — Centro
Tel. 220-3444
Airport: 398-3168

Iraqi
Av. Rio Branco, 251 — Centre
Tel. 262-1123. Telex: 33246
Airport: 398-3541

Japan Air Lines
Av. Rio Branco, 108 — Centro
Tel. 221-9454 Telex: 23560
Reservations: 221-9663

KLM
Av. Rio Branco, 311 — Centro
Tel. 210-1342. Telex: 23276
Reservations: 220-1347
Airport: 398-3700
Freight: 393-6845

Ladeco
Av. Rio Branco, 277 — Centro
Tel. 220-0299. Telex: 32886

Lan Chile
Rua São José, 70 — Centro
Tel. 221-2882
Airport: 398-3799

L.A. Paraguayas
Av. Rio Branco, 245 — Centro
Tel. 220-4148 Telex: 23990

L.A. Boliviano
Av. Calogeras, 30-A — Centro
Tel. 220-9548. Telex: 30463

Lufthansa
Av. Rio Branco, 156 — Centro
Tel. 262-1022 or 262-0273
Telex: 22560
Airport: 398-3620
Freight 383-7396
Information: 521-0239

Mexicana
Rua Uruguaiana, 10/1907 — Centro
Tel. 242-3344. Telex: 32905

Pan American
Av. Pres. Wilson, 165 — Centro
Tel. 240-6662. Telex: 22266
Reservations: 240-2322
Airport Freight: 393-6660 or 393-6737
Airport Information: 398-3307

Pluna
Rua Mexico, 11 — Centro
Tel. 262-4466. Telex: 31501
Airport: 398-3920

Qantas
Av. Ataulfo de Paiva, 226/6 — Leblon
Tel. 511-0045. Telex: 32549

Rio Sul
Aeroporto Santos Dumont
Tel. 262-6911. Telex: 21654
Freight: 220-1453

Royal Air Maroc
Av. Pres. Wilson, 113 — Centro
Tel. 210-1337. Telex: 23458
Airport: 398-3766
Freight: 220-2922

Sabena
Rua da Assembleia, 10 — Centro
Tel. 221-9455. Telex: 23740

SAS
Av. Pres. Wilson 231/21 — Centro
Tel. 210-1222. Telex: 30175
Airport: 398-3708
Freight: 393-6393

Singapore Airlines
Av. Treze de Maio, 13 — Centro
Tel. 262-5253 .Telex: 21657

South African
Av. Rio Branco, 245/32 — Centro
Tel. 262-6002. Telex: 33524
Reservations: 262-6252
Airport: 398-3365
Freight: 398-3767

Swissair
Av. Rio Branco, 99 — Centro
Tel. 203-2152. Telex: 23383
Reservations: 203-2144
Airport: 398-3304
Freight: 398-3849

Taba
Av. Franklin Roosevelt, 115/405 — Centro
Tel: 220-2529. Telex: 30802

Tam
Aeroporto Santos Dumont — Centro
Tel. 262-6311. Telex: 23799
Airport: 398-3271

Tap
Av. Rio Branco, 311 — Centro
Tel. 210-2414. Telex: 22134
Reservations: 220-5521
Freight: 393-9383

Transbrasil
Aeroporto Santos Dumont — Centro
Tel: 297-4477
Av. Atlântica, 1998 — Copacabana
Tel. 236-7475
Reservations: 297-4422
Airport: 398-3980
Freight: 393-2165

United Airlines
Av. Beira Mar, 406 — Centro
Tel. 220-3397. Telex: 31783

US Air
Rua Uruguaiana, 10 — Centro
Tel. 221-7373. Telex: 32478

Varig/Cruzeiro
Av. Rio Branco, 277 — Centro
Tel. 297-4400
Rua Mexico, 11 — Centro
Av. Rio Branco, 128 — Centro
Av. Franklin Roosevelt, 194 — Centro
Rua Visconde de Pirajá, 351 —
Ipanema
Tel. 287-9040
Hotel Nacional — São Conrado
Tel. 322-1957
Rua Rodolfo Dantas, 16 — Copa-
cabana
Tel. 541-6343
Aeroporto Santos Dumont —
Centro
Tel. 297-5141
Airport: 398-3258 or 398-3792
Information: 398-3410 or 398-3420
Air Bridge (Rio/São Paulo): 220-
4420

VASP
Av. Alm. Sílvio de Noronha, 369 —
Centro
Tel. 292-2080
Av. N. S. de Copacabana, 262 —
Copacabana
Tel. 292-2112
Rua Santa Luzia, 735 — Centro

Tel. 292-2112
Rua Visconde de Piraja, 444 —
Ipanema
Tel. 292-2112
Av. Nilo Peçanha, 11 — Centro
Tel. 292-2112
Aeroporto Santos Dumont —
Centro
Tel. 292-2112
Airport: 398-5989

Viasa
Rua do Carmo, 7 — Centro
Tel. 224-5345: Telex: 31005
Airport: 398-3808
Freight: 393-5466

Votec
Av. Franklin Roosevelt, 115 —
Centro
Tel. 292-6611 — Telex: 21362
Aeroporto Santos Dumont —
Centro
Tel. 220-9328

Western
Av. Rio Branco, 181/1508 — Centro
Tel. 220-3157. Telex: 35905

Air Taxis and Helicopters

AIR TAXI SERVICES

Costair
Rua Santa Luzia, 651
Centro - 220-0668

Cruzeiro
Av. Almirante Frontin, 381
Centro 270-8582

Lider Taxi
Praça Senador Salgado Filho
Centro - 262-7088

Tam
Aeroporto-Santos Dumont

Centro   220-4660

Votec
Av. Franklin Roosevelt, 137
Centro   292-6611

HELICOPTERS

Gray Line
Sheraton Hotel
Vidigal   294-0393

Votec
Av. Franklin Roosevelt, 137
Centro - 292-6611

Shipping Lines

Since flying has become so fast, cheap and popular, and the distance by sea from Rio de Janeiro to anywhere in the world is so enormous very few shipping lines have survived.

From Rio and Santos a number of cargo ships take a limited number of passengers on their sailings to-and-from the U.S. and

Europe, otherwise traffic is restricted to cruise liners who are either cruising in Brazilian waters or whom have scheduled a stop in Rio as part of their world or South American cruise.

The Captain of the Port of Rio de Janeiro can be contacted on 253-6633 while information about the docks is available on 291-2122.

Abretur
Rua Mexico, 21A
Centro — 217-1840

Commodore Cruise Line
Rua da Assembleia, 93/803
Centro   232-6293

Cori Irmãos
Av. Rio Branco, 4/11
Centro - 223-3222

Expresso Mercantil
Av. Rio Branco, 25

Centro   233-8772

Linea C
Av. Rio Branco, 109
Centro   232-4309

Oremar
Rua da Assembléia, 10/36
Centro   221-9455

Wilson Sons
Av. Rio Branco, 25/4
Centro — 233-4983

Buses

BUS STATIONS

Novo Rio
Av. Francisco Bicalho, 1
São Cristóvão - 291-5151

Buses to all the state capitals most importantly São Paulo and to Asuncion (Paraguay), Buenos Aires (Argentina), Montevideo (Uruguay) and Santiago (Chile).

Menezes Cortes
Rua São Jose
Centro - 224-7577

Central bus terminal for downtown! Rio better known as Castelo, Air-conditioned buses run from Menezes Cortes to all parts of the zona sul as well as Petropolis and Teresopolis (Tel: 243-5414 & 263-8792).

BUSES — AIRPORT

Air conditioned buses run from Rio's two airports to various points in the city including most of the main hotels.

If you have any doubt about where the bus is going, write the name of your destination on a piece of paper and show it to the driver.

Aeroporto Internacional — Alvorada: International Airport (Galeão), Av. Brasil, Rodrigues Alves (Docks), Venezuela, Praça Mauá, Rio Branco (downtown), Beira Mar, Praia do Flamengo, Praia de Botafogo, Rio Sul, Princesa Isabel, Atlantica, R. Elizabete, Vieira Souto, Delfim Moreira, Niemeyer, Hotel Sheraton, Hotel Nacional, Inter-Continental, Auto-estrada Lagoa-Barra, Joá, and on to Alvorada.

Aeroporto Internacional — São

Conrado: Same route as above from the international airport as far as the Inter-Continental. End of the line is Praça São Conrado.

Aeroporto Internacional — Aeroporto Santos Dumont: Express bus service linking the International Airport and the Santos Dumont Airport downtown.

Aeroporto Santos Dumont: A number of services run from Santos Dumont to all points in the city.

BUSES — CITY

I am against tourists using any of the local bus services except the executive air-conditioned service.

Rio's normal buses are badly driven, the scene of most crimes against tourists and locals, and will probably end up getting you lost.

Other forms of transport in Rio, including taxis, are cheap so there is no real excuse for tourists to use the normal bus services, the exception are those that link with the Metro (subway) at Botafogo and are clearly marked "Metro". At present there are two lines: the M.21 and M.22 both of which are circular routes so make sure that you are heading in the direction you want! To-or-from the station.

The other acceptable form of bus transport is the efficient air-conditioned service which runs to the Castelo (Menezes Cortes) bus terminal downtown. Buses going downtown are marked "Castelo". The main routes are:

Castelo — Hotel Nacional: Graça Aranha, Pres. Wilson, Beira Mar, Praia do Flamengo, Osvaldo Cruz, Praia do Botafogo, San Clemente, Humaita, Jardim Botanico, Praça Santos Dumont, auto-estrada, Lagoa/Barra, Dois Irmãos Tunnel, Hotels Nacional and Inter-Continental.

Castelo — Urca: Graça Aranha, Nilo Peçanha, Rio Branco, Clotilde Gulmarães, Passagem, Gen. Severiano, Venceslau Bras, Pasteur, Ramon Franco, Mal. Cantuaria, João Luis Alves, Candido Gafree, João Luis Alves.

Castelo — Copacabana: Graça Aranha, Calogeras, Beira Mar, Praia do Flamengo, Praia de Botafogo, Rio Sul, Princesa Isabel, Barata Ribeiro, Raul Pompeia, Francisco Otaviano, Av. N.S. de Copacabana.

Castelo — Jardim de Alah: Graça Aranha, Calogeras, Beira Mar, Praia do Flamengo, Praia de Botafogo, Rio Sul, Princesa Isabel, Atlantica, R. Elisabete, Prudente de·Morais, Epitacio Pessoa.

Castelo — Leblon: Graça Aranha, Calogeras, Beira Mar, Praia do Flamengo, Praia de Botafogo, Rio Sul, Princesa Isabel, Barata Ribeiro, Toneleros, Pompeu Loureiro, Henrique Dodsworth, Epitacio Pessoa, Borges de Medeiros, Gen. San Martin, Visc. de Albuquerque, Ataulfo de Paiva, Dias Ferreira.

Castelo — São Conrado/Barra Shopping: Graça Aranha, Calogeras, Beira Mar, Praia do Flamengo, Praia de Botafogo, Rio Sul, Princesa Isabel, Atlantica, R. Elisabete, Vieira Souto, Delfim Moreira, Niemeyer, Hotel Sheraton, Hotel Nacional, Inter-Continental, Estrada da Gávea, Praça São Conrado, Americas, Barra Shopping.

Castelo — Bairro Peixoto (Copacabana): Graça Aranha, Calogeras, Beira Mar, Praia do Flamengo, Praia de Botafogo, Rio Sul, Princesa Isabel, Barata Ribeiro, Figueiredo Magalhães, Praça Ver. Rocha Leão.

Castelo — Leme: Graça Aranha, Calogeras, Beira Mar, Praia do Flamengo, Praia de Botafogo, Rio Sul, Princesa Isabel, Prado Junior, Atlantica, Praça Alm. Julio Noronha.

Note: Because of the expressway it is difficult for the buses to stop along the length of Praia do Flamengo and Praia do Botafogo.

BUSES — BEACH (JARDINEIRA)

One of the big successes in Rio's tourist world in 1985 was the introduction of the *Jardineira* bus service which runs the length of the coast from Leme to São Conrado.

The *Jardineiras* are specially designed open sided buses, a modern day equivalent of the street cars if you like, which hold 36 seated passengers and if necessary a further 34 standing.

The buses work on a flat fare basis and tend to cover their route at a more leisurely rate than the normal buses.

The *Jardineiras* have their own special stops which are clearly marked along the routes and at 500m intervals along the sea front and in front of the main hotels.

Due to the success of the *Jardineiras* several routes have been added to the original so you now must make sure you get on the right one.

At the time of going to press there were three *Jardineiras* routes. The original, and most interesting, is the "500 / São Conrado-Praia Vermelha" which links the São Conrado Fashion Mall behind the Inter-Continental and Nacional hotels with Sugar Loaf; the "700 / São Conrado/Bosque da Barra" which links the Fashion Mall with Barra; and the "900 / Ilha do Governador".

In their first years of operation the *Jardineiras* have possed no security problems for the passengers. I hope it stays that way.

BUSES — SURVIVAL

If you are going to be a resident in Rio, rather than a tourist, you will soon learn the dos and don'ts as far as the buses go.

Bus routes are posted on the back door of the bus and if you have any doubt you only need to shout the name of your destination to the conductor (ticket seller) who sits at the back of the bus.

Should you insist on travelling on the normal Rio buses here are a few of the facts you should watch for.

— Buses are very cheap. You pay the conductor at the back and the price will be posted behind him. The price, even with inflation, will probably be less than Cz$3 so a Cz$5 or Cz$10 note is a good one to have to hand when you board the bus. You will not be popular if you delay the bus by digging in to your bag to find the money, you will also be showing potential thieves exactly where your wallet is.

— Buses are a favorite location for holdups and robberies so watch yourself. Get on the bus with your fare in hand. Pay and go through the turnstyle. Do not hang around at the back of the bus. If you are going to rob a bus you are not likely to want to pay the fare are you?

— Watch yourself going through the turnstyle. You are being funnelled through a small opening, the perfect location for pickoockets to work, often in league with the conductor and driver. Keep your bag and wallet in front of you.

— Never flash large sums of money, cameras, or other valuables about on the bus. Someone will take them from you and jump off the bus. I repeat, never take an expensive camera on the bus that is not hidden in a bag.

— Rio's buses are designed to get people from A to B. They are not intended for tourists so don't go sightseeing on them. Use them for travel when you don't have your camera etc. with you.

— If you pay 10 cents for a bus ride instead of $2.50 for a cab you must expect what you get. The choice is your's so make it sensibly.

Car Hire/Car Rental

Besides the international airport, most of the major car rental companies, including Hertz, Avis. Budget and Localiza have chosen to group together close to Av. Princesa Isabel, the road which runs alongside the Meridien Hotel away from Copacabana beach.

Prices in Rio range from $19 a day for a small Volkswagen or Fiat all the way up to $50 for a limousine.

The top car rental companies accept the majority of international credit cards and restrict the minimum age of the driver to 25 although at Localiza and Hertz the age is 21.

Strictly speaking to drive in Brazil you should hold an international driving license issued in your country of origin but for a short rental the companies will accept your normal standard driving license although I can't promise that the Brazilian police will have the same attitude.

Reservations for car rental should be made in advance to avoid disappointment and can be made in any hotel or if you wish direct with the companies.

The main car rental companies are:

Avis
Av. Princesa Isabel, 150
Copacabana   542-4249
Toll Free: 011 800 8787
International Airport: 398-3083

Budget
Av. Princesa Isabel, 250
Copacabana   275-3244

Hertz
Av. Princesa Isabel, 334
Copacabana   275-4996
Toll Free: 011 800 8900
International Airport: 398-3162

Interlocadora
Av. Princesa Isabel, 186
Copacabana   275-6546

International Airport: 398-3181

Localiza (National Car Rental)
Av. Princesa Isabel, 214
Copacabana   275-3340
Toll Free: 031 800 2322
International Airport: 398-4456

Locarauto (Ansa International)
Rua Francisco Manoel, 81
Benfica   228-5192
Toll Free: 011 800 8188
International Airport: 398-3783

Nobre
Av. Princesa Isabel, 150
Copacabana   541-4646
International Airport: 398-3862

Motorcycle Rental

Unless you are an extremely competent driver I firmly suggest you avoid the urge to take to the roads of Rio on a motorbike. Your chances of survival are at best slim.

If you insist in your madness two of the main bike rental companies are Escobar at Av. Princesa Isabel, 323 (Tel. 542-2193) and Mar e Moto at Av. Bartolomeu Mitre, 1008 in Leblon (Tel. 274-4398).

To hire a bike you must be over 21 with the appropriate licence. Prices range from $10-a-day for 125cc to $25-a-day for 400cc.

Taxis

It is never difficult to get a taxi in Rio except downtown in the rush hour when it is raining.

The standard taxis are yellow in color and range from small Fiats all the way up. When you enter the cab the meter should be reset and the flag "1" showing. Flag "2", which represents a 20% increase in the fare, should only be used after 11 p.m., on Sundays and holidays, after the end of Leblon, and as a Christmas bonus during parts of December.

Because of the changes in prices the authorities have given up trying to regulate the meters, the taxis are therefore issued with a table of prices relative to what is shown on the meter. To protect the customer the correct table must be fixed to the back left-side window.

If you need to complain about one of the standard taxis the number to call is 269-5212.

Rio also has a very efficient radio taxi service, which although more expensive, offers larger more comfortable cars. Radio taxis are the fastest and best way to get to the airport.

The main radio taxi companies are:

Coopertramo — 260-2022
Cootramo — 270-1442
Transcoopass — 270-4888

Subway and Railway

Rio has one of the most modern, clean and efficient subway systems in the world.

Although not one of the largest systems Rio's metro can whisk you from Botafogo to downtown in under ten minutes. If you are going anywhere in Rio and can take the metro do so, it is the safest form of transport.

Open Monday through Saturday from 6 a.m. to 11 p.m. the metro starts at Botafogo (take a cab or one of the buses marked "Metro"). From Botafogo the trains go to Flamengo — Largo do Machado — Catete — Gloria — Cinelândia — Carioca — Urugaiana — Presidente Vargas — Central — Praça Onze — Estácio — Afonso Pena — São Francisco Xavier — Saens Pena. At Estácio you can change to "Linha 2" (Line 2) which goes on to São Cristóvão and Maracanã.

The metro is flat rate and you can buy a return *Ida e Volta*.

Besides Botafogo, which is the nearest station to the hotels in the zona sul, the following metro stations are of importance:

Catete: Opposite the Museum of the Republic. This station should be used for the Novo Mundo hotel.

Gloria. Closest station to the Gloria Hotel and the Marina.

Cinelândia: Bottom of Rio Branco in Centro. Many of the airlines have their offices within walking distance of Cinelândia and Carioca. Station for the Teatro Municipal, Sala Cecilia Meirelles and the

National Museum of Fine Arts. Closest station to the Santos Dumont airport.

Carioca. Middle of Rio Branco. Station for the Metropolitan Cathedral, Castelo Bus Terminal, Praça XV and Largo da Carioca.

Uruguaiana: Top end of Rio Branco. Station for Candelaria and the São Bento Monastery. Nearest station to Praça Mauá where the ships dock.

At Carnival you should take the metro to Central if you are in one of the uneven numbered stands and Praça Onze if in the even numbered stands.

Rail Terminals

Trains for São Paulo and Belo Horizonte leave from the Dom Pedro II Station in Praça Cristiano Ottoni in Centro. Tel.: 233-4090 or 233-3277.

Distances from Rio

DISTANCES FROM RIO DE JANEIRO IN AIR MILEAGE

Amsterdam — 5938
Berlin — 6207
Buenos Aires — 1231
Cape Town — 3773
Chicago — 5228
Copenhagen — 6321
Frankfurt — 6237
Hong Kong — 11002
Lima — 2351
London — 5751
Madrid — 5045
Melbourne — 8218
Mexico — 4769
Montreal — 5082
Moscow — 7162
New York — 4805
Paris — 5681
Rome — 5704
San Francisco — 6621
Stockholm — 6638
Santiago — 1820
Tokyo — 11535

DISTANCES FROM RIO DE JANEIRO (BRAZIL) KM

Belem — 3242
Belo Horizonte — 442
Brasilia — 1145
Curitiba — 837
Fortaleza — 2851
Foz do Iguaçu — 1500
João Pessoa — 2574
Manaus — 4412
Natal — 2750
Porto Alegre — 1550
Recife — 2461
Salvador — 1691
Santarem — 3869
Santos — 501
São Paulo — 429
Vitoria — 513

Times Differences

In 1985 Brazil introduced "summer time" to help save energy. In 1986, summer time came into effect on November 14 and ends on February 14, 1987. During the period of summer time Brazil's clocks go forward one hour leaving the time difference between Brazil and most of Europe as three hours instead of four.

ST in the table below denotes "summer time" for that country.

Argentina. 0
Australia (Victoria). +13 (ST +14)
Austria. +4 (ST +5)
Belgium. +4 (ST +5)
Bolivia. −1
Canada (Eastern). −2 (ST −1)
Chile. −1
Colombia −2
Denmark. +4 (ST +5)
Egypt. +5
Equador. −2
Finland. +5
France. +4 (ST +5)
Great Britain. +3 (ST +4)
Greece. +5 (ST +6)
Holland. +4 (ST +5)
Hong Kong. +11
India. +8.30
Ireland. +3 (ST +4)
Israel. +5
Italy. +4 (ST +5)

Japan. +12
Mexico. −3
Norway. +4 (ST +5)
New Zealand. +15 (ST +16)
Paraguay. −1
Peru. −2
Portugal. +4 (ST +5)
South Africa. +5
Spain. +4 (ST +5)
Sweden. +4 (ST +5)
Switzerland. +4 (ST +5)
Union of Soviet Socialist Republics
(Moscow). +6
United States of America
  − Eastern Time. −2 (ST −1)
  − Central Time. −3 (ST −2)
  − Mountain Time. −4 (ST −3)
  − Pacific Time. −5 (ST −4)
Uruguay. 0
Venezuela. −1
West Germany. +4 (ST +5)

Leaving Rio de Janeiro

INTERNATIONAL TRAVEL — BY AIR

Most international travellers leave Rio from the International Airport on Ilha do Governador.
The quickest and safest way to get to the airport is by radio taxi which can be booked in advance.

If you are staying at a hotel ask at the desk about getting to the airport, you may find the hotel has a bus scheduled to go at the time you want.

If money is running short take a normal cab to the Santos Dumont Airport downtown, and then catch the regular express bus service which links the two airports.

Most overseas flights to the U.S. and Europe leave Rio at night, it is therefore advisable to get to the airport in good time to avoid the crush to go through emigration. Remember to keep some cruzeiros in case you have to pay the airport departure tax which is normally a cruzeiro value of about $8.

For emigration you need your passport, air ticket, and the form you filled in and had stamped on arrival.

Before passing through emigration pick up any magazines or books you need, the book stalls before you go through carry a much larger stock and selection.

At the airport there are shops for last minute gifts, and this includes coffee in special travel packs.

If you are being seen off by friends you can enjoy a drink or meal in the restaurant on the third floor. This restaurant also operates through emigration. If you don't have people with you go straight through.

Through emigration there are a number of duty free shops that cover both national and international goods. National goods include jewelry, drink, clothing and leather goods while the international duty free shop carries a full range of perfumes, cosmetics, gifts, calculators, watches, photographic equipment, tobacco, cigarettes, and liquor. The shop will advise you about the duty free allowance at your next port of call. Please note, however, that the duty free shops can only accept major international currencies and credit cards; they can under no circumstance accept cruzeiros. This is not their rule, but a Gorvernment regulation. If you have cruzeiros left use them in the book shop, on the plane, or in the shops before passing through emigration.

INTERNATIONAL TRAVEL — BY BUS

Despite the distance, it is possible to leave Rio for another country by bus. Buses leave the Novo Rio bus station (Av. Francisco Bicalho, 1 — São Cristóvão) daily for Asuncion, Buenos Aires, Montevideo and Santiago.. Reservations can be made in advance at most travel agents. Emigration formalities take place at the respective borders.

NATIONAL TRAVEL — BY BUS

The Novo Rio bus terminal is also the terminal for all buses leaving Rio for the other state capitals, including São Paulo. All seats can be booked in advance at most travel agents.

For any further information about bus times etc. get someone who speaks Portuguese to call the bus station on 291-5151.

NATIONAL TRAVEL — BY AIR

Brazil has an internal air service that is second to none. Three major companies fly internally, Varig/Cruzeiro, Transbrasil and Vasp, and they are supported in different regions by Nordeste, Rio Sul, Taba, Tam, and Votec.

All long distance internal flights leave from Sector A of the international airport on Ilha do Governador. (See "International Travel — By Air"). Seats can be booked at any travel agent or the airport itself.

AIR BRIDGE (SHUTTLE): SÃO PAULO, BELO HORIZONTE, BRASILIA.

Because of the levels of traffic on certain routes, Cruzeiro, Transbrasil Varig and Vasp have joined forces to organize walk-on/walk-off air bridges, which can be booked in advance if required.

From the international airport on Ilha do Governador jets link Rio to São Paulo, Brasilia and Belo Horizonte, while Electras link Rio's downtown airport of Santos Dumont with São Paulo.

Flight time is 55 minutes to São Paulo, 50 minutes to Belo Horizonte, and one-and-a-half hours to Brasilia.

The approximate dollar cost of a return flight to São Paulo is $75; to Belo Horizonte, $70; and to Brasilia, $155.

Air Pass

If you are considering travelling on to explore the rest of Brazil, you should purchase a Brazilian Air Pass from your travel agent before arriving in Brazil. The air pass can only be sold outside Brazil and to non-residents.

. The Brazilian Air Pass comes in two forms, and can be purchased for the flights of Transbrasil, Varig-Cruzeiro, and Vasp, each pass only being valid for the flights of the issuing carrier.

The most complete air pass sells for $330 and allows 21 days of unlimited travel within Brazil, although the same route cannot be flown twice in the same direction. The cheaper pass costs $250 and is valid for 14 days allowing visits and stopover at four cites in addition to your point of entry, which is likely to be Rio de Janeiro. Both passes start from the day of your first internal flight and the routing can be reserved in advance before you arrive in Brazil or at the time in Brazil.

Considering the size of Brazil, and the cost of internal flights, the air pass offers excellent value. It is also worth noting that if an air pass is unused it can be cashed in for a full refund, and so is a worthwhile investment even if you are not sure that you will want to travel.

Remember to confirm all your flights at least 72 hours before flying.

That includes international and internal flights.

J

General Information

Telephone Services

Currency Exchange

Business Rio

Health Matters

Useful Words and Phrases

Foreign Consulates

Brazilian Contacts Abroad

Annual Events and Holidays

Emergency Services

General Information

BABY SITTING

Castelinho
Rua Barão da Torre, 468
Ipanema — 287-5397

BREAKDOWN SERVICE

Auto-Socorro Botelho
Rua Sá Freire, 127
São Cristovão — 580-9079

Auto-Socorro Gafanhoto
Rua Aristibes Lobo, 156
Laranjeiras — 273-5495

Auto-Socorro Gafanhoto
Av. das Americas, 1577
Barra — 399-2192

Golden Tour
Rua da Passagem, 35
Botafogo — 295-9494

BUFFET HIRE

See shopping section.

CHURCHES (ENGLISH SPEAKING)

Christ Church
Rua Real Grandeza, 99
Botafogo — 226-2978

Our Lady of Mercy (*Roman Catholic*)
Rua Visconde de Caravelas, 48
Botafogo — 246-5664

Union Church
Rua Parque da Lagoa de Marapendi
Barra da Tijuca — 325-8601

International Baptist Church
Rua Desembargador Alfredo Russel, 146

Leblon — 246-7677

Associação Religiosa Israelita
Rua General Severiano, 170
Botafogo — 295-6444

CHURCHES (HISTORIC)

Brazil is predominately Roman Catholic therefore it is not surprising that the city's most famous and historic churches are all Catholic.

Candelaria
Praça Pio X — Centro.
Sunday: 10 a.m., 11 a.m. & noon.

Metropolitan Cathedral
Av. Chile — Centro.
Sunday 10 a.m.

São Bento
Rua Dom Gerardo — Centro,
Sunday: 10 a.m.

Santo Antonio
Largo da Carioca — Centro
Sunday: 10 a.m. and 5 p.m.

COMMERCIAL HOURS

Banks: Monday through Friday from 10 a.m. to 4:30 p.m.
Gas Stations: Monday through Saturday from 6 a.m. to 8 p.m. Should change to a 24-hour service during 1987.
Offices: Monday through Friday from 8 a.m. to 6 p.m.
Shopping Centers: Monday through Saturday from 10 a.m. to 10 p.m.
Stores: Monday through Friday from 9 a.m. to 7 p.m. Saturday from 9 a.m. to 1 p.m.
Supermarkets: Monday through Saturday from 8 a.m. to 10 p.m.

CONVERSION TABLES

Length

Cm	Inches/Cm	Inches
2,54	1	0,394
5,08	2	0,787
7,62	3	1,181
10,16	4	1,575
12,70	5	1,969
15,24	6	2,362
17,78	7	2,765
20,32	8	3,150

22,86	9	3,543
25,10	10	3,937
50,80	20	7,874
76,20	30	11,811
101,60	40	15,748
127,00	50	19,685
152,40	60	23,622
177,80	70	27,559
203,20	80	31,496
228,60	90	35,433
254,00	100	39,370

KM	Miles/Km	Miles
1,609	1	0,621
3,219	2	1,243
4,828	3	1,864
6,437	4	2,485
8,047	5	3,107
9,656	6	3,728
11,265	7	4,350
12,875	8	4,971
14,484	9	5,592
16,093	10	6,214
32,187	20	12.427
48,280	30	18,641
64,374	40	24,855
80,467	50	31,069
95,561	60	37,282
112,654	70	43,496
128,748	80	49,710
144,841	90	55,923
160,934	100	62,137

Weight

Kilos	Pounds/Kilos	Pounds
0,454	1	2,205
0,907	2	4,409
1,361	3	6,614
1,814	4	8,819
2.268	5	11,023
2,722	6	13,228
3,175	7	15,432
3,629	8	17,637
4,082	9	19,842
4,536	10	22,046
9,072	20	44,092
13,608	30	66,139
18,144	40	88,185
22,680	50	110;231
27,216	60	132,277
31,752	70	154,324
36,287	80	176,370
40,823	90	198,416
45,359	100	220,462

Volume

Litres	Gallons/Litres	UK Gallons
4,546	1	0,220

9,092	2	0,440
13,638	3	0,660
18,184	4	0,880
22,730	5	1,100
27,276	6	1,320
31,822	7	1,540
36,368	8	1,760
40,914	9	1,980
45,460	10	2,200
90,919	20	4,399
136,379	30	6,599
181,839	40	8,799
227,298	50	10,998
272,758	60	13,198
318,217	70	15,398
363,677	80	17,598
409,137	90	19,797
454,596	100	21,997

CORRESPONDING SIZES

Women's Dresses

American	British	Brazilian
6	32	38
8	34	40
10	36	42
12	38	44
14	40	46
16	42	48

Women's Shoes

American	British	Brazilian
4-4 1/2	3	34
5-5 1/2	4	35
6-6 1/2	5	36
7-7 1/2	6	37
8-8 1/2	7	38

Men's Suits

American	British	Brazilian
36	36	46
38	38	48
40	40	50
42	42	52
44	44	54
46	46	56

Men's Shirts

American	British	Brazilian
14	14	36
14 1/2	14 1/2	37
15	15	38
15 1/2	15 1/2	39

16	16	40
16 1/2	16 1/2	41
17	17	42

Men's Shoes

American	British	Brazilian
7	7	39
8	8	40
8 1/2	8 1/2	41
9-9 1/2	9-9 1/2	42
10-10 1/2	10-10 1/2	43
11-11 1/2	11-11 1/2	44

CREDIT CARDS

Most major international credit cards are accepted in Brazil although their Brazilian equivalents are restricted to internal use.

American Express, Diners and *Visa* all operate in Brazil. *American Express* can be contacted on 552-2243, *Diners* on 221-8942, and *Visa* (*Credicard*) on 292-7172 (Stolen *Visa* cards: 011-800-3788).

Your credit card receipts from stores and restaurants will be priced in cruzados although you will finally be billed in the currency of your own country, the official exchange rate having been taken into consideration.

DRINKING WATER

Although Rio's water is treated it is best to avoid drinking it except to clean your teeth. Stick instead to bottled mineral water that can be purchased in any supermarket or drugstore and is sold in every restaurant. Bottled water in Brazil comes with gas (*com gas*) or without (*sem gas*).

Mineral water in Brazil is not expensive, your holiday is and so is your health. Think about it.

DRUGSTORES/CHEMISTS

See shopping section.

DRY CLEANERS

See shopping section.

ELECTRIC CURRENT

Rio's current is 110 volts (60 cycles) but many of the larger hotels offer 220 volts as well. If you have any doubts check with the front desk or the owner of the house or apartment. Transformers to boost the current from 110 volts to 220 volts are available in most electrical supply stores.

Remember not all of Brazil is 110 volts so do ask.

ESTATE AGENTS

Rio has numerous estate agents who advertise their properties, both for rent and sale, in the newspapers. The best newspapers to check on Thursday, Saturday and Sunday are the *Jornal do Brasil* and *O Globo* and on Thursday the *Latin America Daily Post*.

In the Brazilian press look in the *Classificados* section under *Imoveis — Venda* (sale) and *Imoveis — Aluguel* (rent).

Some of the major agents with apartments for rent are:

Ferreira
Rua Pompeu Loureiro, 56
Copacabana — 257-8960

Golden
Rua Visconde de Piraja, 207
Ipanema — 267-7893

Mansion House
Rua Visconde de Piraja, 580/317
Ipanema — 239-7994

Marcub Cavalcanti
Av. Atlantica, 4240/326
Copacabana — 227-8474

Predial Leme
Av. Princesa Isabel, 7
Copacabana — 275-5449

Solar
Rua Visconde de Piraja, 156/610
Ipanema — 267-6894

Swiss
Rua Visconde de Piraja, 580/321
Ipanema — 239-4646

Toby
Rua Miguel Lemos, 67
Copacabana — 521-2541

FLOWERS

See shopping section.

FORMAL WEAR HIRE

See shopping section.

GAS STATIONS

The law which regulates the opening hours of Brazil's gas stations is always changing it would seem. At the time of going to press the gas stations open Monday through Saturday from 6 a.m. to 8 p.m. for both petrol (*gasolina*) and alcohol. It is hoped, however, that during 1987 the law will change to allow the gas station to open around the clock, seven days a week.

KENNELS

Canil Bruno Tausz
Estrada de Bandeirántes, 12,307
Jacarepagua — 342-6793

Canil Morumbi
Estrada do Rio Grande, 3604
Jacarepagua — 342-9164

LOCKSMITHS

The following locksmiths are situated in Rio's zona sul and operate 24-hours-a-day, including weekends and holidays.

A Carioca: 257-2221 (Copacabana). 225-1271 (Catete) and 294-1749 (Leblon).
Trancauto: 391-0770, 391-1360, 288-2099 and 268-5827.
Barra Mar Chaveiros: 325-0789 and 325-4596 (Carrefour and Freeway).

(The Portuguese word for locksmith is *chaveiro*).

MOVING

See "Removals"

NEWSPAPERS

Brazil has many fine newspapers but as in the U.S. the size of the country dictates that the majority must be regional.

In Rio the big two are *O Globo* and *Jornal do Brasil*. Both contain a high level of journalism and excellent entertainment sections which will bring you up to date with what is happening in Rio today — and you won't have to read Portuguese to understand them. *Cinema* is cinema; *show* is show; *teatro* is theatre; *musica* is classical and erudite music; *opera* is opera; *dança* is dance and ballet; and *televisão* is television. *O Globo* and *Jornal do Brasil* have good business pages which include normally in a box headed "Indice", the latest dollar rate on both the official and parallel markets (Dolar — Dolar Paralelo).

Brazil also has its own English language newspaper, the *Latin America Daily Post,* which is published Tuesday through Saturday to keep you in touch with what is happening in the U.S. and the rest of the world in both general, business and sports news.

1987 sees the launch of *Rio Life*, a newsletter designed specifically for the English speaking foreign community resident in Rio.

Foreign newspapers and periodicals are not difficult to find in Rio. Besides the *Latin America Daily Post* you will also find at most hotels and good newsstands the international editions of the *Miami Herald* and *Herald Tribune* which are flown in each morning from Miami and distributed by noon.

Time, Newsweek and *The Economist* can also be found at most of the newsstands around town. These same newsstands normally stock a further range of English language publications especially the stands on the corner of Av. Prado Junior and Av. N.S. de Copacabana; in Praça Serzedelo Correia (Copacabana); Praça General Osorio and Praça da Paz (Ipanema), and on the corner of Av. Ataulfo de Paiva and Rua Rita Ludolf (Leblon). The newsstands in Av. Rio Branco (Centro) and the bookshop in Carrefour are also worth checking for foreign language publications.

Most of the major hotel book stores carry a selection of English language literature, as do many of the better book shops around town.

Foreign publications are one of Brazil's few imports so be warned they are costly relative to what you would pay back home. It is still reassuring, however, to know that if you want a book or publication you can find it in Rio.

One of the main importers and distributors of foreign publications is the *South American Distribution Service* which also operate a very efficient subscription service which is payable in cruzados. *South American Distribution Service* can be contacted at Av. N.S. de

Copacabana, 605/1106 or by calling 255-6125.

Finally, if you are heading on down to São Paulo the papers to pick up with the best entertainment section are the *Folha de São Paulo* and the *Estado de São Paulo*.

PHOTOGRAPHIC

See shopping section.

POLICE STATIONS (DELEGACIES POLICIAIS)

Rua Hilario de Gouveia — Copacabana.
Av. N.S. de Copcabana, 1260 — Copacabana.
Rua Humberto de Campos. 315 — Leblon. (Also Poltur, the tourist police, Tel: 259-7048).
Rua Major Vaz — Gavea.

PORTUGUESE LANGUAGE SCHOOLS

If you are coming to Brazil for any lenghth of time you will soon discover the importance of learning the Portuguese language. The following schools offer courses for foreigners.

Berlitz
Rua Alm. Barroso, 139/3°
Centro — 240-6606

Berlitz
Rua Visconde de Piraja, 365
Ipanema — 267-1249

Feedback
Rua da Quitanda, 74/1°
Centro — 221-1863

Feedback
Av. Princesa Isabel, 7
Copacabana — 275-8249

Feedback
Rua Visconde de Piraja, 595/207
Ipanema — 259-5296

Feedback
Rua Barão de Itambi, 58
Botafogo — 551-0049

Feedback
Rua Armando Lombardi, 800/100
Barra da Tijuca — 399-5766

The Group
Av. Rio Branco, 135/201
Centro — 221-7146

The Group
Gavea Shopping Center
Gavea — 274-6449

I.B.E.U.
Av. N.S. de Copacabana, 690
Copacabana — 255-8939

POSTAL SERVICES (*CORREIOS*)

The opening times of Rio's many post offices vary but are usually 8 a.m. to 6 p.m. Monday through Friday and until 12 noon on Saturday, although, for example, the post office in Praça Serzedelo Correia in Copacabana is open Monday to Friday from 8 a.m. to 8 p.m., on Saturday from 8 a.m. to 6 p.m. and on Sunday from 8 a.m. to 12 noon.

The only post office open 24-hours-a-day is at the International Airport.

The main post offices in the *zona sul* are as follows:

Copacabana & Leme

Av. Princesa Isabel, 323A.
Av. N.S. de Copacabana, 540 (Praça Serzedelo Correia.)
Rua Dias da Rocha, 45 (Between Santa Clara and Contante Ramos).
Av. N.S. de Copacabana, 1298 (Between Francisco Sá and Julio de Castilhos).

Ipanema & Leblon

Rua Prudente de Morais, 147 (Praça General Osorio).
Rua Visconde de Piraja, 452 (Between Maria Quiteria and Garcia d'Avila).
Av. Ataulfo de Paiva, 822 (Praça Antero de Quental).

Jardim Botanico

Rua Jardim Botanico, 643

Barra da Tijuca

Barra Shopping.

Telex Service

Telexes can be sent from the post office at Av. N.S. de Copacabana, 540 (Praça Serzedelo Correia).

Telegrams

To send a telegram you can use any post office or phone 135 (national) or 000222 (international)

REMOVALS & STORAGE

Fink
Rua Senador Dantas, 74/16°
Centro — 210-1212

Four Winds
Rua Sargento Silva Nunes, 161
Ramos — 260-7233

Metropolitan
Av. Brasil, 2021 – 580-2868

Transworld
Rua Miguel Couto, 134/1002
Centro – 263-8112

SCHOOLS (ENGLISH SPEAKING)

British School of Rio de Janeiro
Rua da Matriz, 76/86
Botafogo – 226-3495
(Note: The main entrance is actually in Rua Real Grandeza, 99)

Escola Americana
Estrada da Gavea, 132
Gavea – 322-0825

Our Lady Of Mercy School
Rua Visconde de Caravelas, 48
Botafogo – 246-8060 and 266-5495

St. Patrick's School
Av. Ataulfo de Paiva, 1120
Leblon – 274-0033

TIPPING

Tipping is a difficult art in Brazil but keep in mind that it should be an expression of pleasure for services rendered. Tip because you want to not because you feel you should.

When tipping in Brazil you must remember the educational level of the person you are dealing with as well, and more importantly their wage level.

The minimum wage in Brazil, which a large portion of the people you tip will be earning, is about US$50 a month. Tips should be in line with this. 30 cents for the man who looks after your car for example.

At the other end of the scale you will be meeting people that are well educated and who would prefer no tip at all to receiving 30 cents. These are your tour guides, front desk managers, etc. If you want to make the tip extra special give it in dollars and of the amount you would expect to tip at home.

These guidelines will give you some idea of what to tip.

Restaurants – While it is illegal, most restaurants add 10% to the total of your bill and if they don't they will be quick to let you know. If the service has been above average you should round the bill up to the next suitable figure. For example Cz$232 to Cz$235 or Cz$240 if the service was exceptional.

Taxis – Brazilians rarely tip taxi drivers although they may round the

total up. Cz$28 to Cz$30 for example. As a visitor I always think it is nice to tip the driver if he has been helpful and hasn't tried to take you half way around the city to get to your destination.

Women's Hairdressers – 10% to the hairdresser, 50 cents to the shampooer, 75 cents to the manicurist.

Men's Haidressers – 10% to the hairdresser.

Car Park Attendant (*Unofficial*) – 30 cents.

Hotels – Nearly all hotels add a service charge to the bill, probably 10%, but as it is unlikely that the staff will receive this you should remember to tip accordingly in the bar and restaurant. What you tip at the end of your stay to individuals should reflect the service they have given during your visit. If the girl at the pool bar has been particularly helpful then tip accordingly, it will be highly appreciated.

TIRE REPAIRS

See "Tyre Repairs".

TOURIST INFORMATION

Rio has a split personality when it comes to tourist information. The city is looked after by *Riotur*, the state by *Flumitur*, and the country by *Embratur*.

Riotur and *Flumitur* are located downtown in the Candido Mendes building close to the main bus station. Menezes Cortes, while *Embratur* is in Praça da Bandeira on the way to the Maracana stadium (between the metro stations of São Cristovão and Estacio).

Riotur
Rua da Assembleia, 10/9º
Centro – 297 7117
Information: 242-8000

Flumitur
Rua da Asembleia, 10/7º
Centro – 221-8422
Information: 252-4512

Embratur
Rua Mariz e Barros, 13
Praça da Bandeira – 273-2212

TOW TRUCKS

See Breakdown Service.

TV RENTAL

See shopping section.

TYRE REPAIRS

The best, and cheapest, tyre repair offices are located in Av.

Mem de Sá in Centro just beyond the *Aqueduto da Carioca*.

A 24-hour-a-day service is offered at Av. Princesa Isabel, 272 in Copacabana (541-7996).

Telephone Services

Despite what the majority of guides would have you believe, Brazil has a very efficient telephone service which allows you to dial direct to virtually any point on the globe.

INTERNATIONAL CALLS

International calls from Brazil are the responsibility of Embratel. You can dial direct, which is cheaper, to most countries in the world by first dialling 00 then the country's own code followed by the area code and number you want. For example if you were calling the number 123 4567 in New York you would dial 00 1 212 123 4567. The telephone directory has a full list of country codes and the major area codes but this information is also available free of charge from the international operator on 000333. The operators speak English and also offer a free translation service in French, Japanese, German, Italian and Spanish. If you already know the number but wish to call person-to-person or collect then call the operator on 000111.

The main international country codes are:

Argentina — 54
Austria — 43
Belgium — 32
Canada — 1
Chile — 56
Colombia — 57
Denmark — 45
Equador — 593
Finland — 358
France — 33
Great Britain — 44
Greece — 30
Holland — 31
Ireland — 353
Israel — 972
Italy — 39
Japan — 81
Mexico — 52
Norway — 47
Paraguay — 595
Peru — 51
Portugal — 351
Spain — 34
Sweden — 46
Switzerland — 41

U.S.A. — 1
Venezuela — 58
West Germany — 49

SHORE TO SHIP

Brazil is a member of INMARSAT, the International Maritime Satellite Organization, and can therefore link you direct to any ship sailing anywhere in the world. For more information call 000111.

LOCAL CALLS

Local calls within Brazil are made just as you would at home. Area codes are listed in the telephone directory the main ones being: —

Rio de Janeiro — 021
São Paulo — 011
Brasilia — 061
Belo Horizonte — 031
Porto Alegre — 0512
Recife — 081
Salvador — 071
Manaus — 092
Foz do Iguaçu — 0455

The following services are in Portuguese, if you need help from the operator in English call 000333 and explain your problem.

Operator — 100
When no direct dial service — 101
Directory Enquiries — 102
Price of Call — 108
Time — 130
Wake Up Call — 134
Telegram (National) 135
Telegram (International) — 000222

WHERE TO PHONE FROM

If you do not have a phone where you are staying the city is well equipped with pay telephones. To use these you must first buy a *ficha* which you place in the machine before dialing. To call collect from a pay phone dial 107.

As most pay phones are located in the open street the chances are that for an important call, especially an international one, you require a quieter enviroment, this can be found at Telerj and Cetel's *Postos de Serviços* found throughout the city.

International Airport — Open 24 hours

Santos Dumont Airport — Open 6 a.m. to 11:30 p.m.

Centro (Praça Tirandentes, 41) — Open 24 hours

Centro — (Terminal Meneses Cortes) — Open weekdays from

6:30 a.m. to 10:30 p.m.

Copacabana (Av. N.S. de Copacabana, 462) — Open 24 hours

Ipanema (Rua Visconde de Piraja, 111) — Open 6:30 a.m. to 11 p.m.

Rodoviaria Novo Rio (Bus Terminal) — Open 24 hours

Barra da Tijuca (Barra Shopping) — Open 10 a.m. to 10 p.m. (except Sunday).

Currency Exchange

Up until March 1986 Brazil had suffered for a number of years from galloping inflation which was about to hit over 500% in the year. On February 28, 1986 the Brazilian government brought in a sweeping economics package that effectively outlawed inflation and changed the Brazilian currency from the cruzeiro (Cr$) to the much stronger cruzado (Cz$).

Inflation over the years has not affected the foreign visitor because regular devaluations of the cruzeiro against the American dollar kept Brazil cheap, the same thing is now happening with the cruzado.

The inflationary economy of Brazil is one of the most complicated in the world and nearly impossible for the casual visitor to understand, even the mighty International Monetary Fund have their problems. There are certain things however that are important for every visitor to know, and number one on that list is the parallel dollar market.

Brazilian individuals and companies are severely restricted as to the number of dollars they can obtain "officially" in any one year. The market price of the cruzado does not therefore reflect its true value against the dollar which normal demand would push higher. The result is that in Brazil you end up with two values for the dollar and every other strong currency.

Firstly you have the official bank rate. This is the official exchange rate for the cruzado set by Brazil's Central Bank. If you exchange any dollars, or any other currency, with a recognized bank or hotel then this is the rate you will receive. If you change money this way keep the receipt because at the end of your stay you can turn up to one third of the money back into its original currency if you have over estimated your needs.

The second market for dollars and other currencies is the parallel market, or as it is sometimes known the "Black Market". Technically by Brazilian law everyone is quite free to buy and sell as many dollars as they want, this second market has thus sprung up to cater for the demand that the bank's can't fulfil because of legal restraints. During the year the gap between the "official" and "parallel" rates rises and falls depending on supply and demand. The differential at any one time can be over 100%.

When Brazilians talk about a dollar value they invariably mean the parallel market rate and not the official one. In the guide I have always quoted prices at the official rate and so you should adjust accordingly. Where I say a room at a hotel costs $50, that at the time of writing may have meant in official cruzado terms Cz$ 705,00, but to get those Cz$ 705,00 in Brazil you would have only had to change $30 on the parallel market. That is why Brazil is so cheap today for the foreign visitor.

At your hotel, through no fault of their own, they will have to display the official rate of the day. If you wish to change your dollars over the desk this is the rate you will receive. The hotels would love to be able to offer you the parallel rate but to do so would be illegal.

The main group of *bureaux de change* who operate in the parallel market used to be found at the Praça Maua end of Av. Rio Branco in the city, and while they still operate there today there has, in recent years, been a significant switch as they have gone in search of the tourist dollars. You can now therefore find the parallel rate offered in most travel agencies and exchange houses in the Copacabana and Ipanema area. One of the best run operations is Casa Piano in Praça da Paz in Ipanema. Exprinter is another reliable name and one of their branches can be found directly behind the Meridien in Rua Gustavo Sampaio.

The daily rate for both markets are published in the business pages of the *Jornal do Brasil* and *O Globo* in a box headed "Indice" or "Indicatores". In the box you will see "Dolar" and "Dolar Paralelo", these are your two rates of the day.

There can be a danger for visitors to become preoccupied with the varying exchange rates, preoccupied to an extent that they waste half their holiday chasing across town to make an extra 30 cents. Everything must be kept in perspective and that includes the fact that your time, especially if it is limited, is money. You should therefore seek out the parallel rate local to your hotel. The man most likely to know is the hotel porter who will probably offer a rate just below the rate posted in the paper. Basically the hall porter, or whoever, will be exchanging your money in the knowledge that they can make a small profit if they go downtown and change it that day, or an even larger one if they hold on to the dollars until another devaluation takes place. But this is their worry and should not be yours.

If you insist on using dollars in the shops expect to be offered a rate somewhere between the official and parallel rate.

If you holiday in Brazil on the official rate you will have a very cheap vacation, if you holiday on the parallel rate it will be a give away. Either way you can't lose so just keep in mind that you are in Rio to have a holiday and not gain an economics degree in inflation accounting.

Business Rio

If you do not belong to a large multi-national and are visiting Brazil, on a fact finding mission for a company, you may find yourself at a loss to find the information you require.

The quickest introduction to business in Rio is through the Commercial Section of your respective Consulate General (See Foreign Consulates).

The Commercial Consul should be able to put you in touch with the companies and officials that you need to see.

Another entry in to the world of business in Rio are the American and British Chambers of Commerce. The American Chamber can be found at Praça Pio X, 15/5th Floor (Tel: 203 2477) while the British is located at Rua Real Grandeza, 99 (Tel: 226 0564). Because the British Chamber is only a branch office you may get more information from the head office located in São Paulo at Rua Barão de Itapetininga, 275 (Tel: 011 255 4286 or 011 255 0519).

The following addresses may also be of use to visiting businessmen and women:

BANKS

Boston
Av. Rio Branco, 110
Centro — 291-6123

Bozano Simonsen
Av. Rio Branco, 138
Centro — 271-8000

Chase Manhattan ·
Rua Ouvidor, 98
Centro — 216-6112

Citibank
Rua da Assembleia, 100
Centro   276-3636

Lloyds
Rua da Alfandega, 33
Centro   211-2332

Standard Chartered
Rua da Ajuda, 35/Cob.
Centro — 262-4172

Other banks can be found in the Yellow Pages (*Lista Telefonica Classificada*) under *Bancos*.

ACCOUNTANTS

Arthur Andersen
Av. Almirante Barroso, 52
Centro   292-3933

Arthur Young
Av. Rio Branco, 128/16°
Centro   203-2424

Coopers & Lybrand
Av. Rio Branco, 110/23°
Centro   224-6272

Deloitte, Haskins and Sells
Rua da Candelaria, 60/8ª
Centro — 233-6122

Ernst & Whinney
Av. Almirante Barroso, 63/17°
Centro   240-9442

Pete Marwick Mitchell & Co.
Av. Rio Branco, 110/40°
Centro   231-1897

Price Waterhouse
Rua Almirante Barroso, 139/9°
Centro · 292-6112

CREDIT INFORMATION

Dun & Bradstreet
Rua Dom Gerardo, 35/2°
Centro   233-4122

BUSINESS CONSULTATNTS

B.B.M.
Av. N.S. de Copacabana, 605/1204
Copacabana — 255-4433

Healey Associates
Av. Rio Branco, 45/1305
Centro   253-4771

LAWYERS

Daniel & Cia.
Rua da Alfândega, 108/7°
Centro — 221-7758

Garcia & Keener
Av. Rio Branco, 99/15°
Centro — 203-2466

Neves, Salgado, Correa-Lino &
Cobra
Praça Pio X, 15/3°
Centro — 263-6768

Stroeter, Trench & Veirano
Av. Nilo Peçanha, 50/17ª
Centro   262-2622

Other lawyers can be found in the Yellow Pages (*Lista Telefonica*) under *Advogados*.

INSURANCE

Adams & Porter
Av. Beira Mar, 200/10°
Centro — 262-7772

Johnson & Higgins
Av. Rio Branco, 125
Centro — 297-5122

Phoenix
Rua Conselheiro Saraiva, 28/7°
Centro   233-7477

Steamship Mutual
Av. Rio Branco, 151/1505
Centro   221-6074

Tudor-Marsh & McLennan
Rua Teofilo Otoni, 63
Centro   296-1182

Yorkshire-Corcovado
Av. Almirante Barroso, 52/24°.
Centro   292-1125

TRANSLATORS AND TRANSLATIONS

Berlitz
Rua Almirante Barroso, 139/302
Centro — 240-6606

Feedback
Rua da Quitanda, 74
Centro — 221-1863

For other translators see the Yellow Pages (*Lista Telefonica Classificada*) under *Tradutores* and *Tradutores Publicos*.

COURIER SERVICES

Contact the appropriate international airline who should be able to inform you which courier service goes to the destination you want; it is quite possible that the airline's own urgent small package service is all that you require.
The main couriers services operating in Brazil are:

DHL
Rua Teofilo Otoni, 15
Centro — 263-5454

World Courier
Rua 7 de Setembro, 111/701
Centro — 224-7113

SECURITY PRINTING

Thomas de la Rue
Rua Peter Lund, 146
São Cristovão — 580-4118

CHARTERED SURVEYORS

Richard Ellis
Av. Paulista, 1294/6°
São Paulo   (011)283-2266

Conferences, Congresses and Trade Fairs

Since 1984 the responsibility for coordinating and organizing conferences, congresses, conventions and trade fairs has fallen to the Rio Convention Bureau located at Rua Visconde de Pirajá, 547 (6th floor) in Ipanema. Tel: 259-6165. Telex: 021 34223.

With its abundant supply of good hotels and sophisticated night life, Rio is quickly becoming known as the ideal location for conferences, congresses, etc. of any size.

Rio's greatest asset is the much under used Riocentro in Barra which was obviously built with an eye on the future.

Riocentro boasts a main exhibition hall with a covered area of more than 30,000 m², a fully equipped conference center with a main hall area of over 4000 m²; heliport and parking facilities for more than 6000 cars.

Information about Riocentro is available from the Rio Convention Bureau or direct from the center at Estrada RJ-089, 6555 in Jacarepagua. Tel: 342 3535 or 342 5353. Telex: 021 21669.

The main hotels with facilities for smaller conferences and conventions are:-

Caesar Park
Copacabana Palace
Gloria
Inter-Continental
Meridien
Nacional
Rio-Palace
Sheraton

A full list of up-and-coming conferences etc. is included at the end of this book under ''Events and Holidays''

Health Matters

Heath worries can be the major concern for many overseas travellers but in Rio you can put your mind at rest. The city has numerous excellent hospitals and some of the world's best and most distinguished doctors many of whom are English speaking.

Since 1982 Rio has been lucky enough to have an organization called the Rio Health Collective.

The Rio Health Collective offers a central information and referral system for physical and mental health problems; workshops and group counselling in relocation adjustment; tropical health care; first aid courses; cardiopulmonary resuscitation classes; a heart saver course; as well as infant, pre-natal, and post-natal care; a well baby center; nurse companions and health talks given by the Health Collective's member doctors. The organization is non-profit making

and its phone-in referral service, which provides the names of qualified medical and health professionals who speak other languages in addition to Portuguese, is free.

If you have any questions about health and medicine in Rio the people for you to contact are the Rio Health Collective between 9 a.m. and 2 p.m. on 511-0940.

After 2 p.m. the Health Collective's answer-phone will give you the phone number of the duty-officer who will answer all queries between 2 p.m. and 9 a.m.

The Rio Health Collective's office is located at Av. Ataulfo de Paiva, 135 (room 1415) in Leblon.

If you can not get in contact with the Rio Health Collective you should call your consulate who will have a list of doctors who speak your language.

However, if you speak Portuguese you also have the opportunity of calling Golden Cróss, Brazil's largest health insurance service, who operate a 24-hour free referral service. In Rio, Golden Cross can be contacted on 286-0044, or outside Rio on their Toll Free number (021) 800-3070.

EMERGENCY SERVICES

If it is an emergency and you can't contact the Rio Health Collective or your Consulate then contact the following hospitals, although it is unlikely that anyone will speak English on the telephone.

Miguel Couto
Rua Bartolomeu Mitre
Leblon — 274-2121

Lourenço Jorge
Av. Sernambetiba, 610
Barra da Tijuca — 399-0123

Souza Aguiar
Praça da Republica
Centro — 296-4114

It is more likely that you will find English speaking doctors of a very high level at the following private clinics.

Sorocaba Clinic
Rua Sorocaba, 464
Botafogo — 286-0022

Centro Medico Ipanema
Rua Anibal Mendonça, 135
Ipanema — 239-4647

São Bernardo Clinic
Av. das Americas, 3250
Barra da Tijuca — 325-6611

HEART

For cardiac or respiratory problems you should contact one of the following clinics:

Cardiocenter
Av. Rio Branco, 156/3310
Centro — 262-0085

Eletrocor
Rua São João Batista, 80
Botafogo — 246-8036

Pro Cardiaco
Rua Dona Mariana, 219
Botafogo — 246-6060

Prontocor
Professor Saldanha, 26
Lagoa — 286-4142

Rio Cor
Rua Farme de Amoedo, 86

Ipanema — 521-3737

Uticor
Rua Soares Cabral, 36
Laranjeiras — 265-6612

Urgecor
Estrada Tres Rios, 563
Jacarepagua — 392-6951

CHILDREN

If the problem is with a child contact:

Amiu
Rua Muniz Barreto, 545
Botafogo — 286-6446

Psil
Rua Jardim Botanico, 448
Jardim Botanico — 266-1287

UPC
Rua Barata Ribeiro, 111
Copacabana — 287-6399

URPE
Av. Pasteur, 72
Botafogo — 295-1696

AMBULANCE

Should you require an ambulance and the clinic or hospital does not have one available you should call one of the following private services.

Clinic Savior — 227-5099 or 227-6187
Pullman — 236-1011 or 257-4132

24-HOUR DRUGSTORES (CHEMISTS)

The following drugstores (chemists) operate 24-hours-a-day.

Copacabana (Meridien end): Farmacia do Leme — Av. Prado Junior, 237 (corner of Viveiros de Castro) Tel. 275-3847.

Copacabana (Othon Palace area): Farmacia Piaui — Rua Barata Ribeiro, 646 (corner of Constante Ramos) Tel. 255-7445.

Copacabana (Rio Palace end): Drogaria Cruzeiro — Av. N.S. de Copacabana, 121 (corner of Souza Lima) Tel. 287-3694.

Ipanema/Leblon: Farmacia Piaui — Av. Ataulfo de Paiva, 1283 (corner of Rita Ludolf) — Tel. 274-7322.

Barra da Tijuca: Drogaria Atlas — Estrada da Barra da Tijuca, 18 — Joá Tel. 399-5421.

The Leading Hotels of the World®

RESERVATION CENTERS

For information and reservations at The Leading Hotels of the World,
please telephone any of the offices listed below:

North America

U.S.A., Puerto Rico & U.S. Virgin Islands
(800) 223-6800
N.Y. State, Hawaii and Alaska
(212) 838-3110 collect
Canada
(800) 341-8585
SABRE code LW/APOLLO code LW/PARS code LW
Meetings and Groups
(800) 223-1230 or (212) 751-8915 collect

Europe

Austria	☎	**Vienna** (0222) 55-21-07
Belgium	☎	**Brussels** (02) 218-3131
Denmark	☎	**All Denmark** 0430-0006
England		**London** (01) 583-3050 Telex: 299370
		Prestel 20002
		Meetings & Groups (01) 583-1712
France	☎	**Paris** (6) 079-0000
Holland	☎	**Amsterdam** (020) 435-319
Italy		**Milan** (02) 655-27-02 or 655-70-73 Telex: 325263
Norway	☎	**Oslo** (2) 41-33-16
Spain	☎	**Barcelona** (93) 301-0184
	☎	**Madrid** (91) 401-2412
Sweden	☎	**Stockholm** (08) 215-311
Switzerland	☎	**Geneva** (022) 286-566
	☎	**Zurich** (01) 302-0808
West Germany		**Frankfurt** (069) 290-471 Telex: 411592
		Elsewhere 01-30-21-10 toll free

Middle East

Israel	**Tel Aviv** (03) 241-125 Telex: 33705
Saudi Arabia	**Riyadh** (01) 464-8411 Telex: 200100

Asia

Hong Kong	**Hong Kong** (5) 221-142 Telex: 72602
Indonesia	**Jakarta** (21) 321-307 Telex: 45755
Japan	**Osaka** (06) 453-6501
	Tokyo (03) 585-7510 Telex 25361
Philippines	**Manila** (2) 857-811 Telex: 63756
Singapore	**Singapore** (65) 737-9955 Telex: 21528
Thailand	**Bangkok** (2) 234-9920 Telex: 82997

Australia

Australia	**Sydney** 233-8422 Telex: 27997
	Elsewhere (008) 222-033 toll free

Central & South America

Argentina	**Buenos Aires** (1) 392-0850 Telex: 24686
Brazil	**Rio de Janeiro** (21) 267-0665 Telex: (21) 21204
	São Paulo (11) 251-5021 Telex: (11) 22539
Mexico	**Mexico City** (5) 566-6899 Telex: 17-73401
Venezuela	**Caracas** (2) 316-931 Telex: 23153

☎ International toll free through Service 800

Executive offices and headquarters
747 Third Avenue, New York, N.Y. 10017-2847 U.S.A.
Tel: (212) 838-7874 Telex: 420444; 237158 TWX: 7105815309

DENTISTS

If you require emergency dental treatment you should find help at one of the following specialized clinics:

Assistencia Dentária
Av. das Américas, 2300

Barra – 399-1603

Clinica de Urgencia
Rua Marques de Abrantes, 27
Flamengo   226-0083

Dentário Rollin
Rua Cupértinho Durão, 81
Leblon   259-2647

Useful Words and Phrases

Guide books, in my opinion, are not the place to find such useful expressions as "Can you help me, my grandmother has been struck by lightening while hang gliding?". That sort of phrase is best left to the professional phrase books which you can find in any good book-shop in the zona sul.

Before tackling the Portuguese language it is worth knowing that Rio has its own special, rather lazy, dialect, which is difficult for the newcomer to cut through. For this reason the phrases I do include are short and to the point. They may not be pretty but they should get results.

Do you have....?	*Tem....?*
I want....	*Quero/Queria....*
I don't want....	*Não quero/queria....*
How much does it cost?	*Quanto custa?/ Quanto é?*
Do you speak English?	*Fala ingles?*
I don't speak Portuguese.	*Não Falo portugues.*
Where is....?	*Onde é....?*
What time is it?	*Que horas são?*
At what time?	*À que horas?*
When will it be ready?	*Quando estará pronto?*
Excuse me!	*Com licença*
Good morning.	*Bom dia*
Good afternoon.	*Boa tarde*
Good evening.	*Boa noite*
Thank you.	*Obrigado*
Please.	*Por favor*

WORDS

Yes/No	*Sim/Não*
Big/Small	*Grande/Pequeno*
Good/Bad	*Bom/Mau*
Cheap/Expensive	*Barato/Caro*
Old/New	*Velho/Novo*
Hot/Cold	*Quente/Frio*
Left/Right	*Esquerda/Direita*
Early/Late	*Cedo/Tarde*
Here/There	*Aqui/Ali*
Day/Week/Month/Year	*Dia/Semana/Mes/Ano*
Yesterday/Today/Tomorrow	*Ontem/Hoje/Amanhã*
Help!	*Socorro*

IN THE RESTAURANT

Menu	*Menu/O cardapio*
The bill	*A conta*
Napkin	*Um guardanapo*
Rare	*Mal passado*
Medium	*Ao Ponto*
Well done	*Bem passado*

DRINK

Beer	*Uma cerveja/Um chopp*
Wine (red/white/rose)	*Vinho (tinto/branco/rose)*
Coffee/Tea	*Café/Chá*
Milk	*Leite*
Mineral water (with gas/without gas)	*Água mineral (com gas/sem gas)*

FOOD

Beans	*Feijão*
Bread	*Pão*
Butter	*Manteiga*
Cheese	*Queijo*
Chicken	*Frango*
Chops	*Costeletas*
Dessert	*Sobremesa*
Eggs	*Ovos*
Fish	*Peixe*
French Fries	*Batatas fritas*
Garlic	*Alho*
Ham	*Presunto*
Ice Cream	*Sorvete*
Lamb	*Carneiro*
Lemon	*Limão*
Lettuce	*Alface*
Liver	*Figado*
Lobster	*Lagosta*
Meat	*Carne*
Omelette	*Omelete*
Onion	*Cebola*
Orange	*Laranja*
Oysters	*Ostras*
Pepper	*Pimenta*
Pineapple	*Abacaxi*
Pork	*Porco*
Potatoes	*Batatas*
Rice	*Arroz*
Salad	*Salada*
Salt	*Sal*
Sandwich	*Sanduiche*
Sauce	*Molho*
Sausage	*Lingüiça*
Shrimp	*Camarões*
Sole	*Linguado*
Soup	*Sopa*
Squid	*Lula*
Strawberries	*Morango*
Sugar	*Açúcar*
Toast	*Torrada*
Turkey	*Peru*
Vegetables	*Legumes*
Vinegar	*Vinagre*
Watermelon	*Melancia*

UTENSILS

Knife	*Faca*
Fork	*Garfo*
Spoon	*Colher*
Cup	*Xicara*
Glass	*Copo*
Plate	*Prato*
Toothpick	*Palito*

NUMBERS

One	*Um, Uma*
Two	*Dois, Duas*
Three	*Três*
Four	*Quatro*
Five	*Cinco*
Six	*Seis*
Seven	*Sete*
Eight	*Oito*
Nine	*Nove*
Ten	*Dez*
Eleven	*Onze*
Twelve	*Doze*
Thirteen	*Treze*
Fourteen	*Catorze*
Fifteen	*Quinze*
Sixteen	*Dezesseis*
Seventeen	*Dezessete*
Eighteen	*Dezoito*
Nineteen	*Dezenove*
Twenty	*Vinte*
Thirty	*Trinta*
Forty	*Quarenta*
Fifty	*Cinqüenta*
Sixty	*Sessenta*
Seventy	*Setenta*
Eighty	*Oitenta*
Ninety	*Noventa*
One Hundred	*Cem*
One Hundred and One	*Cento e Um*
Two Hundred	*Duzentos*
Three Hundred	*Trezentos*
Four Hundred	*Quatrocentos*
Five Hundred	*Quinhentos*
Thousand	*Mil*
Million	*Milhão*

Foreign Consulates

ARGENTINA

Praia de Botafogo, 228/201
Botafogo — 551-5798 or 551-5148

AUSTRALIA

Rua Voluntarios da Patria, 45/5th
floor
Botafogo — 286-7922

AUSTRIA

Av. Atlantica, 3804
Copacabana — 227-0040 or 227-
0048

BELGIUM

Av. Visconde de Albuquerque,
694/101
Leblon — 274-6747 or 274-3722

BOLIVIA

Av. Rui Barbosa, 664/101
Botafogo — 551-1796

CANADA

Rua Dom Gerardo, 35/3º
Centro — 233-9286

CHILE

Praia do Flamengo, 382/401
Flamengo — 552-5349 or 552-5149

COLOMBIA

Praia do Flamengo, 82/202
Flamengo — 225-7582

COSTA RICA

Rua Jardim Botanico, 700/215
Jardim Botanico — 259-1748

CZECHOSLOVAKIA

Rua Maria Angelica, 503
Lagoa — 266-2033

DENMARK

Praia do Flamengo, 284/101
Flamengo — 552-6149

EGYPT

Rua Muniz Barreto, 741
Botafogo — 266-5688

EQUADOR

Praia do Flamengo, 382/402
Flamengo — 552-4949

FINLAND

Rua Paissandu, 7/4th floor
Flamengo — 225-6145

FRANCE

Av. Presidente Antonio Carlos, 58
Centro — 220-4529 or 210-1272

GREAT BRITAIN

Praia do Flamengo, 284/2nd floor
Flamengo — 552-1422

GREECE

Praia do Flamengo, 382/802
Flamengo — 552-6849 or 552-6749

GUATEMALA

Rua Garcia d'Ávila, 113
Ipanema — 294-1849

HOLLAND

Rua Sorocaba, 570
Botafogo — 246-4050

HUNGARY

Av. Rui Barbosa, 460/602
Flamengo — 551-2247

IRELAND

Rua Fonseca Teles, 18
São Cristovão — 248-0215

ISRAEL

Av. N.S. de Copacabana, 680
Copacabana – 255-5432
2796

ITALY

Av. Presidente Antonio Carlos,
40/7th floor
Centro — 262-9090

JAPAN

Praia do Flamengo, 200/10th floor
Flamengo — 265-5252

MEXICO

Praia de Botafogo, 28/301
Botafogo — 551-9696

NORWAY

Rua da Gloria, 122/102
Gloria — 242-9742

PANAMA

Av. N.S. de Copacabana, 1183
Copacabana — 267-7999

PARAGUAY

Rua do Carmo, 20/1208
Centro — 242-9671

PERU

Av. Rui Barbosa, 314/2nd floor
Botafogo — 551-6296 or 551-4496

POLAND

Praia de Botafogo, 242/9th floor
Botafogo — 551-8088

PORTUGAL

Av. Presidente Vargas, 62/3rd floor
Centro — 233-7574 or 233-6574

RUMANIA

Rua Cosme Velho, 526
Cosme Velho — 225-0060

SOUTH AFRICA

Rua Voluntarios da Patria, 45/9th
floor
Botafogo — 266-6246

SPAIN

Rua Duvivier, 43/201
Copacabana — 541-2299

SWEDEN

Praia do Flamengo, 344/9th floor
Flamengo — 552-2422

SWITZERLAND

Rua Candido Mendes, 158/11th
floor
Gloria — 242-8035

TUNISIA

Av. N. S. de Copacabana, 906/3°
Copacabana — 235-4060

UNION OF SOVIET SOCIALIST
REPUBLIC

Rua Professor Azevedo Marques, 50
Leblon — 274-0097

UNITED STATES OF AMERICA

Av. Presidente Wilson, 147
Centro — 292-7117

URUGUAY

Rua Artur Bernardes, 30
Catete — 225-0089

VENEZUELA

Praia de Botafogo, 242/5th floor
Botafogo — 551-5698 or 551-5398

WEST GERMANY

Rua Presidente Carlos de Campos,
417
Laranjeiras — 285-2333

Brazilian Contacts Abroad

If you require more information about Brazil before you arrive, or after you leave, then contact your local Brazilian Embassy or Consulate, or write to the Brazilian Tourist Board, Embratur,

Rua Mariz e Barros, 13
Praça da Bandeira.
Rio de Janeiro, 20.220.
Tel: (021) 273 2212
Telex: 021-21066 Etur

BRAZILIAN EMBASSIES

Argentina

Calle Arroyo, 1142.
Buenos Aires   1007

Autralia and New Zealand

P.O. Box 1540
Canberra   2601

Austria

Lugeck 1/V/15
1010 — Vienna

Belgium

350, Avenue Luise
1050 Brussels

Bolivia

Calle Fernando Guachalla, 494
Apartado Posta 429
La Paz

Canada

255 Albert Street, Suite 990
Ottawa KIP 6A9

Chile

Casilla Correo 1497
Santiago

China

Kuang Hua Road, 27
Peking

Colombia

Calle 93, NR 14
Apartado Aerêo 90540
Bogota 8

Cuba

Hotel Habana Libre
Suite 1908
Havana

Denmark

Ryvangs Alle, 24
2100 — Copenhagen

East Germany

Esplanade 11/1110
Berlin
Pankow

Egypt

1125, Av Cornche el-Nie
Maspero
Cairo

Equador
Av. Amazonas, 1429
Quito

Finland

Mariankatu, 7
00170 — Helsinki

France

34, Cours Albert Ler
75008 — Paris

Great Britain

32 Green Street
London — WIY 4AT

Greece

Platia Philikis Eterias, 14
Athens — 138

Holland

Mauritskade, 19
The Hague

India

8, Aurangzeb Road,
New Delhi — 110011

Israel

Hei Beyar, 14
Kikar Hamedinah
Tel Aviv

Italy

Palazzo Pamphilj
14, Piazza Navona
00186 — Rome

Japan

11-13, Kita — Aoyama
2 Chome Minato-Ku-Tokyo 107

Mexico

Paseo de la Reforma, 455
5 Mexico DF

Nigeria

6 Kofo Abayomi Road
Victoria Island
Lagos

Norway

Drammensvein, 82 — C
Oslo — 2

Paraguay

Calle 25 de Mayo
Casilla de Correo, 22
Asuncion

Peru

Comandante Espinar, 181
Apartado Postal, 405
Lima — 18

Portugal

Avenida Fontes Pereira de Melo, 14
Lisbon

Saudi Arabia

Diplomatic Quarter
P.O. Box 94348
Eriyada   166693

South Africa

382 Aires St. Walerkloot Ridge
Pretoria 0181

Sweden

Sturegalan, 12
11436 — Stokholm

Switzerland

Monbijoustr, 65
3006 — Bern

Union of Soviet Socialist Republics

Rua Guertzena, 54
Moscow

United States of America

3006 Massachusetts Avenue, N.W.
Washington D.C. 20008

Uruguay

Boulevard Artiga 1328
Apartado Postal 16022
Montevideo

Vatican

Via della Conciliazione, 22
00193 — Rome

Venezuela

Av. San Juan Bosco
Quinta San Antonio — Altamira
Apartado Postal 3977
Caracas

West Germany

Kennedyallee, 74
5300 Bonn, 2

Brazilian Consulates in the USA

Incredible as it may seem Brazil's most important group of visitors financially, the citizens of the US, require a visa to visit Brazil, even when coming for a holiday.

Brazilian visas are issued to American citizens virtually automatically, which makes the regulation and combined paper work even more ridiculous, and can be applied for from the following consulate in the US.

Atlanta

229 Peachtree Street
N.E. Suite 2420

Atlanta — Georgia
Tel: (404) 659-0660
Telex: 54-2174

Chicago

20 North Wacker Drive
Suite 1010
Chicago — Illinois
60,606
Tel: (312) 372 2179
Telex: (23) 1253863

Dallas

World Trade Center 2050
Stemmons Freeway

Suite 174
Dallas   Texas
Tel: (214) 651 1854
Telex: 23-732241

Houston

1333 West Loop South
Suite 11,000
Houston   Texas
77,027
Tel: (713) 961-3063
Telex: 23-0774359

Los Angeles

Wiltshire Boulevard, 3810
Suite 1500
Los Angeles   California
90,010
Tel: (213) 362-3133
Telex: 23-677309

Miami

330 Biscayne Boulevard, 11th Floor
Miami   Florida
33,132
Tel. (305) 374-2263

Telex:23-264060

New Orleans

World Trade Center
2 Canal Street
Suite 1306
New Orleans   Louisiana
70,130
Tel: (504) 588-9187
Telex: (23) 0587366

New York

630 Fifth Avenue, 27th Floor
New York
10,111
Tel: (212) 757-3080
Telex: 23-125328

San Francisco

300 Montgomery Street
Suite 1160
San Francisco   California
94,104
Tel: (415) 981-8170
Telex: (23) 0330436

Annual Events and Holidays

HOLIDAYS 1987

January 1	New Year's Day	Thursday
January 20	Founding of the City of Rio	Tuesday *
January 25	Founding of the City of São Paulo	Sunday
March 2-3-4	Carnival	Monday — Wednesday
April 17	Good Friday	Friday
April 21	Tiradentes	Tuesday *
May 1	Labor Day	Friday
June 15	Corpus Christi	Monday
September 7	Independence Day	Monday
October 12	N. S. da Aparecida	Monday
November 2	All Souls	Monday
November 15	Proclamation of the Republic	Sunday
December 25	Christmas Day	Friday

Note: * Under the law 7.320 of 11-06-1985 those holidays which fall during the week will be celebrated on the previous Monday. The exceptions are Christmas, Good Friday, New Year's and Independence Day.

Long Weekends: 1987 is a bumper year for long weekends which should be noted in your diary as January 17-19 (Saturday-Monday); February 28 — March 4 (Saturday-Wednesday); April 17-20 (Friday-Monday); May 1-3 (Friday-Sunday); June 13-15 (Saturday-Monday); September 5-7 (Saturday-Monday); October 10-12 (Saturday-Monday).

EVENTS 1987

Clocks Go Back (February 14): Brazil puts its clocks back one hour.

Carnival (February 28-March 3): Rio's Carnival is the biggest and most famous in the world. Once you have seen it you will know why.

Famous Ships in Port (March 1-2): To coincide with Carnival a number of the world's top liners will be anchored in the port of Rio.

Rio Fashion (March): The Rio Fashion Show (Moda Rio) will present the top Brazilian fashion collections for the South American fall and winter at the Hotel Nacional.

Brazilian Grand Prix (April 12): The Formula 1 circus comes to Rio for the eighth consecutive year to race at the city's circuit in Barra da Tijuca. Activities will be centered on the Inter-Continental Hotel.

Soccer Tour (May 19-June 10): The Brazilian soccer team will tour Europe in May and June with games set against England (May 19), Northern Ireland (May 7), Scotland (May 26), Finland (June 3), Italy (June 7) and either Sweden or Czechoslovakia (June 10).

Festas Juninas (June): The saints days of Anthony, John and Peter are celebrated throughout the month of June and early July by traditional parties.

Grande Prêmio Brasil (August 2): Brazil's most important horserace takes place on the first Sunday in August at the beautiful Gávea racetrack.

Marathon (August 22): Rio's eighth marathon will be run in the late afternoon of August 22 over one of the most beautiful courses in th world.

Rio-cine festival (August): Rio's third festival for Brazilian films will take place at various cinemas around the city based on the Ricamar.

Rio Fashion (August): The Rio Fashion Show (Moda Rio) will present the top Brazilian fashion collections for the South American summer at the Hotel Nacional.

III Free Jazz Festival (September 2-7): The third "Free Jazz Festival" is slated for September with the participation of the top names from the US, European and Brazilian jazz worlds.

Feira de Utilidades Domésticas (September): Everything related to the home and leisure can be found at the Domestic Utilities Fair, Rio's largest commercial fair, which fill Riocentro for a period of two weeks.

IV International Festival of Film, TV and Video (November): FESTRIO, one of the six most important film festival's in the world, takes place for the fourth time based on and around the Hotel Nacional.

Feira da Providência (November): Huge charity fair which runs over one weekend at Riocentro attracting over 1.5 million visitors.

CONFERENCES AND CONVENTIONS

For a full list of the conferences and conventions due to take place in Rio in the coming year contact the Rio Convention Bureau at Rua Visconde de Pirajá, 547 in Ipanema. Tel. 259-6165. Telex, 021-34223.

Emergency Services

The following ar the main emergency numbers in Rio de Janeiro. If you have any trouble making yourself understood call the international operator, who will speak English, and ask for their assistance.

International Operator — 000333
Police — 190 (Poltur 259-7048)
Fire — 193
Water — 195
Eletricity — 196
Gas — 197

If your telephone number begins in 3 you have different emergency numbers for water, electricity and gas. They are:

Water — 232-2124
Eletricity — 224-0196
Gas — 372-7669

Other important numbers to have at hand are:

Ambulance (Miguel Couto Hospital) — 274-2121
Rio Health Collective — 511-0940
Golden Cross — 286-0044

Consulates — See Foreign Consulates
Tourist Information (Riotour) — 242-8000
Comlurb (Refuse Collection) — 234-2000
Detran — 231-1820
Taxi Complaints — 269-5212
Captain of the Port — 253-6633

The most important emergency address and telephone number for the foreign visitor is that of the special police unitl Poltur which operates specifically to help visitors in trouble.

Poltur are based in Leblon at Av. Humberto de Campos, 315 (corner of Av. Afrânio de Melo Franco, almost opposite the Scala showhouse). Tel. 259-7048. The service operates seven days-a-week, 24 hours-a-day.

MAPS

MAPS

1. ACCESS

2. CENTRO

3. CENTRO

4. CENTRO

5. BOTAFOGO

6. FLAMENGO

7. COPACABANA

8. COPACABANA

9. LEME / URCA

10. LAGOA

11. IPANEMA

12. LEBLON

13. JARDIM BOTANICO / GÁVEA

14. SÃO CONRADO / BARRA

LAND MARKS

🏠 HOTELS & RESTAURANTS

1 . COPACABANA PRAIA . mp 7

2 . RIO PALACE · LE PRÉ CATELAN . mp7

3 . RIVIERA . mp7

4 . MIRAMAR · LUXOR REGENTE . mp7

5 . DEBRET . mp 7

6 . SAVOY OTHON . mp7

7 . OTHON PALACE . mp 7

8 · BANDEIRANTES OTHON . mp7

9 . CALIFÓRNIA . mp 8

10 . OLINDA . mp8

11 . TROCADERO . mp8

12 . COPACABANA PALACE · EXCELSIOR . mp 8

13 . OURO VERDE . LANCASTER . mp8

14 . LE BEC FIN . mp 8

15 . RIO COPA HOTEL . mp 8

16 · MERIDIEN · SAINT HONORÉ . mp9

17 · LEME PALACE . mp9

18 . THE LORD JIM . mp11

19 . PRAIA IPANEMA . mp 11

20 . THE CATTLEMAN mp11

21 . ANTONINO . mp11

22 · HIPPOPOTAMUS · SAL E PIMENTA . mp11

23 · EVEREST · IPANEMA INN . mp 11

24 · CAESAR PARK · mp11

25 . EQUINOX . mp11

26 · SOL IPANEMA . mp11

27 · LE STREGHE . mp 11

28 · FLORENTINO . mp12

29 · ANTIQUARIUS . mp 12

30 · MARINA PALACE . mp.12

31 . TROISGROS . mp13

32 . EL CORDOBÉS . mp13

33 . INTERCONTINENTAL . mp 14

34 · NACIONAL . mp 14

● CINEMAS

1. VENEZA – mp.5

2. STUDIO COPACABANA – mp.7

3. ROXY – mp.7

4. ART COPACABANA – mp.7

5. COPACABANA – mp.7

6. JÓIA – mp.7

7. BRUNI COPACABANA – mp.7

8. CONDOR COPACABANA – mp.8

9. RICAMAR – mp.8

10. CINEMA 1 – mp.8

11. CINE LAGOA DRIVE IN – mp.10

12. BRUNI IPANEMA – mp.11

13. CANDIDO MENDES – mp.11

14. LEBLON 1 2 – mp.12

15. RIO SUL – mp.13

16. ART FASHION MALL 1 2 3 4 – mp.14

17. BARRA 1 2 3 – mp.14

18. ART CASA SHOPPING 1 2 – mp.14

△ SHOW HOUSES

1. OBA OBA – mp.5

2. PLATAFORMA – mp.12

3. SCALA 1 2 – mp.12

4. CASA GRANDE – mp.12

▲ SUBWAY (METRO) STATIONS

1 . CENTRAL ▪ mp. 2

2 . PÇ. ONZE ▪ mp. 2

3 . PRES. VARGAS ▪ mp.3

4 . URUGUAIANA ▪ mp.3

5 . LARGO DA CARIOCA ▪ mp.3

6 . CINELÂNDIA ▪ mp.3

7 . GLÓRIA ▪ mp.6

8 . CATETE ▪ mp.6

9 . LARGO DO MACHADO ▪ mp.6

10. FLAMENGO ▪ mp.6

11 . BUTAFOGO ▪ mp.5

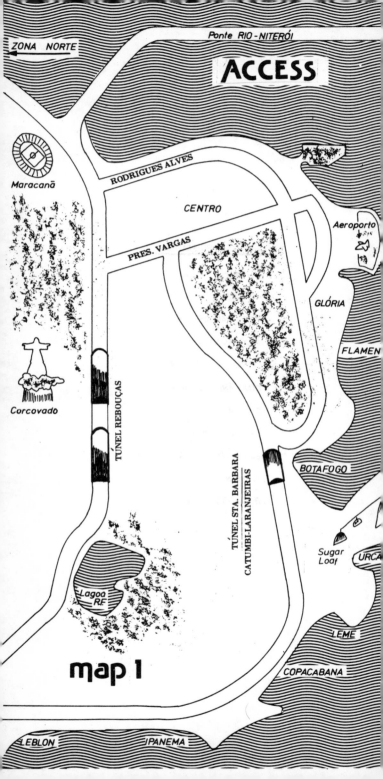

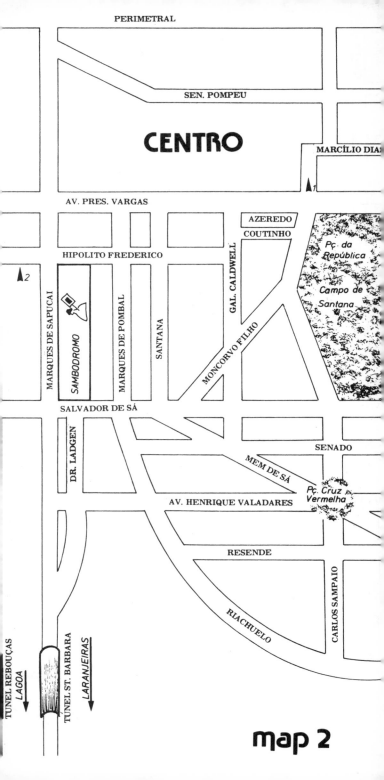

map 2

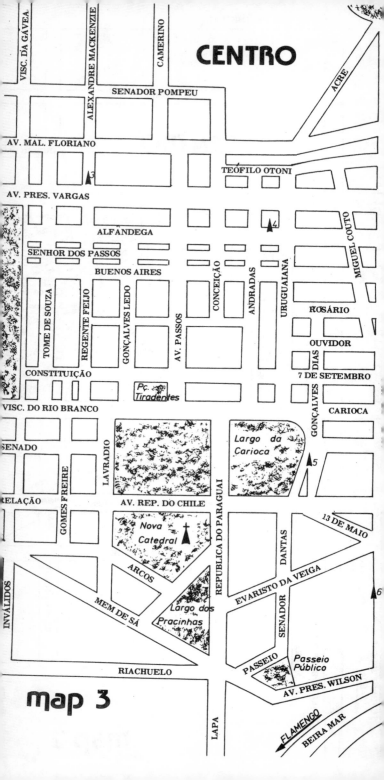

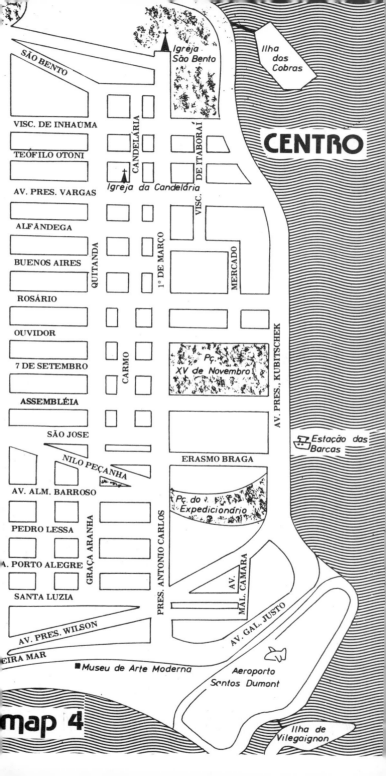

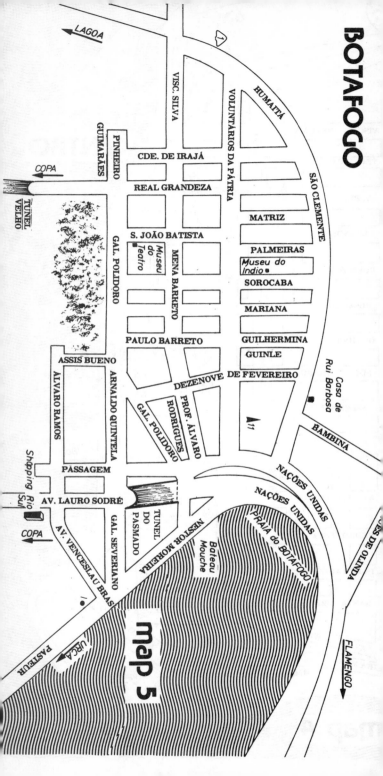

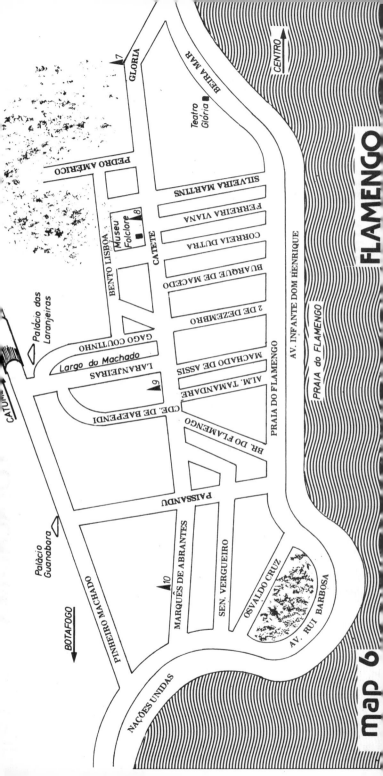

FLAMENGO

map 6

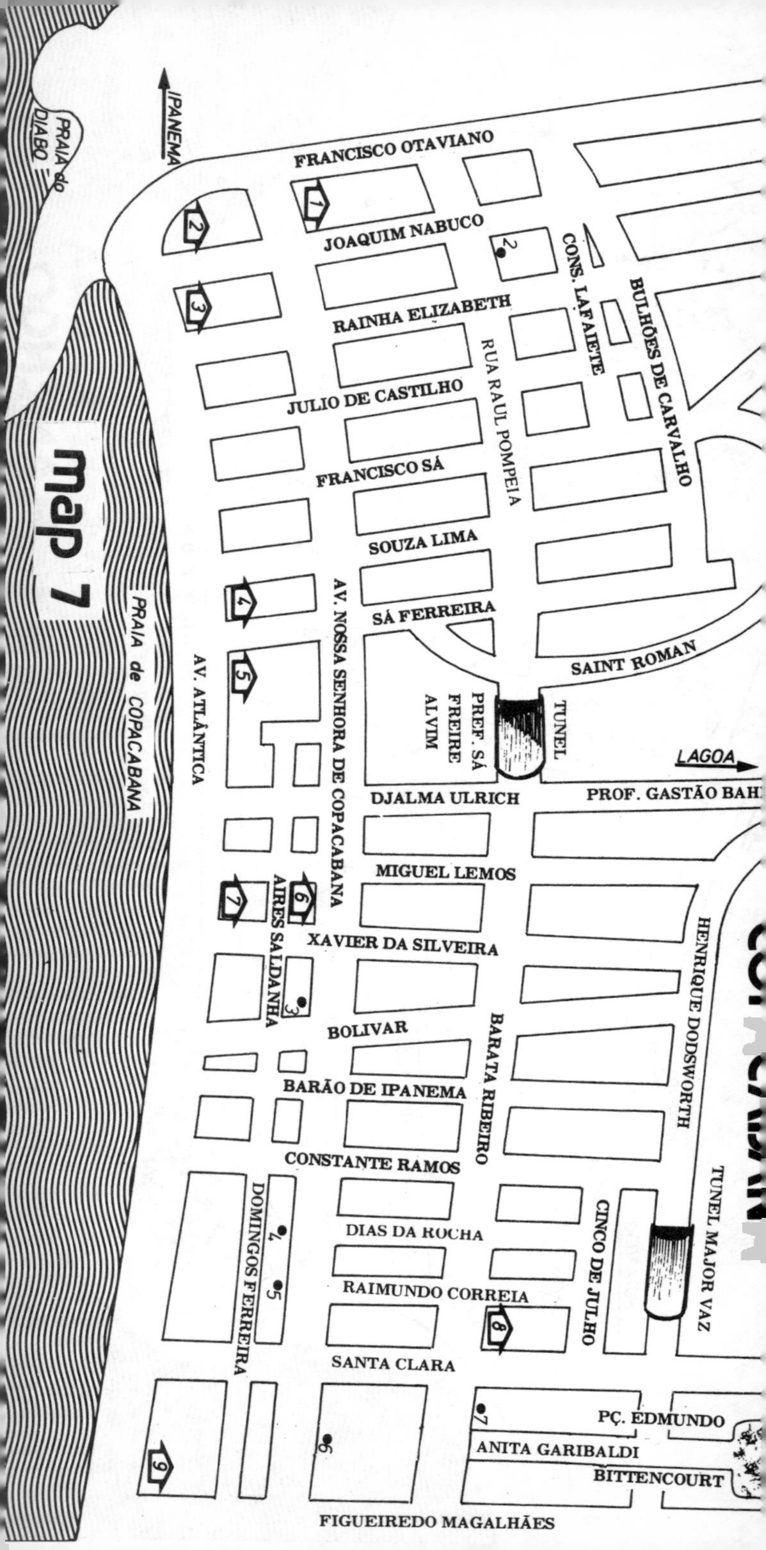

map 7

PRAIA do DIABO

IPANEMA

PRAIA de COPACABANA

AV. ATLÂNTICA

AV. NOSSA SENHORA DE COPACABANA

FRANCISCO OTAVIANO

JOAQUIM NABUCO

RAINHA ELIZABETH

JULIO DE CASTILHO

FRANCISCO SÁ

SOUZA LIMA

SÁ FERREIRA

DJALMA ULRICH

MIGUEL LEMOS

XAVIER DA SILVEIRA

BOLIVAR

BARÃO DE IPANEMA

CONSTANTE RAMOS

DIAS DA ROCHA

RAIMUNDO CORREIA

SANTA CLARA

FIGUEIREDO MAGALHÃES

CONS. LAFAIETE

BULHÕES DE CARVALHO

RUA RAUL POMPEIA

SAINT ROMAN

PREF. SÁ FREIRE ALVIM

TUNEL

LAGOA

PROF. GASTÃO BAH

AIRES SALDANHA

BARATA RIBEIRO

HENRIQUE DODSWORTH

CINCO DE JULHO

TUNEL MAJOR VAZ

DOMINGOS FERREIRA

PÇ. EDMUNDO

ANITA GARIBALDI

BITTENCOURT

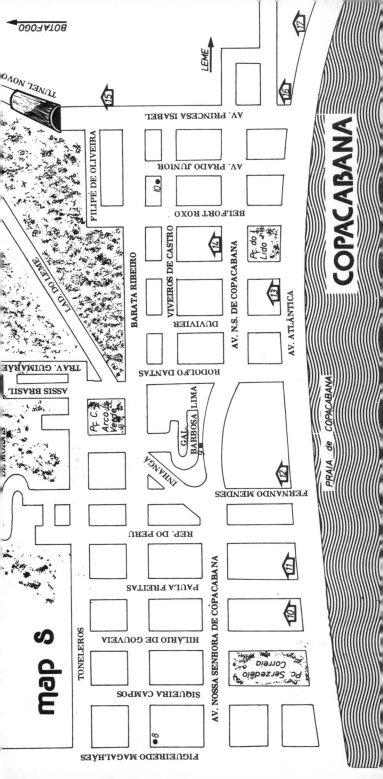

map 5

COPACABANA

PRAIA de COPACABANA

BOTAFOGO

TUNEL NOVO

LEME

AV. PRINCESA ISABEL

AV. PRADO JUNIOR

BELFORT ROXO

AV. N.S. DE COPACABANA

AV. ATLÂNTICA

FILIPE DE OLIVEIRA

VIVEIROS DE CASTRO

DUVIVIER

RODOLFO DANTAS

FERNANDO MENDES

REP. DO PERU

PAULA FREITAS

HILÁRIO DE GOUVEIA

SIQUEIRA CAMPOS

FIGUEIREDO MAGALHÃES

TONELEROS

AV. NOSSA SENHORA DE COPACABANA

BARATA RIBEIRO

LAD. DO LEME

TRAV. GUIMARÃES

ASSIS BRASIL

DE MORAIS

Pç. C.
Arco
Verde

INHANGA

GAL.
BARBOSA LIMA

Pç. do
Lido

Pç. Serzedelo
Correia

15

16

17

14

13

12

11

10

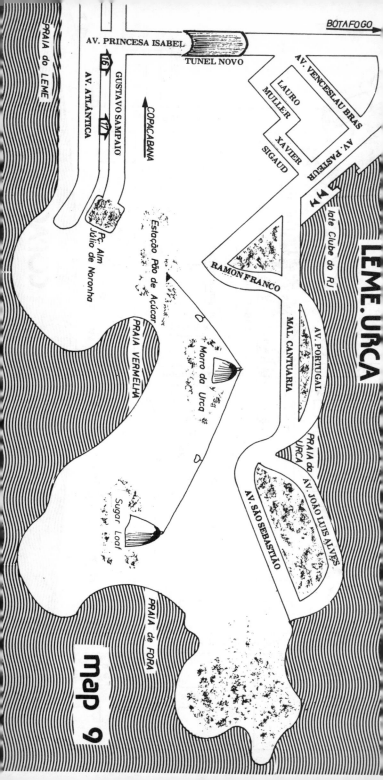

LEME.URCA

map 9

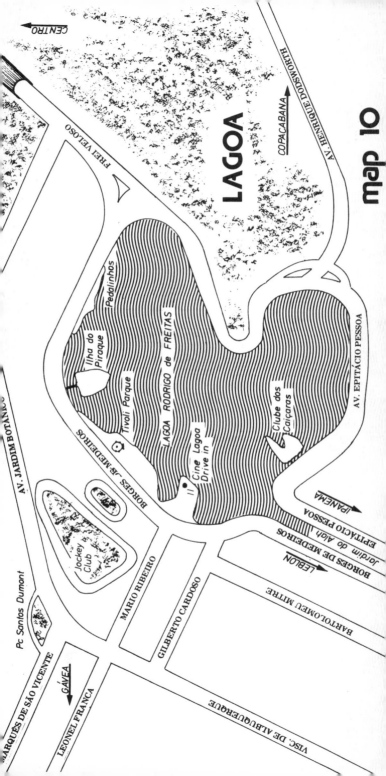

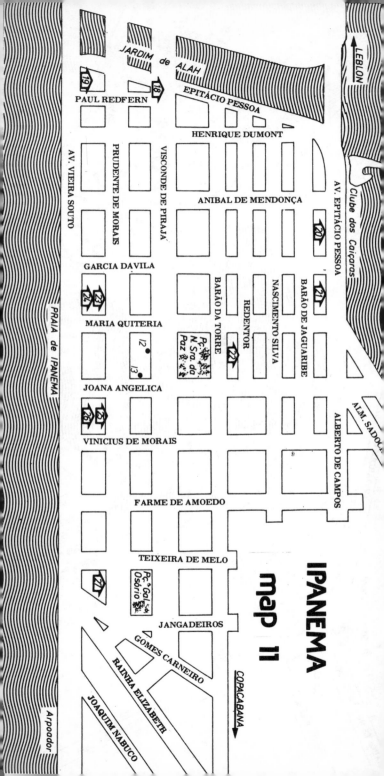

LEBLON

map 12

IPANEMA

JARDIM de ALAH

AV. BORGES DE MEDEIROS

PROF. ANTONIO MARIA TEIXEIRA

ALM. PEREIRA GUIMARÃES

AV. AFRANIO DE MELLO FRANCO

ALM. GUILHEM

CARLOS GOIS

CUPERTINO DURÃO

JOSÉ LINHARES

JOÃO LIRA

AV. ATAULFO DE PAIVA

SAN MARTIN

DELFIM MOREIRA

BARTOLOMEU MITRE

Pç. Antero de Quental

GAL. URQUIZA

GAL. VENANCIO-FLORES

GAL. ARTIGAS

RAINHA GUILHERMINA

ARISTIDES ESPINOLA

RITA LUDOLF

Pç. Atahualpa

CDE. BERNADOTTE

DES. ALFREDO RUSSEL

HUMBERTO DE CAMPOS

JOÃO DE BARROS

PROF. ARTUR RAMOS

DIAS FERREIRA

VISC. DE ALBUQUERQUE

GAVEA

PRAIA da LEBLON

SÃO CONRADO

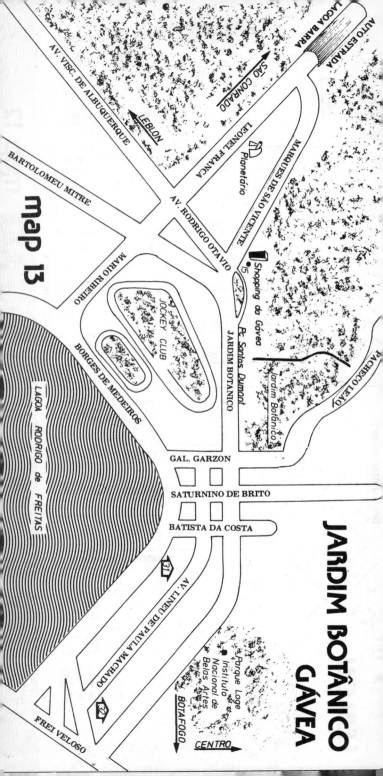

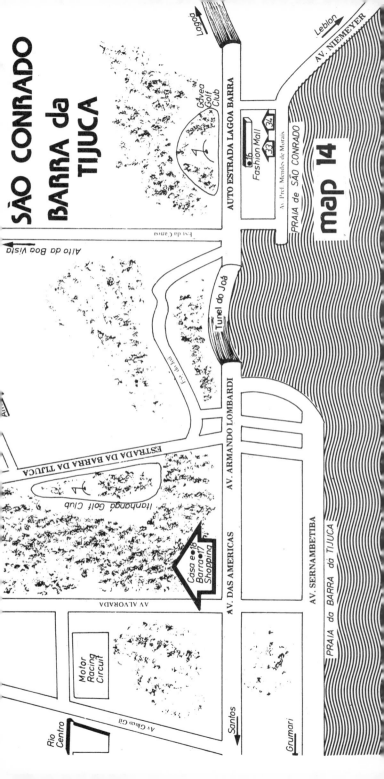

Index

A

Accountants; J – 11
Aerolineas Argentinas; I – 2
Aeroperu; I – 2
Air France; I – 2
Airlines; I – 3
Air Pass; H – 12, I – 12
Airports; A – 7, I – 2
Air Taxis; I – 4
Albamar; C – 14, G – 8
Alitalia; I – 2
Amazon; H – 25
Ambulance; J – 14
Angra; H – 6
Annual Events; J – 21
Apart Hotels; B – 21
Arco de Telles; G – 9
Arpoador; D – 10
Arrival in Rio; A – 4, A – 7
Art & Antiques; D – 25, F – 9
Author's Tour; D – 6
Avianca; I – 2

B

Baby Sitting; J – 2
Ballet; C – 72, E – 2
Banks; J – 11
Barra da Tijuca; A – 10
Barra da Tijuca Beach; D – 11
Barra da Tijuca Restaurants; C – 12
Barra Shopping; C – 18, F – 2
Bateau Mouche; C – 54, D – 13
Beaches; D – 9, G – 12
Beach Wares; D – 12
Bikini; F – 18, G – 12
Billiards; E – 2
Boat Hire; E – 2
Bonde; D – 20
Botafogo; A – 9
Botafogo Beach; D – 9
Botafogo Restaurants; C – 11
Botanical Garden; D – 14
Boutiques; F – 13, F – 17
Bowling; E – 3
Brasília; H – 19
Brazilian Consulates; J – 20
Breakdown Services; J – 2
Bridge; G – 8
British Airways; I – 2
Buffet Hire; F – 10
Bus Stations; I – 5
Busses; A – 11, I – 5
Business Consultants; J – 12
Butchers; F – 10
Buzios; H – 2

C

Caesar Park; B – 8
Camping; E – 3, F – 10
Carnival; C – 79
Carnival – Balls; C – 80
Carnival – Dates to the Year 2000; C – 87
Carnival – Parades; C – 83
Casa Shopping; F – 3
Cassino Atlantico; F – 3
Carrefour; F – 3
Caipirinha; G – 13
Candelaria; G – 9
Canga; G – 12
Car Hire / Car Rental; I – 8
Carmen Miranda Museum; D – 24
Central Brazil; H – 17
Centro; A – 9
Centro – Restaurants; C – 11
Chacara do Ceu Museum; D – 26
Chemist; F – 10, J – 14
Children's Clothes; F – 10
Chinese View; D – 8
Chinese Restaurants; C – 61
Churches; J – 2
Cigarettes; F – 10
Cinemas; C – 75
City Museum; D – 24
Clubs; E – 11
Coffee; G – 13
Colonial Tour; D – 21
Commercial Hours; J – 2
Computers; F – 10
Consulates; J – 17
Conversion Tables; J – 2
Copacabana; A – 10, F – 7
Copacabana Beach; D – 9
Copacabana Palace Hotel; B – 9
Copacabana Restaurants; C – 11
Corcovado; D – 4
Corresponding Sizes; J – 4
Costa Verde; H – 6
Credit Cards; J – 5
Credit Information; J – 12

D

Dancing; C – 69
Darts; E – 3
Delicatessens; F – 10
Department Stores; F – 5
Discotheques; C – 69
Distances; I – 10
Dona Marta; D – 7
Dress; A – 3
Drink; F – 10
Drinking Water; J – 5

Drugs; A — 3
Drugstores; F — 10, J — 14
Dry Cleaners; F — 11
Duty Free; A — 7, H — 24

E

Electric Current; J — 5
Electronics; F — 11
Emergency Services; J — 23
Erudite Arts; C — 72
Estate Agents; J — 5
Exchange (Money); A — 3, J — 10

F

Fancy Dress; F — 11
Fashion Mall; F — 3
Favelas; G — 13
Feijoada; G — 14
FestRio; C — 76
Figa; G — 14
Film Festival; C — 76
Fiscal Island; G — 8
Fishing; E — 3
Flamengo; A — 9
Flamengo Beach; D — 9
Flowers; F — 11
Food and Fruit Markets; F — 11
Foreign Newspapers; F — 11
Formal Wear Hire; F — 12
Foz do Iguaçu; H — 20
Funfair; D — 21
Furniture; F — 12

G

Gas Stations; J — 6
Gavea Golf; E — 4, E — 11
Gavea Shopping; F — 4
Gay Rio; C — 78
Gifts; F — 12
Gloria Church; G — 7
Gloria Hotel; B — 11
Golf; E — 4
Grumari Beach; D — 11
Guarana; G — 15
Gymnastics; E — 4

H

Hairdressers; F — 12
Hammocks; F — 12
Hang Gliding; E — 4
Health; J — 13
Helicopter Hire; I — 4
Helicopter Tour; D — 14
Hi-Fi; F — 12
Hippie Fair; D — 15, D — 25
History of Rio; G — 2
Holidays; J — 21
Horse Racing; E — 4
Horse Riding; E — 5
Hospitals; J — 14·
Hotel Numbers; B — 4

Hotels; B — 2
Hotels By Area; B — 5
Hotelçs By Category; B — 5
House of the Viceroy; G — 8

I

Iberia; I — 2
Ice Skating; E — 6
Imported Fodstuffs; F — 12
Insurance; J — 12
Inter-Continental Hotel; B — 11
Ipanema; A — 10
Ipanema Beach; D — 10
Ipanema Restaurants; C — 12
Ipanema Shoping; F — 5
Itanhanga Golf; E — 4, E — 11
Itaipu Dam; H — 23
Itamaraty Palace; D — 23

J

JAL; I — 3
Jardim Botanico; A — 10
Jardim Botanico Restaurants; C — 11
Jardineira; I — 6
Jazz Bars; C — 66
Jewelry; F — 8, G — 15
Jewelry Tour; D — 15
Jockey Club; C — 36, D-16, E — 4
Jogo do Bicho; G — 15

K

Karaoke; C — 68
Kennels; J — 6
KLM; I — 3

L

Lagoa; A — 10
Lagoa Restaurants; C — 11, C — 12
Lan Chile; I — 3   ·
Language; A — 3
Largo da Carioca; G — 10
Largo da Lapa; G — 10
Lawyers; J — 12
Leaving Rio; I — 11
Leblon; A — 10
Leblon Beach; D — 10
Leblon Restaurants; C — 12
Leme Beach; D — 9
Liquor; F — 12
Lobsters; F — 13
Locksmith; J — 6
Lufthansa; I — 3

M

Macumba; G — 15
Mairynk Chapel; D — 7
Manaus; H — 25
Maracanã Stadium; D — 16, E — 8
Marathon; E — 6